Death Talk

Death Talk

The Case against Euthanasia and Physician-Assisted Suicide

MARGARET SOMERVILLE

McGill-Queen's University Press
Montreal & Kingston · London · Ithaca

© McGill-Queen's University Press 2001
ISBN 0-7735-2201-8 (cloth)
ISBN 0-7735-2245-X (paper)

Legal deposit third quarter 2001
Bibliothèque nationale du Québec

Printed in Canada on acid-free paper

McGill-Queen's University Press acknowledges the financial support of the Government of Canada through the Book Publishing Industry Development Program (BPIDP) for its publishing activities. It also acknowledges the support of the Canada Council for the Arts for its publishing program.

National Library of Canada Cataloguing in Publication Data

Somerville, Margaret A., 1942–
    Death talk: the case against euthanasia and physician-assisted suicide
    Includes bibliographical references and index.
    ISBN 0-7735-2201-8 (bound)
    ISBN 0-7735-2245-X (pbk.)
    1. Euthanasia. 2. Assisted suicide. I. Title.
    R726.S64 2001   179.7   C2001-900477-X

This book was typeset by Dynagram Inc. in 10/12 Baskerville.

FOR MY PARENTS,

GERTRUDE HONORA GANLEY

AND

GEORGE PATRICK GANLEY,

IN MEMORIAM

Contents

Acknowledgments

The research on which this book is based spans a period of more than twenty-five years. Consequently, I owe a debt of gratitude to many people who have helped me. First, I am grateful to my colleagues at the Faculty of Law, Faculty of Medicine, and Faculty of Religious Studies at McGill University who have given me the privilege of engaging with them in "working conversations" about the issues raised by euthanasia and, in doing so, have provided important insights. In particular, I thank Professor Katherine Young of the Faculty of Religious Studies; Dr Balfour Mount, Dr Donald Boudreau, Dr Norbert Gilmore, and Dr Bernard Lapointe of the Faculty of Medicine; Professor Ron Sklar and Professor Rod Macdonald of the Faculty of Law; and Professor Ron Melzack of the Faculty of Arts (Department of Psychology). And, from outside McGill, Dr John Keown of Queen's College, Cambridge University, and my Australian colleagues Dr Mary Brooksbank, Dr Elizabeth Hepburn, and Dr Norelle Lickiss gave generously of their time and learning.

I was fortunate to have many opportunities to participate in conferences and seminars on death and dying, palliative care, and pain-relief treatment. In doing so, I met an extraordinary group of people who epitomize the best of the human spirit in dealing with some of the most difficult situations we face as human beings. In particular, in this regard, I would like to thank Dame Cecily Saunders, Dr Edmund Pellegrino, Dr Marie de Hennezel, Dr Kathy Foley, Dr Leon Kass, and Mrs Kappy Flanders, who, in many and varied ways, all provided inspiration.

I also acknowledge with thanks Dr Robert Almeder, Dr Constantine Falliers, Dr James Humber, Dr Gregg Kasting, Dr Torsten Nielsen, Engelbert Schucking, the late Marilynne Seguin, and Dr Sylvia Stolberg. Their articles, which are printed here, provided the basis on which I developed some of the approaches I have taken in the euthanasia debate.

Only authors properly know the debt of gratitude they owe to their editors, and I owe such a debt to Dr Paul Nathanson and Rosemary Shipton. Paul offered wise counsel and made a major contribution in helping me to structure the manuscripts that make up this book. I learned much that will be useful well beyond its pages from his careful, perceptive, challenging input. I was challenged for a second time by Rosemary, and I am most grateful for the important improvements she made. My thanks are also owed to Maureen Garvie for her painstaking work on the index. And I thank McGill-Queen's University Press, in particular Philip Cercone and Joan McGilvray for their assistance and patience.

As law student researchers, Ramona Rothschild and Hoi Kong once again contributed by chasing down hard-to-find sources and notes, and I thank them. I am also grateful to former research assistants who contributed to certain chapters. They include Ann Crawford, Claire Fitzgerald, Ann Gossage, John Kennedy, and Galina Mikhlin. My thanks also to Sharifa Janmohamed, Khandan Movafegh, and Valerie Shoffey, who, over the years, made my working life much easier.

And, finally, my deepest gratitude to Eileen Parle, who unfailingly exhibited grace under pressure. I thank her for the long hours she spent organizing the manuscript and for her perceptive questions about the text.

Prologue

We all need to engage in "death talk" if we are to accommodate, with some degree of comfort, the inevitable reality of death into the living of our lives. And we must do this both as individuals and as members of society. Until the last few decades, most of us participated in death talk as part of our religious practice. Today, in industrialized Western societies, the euthanasia debate provides a prominent context for such talk. This book contains a collection of papers, which I have written over the last twenty years, on euthanasia and physician-assisted suicide, and the debate that has surrounded these issues.

Death confronts us with terror and aloneness, even if we are accompanied by loving others. We can respond in two ways. In the first, we can take control of death and view it – and life – in a reductionist way. Euthanasia[1] is often a manifestation of this approach. Many advocates of euthanasia, while they value human life and respect it within given parameters, do not view it as having any intrinsic value, mystery, or meaning. Rather, they value human life for what it provides, and believe that, when the human machine deteriorates beyond some point – when we, or others, judge the quality of life as "not worth living" – euthanasia allows a dignified exit from life. One politician of this school of thought (Mr Jeff Kennett who was then premier of the state of Victoria in Australia) summed it up in this way: When you are past your "use-by"/"best-before" date, you should be checked out as quickly, cheaply, and efficiently as possible.

This politician's consumer-market-values approach to death – perhaps even seeing the morality of death as being worked out in the morality of the market place – can be compared with the approach and attitudes to death captured in a beautifully bound large book placed on a stand in the non-denominational chapel of an Australian hospice. The messages written in this volume by people – from small children who have just learned to write to spouses whose lifetime partners are dying – capture an intangible reality that I am unable to describe but that can be experienced in reading the entries. The impression about what human death and dying involves that I was left with was the polar opposite of the one generated by the politician's remarks.

This reaction opens up the other way to deal with death: to search for meaning in it. People who do so often view human life as having intrinsic value, encompassing a mystery (at least the mystery of the unknown), eliciting a response that contains wonder and awe. They believe that legalizing euthanasia would put at high risk the likelihood that we will find meaning in death, and that this possibility threatens our ability to find it in life. "Death talk" and "life talk" are two sides of the same coin, and the content of these two forms of talk is inextricably intermingled: death talk forms part of life talk and vice versa. We run serious risks as individuals and societies, moreover, if we fail to balance one with the other. In this book, I want to balance the death talk articulated in the euthanasia debate with life talk and to articulate the harmful impact that accepting euthanasia would have on the latter's content.

One of the great difficulties in the euthanasia debate is that we lack a secular vocabulary that can adequately capture the non-physical – the metaphysical – realities we need to create, protect, and live in if we are to experience fully human lives. Traditionally, we have used the language of religion to create the intangible, invisible, immeasurable reality that is essential to our human well-being, both as individuals and as a society. Often, we still need to employ the vocabulary of that language to capture the dimension of "*human spirit*" – which we need, whether we are religious or not. The use of this language can cause difficulties for those who reject religion and the supernatural because they see this vocabulary as invoking these entities. But in using this language in a secular context, I do not intend to base my arguments on religion or to rely on the supernatural.

By the human spirit I mean the "deeply intuitive sense of relatedness or connectedness to the world and the universe in which we live."[2] To recognize this dimension of ourselves is to recognize that we are more than "gene machines" and more than just logical, rational beings. We can create this dimension through shared language in the broadest sense of both words. Indeed, one challenge of "globalization" is to find a language and vocabulary that will cross the boundaries of religion and of ethnic and national origin (the boundaries of culture) and capture the profound realities of the human spirit that can give meaning to our lives – and deaths. The euthanasia debate is one important context in which we have an opportunity to contribute to finding this common human spirit and the shared language that will elicit and describe it.

We are story-telling animals. Some of our most important shared stories are in the form of metaphor, parable, and poetry. We communicate through imagination and intuition as much as reason and cognition. And we can find and communicate certain realities only indirectly, not directly. Some kinds of knowledge can be sought only by setting up metaphorical-metaphysical spaces within which we hope to encounter them. This is true with regard to knowledge and wisdom about death.

Setting up a space of that kind depends on having a sense of belonging to a community. Many of us have lost this sense and, consequently, have difficulty finding or entering the metaphorical-metaphysical space we need when we, or those we love, are dying. In facing the circumstances of death, it can be much harder for us than it was for our ancestors to fulfil the need to cry and to laugh through the tears; to come together to share the pain of loss and the joy of memory; and to participate with others in poetry, ritual, and song. Euthanasia is one response to this loss.

Our fear of death might be getting in the way of our ability to see death as a means of finding connection with others, forming community, experiencing transcendence (a feeling of belonging to something bigger than ourselves), and leaving a legacy. These are all means of helping people to experience a "good death." Euthanasia also is connected with our fear of death and of overcoming it, and likewise has the goal of providing people with a good death. But euthanasia blocks our access to a good death through the other ways outlined, which means that we lose important opportunities for experiencing such a death.

We must, to paraphrase the words of an Australian aboriginal elder who was speaking to white Australians, find a "new dreaming" – especially one that can hold us when we are facing death. We must be able to experience belonging to something bigger than ourselves; a sense of hope – a connection with the future; and a sense that we are loved and can love in return. All these feelings are possible for dying people – but, probably, only if those who care for and relate to them can also give and accept the experiences that generate them. Calls to legalize euthanasia often reflect a loss of these possibilities for dying people or those close to them – or, at least, a fear of their loss.

* * *

In this book I explore the causes, scope, and impact of the contemporary euthanasia debate. I argue in chapter 1 in Part One that this debate is part of the search for a new cultural paradigm on which to base the societal structure. This search is also being undertaken in the context of genetics and reproductive technologies. What we do and choose not to do in relation to both the passing on of human life (genetics and reproductive technologies) and the ending of it (euthanasia) will create the metaphysical reality, the sense of meaning, within which we live our lives. We have always used birth and death, the two great "marker events" of human life, as central to our search for meaning.

As long as we humans have been around, we have become ill, aged, suffered, and died, and others have always been able to kill us. Euthanasia is not a new question. But our kind of society has rejected it for over two thousand years. Why, then, has the legalization of euthanasia been seriously considered in industrialized Western societies within the last twenty years? These are the same societies, moreover, that have made astonishing advances in the ability to relieve pain and suffering. Not all of us agree on the reasons, though most of us admit they are multiple and complex. These factors are explored in chapter 6, "Legalizing Euthanasia: Why Now?" one of several chapters in Part Two on the evolution of the euthanasia debate.

One reason the euthanasia debate might have emerged now in industrialized Western countries is that recent extraordinary medical successes have expanded our life span and changed the diseases from which we are most likely to die from acute ones (which killed us quickly) to chronic ones (which do not). In general, people who die of chronic diseases cost the health-care system much more than those who die suddenly. We are also aging populations, which means that more of us are likely to die of chronic diseases. In short, our medical successes benefit us, but they also present us with their cost and the need to recognize our inability as a society to provide all the health care that might benefit everyone who wants it. It is, and should be, very difficult to face someone whom we know we could help with very expensive medical treatment and refuse access to it. Recently, the connection between euthanasia and the saving of health-care resources has been articulated in public forums, although the topic has always been discussed privately. In chapter 2, I address the question, "Should the Grandparents Die?"

The reasons behind calls for the legalization of euthanasia are complex, as is the debate itself. Consequently, we need to be aware of the ways in which the case for one side or the other is promoted. The case for legalization has been promoted, for instance, through confusion with other acts or situations that do not, in general, raise ethical and legal difficulties. This confusion must be identified and carefully explored. I aim to demonstrate in chapter 7, "Euthanasia by Confusion," that such an investigation could make us see some of the arguments differently. Another reason given for the need to legalize euthanasia is that it is necessary to relieve pain. In Part Three I discuss pain and pain-relief treatment, and their relation to euthanasia. We have been grossly negligent, even malevolent, in our failure to treat pain. And, looking back, I find it difficult to imagine how we could have been so inhumane. Increasing sensitivity to the pain of others, especially on the part of health-care professionals, has been a major advance of the last twenty years. This awareness is particularly true with respect to those who are unable to communicate their pain easily, whether because they are too young, too old, or of a different cultural or linguistic background.

Because euthanasia is a topic of debate, it matters how we carry out that debate. Often this debate centres around what is required to respect dying people. The chapters in Part Four deal with that issue. Some of these chapters consist of my responses to others' contributions, some of which were, in turn, responses to mine. They also include my reviews of two books written by advocates of legalization.

The two chapters in Part Five deal with euthanasia in the "public square." Much of the euthanasia debate is carried out in the mass media. Consequently, journalists' values, media ethics, and the messages that are conveyed to the public are important considerations.

Finally, in Part Six, I examine some foundational concepts in health ethics and law that are relevant to the euthanasia debate. Chapter 21 explores some of the concepts that govern decision-making concerning medical treatment at the end of life – autonomy, self-determination, competence, and voluntariness. The approaches taken to these concepts in law, psychiatry, and ethics are compared and contrasted.

In exploring euthanasia, we need to undertake a broader analysis than one based merely on ideas that are familiar to people living in an industrialized Western democracy. Human rights was one of the most important global concepts of the second half of the twentieth century, and, in recent years, human rights in health and health care have been a focus of attention. Human rights is not, however, a universally accepted concept in all circumstances – in part because the language of "rights" can seem too Western and too legalistic to some other societies and cultures. We have always recognized that human rights necessarily encompass human responsibilities, and yet, in the West, we have been nervous of expressly naming the latter for fear they could be used as instruments to deny human rights. Governments might argue that human rights depend on fulfilling human responsibilities as defined by the state. In chapter 22, on human rights in health and health care, I identify a concept of "*human ethics*". This concept is not meant in any way to detract from the importance of human rights. Indeed, the contrary is true. The idea is that human ethics might be a more neutral and a more universally acceptable term than human rights, at least that term standing alone. In short, human rights and human responsibilities both express the concept of human ethics – and it expresses them; they are interchangeable. Adopting the concept of human ethics would mean that, even if a state does not recognize human rights (legally enforceable claims of individuals or groups against the state), it would still be bound by fundamental principles of human ethics. One of those principles, I believe, is that, except in essential self-defence, we must not kill each other – not even for reasons of the utmost mercy and compassion. Consequently, euthanasia would contravene the requirements of human ethics.

* * *

The euthanasia debate has much to teach us. Those who oppose euthanasia might wish that the debate had never emerged, yet, provided the outcome remains that euthanasia is prohibited, the net result of this debate might be beneficial. We have already learned much. We know, for example, that people who want euthanasia have lost all hope. When we are terminally ill, by definition, we cannot, apart from a miracle, hope for long-term survival. Yet there are things we can still hope for – to see a loved person, to see the next sunrise and hear the dawn chorus of birds, to cuddle a kitten or pat a friendly dog. Hope is our connection with the future, and that future need not be distant to play its essential role in allowing us to experience hope. Hope is our connection with life and with the continuation of life – even when we know we will die (which is true for most of us for most of our lives).

Euthanasia confirms the power of death over hope, of death over life. It fails to recognize the great mystery that allowing death to occur, when its time has come, is an act of life. Euthanasia is an act of death. There is a vast difference between natural death and euthanasia. In our often unsubtle, un-nuanced, very physically oriented, non-metaphysically sensitive world at the dawn of a new century, many of us are failing to recognize how some deaths, and some forms of death, are compatible with life and hope, but others, especially those resulting from euthanasia, are not. It might be that in less sophisticated times, certainly in less scientifically sophisticated ones, we comprehended this distinction through our intuition. We knew through *true simplicity*.

Often, when we gain knowledge, we move from true simplicity to a *chaos* phase in which we find it difficult to structure our new knowledge and to formulate appropriate responses. It is only when we can structure the chaos to understand the deep roots and complexities involved in what we do, and the symbols and values affected, that we can make decisions on an adequate and comprehensive basis. These decisions are often similar to those made on the basis of true simplicity, but the resemblance is superficial. These decisions are based on *apparent simplicity*, which comes with deep understanding.

I believe we have moved from a stage of true simplicity concerning how our societies should handle human death to one of chaos, which is the context of the euthanasia debate. We should now move to a stage of apparent simplicity in which we will recognize the complexity and mystery of death, which exactly mirrors the complexity and mystery of human life. Our decisions at this third stage should be ones that respects the mystery of our humanness, while recognizing the suffering of terminally ill and dying people and our most serious obligations to relieve it. This transition requires that we respect death, and that, in turn, requires that we live out our own lives to their natural ends. In saying this, I do not mean to romanticize or glamorize death. On the contrary, we need to be realistic, to accept that death can be horrible. Rather, I am proposing that we accept and respect death, despite the horror and fear it can engender, because if death has no meaning, life has no meaning. We do not need to be religious or to believe in the supernatural to adopt the concept of respect for human life and human death proposed here. We do, however, need to recognize a "human spirit" – that it can be damaged or even annihilated, and that we have obligations to protect it. We should reject euthanasia because it is incompatible with fulfilling these obligations.

Death is one of the oldest focuses of human fear, curiosity, and philosophical debate. It is the last great act of life. It must remain so, if we are to live fully human lives and pass on the capacity and opportunity for doing so to our descendants. We are not, and never should be, supermarket products to be checked out by others according to a "best-before date." All of us need to see ourselves as having one of our hands in the earth – to which we will return – and the other reaching up to the stars – from which, contemporary cosmologists tells us, we probably came. Respect for human death also matters greatly to society: it is fundamental to maintaining a high ethical tone. We must not let our justified fear of death overwhelm our sense of the mystery of death and of life. If we do, the loss and harm to each of us and to society will be beyond our present imagining.

PART ONE

Euthanasia and the Search for a New Societal Paradigm

1 Euthanasia,[1] Genetics, Reproductive Technologies, and the Search for a New Societal Paradigm

We live at a time of unusually intense activity with respect to the evolution of a new cultural paradigm (on which to base a new societal one): the store of values, attitudes, beliefs, commitments, and myths. This paradigm is the shared story – the shared culture – that informs both our collective and our individual lives. Societal phenomena that have given rise to the need for a new paradigm include mind-altering scientific and technological advances, especially genetics and reproductive technologies; a preoccupation with real as well as symbolic individual and communal death;[2] the technological reality of a global community that lacks an accompanying emotional and cultural reality; the search for universal principles of ethics; and the need for universal implementation of fundamental human rights.

With this context in mind, I want to examine two debates. One focuses on genetics and new reproductive technologies; the other on euthanasia. These debates involve attempts to define both the nature and meaning of human life and the fundamental principles on which societies are or should be based. They raise questions that are crucial to any new societal paradigm. Moreover, these debates involve our individual and collective pasts (the ethical, legal, and cultural norms that have been handed down to us as members of families, groups, or societies); the present (whether we will change those norms); and the future (if we do change them, the impact that this change would have on those who come after us).[3] It can be seen as no accident that we are concurrently debating both eugenics (good genetics, or good at birth and, therefore, good life) and euthanasia (good death, or good at death – that is, of no trouble to anyone else). These debates are connected also in another way. People have always sought meaning and value through the meanings and values with which they surround the two great events of each and every human life: birth and death.[4] The stances adopted in one are likely to be adopted in the other, at least if we take a consistent approach.

Consider, for instance, the postmodern concept of individualism. In the West, we live in an era of intense individualism. This prevailing attitude has been described as "individualism gone wild" because it often excludes any sense of community. Many arguments that favour the availability of, and especially unrestricted access to, reproductive technologies, genetic technology, and euthanasia are based on claims of respect for individual rights. Advocates believe that these claims are essentially matters of personal morality and that they involve only, or at least primarily, individuals. Our obligation, therefore, is just to use science and technology to avoid or to relieve individual suffering, whether from disease, infertility, or terminal illness. I propose that this view is mistaken, because these issues are of at least equal importance to society – especially with respect to the formation and maintenance of values and symbols, and to the societal paradigm based on them.

Modern science and technology, in particular the new genetic and reproductive technologies, have changed many important aspects of our individual and collective lives from matters of chance to matters of choice.[5] Societies with the greatest access to these technologies are postmodern (or, possibly, "post-postmodern"), democratic, pluralistic, and secular.[6] The new realities include a previously unimaginable level of control over life and death. Consequently, these technologies have profound effects on the intangible fabric that constitutes any society – its attitudes, values, beliefs, and symbols, as well as its "ethical and legal tone" and, for some people, its "space for spirit." The latter, I would emphasize, need not involve the supernatural or the religious. Some reconciliation of these "new" realities with the "old" ones is necessary, especially in the context of evolving a new societal paradigm. In doing so, three positions – based on three world views – are possible.

The *"pure science" position* is that life is merely a scientific phenomenon; new discoveries in genetics have explained everything there is to know about us as humans. This is a profoundly biological view of human identity. According to the "gene machine" approach, we are nothing more than the biologically active products of our genes. This position is not limited to notions of our physical characteristics. It is the founding principle of theories of human behaviour – sociobiology, for instance, and new subcategories such as evolutionary psychology.[7] Even the functions that we see as most distinctively human – our moral and altruistic attributes – are genetically programmed responses; they are merely expressions of genes that have been selected for the better survival of the animal that carries them, including human beings.

From this point of view, the highest and most characteristic human attributes are their logical, cognitive, and rational ways of functioning. Correlatively, this position assumes loss of human identity (and, therefore, the worth or value associated with it) if these functions are irreversibly lost.∘ It leaves no room for mystery in human existence. It ∘ allows no "space for spirit." In the context of evolving a new societal paradigm, we need to ask whether our political and legal systems are based on that stance and, if so, to consider the broad implications.

The *"pure mystery" position* espouses concepts such as "creation theory," which is a denial of evolution and, for many people, the deliberate adoption of an anti-scientific stance. In fact, advocates often decry science. However, because of an unmitigated and intense emphasis on the sanctity of life, some of them would, for instance, refuse to recognize an informed decision to forgo medical treatment; paradoxically, from the perspective of their attitude to science, they would require that the use of sophisticated medical technology be continued as long as any vestige of life remains.

Those who adopt this approach almost always derive it from fundamentalist forms of religion. In this respect, they have something in common with those who support regimes, often totalitarian ones, that claim political authority on the basis of fundamentalist religion and exploit it to establish their own paradigms. These two groups differ dramatically, however, in some crucial aspects of their basic world views. The former seeks to establish its beliefs, through the democratic political process, as informing principles of the governing paradigm; the latter, by definition, eschews democracy and imposes its beliefs.

The *"science spirit" position* manifests some aspects of both the pure science and the pure mystery position and seeks a structure that will accommodate them, though sometimes they seem to be an impossible combination. Proponents are excited by the amazing achievements of science and, like those who adopt the pure science position, they seek a deeper and deeper comprehension of physical and human reality through science. They are awed by the wonder of what it can reveal. "As ∘ the radius of knowledge expands," they say, "the circumference of ignorance increases." In other words: the more we know, the more we know that we do *not* know. For some people, the awe inspired by the mystery of this unknown can engender a sense of the human spirit or even of something beyond it. They believe that we can sense this mystery through our intuitions, both scientific and spiritual. They try to integrate it with scientific knowledge and perceptions. Consequently, people who hold this third position respect the mystery of human life and death. This respect can translate into a sense of what could be called the "secular sacred." ∘

Recognition of the awesome knowledge opened up by science, and also that we have a "space for spirit," gives rise to an intangible conceptual reality that is more than the sum of its parts and different from each of these parts and from the other two positions. There is an image that, though admittedly nebulous and abstract, could capture the difference between "pure science"and "pure mystery" on the one hand and "science spirit" on the other. Each of the former world views could be described as two-dimensional and the latter as three-dimensional. It could even be that an inherent tension between science and spirit is necessary to create a third dimension: a space that can hold us as fully living human beings (and fully human living beings) and allow us to escape the linearity of the other positions.

To accept this third position means there is more we can do with science and technology than we ought to do; there are some things, moreover, that we ought not to do if we are to respect space for spirit. It is open to debate what these things are, of course, but examples can be given. For instance, some people believe we should never use our new genetic technology to alter the human germ-cell line – the genes that, being passed on from one generation to another, are the fundamental units of heredity. Others believe that non-therapeutic research on human embryos, which has been made possible through reproductive technology, should be prohibited. Likewise, some people believe that there are fine, but immensely important, distinctions to be made in grey areas of decision-making at the end of life. They would accept refusals of medical treatment even when these refusals result in death. They would accept the need to give pain-relief treatment even if that would shorten life. But they would not find it acceptable to give a lethal injection and deliberately end life.

We need a framework that would accommodate both science and spirit. First, however, we must understand the nature of that spirit. The currently widespread search for ethics could be one important response to perceiving this need and fulfilling it. Second, we must avoid the grave danger of being summarily dismissed for speaking of spirit. Some advocates of the pure science position automatically dismiss those who refer, directly or indirectly, to spirit or religion.[8] This is a doctrinaire response, similar in tone though not in content to that of religious fundamentalists. We must incorporate spirit indirectly by trying to ensure that our structures do not destroy the opportunity for its inclusion. Otherwise, spirit could seem very uncertain, a state that could, in turn, provoke anxiety. This uncertainty is used by those who advocate the pure science position as a basis to challenge the science spirit position, as we will see. Some people feel extreme discomfort with any concept that involves the idea of a space for spirit, especially any reference to this idea in the context of public policy. I would point out to them that imagination and creativity are important components of spirit. Few people would disagree that we should do all we can to protect and foster these qualities.

In short, we need to create a framework that will accommodate *all* our important dimensions. These dimensions extend beyond those of biological machines. Only with that framework will it be possible to tell a collective story, to create a new paradigm, of sufficient depth, breadth, and richness to capture our collective mind, heart, and imagination.

To establish this framework would require us to ask many questions – and they should be the right ones. It would require us also to recognize that, in some or even most instances, there might be no single right answer, and possibly not even a choice among several right answers. We would need the courage to live with uncertainty in both the scientific and "(human) spirit" dimensions. And we need a framework that will help us find a way of living, both as individuals and as local and global societies, at the highest level of our ethical, scientific, and (human) spirit potentials – despite the inevitable uncertainty.

This goal leads to the identification of a feature that is common to both the pure science position and the pure mystery position, and which differentiates them from the science spirit position. For their adherents, each of the former positions is of certain content; in this respect, both can be described as fundamentalist. But the content in one case is the polar opposite of the other: pure science as compared with pure mystery. The science spirit position can be much less certain in terms of its content and, therefore, advice on how to act in specific circumstances. It takes more courage, not less, to live with uncertainty, although people who espouse clear and adamant views often *seem* more courageous. In contrast, those taking a position that incorporates uncertainty, such as the one described here, can be considered compromisers and, therefore, weak or inconsistent; they are often condemned for relying on semantic distinctions that they believe to be both crucial and profound. Politicians know that decisiveness and "doing something," even if it turns out to be the wrong thing, are preferable in terms of public opinion to appearing uncertain or to admitting lack of knowledge. In the political context, it would take special courage to adopt the science spirit position.

I propose that irreconcilable world views (different aspects of which are reflected in each of the pure science, pure mystery, and science spirit positions) are now competing for recognition as the basis of a new societal-cultural paradigm. The conflict creates problems for local societies, as well as seemingly insurmountable barriers to the creation of a global society. This barrier prevents the formation of a universal paradigm, which, in some form, is essential for the establishment of a global society. But two endeavours – the current search for some universal ethical principles and calls for universal respect for fundamental human rights – might reflect a recognition of the need to deal with conflict among the various world views. Dealing with this conflict would require identifying both where we agree (which might, in turn, require that we search below the surface of our attitudes) and where we disagree. In the latter case, we would need to promote "active tolerance"and learn to live with unresolvable conflict. What follows is an example of how we can search for agreement.

Basic to the conflict between the pure science position and the science spirit position is whether people are in any sense sacred. Just as there is no necessary connection between accepting a space for spirit and being religious, neither is there any necessary connection between having a sense of the sacred and belonging to an organized religion. New genetic and reproductive technologies have caused us to recognize the vast extent to which we share our genome with the genomes of other species. One result is a sense that we understand enough about the origin and nature of human life to manipulate or even "create" it. This attitude has damaged, although it need not have, a sense of the distinctive sacredness of human life. One expression of this loss is manifested in concepts such as Peter Singer's "speciesism," which are based on the idea that distinguishing between humans and other animals is a form of wrongful discrimination. Therefore, it can be argued that we should not regard ourselves as sacred if we do not regard other animals that way. If we believe that it is ethical to carry out research on animal embryos, resulting in their destruction, it is ethical to do the same with human embryos. In a similar vein, it can be argued that if we provide merciful euthanasia for animals, there is no justification for denying it to people.

•The alternative is to regard people either as uniquely sacred or as sacred in some unique sense. The latter is preferable, because it allows us to regard all life as sacred, in a broad sense, while still allowing us to regard human life as worthy of special respect. As I have said, doing so does not necessarily mean invoking the supernatural or adopting a religious stance – not if we think in terms of the secular sacred. If advocates of both the pure science view and the science spirit position were to adopt that concept, it would reduce the scope of the disagreement. There are some indications that this concept is becoming widely accepted, at least in relation to life in general. If so, somewhat paradoxically, we could rediscover the special sacredness of human life by rediscovering the sacredness of all life.

We have allowed science to obscure the sacred. The environmental protection movement, which has an increasingly powerful and sophisticated scientific component, represents a strong countervailing trend. Recognition of our inherent dependence on the planet's ecological health has fostered a sense of the "secular sacred" (which might be either the resurrection of an ancient sense or a new development) by focusing attention on the absolute necessity of respectful human-Earth relations.[9] Moreover, as environmental science has tended to show us, our new science can be linked with eliciting a sense of the sacred – it just depends on how we view it. For example, we can experience a deep sense of awe and wonder in recognizing that all life arises from so few, shared, basic components, yet is manifested in such extraordinary variety. Recognition of the mystery that is entailed could, in turn, open up the possibility of reducing the disagreement and conflict not only between the pure science position and the science spirit position but also between these positions and the pure mystery one.

There is an important link between the contemporary societal debates about the new science and about euthanasia. In debating how we should develop, use, and regulate science and technology – especially genetic and reproductive technologies – we are debating much more than simply the appropriate *use* of science and technology. We are debating matters that include the nature of individual human identity, the ethical and legal tone of society, and the new paradigm for a global community which will guide us into the future and be handed on to those who follow us. The same is true for the debate over euthanasia.

We need a new era of joyful trusteeship of both our own and other life forms. We need a global paradigm that would foster this trusteeship. In the future we might focus on trust and responsibility more than on rights. And that might turn us back – or, perhaps more accurately, send us forward – to a new sense of community. The gains that have been made through a focus on individualism, especially in terms of respecting and protecting individuals as such, would not be lost; on the contrary, they would be enhanced by the necessary fullness and meaning that a sense of human spirit and community gives to the life of everyone.

PART TWO

Evolution of the Euthanasia Controversy

2 Should the Grandparents Die? Allocation of Medical Resources with an Aging Population

The question in my title – a deliberate inversion of the famous question asked by Helga Kuhse and Peter Singer: "Should the baby live?"[1] – is being asked more and more often. As Gerald Gruman has observed, "It is questionable if today the young comatose patient is the prototype for the discussion of issues of death and dying. A more probable crucial issue is that of the elderly: a reservoir of relatively defenceless persons, perceived, through bigoted 'ageism,' as unproductive and pejoratively dependent. In them, modernization has created a population stratum that, in a state of nature or conditions of scarcity economics, 'ought' to be dead."[2]

Frequent topics of discussion today include the medical needs of aged people, and how we, as individuals and as societies, will fulfil these needs in an era characterized by a real or a perceived scarcity of medical resources. The "scarcity" is often a given in discussions of allocation. But what is meant by that word? What constitutes a scarcity? What causes it? Can it be alleviated by, for example, greater emphasis on preventive medicine? How do answers to these questions affect responses to the following questions: Should the grandparents be allowed to die? Should the grandparents die? And which of these two questions, if either, is appropriate? The conduct that would be mandated, permitted, or prohibited by the same answer to both, whether positive or negative, would not be the same.

Resources can be unavailable because they do not exist or because they are unavailable in practice. Unavailability can be either avoidable or unavoidable. Monetary resources, theoretically, always exist; the issue is their allocation *to* and *in* medicine. But the fundamental issue that must be addressed in every case, whether monetary or non-monetary, is whether the decision is acceptable in both process and outcome.

Allocation depends on a range of factors, including perceptions of a non-allocation decision that imposes harm or the risk of harm. The harm or risk can be perceived as being imposed by choice or by chance, directly or indirectly, through an act or an omission, by an overt or a latent decision-making process, by identified or unidentified allocators, and on identified or unidentified victims. To the extent that a harm or risk is, or appears to be, imposed by choice, directly, by an act, through overt decision-making, by an identified allocator, or on an identified victim, it is likely to be considered unacceptable. Conversely, to the extent that a harm or risk is, or appears to be, imposed by chance, indirectly, through an omission, through latent decision-making by an unidentified allocator, or on a victim unidentified at the time risk is created, it is likely to be considered acceptable. In short, seriousness and probability of risk and harm do not alone determine the acceptability of a decision that leads to their imposition. Features of the decision-making process that results in that outcome, too, are very important.

Another important factor is the difficulty presented by uncertainty. People might choose an approach to allocating health-care resources that promises to minimize this problem. They might focus only on demography, for instance, in allocating scarce medical resources to an aging population, thereby creating a greater sense of certainty and security. People might seek a "right" answer through demographic manipulation, because right (in the sense of apparently certain) answers are not available when other approaches are used. This approach enables them also to avoid facing "the challenges of competing social and political claims for health care resources."[3]

In some cases, we might have to alter our thinking. To cite but one example, there can be an almost conditioned response that inexpensive alternatives are less beneficial than expensive ones. In fact, however, some cost-saving alternatives can confer additional benefits. For instance, hemodialyzer reuse can be no more risky than the use of new dialyzers for each treatment, and could even be safer.[4]

The initial characterization of a problem influences both questions and answers – and outcomes as well. There is an important difference in the *prima facie* presumption governing decision-making when one refers to "medical resources" rather than "scarce medical resources" (the term more often used). Likewise, characterization of medical resources can be used to make them unavailable. A treatment can be identified as "experimental" or "extraordinary" to deny either access to it or the responsibility to continue providing it. Health-care insurance might not cover the costs of experimental treatment; consequently, to impose that label can be a money-saving device. Similarly, it can be held that there is no legal or moral obligation to provide "extraordinary" treatment. This category (which is much less used now them it was in the past) might include life-support treatment when patients' wishes are unknown. Non-allocation, whether through laudably reflecting respect for the wishes of competent patients who refuse treatment or the "best interests" of incompetent patients whose wishes are unknown, has the secondary effect of saving money.

DISCRIMINATION ON THE BASIS OF AGE

A semantic trap lies in the common formulation of the problem of "scarcity" as one of allocating resources to or among aged people. This terminology implies that "we" decide what to do to "them." In reality, we are a community, a global, dynamic whole, and aged people are part of that whole. That is why the title of this chapter refers to the allocation of medical resources *with* an aging population. I want this terminology not only to reflect or create a more neutral approach to age in allocating health care resources, but to cause the people needing medical care to be integrated as members of the general community.

Initially, we might consider "the aged" as a separate group in order to study them and their needs or for altruistic or paternalistic reasons. But the danger in distinguishing them as a group and treating them differently on that basis is in creating an opportunity to stigmatize them and discriminate against them.

Discrimination – whether intentional or accidental, conscious or unconscious, acceptable or unacceptable in terms of motive – can lead to unjust decisions. Surgery might be considered less desirable for old people than for young ones because the risk-benefit calculus is less favourable for the former than for the latter. But this denial could be based on wrongful discrimination on the basis of age rather than on valid medical justifications. Also, care should be taken to prevent unjustified paternalism from governing decisions. The paternalistic tendency to infantilise old people is regrettable. Yet, even though "paternalism" has come to be a dirty word, there is as much danger in excluding it entirely as in overusing it. So we need to find the right balance of autonomy and paternalism.

Should legislation prohibiting discrimination on the basis of age outlaw it at any age or only within an age range – up to the age of sixty-five years, for example, or only between forty-five and sixty-five, or only after the age of majority? When does discrimination (and most people discriminate a great deal of the time) become legally wrongful discrimination? The basis for discrimination, the situation in which it occurs, and its effects are all relevant. Most jurisdictions that prohibit discrimination include that on the basis of age or of physical or mental handicap (a provision that could be relevant to some aged people). Denying aged or handicapped people access to needed health care on the basis of these characteristics would almost certainly fall within the definition of prohibited discrimination. In general, the burden of proof of a *prima facie* case of discrimination is on the plaintiff. If the case is established, the defendant must show that discrimination either did not occur or that, if it did, it was justified.

Prohibition of discrimination does not provide a guarantee of access to medical care, because rights against discrimination are of "negative" content, not "positive." One has the right to be treated no worse than anyone else, not a claim to be treated better than others and according to one's needs. Because old people might need more health care than other members of society, protection against discrimination might not provide an adequate safeguard or remedy.

The crucial question becomes: Are there rights of access to health care? Most jurisdictions do not legislate a legal right of access to health care. The Quebec Health and Social Services Act[5] is one notable exception. In other jurisdictions, one might ask whether a government-funded health-care system that is required by law[6] to be universal (applicable to all residents), comprehensive (applicable to all illnesses), portable (applicable in all provinces), accessible, and publicly administered implies or amounts to "holding out" that there is a legal, moral, or even "political" right of access to necessary health care. In Canada, we hear frequent declarations by government and government-supported institutions that all people are, should be, and will be provided with necessary health care. Do these statements, in an era of limited medical resources, establish a right of access?

Redefining what is necessary treatment is one way to maintain the appearance of a right of access to health care while not providing access to all useful treatments. This approach can be a politically feasible option, but is it honest? What harm does it perpetrate? Sometimes – in fact, often – people are better off knowing that treatment is possible but not provided than they are believing, wrongly, that everything possible has been provided. In the former case, they can at least take steps either to challenge the decision to deny treatment or try to obtain it elsewhere; in the latter circumstances, they might not even be aware that treatment is being denied or that it exists.

To avoid all these situations, jurisdictions could mandate that patients must be informed when treatment indicated as appropriate will not be provided. This disclosure gives them opportunities to challenge the denial of treatment or to seek it elsewhere. "Treatment indicated as appropriate" should be defined to include all treatment that might benefit patients.

JUSTIFICATIONS FOR DISCRIMINATION

Sometimes discrimination can be justified. Several justifications, some of them very controversial, have been proposed in relation to withholding some medical care from elderly people.

Fair Innings

The "fair innings" concept means that people should no longer have access to life-prolonging treatment after a specified age – except to reduce their suffering. One issue is whether the fear of future denial constitutes present suffering; if so, it should be alleviated under the suffering-reduction exception. Fair innings is an absolute, not a relative, concept. Among those who have passed the "marker event," there would be no allocation according to age even of "spare" resources. All would be equally unentitled.

One can ask whether fair innings can be justified on the basis that it reflects life expectancy. Young people have longer life expectancies than old people, the argument goes; to invest medical resources in the former, therefore, is justified discrimination. But this variation is true only in statistical terms and in general; the life expectancy of any particular young person might in fact be lower than that of an old person. But does the application of fair innings to everyone make it acceptable? Or would letting people agree to have fair innings applied to themselves, in return for additional benefits at a younger age, make it acceptable?

I suggest that if discrimination on the basis of age in allocating medical resources is acceptable at all, it is acceptable only when it is the least invasive and least restrictive alternative reasonably available and is likely to be effective in achieving a justifiable aim. What would constitute such an aim is, of course, a value judgment on which we will not all agree.

Non-maleficence Compared with Beneficence

Some argue that it is acceptable to withhold a health-care benefit, but not to inflict harm. If so, when is withholding a benefit maleficence? I suggest that one is inflicting harm if the benefits withheld are of a kind usually provided, involve no special or unusual risks, and are readily available.

Similarly, some argue as follows: although harm-inflicting omissions are justified, harm-inflicting acts are not. This distinction might reflect a psychological reality, in that we bond psychologically with those people affected by our interventions, but not with those on whom we fail to intervene, especially when we are strangers with no previous emotional ties. We are more comfortable with harm-inflicting omissions, therefore, than acts. Moreover, the distinctions between maleficence and beneficence and between act and omission involve value judgments. And they can depend on the definitions of key terms and existing situations. These factors, in turn, will indicate whether or not conduct is morally and legally acceptable.

Opportunity Costs

In considering the costs of allocating medical resources to aged people, we must take into account the loss of the alternative benefits that these same funds could have generated. We might well find that no "no harm" options are available.

Making decisions under these conditions is often indirect and hidden, features that have been criticized as harmful. Yet direct and overt decisions, too, can involve harm. A direct, overt decision not to allocate resources for some purpose creates and symbolizes lack of caring for that purpose. This dearth of caring is especially likely to be recognized when the non-allocation harms a person or a group that can be identified before any decision is made.

Economic Costs

All medical care costs money, but the care of elderly people can be exceptionally costly. The same treatment can cost more for an older than for a younger person because the former needs more intense care and recovers more slowly. Yet similar cost discrepancies can exist between other groups, neither of which is aged. For instance, it might cost more to care for a sick baby than for a twenty year old with a similar condition. We would not be justified in discriminating against aged people, then, at least not on the basis of a cost discrepancy. Moreover, if different age groups receive different levels of care, these discrepancies will have to be justified to avoid the risk of discrimination.

Finally, we could wrongfully consider the cost not only of saving the lives of old people but of maintaining them thereafter. Cost-reducing incentives for health-care professionals or institutions – such as diagnostic-related groups or prepayment in health maintenance organizations – will make this an increasingly important feature of decision-making.

Treatment might be withheld not because it costs too much initially but because decision-makers believe the ongoing care would constitute too great an economic drain. We need to be extremely careful that decisions are not wrongfully influenced by such "second order" considerations.

We need also to consider alternative ways of paying the costs. Could some entity or person other than the health-care system be required to pay? Increasingly, children are required to provide necessary care for their parents when the latter are unable to do so (the corollary of parents' duties to support minor children).[7] The real difficulty arises when neither the "system" nor an alternative payer is able to pay.

Life Expectancy and Quality of Life

Both short life expectancy and inadequate quality of life can be used as justifications for withholding treatment, whether from old people or others. But how are these factors to be assessed? How can we compare one person's quality of life with another's? And can we compare quality with quantity? Is there a minimal or minimum extension of life that is not worth having or not worth the cost involved? Semantics can be used to justify withholding treatment. Provided that this form of analysis is undertaken honestly, with integrity and according to careful analysis, it can provide helpful insight and assist in making decisions. For example, one can define a treatment as being intended either "to prolong living" or "to prolong dying," and withhold it in the latter situation. Such a withholding could be justified when someone is terminally ill, death is imminent, and the suffering involved in treatment far outweighs any benefits it could confer. As both ethics and the law have developed it would be, however, for the patient (or the legal representative of an incompetent patient) to make the latter decision.

ALLOCATION SCHEMATA THAT ARE NEUTRAL IN THEORY BUT NOT IN EFFECT

Some allocation schemata, though meant to apply generally, might nevertheless deprive old people of treatment. The use of quality of life and quantity of life as criteria could "rank the disabled elderly a low priority, as the gains in terms of complete restoration of health would be small and residual disability high."[8] Refusing to allocate resources to patients with self-inflicted conditions, such as those arising from smoking or alcoholism, could affect older people, too, because these conditions tend to develop later in life.

LEVELS OF DECISION-MAKING

Decisions are made on at least three levels: individual, institutional, and governmental. The ethical principles that apply at each level are not necessarily the same.

Individual Level

Individuals involved in making decisions about medical treatment include the patients themselves, their physicians, other health-care professionals, and sometimes the families. Most important are the patients. But, in terms of the quantity of resources deployed, physicians are most important. Of course, patients, their families, and sometimes their representatives or advocates can influence physicians. More demanding patients or their representatives are more likely to obtain scarce resources.

Edmund Pellegrino has analyzed the physician's role as that of "gatekeeper."[9] He has identified three categories of gatekeeping. Physicians are unavoidably "*de facto* gatekeepers" because their decisions determine the flow of 75 per cent of health-care expenditures. In this capacity, they have a duty to ensure that the money is spent effectively and beneficially. Depending upon the definition used, sometimes only the latter goal is achievable. Palliative care is highly beneficial, but ineffective in some important senses of that word; it neither cures illness nor prolongs life. It is, however, highly effective in relieving suffering and pain and improving the quality of life of dying people. If we see health care as an investment – if we believe that treatment must somehow augment the productivity of patients – we are likely to provide it only when it is both beneficial and effective. In contrast, if we see health care as a social good, we are more likely to consider the benefit it confers as justification for its cost.[10] Physicians can be involved in "negative gatekeeping" too, as when they benefit from constraining the use of resources. Conversely, "positive gatekeeping" happens when they benefit from increasing the use of resources.

As Pellegrino notes, negative and positive gatekeeping dilute the physician's duty as primary advocate of the patient's interest. To avoid the ethical problems inherent in the gatekeeper role, he suggests that institutions establish decision-making structures based on a hierarchy of services and a rationing principle set by public policy, one that is communicated to all who seek care.[11]

Institutional and Governmental Levels

The principles that should apply at the institutional or governmental level might well differ from those that apply at the individual level.[12] Giving primacy to utility and efficiency can be seen as acceptable for governments, for example, but not for individuals. Why is this so, when the results – harming people or depriving them of resources – are the same? It could be that it is easier to deny medical resources to a class than to an individual, and easier for a group than for an individual to make that decision. These different responses would be consistent with Guido Calabresi's theory that we find it easier to harm unidentified victims,[13] and with the concept that higher levels of risk are considered tolerable when a decision to impose risk is a shared responsibility. Moreover, governments have ethical obligations that can sometimes conflict: providing health care for society as a whole and for each individual. The former might justifiably be given priority by them.

It could be argued that the individual ethic should be the same or at least consistent with the communal one. Then we would have to argue over the appropriate content of this ethic. Or we could suggest that one of the two show a stricter degree of respect for persons and for life in terms of providing access to health care – or at least by not denying it. Alternatively, inconsistency could be seen as desirable and, here several perceptions are possible. According to one, inconsistency provides the best of two worlds: appropriate symbolism and also a "way out" in some circumstances. Inconsistency of this kind can either reflect or cause change, because an individual ethic is likely to change faster than a communal one, and because the former can influence the latter (which might change more slowly and less extensively). Yet another view would be that a community ethic is merely fiction, albeit one that is necessary for societal coherence and education, and that the ethic applied in practice is an individual one. Or a communal ethic could be considered an amalgam, or "mean," of various individual ones and, therefore, not applicable in individual cases.

LOGICAL AND INTUITIVE DECISION-MAKING

It is not enough to make decisions about the allocation of medical resources only on a logical, or rational, basis. We need a decision-making structure that will accommodate and integrate intuition and "examined emotions" as well as logic. (I use the term "examined emotions" to distinguish between emotional responses that people review – in connection with their sources, appropriateness, and validity – and unexamined emotionalism.) Moreover, that structure must facilitate both horizontal and vertical analysis. Horizontal analysis helps to identify additional factors relevant to the decision, often not readily obvious ones. Vertical analysis examines not only the conscious level of a decision but also its origins and causes, and its less immediate or direct effects. The latter would include intangible factors such as symbolism and the values being explicitly or implicitly brought into play.

To summarize: A rational and largely demographic approach to allocating health-care resources with an aging population is inadequate by itself. We must give a great deal of attention also to how people feel about the provision or non-provision of health care, and such extra-demographic factors as the social and political context of health care.[14] In other words, we must avoid "too ready a belief that the right answer as to what is better and appropriate can be found from analysis [only] of objective data ... [R]eaching solutions will require as many decisions about values as about facts."[15]

There might be no "right" answer either to the allocation problem in general or to any particular case – that is, none that provides a "no harm" option. An adequate decision-making structure, however, could be expected to result in a "right" *process* by ensuring that every issue is dealt with fully, fairly, and openly.

Some argue that including examined emotions would open up a slippery slope of ungovernable decision-making with undesirable outcomes. But most decision-making involves some slippery-slope aspects; handling these factors is simply a matter of control and good judgment rather than avoidance. Feelings exist and can be ignored only at our peril. Moreover, including examined emotions in the decision-making process does not mean that reasoning and rationality are excluded. Each component is necessary, but not, by itself, sufficient. The inclusion of all these components could lead to conflicts that would have to be resolved or tolerated. But it is better to face conflict than to avoid it by artificially excluding factors. Indeed, the effort to resolve conflicts could prove unexpectedly fruitful, giving decision-makers greater insight into situations or into the implications of their decisions.

TRUST

Trust[16] is another important component in making decisions about the allocation of medical resources. Individuals and communities must be able to trust those who make these decisions and the mechanisms they use to do so. Some decision-makers are paternalistic and require "blind trust" (I know what is best for you; simply trust me, because I will act in your best interests); others are egalitarian and use the model of "earned trust" (Trust me, because I have proved to you that you can trust me). Trust is necessary between health-care professionals and their patients, colleagues, institutions, and communities, but also between communities and governments. Health care allocation decisions can prevent the establishment of trust or threaten the trust present in each of these relationships. Moreover, maintaining trust in the context of health care can be a very important factor in maintaining the more general ethical fabric of every community.

By understanding the importance of trust, we will be much less likely to ignore the harm or suffering allocation decisions might cause. Instead, when these decisions risk imposing or do impose harm, we would recognize a duty to seek ways of avoiding that harm, in particular by carrying out research.

CONCLUSION

Unfortunately, we might not be able to find any "right" answers – ones that harm no one – in allocating medical resources with an aging population. We are able, however, to use "right" principles and processes. General goodwill and personal conscience and integrity are essential, but not sufficient, approaches or safeguards. Examined cognitive and emotional responses are necessary, along with structured and disciplined procedures. To develop these responses and procedures is a major challenge for contemporary health law and ethics. Development is essential in the search for answers to the companion questions mentioned at the beginning of this chapter: Should the baby live? and Should the grandparents die?

3 The Song of Death: The Lyrics of Euthanasia

This chapter began as one lecture in a series on medical decisions at the end of life. In preparing what follows, two common but powerful and important insights were strongly reinforced. First, the debate about euthanasia concerns much more than that matter itself, for individuals and for society; second, the role of language is immensely important in formulating both the questions and the responses to them. Any consideration of euthanasia requires both thinking and feeling – and language affects not only how we think and feel but also whether these functions are integrated or separated.

To explore some of the complex dilemmas and interactions that confront us in dealing with euthanasia, we need to examine the way in which language is used in this context – including, but not limited to, its use in the law. Language is used in describing and formulating the issues presented by euthanasia, in handling these issues and in eliciting responses to the approaches taken. We should include an exploration of how language is used to label or characterize situations in order to deal with them. Moreover, we should recognize that language is relevant to "talking about" euthanasia and to "doing" it.[1] One of most striking examples of the use of language in these ways is the book *Final Exit*.[2] It "talks" about euthanasia in order to advocate it. But its language can be directly involved in "doing" euthanasia, too. For example, people have been found dead with the book beside them, open at the pages containing detailed instructions that they have followed to kill themselves.

DEFINITION

Nowhere is the use of language more important and, sometimes, more confused and confusing than when it is used for the purpose of definition. This confusion is especially true with respect to euthanasia. Even with an overriding aim of neutrality and precision, it can be difficult to define, accurately and clearly, which interventions or non-interventions constitute euthanasia and which do not. But a definition is necessary.

The etymological origin of this word means "good death." The use of the word, quite apart from its definition (of what does and does not constitute euthanasia), merits careful consideration. For everyone, at some level, death is "bad," in the sense of sad. But some ways of dying are "less bad," or less sad, than others. These are "good deaths." We all hope to be included among those who have "good deaths," with assistance if necessary. Where we disagree is on what limits to assistance, if any, there should be.

It is interesting that people who advocate the legalization of euthanasia, as well as some of those who oppose doing so, have argued for a wide definition. They propose that it should include all medical interventions or non-interventions that would shorten life or that would not prolong it.[3] But each group has adopted this position for exactly the opposite reason. The pro-choice group argue for a broad definition in order to allow all interventions or non-interventions that would promote a "good death," including those undertaken with the primary intention of killing people. Some of those who oppose euthanasia (especially some pro-life groups) argue for a broad definition in order to prohibit all interventions or non-interventions that would shorten life – not only those undertaken with the primary intention of killing people.

I have argued elsewhere[4] that pro-life groups that take this position have harmed the cause of those who oppose euthanasia, in the narrow sense defined below, but would allow valid refusals of treatment, withholding or withdrawal of medically futile treatment or treatment that would cause far more harm than benefit, and access to treatment, even if it would shorten life, if such treatment were necessary to relieve pain or other symptoms of serious physical distress (for example, intractable vomiting).[5] To define these interventions or non-interventions as euthanasia forces people to take a position either for or against *all* interventions or non-interventions that could result in the shortening of life; it does not allow them to take a separate position on euthanasia in a narrow sense. In other words, according to this approach, people must be either for all such interventions or non-interventions or against all of them. I propose that the acceptability of each intervention or non-intervention at the end of life varies according to moral, ethical, legal, medical, social, and societal points of view – and they should not, therefore, be dealt with as a unified whole. In short, the full spectrum of questions raised by medical intervention or non-intervention at the end of life should not be included in one term, as occurs when the word "euthanasia" is used to cover all means of promoting "good" (or less "bad") deaths, as the pro-choice groups argue, or all interventions or non-interventions that could result in shortening of life, as some pro-life groups argue. The terms in this most important, sensitive, nuanced, and delicate area of decision-making should be used precisely.

With the above cautions in mind, I suggest that euthanasia be defined in somewhat legalistic terms as

an intervention or a non-intervention by one person to end the life of another person, who is terminally ill, for the purpose of relieving suffering, with the intent[6] of causing the death[7] of the other person. But an intervention does not constitute euthanasia when the primary intent is either to provide treatment necessary for the relief of pain or other symptoms of serious physical distress, or the non-provision or withdrawal of treatment is justified, in particular, because there is a valid refusal of treatment or the treatment is medically futile (that is, would have no useful physiological effect.)[8]

In less legalistic language, this definition can be restated as an intervention or non-intervention to end the life of someone else who is terminally ill; the goal is to relieve suffering by causing death. Euthanasia is not involved if the primary goal is not to cause death, but to treat pain or other symptoms of serious physical distress; nor is euthanasia involved if not providing treatment, or withdrawing it, is justified either because of a valid refusal of treatment or because the treatment is medically futile – that is, it would have no useful physiological effect. Unless otherwise indicated, this definition of euthanasia is used throughout this book.

This definition excludes the provision of reasonably necessary treatment, which could or would shorten life, for the relief of pain or other symptoms of serious physical distress – provided that the primary intent is to relieve pain or other symptoms of serious physical distress and not to cause death. Although, in legal terms, an intent to cause death could be present, the law does not take this intent into account provided the physician does not want this outcome. The definition excludes also the justified withholding or withdrawal of treatment. In other words, it excludes valid refusals of treatment from euthanasia,[9] and thus allows them for three reasons. First, these cases do not involve the intent of causing death (although they do involve the intention of allowing people to die). Second, the primary intent is either to respect the right to refuse treatment or not to impose futile treatment. Third, death is not caused, from the legal perspective, by the failure to provide or by the withdrawal of treatment; rather, it is caused by the patient's underlying disease.

The proposed definition covers both voluntary and involuntary euthanasia (euthanasia with or without personal informed consent); it is limited to terminal illness; and it requires the relief of suffering as the goal of euthanasia.

Compare this definition with one used in 1985 by the Netherlands' State Commission on Euthanasia: "Euthanasia is the deliberate action to terminate life, by someone other than, and on the request of, the patient concerned."[10] The latter covers only voluntary euthanasia – on the request, and with the consent of, a competent person. Although voluntary euthanasia has just been fully legalized in the Netherlands, there is an ongoing debate about involuntary euthanasia. Disturbing evidence had come to light. Some Dutch physicians had been using the definition then currently accepted in their country to argue that "involuntary" interventions undertaken with the primary intention of causing death did not constitute euthanasia. Why not? Precisely because they were involuntary.[11] Involuntary euthanasia was not prohibited, according to these Dutch physicians, because it was not mentioned by the then current guidelines permitting euthanasia. As a result, they did not believe that these interventions required compliance with the guidelines and procedural safeguards applicable to euthanasia – especially those requiring that patients be competent and consenting and that every case of euthanasia be reported. This is a striking example of how powerful definitions can be. In fact, it turns the definition of euthanasia on its head to achieve exactly the opposite results from those intended – that only voluntary euthanasia would be undertaken, and only by complying with strict procedural safeguards. As Maurice de Wachter warns, "definitions are not morally neutral. They are not just innocent tools that allow us to describe reality. Rather they shape our perceptions of reality"[12] – and, one could add, our actions based on those perceptions.

The Dutch definition of euthanasia that was used in practice, prior to the recent legislation being enacted, did not necessarily limit euthanasia to terminally ill people. Although judicial guidelines[13] in the Netherlands allowed euthanasia only for terminally ill people, it was considered legitimate in the case, for example, of a quadriplegic young woman who requested it, but whose condition did not fall within any usual definition of terminal illness.[14] There are arguments for and against including terminal illness as a criterion in the definition of euthanasia. One argument against it is that terminal illness is difficult to define. In theory, it is an arbitrary point on a continuum; at one extreme, after all, life can be seen as a fatal illness. In practice, it is even more difficult to apply. It could be difficult to say that patients are very likely to die soon, when that prediction is required for them to qualify as terminally ill patients. But physicians could be allowed to declare patients terminally ill. Although this requirement would restrict euthanasia in general, because there would have to be some objective reality to any finding that a patient is terminally ill, it might be too open-ended and liable to abuse. And what if a definition that included terminal illness as a criterion were used in the same way as voluntariness in the Dutch definition was? This definition, which insists that euthanasia be voluntary, was, as we have seen, interpreted to mean that involuntary euthanasia is somehow not regarded as euthanasia. Likewise, killing people who are not terminally ill might somehow not be regarded as euthanasia. These cases might not be regarded as homicide, moreover, because they have all the features – other than terminal illness – required to classify them as euthanasia, not homicide.

The definition in the Dutch guidelines that preceded the new legislation (which does not essentially change the grounds for euthanasia or physician-assisted suicide) did not expressly require severe and untreatable suffering. Nonetheless, this was one of the conditions required if Dutch physicians were to be immune from criminal prosecution for euthanasia.[15] Also, the Dutch definition did not limit the carrying out of euthanasia to physicians; but that, too, was required for immunity according to the Dutch guidelines[16] and is required under the new legislation.

The Dutch definition of euthanasia extended only to acts, although "the deliberate action to terminate life" could include withdrawal or omission of treatment (for example, unplugging a respirator or withholding artificial hydration and nutrition). The possibility of carrying out euthanasia in these latter ways leads to the much criticized active/passive (act/omission) distinction – the distinction between "active euthanasia" (actively killing) and "passive euthanasia" (killing either by not providing or by withdrawing treatment). The distinction can be artificial,[17] so the terms should be abandoned in order to define euthanasia precisely.[18] Some failures to provide treatment or withdrawals of treatment should be classified as euthanasia, but not others. In particular, respect for valid refusals of treatment should not be classified as euthanasia. Examples would include a competent adult patient's informed refusal of life-support treatment[19] or of blood transfusions for religious reasons.[20] Making this distinction does not mean that one may not disagree with both euthanasia and respecting the right to refuse treatment. One may do so, but it is still important

to distinguish them. Euthanasia involves the intention of causing
death; apart from necessary treatment for the relief of pain, which
could be given with this intention, euthanasia is always wrong. Withholding or withdrawing treatment involves an intention of allowing
people to die. This conduct is not justified when it can be regarded as
constituting, or as equivalent to, the intention of causing death. That
is euthanasia. Allowing someone to die is justified when it results from
a valid refusal of treatment or from the fact that treatment is withdrawn (the continuation of which would be medically futile). That is
not euthanasia.

In short, one can have euthanasia, in the narrow sense of this term,
by omission as well as by act. What is important is to distinguish omissions that constitute euthanasia from omissions of treatment that do
not constitute euthanasia.

There is sometimes a fine line between having the intention of allowing someone to die and having the intention of causing someone
to die. This is especially true in relation to withdrawing or not providing treatment except when competent patients refuse treatment or
give "advance directives" to this effect. But the important point is that
there is a line. I suggest that the nature of interventions on one side of
this line is different in kind from those on the other side. Elsewhere, I
have described these demarcations as "marker events."[21] What occurs
on one side can be seen as different in kind, especially with regard to
avoiding precedents, from what occurs on the other. The marker event
for distinguishing euthanasia from other medical interventions at the
end of life is a *mens rea* (state of mind) of a primary intention to cause
death and an *actus reus* (conduct) of an act or omission that causes
someone else's death.

How can we justify failure to provide treatment or withdrawal of
treatment in cases that involve a valid refusal of treatment or in which
the treatment is medically futile or disproportional?[22] These cases can
be dealt with on the basis of either intention or causation. They are
characterized by the intention of allowing someone to die when it is
certain, or almost certain, that death will result from the act or omission in question. But not all acts or omissions that allow someone to
die are equivalent to the intention of causing death. Not all, in other
words, are culpable. Acting on a valid refusal of treatment is a non-cul-
pable act or omission, although it involves the intention of allowing
someone to die. Indeed, *not* acting in this way could be culpable. To
impose treatment on a patient who refuses it is usually regarded by the
law as battery[23] and could constitute criminal assault.

Yet another possible legal analysis resulting in the same outcome is
that there is sometimes no duty to treat or to continue treatment. In
such situations, omitting treatment, even if it results in death, is not

legally actionable. But that is not a strong argument. When there is a "treatment relationship" with a physician, omissions are unlikely to be considered "mere" omissions that do not attract legal liability. Consequently, these omissions would have to be justified on some other basis, such as a valid refusal or the futility of treatment. An alternative, or additional, analysis leading to the same result is that the intentional act (for example, turning off the respirator) is not, in law, the cause of death; the patient dies from some underlying disease. Those who oppose euthanasia, but agree to respect refusals of treatment, even when the omission of treatment could or would result in death, might have made a mistake in denying that, as in euthanasia, their actions would involve the intention of allowing someone to die or even to cause death. They do involve that intention, but intention alone does not make an act culpable. The act must be regarded by the law as the cause of a prohibited outcome – in this case, someone's death. Death is caused in fact by the act of treatment withdrawal and by the underlying disease. In contrast, death is caused in law by the underlying disease only, when withdrawal of treatment is justified and this "cause" is not one that attracts legal liability. In other words, withdrawal is not regarded in law as the cause of death.[24] This scenario can be compared with giving someone a lethal injection. The injection is the sole cause of death. It is clearly the cause in both fact and law. It is a "cause" that attracts legal liability.

The argument that there is no justifiable distinction between "active" and "passive" euthanasia (which is correct if euthanasia is involved in each case), and, therefore, that there is no justifiable distinction between euthanasia and respecting the refusal of treatment,[25] has been put to a further use. It could be that confusion between passive euthanasia and respecting the refusal of treatment has been generated deliberately in the case of pro-choice on euthanasia groups to convince people that agreeing with a right to refuse treatment means that they – as logical, rational, and consistent thinkers – must agree with euthanasia and that, in respecting the right to refuse treatment, they are committing euthanasia.[26] Also implied is the fact that, if they feel comfortable with having carried out "euthanasia" of this kind – by respecting refusals of treatment – they should feel equally comfortable carrying out euthanasia as I have defined it. Similarly, some groups in the anti-euthanasia movement seek to eliminate any distinction between active and passive euthanasia. Their purpose is the same: to argue that agreeing with passive euthanasia necessarily implies agreeing with active euthanasia – if one is to be logical, rational, and consistent. But they do so to promote the opposite result: both active and passive euthanasia should be opposed and prohibited.

There is another pro-euthanasia argument, a sophisticated one. And it, too, is based on regarding the right to refuse treatment as a form of euthanasia. This argument appeared in the *Harvard Law Review*[27] and may be summarized as follows: to recognize a refusal of treatment recognizes a "right to die." If there is a "right to die," there are no convincing moral, political, social, or legal distinctions between allowing people to die from underlying diseases through non-treatment, following their refusal of it, or helping them to die with active assistance.[28] This "right to be assisted in dying" purportedly includes a person's right to choose and to control the time, place, conditions, and manner of dying, whether through passive or active means.[29] This argument interprets recognition by some courts of a "right to die" as encompassing not only a right to be allowed to die (for instance, by refusing treatment) but also a right to be assisted in dying (including by providing euthanasia).[30] But none of the cases in which courts have referred to "a right to die" has contemplated legitimating euthanasia by using that term. One question, therefore, is whether these cases really do provide any precedent for a "right to die with assistance."

The term "a right to be assisted in dying," standing alone, is ambiguous. It could be meant to articulate only a right to palliative care and, as Alexander Morgan Capron eloquently states, "There are so many things – including simple companionship and love – that one might do to 'aid' a dying person, that the phrase 'aid-in-dying' cannot help but disguise more than it reveals."[31] The *Harvard Law Review* article is clear, however, on what is meant: physicians should be legally immune for killing patients, when doing so fulfills specific conditions.[32] It is possible also that a right to die could have the juridical correlate of an obligation to kill a person who wanted to die. But this possibility is rejected: "The right to die with assistance would provide only a right against state interference, not a right to force an unwilling physician to assist in a patient's suicide."[33]

I will discuss the "language of euthanasia" in more detail later, but the use of language in this article merits notice. It is much more difficult to oppose a "right against state interference" in medical decisions at the end of life (a characterization that can include euthanasia, that is, a lethal injection) than immunity for physicians who kill patients. Yet the two can be identical in content and in result.

The right to die with assistance is supported in the *Harvard Law Review* article, ironically, by a close investigation of how American courts have *not* recognized an absolute right to refuse treatment and then by equating this limited right with a "right to die." The authors demonstrate that American courts have put conditions on exercising the right to refuse treatment and, therefore, on the right to die. In particular, the courts have balanced the exercise of this right against "state interests in preserving life, protecting third parties, and preserving the medical profession's ethical image"[34] – any one of which can be given priority. These cases show, the authors propose, that in some situations (those that involve no overriding state interests), but not all (those that do), decisions to refuse treatment that would result in death are respected. There is, therefore, a "right to die." If none of these same state interests would be contravened by "assisting death" (and they propose, they would not be in some cases), there would be no reason not to assist death by "active means."

This position can be compared with that of the common-law jurisdictions of Canada and the civil-law jurisdiction of Quebec, in all of which the right to refuse treatment tends to be regarded as much more absolute[35] and, possibly, of a different nature or origin. The Canadian approach has been to focus on a right not to be touched without consent – the right to inviolability[36] – rather than on any "right to die." This approach, which recognizes a more absolute right to refuse treatment, pursuant to respect for a right to inviolability, does not lend itself so readily, if at all, to the type of argument outlined above.

There is a valuable lesson to be learned from the possible consequences, such as those I have described, of promoting a non-absolute approach to the right to refuse treatment. What would appear initially to be a more life-favouring position (and one promoted by some pro-life groups) – that the right to refuse treatment is not absolute – can in fact be used to achieve exactly the opposite outcome. It can be used in support of the pro-choice on euthanasia position, as, for example, in the *Harvard Law Review* article referred to above.

Pain-relief treatment that could or even would shorten life – but is reasonably necessary to relieve pain – can raise difficulties with respect to the intention of causing death and potential criminal liability. Such treatment must be able to be given with legal immunity. When the motive is to relieve pain and not to kill, the intervention must be regarded as justified – despite the possible presence in a technical, legal sense of an intention to cause death.[37] Motive can be regarded as an excuse or a justification – a defence – protecting against or negating, respectively, criminal or other liability. This analysis is the one most consistent with traditional theory in criminal law.[38] Providing adequate pain-relief treatment could also extend life, because patients would be less physically and psychologically distressed. In that case, failure to provide pain relief could shorten life.

This topic is a critical one in the context of euthanasia. Fear of being left in unbearable pain – or, even more horrific, the reality of being in that situation, which still happens far too often – is probably a strong impetus for many to argue that euthanasia should be made available. We should be acutely aware that some attitudes and systems discourage the provision of adequate pain-relief treatment. I learned of a case in which a man, dying of disseminated carcinoma, was being given Tylenol for severe pain. A physician on night rotation changed the order to morphine. The next night, the doctor was again called to see the man, because he was in very severe pain. She found that, during the intervening day, the man's attending physician had cancelled the order for morphine and had written another for Tylenol. When questioned, the attending physician said that he thought the man was "a complainer" and, in any case, he did not want to have "addicted patients." These are two responses that one would hope not to hear from any physician practising medicine in the new millennium. In another case, a young resident physician gave a dose of potassium chloride to a dying patient in severe pain because the hospital ward's supply of morphine had run out that night and no more could be obtained until the hospital pharmacy opened the next morning. We must ensure not only that health-care practitioners are humane but also that we have humane systems in health-care institutions.[39]

Leaving people in pain is both a human tragedy and a breach of the most fundamental concepts of human rights and human ethics. It should be treated as legally actionable medical malpractice and possibly as a crime. Providing reasonably necessary pain-relief treatment, even that which could shorten life, must not be considered criminal. This topic is explored in much greater depth elsewhere.[40] My point here is that those who oppose euthanasia, but fail to ensure that adequate pain-relief treatment is provided (or, even worse, oppose doing so if that could shorten life), do much to promote the case for euthanasia.

Whether one believes that euthanasia should be available to those who request it or that it should be prohibited, we should deal individually with each medical intervention that takes place at the end of life. In particular, situations that involve the intention of causing death should be dealt with separately from other situations in which there is no such intention. And, within the former group, further distinctions are necessary. In this discussion, the terminology must be very clear. Consequently, the word "euthanasia" is used in the strict sense of the definition given above. The paradigm case of euthanasia is giving a lethal injection with the intention of killing the person. We all agree that this act is euthanasia.

A narrow definition is needed because euthanasia is different in kind, and not merely in degree, from other measures that can mean also that life is not prolonged, or even that death is "caused" (in the sense that it occurs sooner than it would otherwise do). In particular, I argue that the "analogy between forgoing treatment and active euthanasia is simply false."[41] Most people who favour euthanasia would disagree with that statement. They would argue that the outcome is the same – death – and that once allowing death to occur is justified, how this is brought about is morally, and ought to be legally, irrelevant.[42] Recognizing, for the sake of discussion, that this argument could be true does not justify making it true by treating all interventions at the end of life as the same – regardless of whether they involve the intention or primary intention of causing death. Each category of intervention requires separate justification.

If one imagines a continuum, with a very liberal pro-euthanasia position at one end and a very stringent pro-life position at the other, the position I advocate is somewhere in the middle. This position is much more difficult to articulate, define, and defend than that of either pole, for attack can come from both sides. For this reason alone, some people choose one pole or the other. I have suggested elsewhere that living in "the purple-pink middle" represents what we see, at least initially, as an "impossible combination" of attitudes, values, and beliefs.[43] But even though the centre is usually the most difficult position, it could be the most honest one, too, in that it accommodates and even reconciles what we say and what we do. I propose that the most ethically and legally acceptable position with respect to decisions about interventions or non-interventions at the end of life, even when these approaches could or would shorten life, can be set out in three principles. First, to recognize a right to adequate treatment for the relief of pain or other symptoms of serious physical distress and a right to refuse treatment. Second, to accept that there is no obligation to provide a medically futile treatment. And, third, to prohibit all other interventions or non-interventions undertaken with the intention of causing death.

THE EUTHANASIA DEBATE IN CONTEXT

The discussion of euthanasia is widespread. Its venue ranges from cartoons to the pulpit to Parliament. For example, a *Far Side* cartoon shows an old rooster lying in bed, hooked up to many life-support machines, being visited by his hen wife. She says to him: "It is a miracle you have survived, George. Just yesterday, we were wondering whether or not to wring your neck."[44] Media coverage has been intensive, although there is considerable misconception as to what constitutes euthanasia. Often, euthanasia is confused with respecting refusals of life-sustaining treatment. Is that intentional?[45]

Political debate has been intense. In 1988 California's Humane and Dignified Death Initiative (Physician Assisted Death Bill) failed to obtain sufficient signatures for submission on a ballot; in 1992 the sequel was defeated by a margin of 54 per cent to 46 per cent.[46] In 1991 Washington State's Initiative 119 was rejected by voters. That same year, two private members' bills were introduced into the Canadian Parliament. One sought to clarify that those who respect the right to refuse treatment or who provide pain-relief treatment (including treatment that could shorten life, provided it was necessary to relieve pain) are not liable to criminal prosecution.[47] The other bill went far beyond this position by proposing a system of legalized euthanasia.[48] Both bills lapsed.

Also widespread are academic discussions and research projects on euthanasia. One example is the work of Katherine Young, who investigated self-willed or other-willed death in Eastern religions. Her goal was to gain insight, through comparative and historical methods, into how we are handling, or should handle, euthanasia.[49] Her results showed that euthanasia gains acceptability, at both the individual and the collective levels, when societies can be described as either "too religious" or "too secular." Once again, seeking the balance of the "purple-pink middle"[50] (in this instance, between religiosity and secularity) would be an important safeguard.

Quite apart from the arguments raised for or against euthanasia, and by whom and in what ways these arguments are being explored or promoted, the context or forum itself is not necessarily a neutral factor. For instance, it has been alleged that "the [Dutch] media have been virtually monopolized by the euthanasia proponents, and a whole generation of Dutch people has been raised without even hearing any serious opposition to it."[51]

Some events affect the discussion of euthanasia. Derek • Humphry's book on how to commit suicide, *Final Exit*, which strongly advocates euthanasia, was number one on the *New York Times* best-seller list. That it became a best-seller can be interpreted in radically different ways. On the one hand, it can be seen as evidence that the book is needed and is acceptable. On the other hand, it can be viewed as an indication that the book has a morbid appeal and could foster psychopathological tendencies – for instance, suicide by seriously depressed people – to the grave detriment of people with these tendencies. Certainly, there is a major difference, including one of practical impact, between this book and one that argues the case for euthanasia, but not as a heavily promoted "do-it-yourself" text.

The debate on euthanasia is affected also by its tone, whether impartial or partial, and by a related characteristic: whether the focus is on a theoretical, analytical approach or on a practical, "how to" approach. As Susan Wolf[52] points out, not all contexts or discussions are equally

accessible to or even aimed at everyone. She compares the "propa-
ganda and diatribe"[53] of Humphry in *Final Exit*, which clearly caught
public attention in a major way, with the perceived failure of bioethics
to label the questions raised by euthanasia broadly enough to engage
in the "momentous public debate, with profound ethical, legal, religious, psychological and medical implications."[54] She argues that "bio-
ethicists must strive to reach a popular audience and convey
arguments effectively."[55] In other words, it is their obligation to ensure
that the context of bioethics extends to encompass all who should participate in the debate, including the public. This argument provides an
insight: that defining an appropriate context for the debate can be a
way of expanding or limiting the participants, and that, in turn, will
undoubtedly affect the outcome. This potential for manipulation
should be recognized.

WHY ARE WE TALKING OF EUTHANASIA NOW?

Is it a coincidence that our societies are now engaged in a discussion of
legalizing euthanasia? If not, what has stimulated the discussion? After
all, we have always become ill, suffered, and died. These events are not
new. Why, then, when we have prohibited euthanasia for such a long
time, are we now considering its legalization?

Is It an Indirect Way of Talking about Death?

It could be that "euthanasia talk" is a way of covering up some other reality. There is much discussion of euthanasia, but less of death. Talking
about death is difficult. Indeed, we have been described as a society that
is unusually fearful of death, a death-denying society.[56] This term is interesting because denial requires some minimal level of consciousness
of the "thing" feared, in order to suppress the larger consciousness of it.
Is euthanasia the conscious mechanism that we use to suppress our
larger awareness of death? Is it less frightening to talk of euthanasia than
of death? Consequently, is the discussion of death being carried out in
the context of euthanasia? We used to talk about death in the context of
religion, but some of us no longer adhere to organized religion. Even if
we do, many of us no longer talk about death in that context. In recent
times, we have not talked about death in any context except, possibly, in
the symbolic and ritualized forms of literature and the arts. Could it be
also that talk of euthanasia deconditions us to the fear of death – especially because, at the same time as we speak of the feared "event," we
speak of controlling it through euthanasia? As psychiatrist William

Winslade said, "The need to control death whether by postponing it or hastening it – seems to rest on a deep fear and denial."[57] Could it even be that "euthanasia talk" is a terror-management device for both individuals and society? Social psychologist Jeff Greenberg[58] and his colleagues argue that the thought of death raises the deepest terror, which we then need to manage. We do so by trying to achieve a consensus that affirms our most important values; these values, in turn, provide reassurance. This explanation perhaps accounts for the strong polarization and conflict in the euthanasia debate: each side wants the reassurance of having its values affirmed. It could be that this terror is so great, moreover, that we would rather be dead than living in fear of death (particularly imminent death); euthanasia supposedly allows us to achieve this outcome.

It is possible that advocating euthanasia is linked with a desire for control. Control is related to the relief of suffering. Suffering is present in experiencing a sense of personal disintegration and loss of control over personal fate.[59] To move from chance (which the occurrence of death has largely been) to choice (which is the promise of euthanasia) can be to reduce suffering. People might see euthanasia as a way to avoid present suffering or future suffering (either because they seek euthanasia at the time, or because it allays fear – which is a form of suffering – that they can avoid suffering at some time in the future). Also, euthanasia might fulfill the need or desire for certainty, which is related to the need or desire for control. Stated another way, euthanasia reduces uncertainty, which reduces anxiety, and, consequently, provides reassurance. Then, too, euthanasia could be a "do something" response. When faced with fearful situations, anxiety tends to be increased by inactivity and decreased by activity; in the latter case, we are at least "doing something" to remedy the situation. A feeling of greater control reduces anxiety. It is interesting to note in this context an attitude among physicians, that is expressed when they tell their patients that nothing more can be done: that position might cause some patients to seek euthanasia.[60]

The availability of euthanasia could inflict suffering, too. People might fear that it would be practised in ways that would reduce personal control. Similarly, they might worry about the future use of euthanasia. It has been alleged that some old people in the Netherlands fear physicians and hospitals because they fear being subjected to euthanasia.[61] Instead of giving people more individual control, euthanasia might result, overall, in less control. Even seeing oneself as a burden on society, when old and ill, and wanting to do the "right thing" by requesting euthanasia is a loss of individual control and freedom of spirit. Both the anticipation and the experience inflict suffering. And

allowing euthanasia means that people must choose whether or not to
o use it. They might have to justify their choice to continue living because "the existence of the option becomes a subtle pressure to request
it."[62] Situations of this kind are very likely to be a source of suffering.

Euthanasia might be a vehicle for addressing much wider and
deeper realities that operate at conscious, unconscious, or symbolic
levels. As a result of their research on self-willed death, Young and her
colleagues propose

that "reason alone" has never been the sole guiding principle by which individuals have killed themselves or others when ill or old. Rather, reason has often
been used either to affirm or to cover the operation of deeper values that are
not expressly identified. These have included the heroic ideal of the self-willed
death among warriors threatened with defeat or the derivative ideal among as-
cetics or philosophers of self-willed death to demonstrate their version of courage. Unlike the ancient world's desire for a heroic form of death and Nazi
Germany's legitimation of euthanasia to create a "super race," today's societies
are entertaining the idea of self-willed or assisted death to avoid suffering or
ensure "dignity." Since the pain of dying can be effectively treated in most
cases, what accounts for the current movement to legalise euthanasia?[63]

As well as seeking consensus on values for the sake of consensus, because we need the reassurance that consensus provides, what deeper
values could we be trying to affirm or to hide by arguing for or against
euthanasia?

The analysis of a French psychoanalyst, Marie de Hennezel, is of
great interest in this respect, for it illustrates some of the enormous
complexities we are dealing with. It shows that two emotions in particular, fear and love, and the relation between them, are central to the euthanasia debate. De Hennezel argues "that a fine death is an illusion, a
myth ... which people tell themselves to appease their anguish," and
that our society is "governed by th[e] myth of a good death."[64] She argues that there are two versions of this "myth."[65] One sees a "good
death" as "a discreet and rapid death, unconscious, and, particularly, of
no bother to anyone else." This description corresponds to a world view
in which death is denied, medicine is all-powerful, caregivers see death
as a failure, and death is "experienced in great solitude and with no
guideposts or values." This is a "world of effectivity, efficiency, perfor-
mance, with priority given to cost-effectiveness [and] consumption ...
[a] world of objects not of subjects – in short, a world stripped of souls
and spirit, a world without love." The other version comes from "a new
humanism ... try[ing] to bring life and death together as one. An accompanied death, a socialised death, one experienced in lucidity up to

the end becomes the desired good death." The world view behind this version is a much less certain one. In fact, as de Hennezel says, its essence is recognition of uncertainty about the meaning of life and death, of the need for sensitivity to others, and of the need for enough humility to allow others to experience death in their own ways. It involves recognizing that there are possibilities of the extremes of either "nothingness or ... mystery of the beyond." It is "an appeal to change our way of loving." This "new concept of 'dying well' ... is no longer an illusion or a myth, but a permission to experience one's death as one wishes, to experience it fully, with the assurance of being loved and accepted no matter what. This of course requires that someone else be capable of that degree of true love."[66]

Accepting the propositions set out above could lead to the conclusion that we should reject euthanasia: it is too "easy," in the sense of being a simplistic response to the complexity of death, rational at the cost of ignoring profound emotion, cold and unloving. But those in favour of euthanasia argue exactly the converse: that euthanasia is among the great humanitarian causes.[67] The important point to note here is that, whether we argue for or against euthanasia, our arguments are of this nature. In dealing with euthanasia, we are dealing with some of the most fundamental and critical issues of our humanness, both as individuals and collectively. Whether we are pro- or anti- euthanasia, we agree that it is a central focus in our contemporary discussion of these fundamental issues. Where we disagree is whether allowing or prohibiting euthanasia best promotes the human spirit, humaneness, and humanity.

Is There a Newly Perceived Need for Euthanasia?

Polls in California[68] and the Netherlands[69] have shown that approximately 70 per cent of these populations want euthanasia to be available – and this percentage is increasing. But care should be taken when interpreting polls; responses within the same survey might not be consistent. Some polls on abortion, for instance, have shown that most people approve of abortion on demand, but also that most people do not approve of women having abortions for just any reason – for instance, simply for the sake of convenience.[70] Similarly, surveys on willingness to donate organs give inconsistent results. Between 70 and 80 per cent declare themselves willing to donate, but only between 10 and 20 per cent of these same people have actually done so.[71] In short, there might be a large gap between what people say they are willing to accommodate and what they decide to accommodate when it comes to making actual, rather than hypothetical, decisions. This difference was shown in Washington State by the vote on Initiative 119, A Voluntary Choice for Terminally Ill Persons: Death with Dignity. The polls, before voting on this initiative, indicated that it would succeed, yet it failed by a margin of 54 per cent to 46 per cent. Moreover, the results of polling 2,000 randomly chosen physicians about this initiative, 1,105 of whom responded, show comparable discrepancies and have been described as "mystifying."[72]

Of the physicians who answered, 75 per cent said they did not believe they should have the legal right to give a terminally ill patient a lethal injection. Fully 60 per cent said doctors should not be allowed to prescribe a lethal dose of medication to be self-administered by the patient. And 75 percent said they would not be willing to be personally involved in aiding a patient's death. Yet, in answer to the question, "Should the WSMA [Washington State Medical Association] support or oppose Initiative 119?" respondents were split down the middle, with 543 doctors saying the association should support the initiative, and 562 indicating the organization should oppose it.[73]

These results might contain three important warnings. First, our sense of responsibility for the outcomes of decisions might be diminished when that responsibility is shared with a group and exercised through group decision-making. Second, some physicians might make decisions concerning their own conduct according to their own personal morality, but they might not necessarily want to impose the same morality on others. Third, discrepancies of the type outlined above might show that we may need to talk about doing (or, possibly more accurately, the doing of) things that we ourselves would not do and do not want others to do. In other words, the discussion itself might have a purpose other than promoting the conduct (in this case, euthanasia) that forms its content.

The warnings have been sounded: what we say might not reflect what we are willing to do, and what we say might not be inherently consistent. Yet it remains true that most Western democracies have witnessed a groundswell of popular opinion in favour of euthanasia and its promotion as a choice that should be made available (or at least not prohibited). Why is this support occurring? Why now?

Modern Medical Technology

Some people attribute this perceived need for euthanasia as one more effect of modern medical technology. "Playing God" to sustain patients who would once certainly have been dead might have given us a sense of power over life as well as death. Once we use technology to prolong life, in short, there might be some correlative sense in which we believe that we are entitled to use it also to shorten life. Certainly, we do not need new technology to kill; this possibility is as old as the human species itself.

It could be, however, that a fear of the overuse of medical technology has contributed to calls for euthanasia. This fear is summed up by people who say they would rather be dead than left "to the mercy of doctors 'and their machines.' "[74] The development of rights to refuse treatment has been one response to these fears. Rights are a major currency of the law. In contrast, medicine tends to give priority to fulfilling needs. Fulfilling needs and respecting rights can give rise to conflict, especially in relation to refusals of treatment with modern medical technology. Allowing patients to refuse treatment at the expense of fulfilling major and serious needs (which they have or are perceived to have) has been described as "rotting with your rights on."[75] Whatever we choose as the "correct" approach, it could be very important to ensure that "people die with their rights on." This would help prevent the overuse of medical technology and, equally important, the fear of this overuse – which is not only harmful in itself but also likely to promote the advocacy of euthanasia.

It is true also that developments in medical technology have given rise to "the secularization of the human image"[76] and possibly to a different vision of human identity. Transplantation could mean that we no longer each see the self as one integral whole, for instance, but as a collection of interchangeable parts. That would translate into a modular theory of human identity.[77] This theory has mechanistic connotations, which could be linked with the increasing number of people who consider euthanasia acceptable. We are, in general, unsentimental about disposing of outdated, worn-out, or no-longer-efficient machines. If we see ourselves as machines, at least in some respects, we might apply the same attitude to others. Euthanasia could be an expression in practice of this very attitude.

Individual Rights

Emphasis on the rights of individuals has been a phenomenon of major importance in many Western societies. It might have peaked by now, which means that we must take care to continue to protect such rights. Other concerns also should be incorporated into analysis and practice, but emphasis on the rights of individuals has been essential to ensure respect for each person. And such respect is crucial in the context of health care – if it is to be humane.

Calls for the legalization of euthanasia have often been phrased in terms of respect for individual rights. Most of us recognize a claim to a death that is respectful of the person – sometimes called a "dignified death," although that term can be misleading – but disagree on the limits for achieving this goal. In particular, we disagree on whether anyone has a right to it because that could require actions with which we disagree. And the right of one person necessarily connotes the duty of another, even if only to refrain from doing anything that would infringe on that right. It is important to recognize points of consensus first, when they exist, and only then points of disagreement. The latter, especially with regard to such strongly held beliefs as those on euthanasia, can have a very different tone when discussion begins with agreement rather than disagreement.

I suggest tentatively that the pro-choice on euthanasia stance might result from failure to balance a very strong (and necessary) emphasis on individual rights by any (or at least enough) consideration for communal claims. Communities, too, need protection. Moreover, it can be argued, protecting the community is also a way of protecting the individual.[78] We need protection of our relationships and bonds to others as well as of ourselves. Hermits aside, people need communities in order to develop fully as individuals. The requirement of a balance between individual rights and protection of the community (between individualism and communitarianism) can be compared with Young's finding of an increase in euthanasia whenever societies failed to maintain the balance between religiosity and secularity; movement towards either pole provoked an increase.[79] By analogy, we could postulate an increase in pro-euthanasia sentiment if the claims of individuals become too strong in comparison with those of the community, or vice versa. It could well be that the greatest danger of overusing euthanasia in the future, were it introduced, would come from an overemphasis on communal claims (for example, cost saving in health care) at the expense of individual rights. Such an outcome would be ironic if the introduction of euthanasia were seen as necessary, as often claimed by advocates, to respect and promote individual rights.

In light of this discussion, it is interesting to note that some of the strongest opposition to anonymous HIV seroprevalence surveys (anonymous screenings of populations to establish the incidence of HIV infection) occurred in the Netherlands. There, on the basis of upholding respect for individual rights, "opposition to any compulsory public health measure is so strong that even professional and popular support for blinded studies is unlikely to overcome the barriers."[80] In contrast, these surveys have met with general approval in both the United States and Canada; they have been carried out after careful consideration of the ethical requirements.[81] Could the Dutch situation with respect to euthanasia be related? I argue that a purely individualistic approach to euthanasia is more likely to result in its being seen as justified and acceptable than one in which communal needs, too, are taken into account.

We all recognize the right to life of every individual born alive. But does this mean that everyone has a duty to go on living? There could be a moral duty to do so, depending on the circumstances, but there is certainly no legal duty. Denying a legal duty, though, is not the same as recognizing a claim or a right to have death inflicted – that is, euthanasia.[82] Recognition of a right to life means that, even if one approves of euthanasia, it should not be carried out against the wishes of those concerned. Involuntary[83] or non-consensual[84] euthanasia would be prohibited. But what of avoluntary euthanasia? If euthanasia were allowed, could it be carried out on incompetent people – those unable to consent or to refuse consent? The ethical and legal presumption in favour of life would mean that those who had never been competent must not be subjected to euthanasia unless it were held that the presumption could be rebutted and that, in the circumstances, it would not take priority. Allowing euthanasia for competent people might or might not set a precedent that the presumption in favour of life can be rebutted to allow avoluntary euthanasia. If one focuses on the right of people to decide for themselves, and if one uses this criterion as the basis for rebutting the presumption in favour of life, it would not set a precedent. But if one focuses on the fact that permitting euthanasia for competent people recognizes that the intentional infliction of death is legitimate in some circumstances (for example, to eliminate suffering), it could set a precedent for the legitimation of avoluntary euthanasia of incompetent people whose circumstances are similar to those of competent people who die through euthanasia. Whatever our approach to people who had never been competent, that would still leave the matter of whether previously competent people should be able to give "advance directives" permitting euthanasia if they become incompetent.

We need to consider also the wider effects of recognizing a right to die with dignity and holding that it includes a right to euthanasia. That right could be converted into a duty to die with dignity. And that, in turn, could become a right of society to insist that the people die "with dignity" (which is likely to involve involuntary euthanasia in some cases) or even an obligation to die[85] (the corollary of which is a right to kill through euthanasia). To explore what is implied by some of the positions contemplated here, compare the right to treatment with the right to be offered treatment. The former is sometimes proposed as the basis for a corresponding duty to treat, which is then converted into a right to impose treatment. The corollary of a right to be offered treatment, in contrast, is a duty to offer treatment – which people may either accept or refuse.

It is also worth noting, in relation to "the language of euthanasia," that the language of a right to a dignified death is often, although it need not be, used as a euphemism for euthanasia.

We cannot recognize as rights all the claims of individuals. Moreover, the claims of people, when viewed as a group or a community, can conflict with their claims as individuals. Two questions – whether collective claims should ever be recognized as collective rights, and whether these rights should override individual rights in given circumstances – will not be pursued here. They are relevant to the euthanasia discussion, though, in at least one important way. Even if one accepts that people have a right to a dignified death, that it includes a right to euthanasia, and that the benefits of recognizing this right at an individual level outweigh the harms, the impact at a macro, or a societal, level would still have to be considered. I suggest that the harms and risks to society would outweigh any claim of an individual to euthanasia. Stated another way, we must not consider individual rights, including any right to euthanasia, only from the perspective of individuals; we must consider also the impact at the macro, or societal, level. The need to protect human values, symbols, and networks, which establish the web that constitutes society, must be given proper consideration. Euthanasia is unacceptable at the societal level, even if that were not true at the individual level; its unacceptability at the societal level outweighs the acceptability of the best-case argument for it at the individual level.

Sanctity of Life and Quality of Life

Our society has moved from relying exclusively on a sanctity-of-life, or vitality, principle to relying as well, or sometimes alternatively, on a quality-of-life principle. The latter includes concepts such as "a life not worth living" and even "wrongful life." Initially, wrongful life was a claim for damages in tort, usually on the part of handicapped children; they argued that their very lives – that is, being born – constituted a damage for which compensation should be available through the courts. Although most of these plaintiffs were not successful, some were.[86] Those precedents have been used for a case involving the other end of life. The plaintiff had refused cardio-pulmonary resuscitation, but was given it after a cardiac arrest; when resuscitated, he was hemiplegic. He sued for damages for "wrongful life."[87]

Recognition of the quality-of-life principle is often linked with euthanasia by the same two opposing groups, each of which argues for a broad definition of euthanasia. I refer to the group consisting of some streams in the pro-life movement and the group of people who are pro-choice on euthanasia. The former oppose consideration of quality of life in the context of making decisions at the end of life – especially in connection with euthanasia; the latter would give it priority over sanctity of life. But one does not necessarily advocate euthanasia or oppose sanctity of life if one agrees that quality of life is a valid consideration. Taking quality of life into account is not always unjustified. Indeed, it might be ethically required in making decisions about the allocation of medical resources at a governmental or institutional (macro) level. The need to consider quality of life arises in part from the possibilities made available by modern medical technology. It has been well said that we were once "reasonably well or dead."[88] Today, we can be very sick for a very long time at the end of our lives because life can be prolonged by modern technology. This can create legitimate concerns about the quality of these prolonged lives.

The reasons for our various approaches to quality of life, as is true of various approaches to euthanasia,[89] could be more complex than we realize at first glance. Ethicist Bridget Campion points out that when we describe people with Alzheimer's disease or Huntington's chorea as "better off dead" or "not the person he or she used to be" – implying that these people no longer have a quality of life adequate to make them want to go on living (or even that they should not be allowed to go on living) – we need to inquire what we mean by what these people were. People are always evolving. They are never what they were previously "and many times ... stopped being ... the [people they] used to be."[90] Do these statements indicate that the problem is defined as a lack of evolution, or the potential for evolution, to what we regard as an acceptable quality of life? Is this a good enough reason for saying, sometimes to justify euthanasia, that someone's life is not worth maintaining, owing to "loss of dignity," and may therefore be "terminated"?[91] Can we not accept either ourselves or others simply for being rather than becoming – as human beings rather than human doings?[92] Is it, as novelist Milos Kundera proposes,[93] a state of just being, without potential to become something else, that is unbearable? If so, we need to ask precisely whom we would be treating with euthanasia: the patient, ourselves, or society.

Part of the problem when we react inappropriately in relation to ill or dying people, according to Campion, is that we see examples of lives that terrify us.[94] We see these patients – and ourselves if we were in similar situations – as unlovable. This perception raises fear of abandonment because, in a consumer society, we get only what we pay for. We believe that we need to earn love. If we cannot earn it, we will not be given it. We will die abandoned and unloved, and we would rather be dead than unloved. Euthanasia is a way to ensure that we are already dead before the abandoning and unloving occurs. "The demand for active euthanasia would be greatly reduced if we could alter this perception that love is very tenuous, that it is conditional and must be deserved."[95]

I have noted the possible connection between euthanasia and a mechanistic approach to people. That approach, too, is associated with consumer societies. Characteristically, this type of society disposes of worn-out or useless products. This outcome becomes mandatory when these products result in economic loss. If we see ourselves simply as products, cogs in the wheel of production, then we would be disposed of as cheaply and efficiently as possible once we are no longer valuable products or producers. Although euthanasia is promoted as a merciful response to suffering, and most of those who advocate it have this as a primary aim, euthanasia does fit into this consumer philosophy. Further, the practice of euthanasia could itself be seen as consistent with the philosophy of a consumer society because it means "death becomes a matter of management." This, in turn, means that several "choices become necessary and several practical points must be discussed: the day and the hour of euthanasia; those to be present; the method to be used."[96] The bizarre thought comes to mind that, in the future, people studying for master's degrees in business management could take courses in "death administration."

The connection between an increasing number of calls for euthanasia and the influence of consumerist philosophy (or, more precisely, its domination) becomes particularly convincing, I suggest, if we consider the circumstances of many people with AIDS. Jay Katz describes powerfully how these terminally ill people can find themselves in a situation of intense "pre-mortem loneliness."[97] In this respect, it is of sad interest to note that, according 1989 to a report, "11.2% of Dutch AIDS patients died by active euthanasia."[98] In 1991 one report put the figure at 23 per cent.[99] Either way, these statistics are well above the average for the number of deaths that occur through euthanasia in the Netherlands.[100] People with AIDS have been among the most stigmatized, most likely to be abandoned, dying people. Without minimizing or ignoring the intense physical and mental suffering that AIDS can cause, these other features of their dying could well correlate with an increased likelihood that patients with AIDS will seek euthanasia (or be offered it), especially in a society that is governed by consumerism. People with AIDS can be viewed not only as useless products but also as potentially harmful ones. Moreover, isolating them from society, whether in practice or through symbols, may serve an additional function – that of a purification ritual – and euthanasia may well be part of that process. The calls, often strident, to test the population in general for HIV, to quarantine those who are antibody positive, to exclude them from schools, hospitals, or the workplace (especially if they are health-care professionals) may all originate from a desire, even if unconscious, for symbolic ways of purifying society. Euthanasia could be the ultimate way.[101]

We should consider as well whether language has an impact on the views of and reactions to euthanasia in the context of AIDS. Military terminology, especially, the concept of a war on AIDS, is often used.

Could there be some connection, even if an unconscious one, between this language and the notion that euthanasia is acceptable for patients with AIDS? Could euthanasia in that context even be some form of killing of the enemy, in that the patient with AIDS, not HIV, is mistakenly identified as the enemy?

WHY DO WE WANT TO MEDICALIZE EUTHANASIA?

Does euthanasia seem kinder, gentler, and in a "safer forum" if it is carried out in a clinical context?[102] Does this association show "approval, acceptance and care of the patient"[103] and of the patient's decision for euthanasia? In speaking of physician-assisted suicide, it has been said that "seeking a physician's assistance, or what can almost seem a physician's blessing, may be a way of trying to remove ... stigma and show others that the decision for suicide was made with due seriousness and was justified under the circumstances. The physician's involvement provides a kind of social approval, or more accurately helps counter what would otherwise be unwarranted social disapproval."[104] Could euthanasia provide a precedent for other interventions that would be carried out "in the medical context"? The involvement of American physicians in capital punishment is a case in point. Would it make any difference that these interventions could be given trial runs, or attempts made to make them acceptable, in the clinical, or purportedly clinical, context of euthanasia, before their equally controversial application in the context of capital punishment? These questions might sound alarmist, but we need to ask them and to do so with some degree of equanimity.

It is not uncommon to medicalize situations in order to deal with those that make us feel uncomfortable or that are prohibited outside a medical situation.⌊For example, infringement of even constitutionally protected rights to liberty and security of the person can be justified by virtue of powers given under mental health acts or public health legislation.⌋Interventions are allowed to protect either the patients themselves or others from serious threats to their lives or health. We should be careful in adopting tactics such as medicalization that we do not dull our sensitivity to some of the basic issues involved. It has been said that nowhere are human rights more threatened than when we act purporting only to help others. We assume that acting within a medical context means we have at least a primary intention of doing good. This assumption would apply to euthanasia no less than to other medical interventions. Although it is usually argued that euthanasia is most appropriately provided within a medical context, and that allowing euthanasia promotes human rights, the claim that good would result from legalizing euthanasia would be more clearly tested by dealing with it outside the medical context.[105] We would then need to prove – not simply assume – that making euthanasia available would be to do good, whether to individuals or to society.]

Bill c-261 was proposed legislation on euthanasia in Canada, but was withdrawn. It would have required euthanasia to be dealt with partly outside a medical context. This legislation, possibly unique, proposed "referees in euthanasia." They would issue "euthanasia certificates," which would permit physicians to carry out euthanasia on those with certificates.[106] There was no suggestion that the referees should be physicians. Indeed, application could have been made for reviews by the attorney general of Canada – who is unlikely to be a physician – in cases of negative decisions.

In summary, we might be dealing with euthanasia in a medical context at least partly to eliminate or reduce reactions that we would otherwise have to one person killing another. To the extent that we expect modern medicine to be our source of miracles, moreover, it could be that, when no miracle is possible, death itself can be seen as a miracle – a different kind of miracle, but one still provided by medicine if it occurs through euthanasia carried out by a physician.

WHY DO WE TECHNOLOGIZE EUTHANASIA?

Consider the much publicized case of Jack Kevorkian assisting Janet Adkins's death. Why did Dr Kevorkian and Mrs Adkins resort to a suicide machine that was even given a special, trademarked name, the Thanatron™?[107] One obvious reason was to avoid prosecution for murder by eliminating the possibility that Kevorkian could be held, in law, to have caused Adkins's death. By using the machine, she could be regarded, in law, as causing her own death. In that case, the situation was one of suicide – and assistance in suicide was not then a crime in Michigan[108] – not murder. It is worth noting, however, that even though Kevorkian did not intervene after the initial intravenous lines had been inserted, and even though Adkins herself activated administration of the lethal drugs, a charge of murder was considered. In two subsequent cases, Kevorkian did intervene (in one, to fix a defect in the machine after it had been started); charges of murder were laid against him, but found to be without foundation.[109]

Kevorkian is now serving a ten-to-twenty-five-years prison sentence as a result of being convicted for second-degree murder in another case. He video-taped himself helping Thomas Youk, a seriously ill, fifty-three-year-old man, to take his own life by lethal injection. The film was subsequently shown on television and was used as the basis of the charge against Kevorkian.

There could be a less obvious reason why we technologize euthanasia. We often speak of the technological imperative in medicine. We have technology and, therefore, believe that we must use it. The presence of technology elicits a response to use it. Much discussion in bioethics has been concerned with attempting to work out principles and guidelines for when we ought (there is a duty), "need not" (there is no duty), or ought not (there is a duty not) to use technology. Could the case of euthanasia be a variation on this technological-imperative response? In euthanasia cases, such as those involving Kevorkian, could it be that, rather than a technology preceding and eliciting a response, a desired response – namely, euthanasia – precedes the development of the technology, which is thus developed precisely to generate the desired response?

Does the use of technology somehow come between us and the person to whom we apply the technology,[110] such that we do not feel that it is our act that creates the result – in the case of euthanasia, death of the person – but, rather, that it is caused by the technology? Does the use of technology allow us to distance ourselves, to disidentify in some degree, from the fact that we are killing another person in the act of euthanasia?

When we apply technology to other people, it has been alleged, there is a risk of depersonalizing them – seeing them as mere objects for the application of technology. We find it easier to act towards others in ways about which we have deep concerns, moreover, when we do not regard those affected as people like ourselves. For example, researchers found it very much more difficult, and sometimes impossible, to carry out medical research on people when they were forced to relate personally to their subjects by participating in a detailed informed consent process.[111] This reaction could provide insight into why people would develop technology to carry out euthanasia. Technology allows us to distance ourselves from those on whom we act and to depersonalize them; without doing so, it would be very difficult to kill them. As an aside, it is worth noting here that we can use language to achieve similar effects. The choice of words, or labels, makes it easier to distance ourselves from others and to depersonalize them. One example is the use of derogatory terms for enemies killed in wartime. A more everyday example is the failure to use words such as "person" or "people" when describing an individual or a group. This almost always occurs in connection with derogatory characterizations: criminals, delinquents, mental incompetents – we do not speak of "mental competents," by way of comparison, but rather of "mentally competent persons" – and the aged.

In summary, consider the following statement by George Annas: "Machines have a tendency to depersonalize death and to make us

seem less responsible for it ... The use of military metaphors in medicine tends to obliterate the patient, just as the use of medical metaphors by the military tends to obliterate the horrors of war. In both
cases, we prefer to concentrate on the technology because, unlike
death, it seems clean and controllable."[112]

WHY WOULD EUTHANASIA BE ALLOWED, OR NOT PROSECUTED, BUT NOT LEGALIZED?

The criminal laws of all countries prohibit culpable homicide – murder and manslaughter. Euthanasia, too, is prohibited by these laws, except now in the Netherlands. Most countries prohibit assisting suicide,
although suicide itself is seldom a crime in modern criminal law. In the
Netherlands, euthanasia has been allowed under specific conditions
since the early 1970s, but it is only very recently that it has been legalized even there – at least in a strict juridical sense.[113]

Dutch criminal law, the Penal Code, prohibits murder (which, until
the recent legislation, included euthanasia) in section 293 and prohibits
assisted suicide in section 294. But since the early 1970s, prosecution has
been unlikely,[114] if guidelines established by the Dutch Supreme Court
in a case involving euthanasia by a physician (some aspects of which were
codified as guidelines in 1990 and, subsequently, enacted as regulations
in 1993) were respected. In any case, decisions to prosecute had to be
approved by five senior prosecutors.[115] The jurisprudential bases used to
validate these guidelines were a few articles in the Penal Code "listing
possible grounds for non-punishment" for any offence.[116] The conditions for legitimating euthanasia were, "among other things, that there
be an explicit and repeated request by the patient that leaves no reason
for doubt concerning his desire to die; that the mental or physical suffering of the patient must be very severe with no prospect of relief; that the
patient's decision be well-informed, free, and enduring; that all options
for other care have been exhausted or refused by the patient; and that
the doctor consult another physician (in addition, he may decide to consult nurses, pastors, and others)."[117] One physician has even been disciplined by a Dutch Medical Disciplinary Board for "breach of trust" for
"misleading a patient into supposing he was being given a lethal dose of
drugs, when the doctor knew this was not so."[118] "The doctor was in effect found guilty for 'not ... unlawfully killing his patient.'"[119] In the
Netherlands, moreover, there has been intense debate over whether
euthanasia should be available when the patients concerned are incompetent to consent. As I have already noted, some (probably many) of
these cases have occurred, although they would clearly have been outside the guidelines applicable at the time. These cases included not only
incompetent adults but also handicapped newborn babies.[120]

The new Dutch legislation, the Termination of Life on Request and Assisted Suicide (Review Procedures) Act (2000), codifies and, in some respects, clarifies the existing practice in such respects. Euthanasia may only be carried out on people who, among other requirements, give a fully informed consent either at the time or through a "euthanasia declaration" – that is, they express their wishes about termination of life in advance. Minors sixteen years of age or older can, in principle, decide on euthanasia for themselves. Children aged between twelve and sixteen years may also request euthanasia, but the consent of both parents or the guardian is required. If, however, a physician is convinced that euthanasia is necessary to prevent serious harm to a child who requests it, the physician may fulfill the child's request despite the refusal of consent by the parents or guardian.

What insights does the Dutch approach to euthanasia provide? First, until the recent legislation, the law was not changed to legalize euthanasia, although euthanasia was practised without attracting legal liability. In individual cases, euthanasia was justified (excused?[121]) in situations of "force majeure, in the sense of conflicting duties."[122] The commentary on Dutch law, with respect to what constitutes this defence, is not always consistent or easy to understand, which could reflect some lack of clarity as to either the exact characteristics of the defence or its application in practice. For example, Diana Brahams states that "force majeure," in the sense of irresistible force, was rejected as a defence to criminal liability for euthanasia. She equates the defence of irresistible force with the defence of necessity and, likewise, finds this defence rejected.[123] According to Brahams, a "conflicting duties situation," which she describes as "the emergency defence," was recognized by Dutch courts: "The court ruled that a physician's duty to abide by the law and to respect the life of his patient 'may be outweighed by his other duty to help a patient who is suffering unbearably, who depends upon him and for whom, to end his suffering, there is no alternative but death.'"[124] In contrast, John Keown says that the defence available to Dutch physicians to justify euthanasia was one of necessity (*overmacht*) contained in Article 40 of the Penal Code. In a 1986 case, he says, the Dutch Supreme Court "accepted that the defense of necessity in the sense of 'psychological compulsion' experienced by the doctor was also available."[125]

Is there any equivalent in Anglo-American common law to this "conflicting duties" defence? The only possibility might be a defence of necessity. A defence of necessity is available in Anglo-American common law when the harm done by breaking the law is clearly outweighed by the harm avoided in doing so; when the harm avoided is of a serious nature; when there is no reasonable alternative to breaking the law if the harm is to be avoided; and when the least harmful approach is used. The critical issue is whether the harm done by breaking the law (killing someone) could ever be outweighed by the harm avoided by doing so (relief of suffering). This possibility seems highly unlikely because it is only if the necessity in question is to save a human life that killing may be excused, though not justified, under a common law doctrine of necessity.[126] Leaving aside the morality of euthanasia, the harm done at a precedent-setting and societal level in allowing euthanasia would not, in my view, be outweighed by harm avoided at the individual level.

Before enacting the recent legislation legalizing euthanasia, the legitimation of the euthanasia process that the Dutch used had managed to maintain at least an impression that each case of euthanasia constituted only an individual event – not only in practice but also symbolically – despite the fact that the total number of cases there was probably very high.[127] The previous Dutch system could have helped to achieve this outcome because (as is also true of the new system) each case of euthanasia must be justified individually and reported;[128] each case, technically, was *prima facie* a breach of the law; and, in each case, the conduct could be found unjustifiable and be prosecuted. This approach could more easily generate a sense of the individuality and uniqueness of each case (not one of institutionalization) than if, as is now the situation, euthanasia were generally legalized – but only under specified conditions. Why, however, would the Dutch have adopted this approach, assuming, as must have been the case, that euthanasia was regarded as acceptable by the majority of the public? One reason might have been that this approach confined cases of euthanasia to the micro level; as exceptions to a general principle against the taking of human life, the latter could still operate at the macro or societal level. Now that euthanasia has been legalized directly by the legislature, the impact of euthanasia is likely to be much greater; the general principle or presumption that governs society has been changed to one that says life may be taken in some circumstances.

In short, the previous Dutch approach maintained the symbolism of the sanctity-of-life principle while allowing practices that were inconsistent with it. This same mechanism can be seen in the French legal and medical systems. A report entitled "French Health Ministry Supports Doctor over Euthanasia" reads as follows:

Leon Schwartzenberg, an eminent French Cancer Specialist, has been suspended for one year by the Paris board of the French Medical Association. The suspension follows Schwartzenberg's admission that he had helped an incurable patient to die. Claude Evin, the French Health Minister, has now joined

Schwartzenberg in filing an appeal, and in calling for broad public debate on euthanasia. Evin said: "The main thing is to relieve suffering, even if that means the end of life." Neither Evin nor Schwartzenberg favour a change in legislation, however. Schwartzenberg has said: "*For the French, anything that is law is normal, and euthanasia can never be normal.*"[129]

A similar approach of *de facto*, but not *de jure*, legalization of euthanasia has been advocated for Canada. The proposal of Barry Sneiderman, a law professor who does not oppose euthanasia, is summarized in the headline accompanying an article written by him: "Don't make it murder, but don't make it legal." Sneiderman writes that

In the rare situation in which the physician is driven to desperate measures (as [occurred] in a Montreal case [in which a physician gave a lethal injection of potassium chloride to a terminally ill person with AIDS who was suffering greatly]), the law has the capacity to stay its hand as a merciful response to a merciful act. But that is a far cry from granting physicians the legal authority to practise euthanasia. As philosopher John Rawls says, "It is one thing to justify an act; it is another to justify a general practice." Given the current crisis over a health-care system unable to meet the reasonable needs of all our ailing people, we cannot guarantee that euthanasia would be practised solely as the medical measure of last resort. In short, one cannot say that the time for euthanasia has come to Canada.[130]

In summary, even those who do, or would, allow euthanasia at an individual level recognize the danger at the societal level. An important question, therefore, is whether we can prevent approved micro-level practices from establishing macro-level precedents. Almost certainly, we cannot. Consequently, quite apart from moral arguments, euthanasia should not be allowed even at the micro level.

HIDDEN DECISION-MAKING AND EUTHANASIA

It is often alleged that euthanasia takes place, but that it is performed secretly. It is further alleged that this situation is the result of euthanasia being illegal. Studies show many cases of hidden (at least in the sense of unreported) euthanasia in the Netherlands,[131] however, when it was *de facto* legal. Consequently, the cause of euthanasia being hidden might not be the fact that it is illegal; even if legal, it might still be hidden. In this regard it will be interesting to see whether the new Dutch legislation legalizing euthanasia leads to an increase in the compliance with the reporting provisions by physicians who carry out euthanasia. Modern Western societies usually react strongly against hidden decision-making and actions, but should they always do so? To respond to this question some distinctions must be made. Do we believe that hidden decision-making is wrong in all circumstances or only in some? Or do we believe that most cases of hidden decision-making involve unethical or illegal decisions and that they can be prevented most effectively by eschewing such decision-making? We must be open-minded enough to ask whether there is a place for hidden decision-making and actions by individuals, though not by institutions or society, in some very unusual situations. Also, we must ask whether trying to eliminate all hidden decision-making in connection with euthanasia would do more harm than good. In particular, we must ask whether legalizing euthanasia, to avoid hidden decision-making, would do more harm than good even if we were to achieve our goal.

With those questions in mind, let us compare euthanasia with abortion. Whether or not we agree that abortion is morally acceptable (always, never, or depending on the circumstances), prohibiting all abortions can involve situations that give rise to its being carried out secretly. This recourse causes a major increase in serious risk for women who have abortions. And because this risk might not even deter women from having abortions, it constitutes an argument against using the law to prohibit abortion in the early stages of pregnancy. Another argument is that the law is ineffective in preventing abortion, especially in light of new methods – for instance, the "morning after" or "abortion pill" – that do not require the use of complex medical techniques or sophisticated facilities.

But to accept the idea that laws prohibiting abortion can create unacceptable levels of harm without compensating benefits (protecting fetuses from abortion), or that these laws are totally ineffective, does not address or alter the morality of abortion. No matter whether the law allows or prohibits abortion, those who believe that abortion is immoral must try to convince those who do not so believe and persuade them to alter their conduct accordingly.

Causing euthanasia to be carried out secretly, because it is illegal, is unlikely to produce similar risks and harms to those who seek it – unless one regards as a harm not being killed when one wants to be killed. (Hidden euthanasia is, almost certainly, far less readily available than legalized euthanasia would be; those who would have access under an overt, legalized system of euthanasia might not have access in the absence of one.) I am assuming here that hidden euthanasia involves only those who want to be killed and who would be eligible for euthanasia if it were legalized. Whether or not euthanasia is legalized, these people would die by that means. Some people argue, however, that the potential for abuse is vastly increased by forcing acts of euthanasia to be hidden, as occurs when it is illegal. But it could be argued also that the potential for abuse is increased even more when euthanasia is legal. For instance, the Dutch policy, before the enactment of the recent law legalizing euthanasia, had been criticized "for creating a 'private place' for euthanasia which is both spacious and poorly policed."[132] Further, those in favour of euthanasia often require opponents of voluntary euthanasia to provide evidence of a "slippery slope,"[133] though this is the opposite burden of proof from the expected one. Usually, leaving aside for the moment questions about the morality of euthanasia, those who want to change the status quo – that is, to legalize euthanasia – would be required to show that change would not be dangerous either to individuals or to society (at least no more dangerous than the present situation), and possibly that the proposed change would do more good than harm.

Euthanasia can occur secretly. Deciding not to take all possible measures to prevent it (even though it is illegal and it causes more harm than good) does not mean that one finds euthanasia morally acceptable. If hidden cases were to become known, moreover, they would have to be prosecuted if the general effectiveness and symbolism of the law is to be maintained. The law allows discretion and, in some rare cases involving euthanasia, this discretion might be exercised best by deciding not to prosecute. These cases must be clearly exceptional and very rare, however, if they are not to become a message to health-care professionals that they may carry out euthanasia with impunity. Suspended or light sentences for euthanasia could have the same effect. In handing down a lenient sentence in a euthanasia case, a Canadian court explicitly noted that health-care professionals should not interpret its judgment in this way.[134]

Great care must be taken with some current research on attitudes to euthanasia, surveys that abandon the distinction between euthanasia and other interventions or non-interventions at the end of life. These surveys often promote the idea that there is much hidden euthanasia, that many health-care professionals – physicians and nurses – have carried out euthanasia for a long time. The implication is that this evidence provides support for the idea of bringing the law into line with reality on the grounds that this conduct has "obviously" not caused any harm; that it must be necessary; that those who undertake these interventions are of "good conscience" and good will; and that they are neither sought out nor prosecuted.[135] According to a report from Boston, one in five American physicians has deliberately caused a patient's death. The report refers to terminally ill patients who asked for assistance in committing suicide; but it is not clear what, if any, were the limits to the conduct engaged in by their physicians in order to "help death."[136]

In interpreting these surveys, a much more accurate assessment would have to be made of exactly what the physicians surveyed meant by "helping death." For example, respecting refusals of treatment or giving necessary pain-relief treatment, even if it could shorten life, might have been included. We should acknowledge that there are major legal and ethical differences between these kinds of assistance and, for instance, giving someone a lethal injection. This distinction is true whether or not one agrees with euthanasia.

Even if some physicians are carrying out unethical or even illegal practices, moreover, it does not mean that the law should be changed to legitimate them. Nor does it mean that the law should be used relentlessly to prosecute every last one of them. In some very unusual circumstances, at the level of an individual case, prosecution might be inappropriate. The symbolism created by legal prohibition is required at the macro level. Great care must be taken in handling individual cases not to damage this symbolism. Sometimes these cases must be treated in a way that can seem harsh for the individual involved in order to maintain the message of respect for human life that is contravened by euthanasia.

Some people argue that, because euthanasia is illegal, those who carry it out fear prosecution, yet they should not have to be burdened by fear. But such immensely serious decisions as euthanasia should never be easy. That they are difficult at both cognitive and emotional levels for those who carry out euthanasia is an essential and enormously important safeguard. Even those who feel morally justified in performing it should have to consider the views of society as expressed in its law and be prepared to accept the consequences of not conforming. This approach might seem very "hard hearted." It might be thought to originate in a failure to appreciate the anguish that can arise for those who believe that, in particular cases, the availability of euthanasia is not only morally acceptable but also morally required. I propose, however, that euthanasia is a situation in which accepting it as the appropriate response for dealing with "hard cases" would make very "bad law" for society as a whole.

Leaving aside for the moment the morality of euthanasia, we sometimes have to choose between the law that we need for symbolism – the law that would be best for establishing principles at the macro level – and what would be the best approach in some very difficult individual cases. Euthanasia, in my view, is one of the situations where the needs of the community – society – must take priority over the claims of the individual. We cannot afford to routinize and institutionalize, let alone legalize, killing. That can be avoided, even if some very rare cases are not prosecuted, provided that the cases involved are each regarded as isolated instances, outside the norm. In short, it is simply wrong to argue that, because prohibited conduct occurs – because "everyone's doin' it" – there is justification for legalizing it.

Our most ancient laws and moral proscriptions are against killing, at the very least, members of our own species. It is true that there have always been exceptions to this rule which had to be restrictively interpreted, and their application in any given circumstances clearly justified by the person relying on them as exceptions. The major examples in Western cultures, apart from what were rightly or wrongly considered "just" wars, were self-defence and capital punishment after "fair trials" for offences that "merited" them (not all, or most, or even any of which everyone agrees should still be allowed as exceptions). In any case, these exceptions should not be extended by legalizing euthanasia.

In considering the legalization and institutionalization of euthanasia, we are considering an alteration to the fundamental presumption against killing each other on which the morality and law of civilized society are based. Why are so many of us apparently actively considering a change? Could there be some socio-biological, genetic, or environmental factor that is causing the current rise of interest in and promotion of euthanasia? One would need to examine other periods and other cultures, probably other species, even to begin formulating an answer.[137] But we should be aware that what we perceive or believe our primary motives to be could hide more complex realities. Empathy, compassion, and mercy, though dominant motives for most advocates of euthanasia, might not be the only ones. It is just possible that factors such as an increasingly crowded world or even overwhelming fear about one's own death (especially in the context of a secular, pluralistic, postmodern, and multicultural world) could be involved as well.

THE LANGUAGE OF EUTHANASIA

Language is not neutral. Although this proposition is obvious, it is so important in relation to the euthanasia debate that it merits stating. We form our narratives, and our narratives form us. We are, at least in part, the stories we tell. Stories about "bad deaths" and "good deaths" are especially influential. They give us access to experiential knowledge. They often help us to identify our emotional responses and provide opportunities to examine them. It is essential to acknowledge the necessity of such examination if we are to respond wisely to problems associated with death – including euthanasia. At a conference in Boston,[138] Timothy Quill and Susan Tolle told "stories," in which a potentially "bad death" was converted to a "good death" by their respective interventions. The two speakers were clearly concerned about the doubtful legality of what they had done. These were powerful pro-euthanasia narratives. In contrast, Christine Mitchell read a deeply moving essay written by an intensive-care nurse who created a situation in which the family of a patient were included in his dying through the nurse's unusually sensitive approach. As the nurse said, this man's dying was a very important event not only in his own life but also in the lives of his family and friends. Mitchell proposed that, in characterizing the kinds of death people experience, we should include what their families and friends will remember and weave into their own lives.

With the power of language in mind, I would like to analyze, briefly, one document: a report of the Institute of Medical Ethics Working Party on the Ethics of Prolonging Life and Assisting Death,[139] which was based in London, England. It contains many examples of the way in which language can be used to influence the euthanasia debate, and provides additional insights as to how our reactions to euthanasia can be modified, depending on the way in which it is presented. (The quotations that follow in this discussion, except where otherwise indicated, are all taken from this report.)

The report speaks of "hasten[ing] death by administration of narcotic drugs." This procedure can be compared with the use of curare in the Netherlands, after the injection of a short-acting narcotic, such as pentothal, to induce sleep.[140] One can query the basis of the decision to use only narcotic drugs. Could these drugs be chosen because they are less likely to make people react to euthanasia as a different kind of intervention from, for example, the pain-relief treatment regarded as acceptable and even required? Is the use of narcotics less likely to elicit different emotional reactions from those we have to pain-relief treatment, and more likely to elicit similar reactions of the appropriateness and acceptability of the intervention than would the use of other drugs? Curare, which causes total body paralysis, is used in many surgical operations that require paralysis to give surgeons easier access to, for example, the abdominal cavity. As one Dutch anaesthetist said in conversation, it is not very difficult for an anaesthetist to carry out euthanasia; it simply requires giving "half a general anaesthetic and just not doing the other half – the resuscitation." General anaesthetics are almost always given for therapeutic reasons and to promote healing. Does linking euthanasia with this procedure, even its confusion with it, cause us to see and react to euthanasia as a healing, therapeutic intervention?[141] If so, this association is undesirable – which is not necessarily to say that one would oppose euthanasia if it could not be viewed in this way. Rather, euthanasia itself must be thought and felt about as clearly as possible. To achieve this realization, one needs to

guard against surrounding consideration of euthanasia with circumstances likely to cause confusion between how one thinks and feels
about treatment decisions associated with the end of life apart from
those involving euthanasia, and how one thinks and feels about those
that, in the same circumstances, do involve euthanasia. As Callahan
has said, "it is important in all moral debates to use very accurate terms
that do not anaesthetise our feelings."[142]

The report refers to "assisted suicide" or "homicide upon request,"
and states that "these terms are not used lest their legal implications
confuse the ethical issues [of euthanasia]." This disconnection of law
from ethics, stops the law from informing ethics. Too often, in the
past, we have simply equated ethics and law: we have tended to assume that, if conduct is legal, it is also ethical. This approach can be
characterized as law informing ethics. More recently, we have realized
that ethics must inform law and, indeed, that often the ethical analysis
should be primary and the legal, secondary. But it remains necessary
for law to inform ethics. The approach proposed in the report has the
effect of stopping legal precedent and history from guiding our reactions to and decisions concerning euthanasia. It stops our conditioned response that an act is wrong because the law has always viewed
it as wrong. We need to be aware of this reaction and to consider
whether we are correct in thinking that any given act, including euthanasia, is wrong. But we should not eliminate this reaction in order
to allow ourselves the belief that conduct otherwise considered wrong
is acceptable.

The report continues as follows: "More important is rejection of the
word 'killing.' This word is generally used to indicate a violent act in
war or crime, rather than to describe a gentle act of merciful clinical
care." This description characterizes the act of euthanasia in the way
proposed by those who advocate it. Although the word *merciful* almost
always correctly describes their motives, euthanasia is not an act of clinical care or necessarily a gentle act. I have already discussed some reasons that might cause people to medicalize euthanasia. The danger in •
medicalization is, again, that we could automatically think and feel
about euthanasia in the same way that we think and feel about other
forms of clinical care. This is neither appropriate nor honest, whether
we are pro- or anti-euthanasia.

"If ... the doctor is confident that the patient's disabilities, coupled
with his genuine distress about the trouble and expense of the care he
needs, make continued life devoid of any enjoyment, the doctor's response [whether or not to provide euthanasia] will depend on the
more general question of how he regards his ethical responsibilities in
relation to assisting death." This statement in the report raises many

questions. Economic factors are recognized as being very important, but their introduction as valid considerations in the context of euthanasia is attributed to the altruism of those seeking euthanasia, not to concerns of the family or the society that must pay. This distinction leads to two very different principles on which arguments in support of euthanasia can be based. One is that of individual liberty. The other is the right to kill in the interests of others, such as the family or society. The justifications that are argued in the latter context can include cost-saving, eugenics, justice and punishment (for example, capital punishment), or protection (as in a "just" war). Usually, the justifications within the general category (of acting in the interests of others) that could arguably be relevant to euthanasia are not presented overtly in that context. Even when the interest being promoted in allowing euthanasia might be an interest that of society (for example, saving money), the focus is on the subjects of euthanasia and on their personal liberty (in this case, being allowed to choose euthanasia and avoid the distress, to them, of causing a financial burden to fall on others). In the Netherlands, similarly, there are claims that "the highest terms of praise have been applied to the request to die: this act is 'brave,' 'wise,' and 'progressive.' All efforts are made to convince people that this is what they ought to do, what society expects of them, what is best for themselves and their families. The result is, as [Dutch] Attorney General T.M. Schalken stated in 1984, that 'elderly people begin to consider themselves a burden to the society, and feel under an obligation to start conversations on euthanasia, or even to request it.'"[143]

The two principles that can be argued as justifications for euthanasia – individual liberty and the interests of society – can conflict. For example, if someone's right to live is denied on the basis of society's right to cut it short when required by its larger interests, a choice must be made between the two. In this respect, it is interesting to note the allegation that "a majority of the same [Dutch] public that proclaims support for voluntary euthanasia ... also accepts involuntary active euthanasia – that is, denial of free choice and of the right to live."[144] This statement is very disturbing, and, indeed, many statements by its author have been challenged.[145] Nevertheless, it merits consideration. The claim that "involuntary active euthanasia" is regarded as acceptable might be reflected in Dutch practice to a much greater degree than has, in general, been believed.[146] Acceptance of involuntary active euthanasia could indicate a popular belief that, when conflict arises in the context of euthanasia, perceived societal interests take priority over individual ones – including liberty. It is worth noting that communal interests can be used, as they would be if such a belief were relied upon, to argue for euthanasia. They can also be used to argue against it. My position is that even if one finds euthanasia acceptable at an individual level, it is unacceptable at a societal level. The interests of society should take priority and require that euthanasia remain prohibited. Different communal interests are involved in each case. Those served by allowing euthanasia would be, among others, saving on economic costs to the community. Those served by prohibiting euthanasia would include maintaining the symbolism and practice of not killing other people.

The report proposes that, to assist death, is "a moral advance rather than a moral decline." This statement leads to the argument that it is unethical to prohibit euthanasia. And, indeed, this argument has been espoused.[147] Ethics has long been used to argue against euthanasia; now it is used to also argue for euthanasia. The report also claims that "it would be unjust if only some doctors, as at present, continued to relieve terminal suffering by assisting death in the privacy of the home, while others, especially in hospital, did not do this." In other words, justice requires that euthanasia be available. But what would this proposition mean if applied to other illegal acts? To take an extreme case, if child prostitution is available to some (as it is), does this in itself indicate that it should be available to all? Once again, the fact that euthanasia occurs does not mean that it is morally acceptable or that it should be legalized and institutionalized.

According to the report, the act/omission distinction is not morally relevant; "killing and letting die" are morally equivalent. It states that, "although allowing death to occur often seems less wrong than deliberate killing, intent, circumstances, and outcome all have a role in determining moral judgment on the act. When the intention and outcome of killing and letting die are equivalent (in each case a good intention and a fatal outcome), then the circumstances become the crucial factor in the moral evaluation of killing and letting die." This is situational ethics: there are no absolute rights and wrongs, not even with respect to killing people; the morality of every situation depends on all the circumstances. The report is correct, as discussed previously, that some omissions could constitute euthanasia. These omissions and the act of killing can be morally and even legally equivalent when, for example, there is a duty to treat, and death results from withholding treatment. But there is not always a duty to treat, not when it would be medically futile or when the patient has given a valid refusal of treatment. In summary, not all situations of killing by an act and letting die through an omission are morally equivalent. Moreover, recognition that "there are circumstances, in clinical practice as well as in hypothetical debate, where the logical difference between act and omission, between killing and letting die, might be unable to bear decisive weight ... does not imply that a decision in favour of killing is therefore permissible in situations where a decision not to maintain life is permissible."[148]

From a legal point of view, many of the cases in which the act/omission distinction is relevant involve the connected notions of duty and causation. I have already discussed the latter. As for the former, common law imposes a duty to take reasonable care not to harm others by one's acts. But there is no general duty not to harm others by omissions. One is liable for an omission only if there was a pre-existing duty to act. In other words, one is not liable for "mere" omissions (that is, omissions in a situation involving no duty to act). When there is a pre-existing duty to act, liability for an omission can be avoided if it is regarded in law as not having caused the damage or the prohibited outcome. The court used just this distinction in the case of *Nancy B.*[149] The judge held that a physician who disconnected a respirator, at the informed request of the patient, would not be held in either criminal or civil law to have caused the patient's death.

In some ways the argument based on criticism of the act/omission distinction (that it is irrelevant to distinguish among the various causes of death – withdrawal of the respirator, underlying disease, lethal injection – because, whichever one is involved, the patient ends up dead) says too much. At one point, we all end up dead. But *when* and *how* we die is relevant to whether or not others can be considered morally culpable or held legally liable for causing death. It is true that the legal concept of causation involves an exercise of discretion through which a court can find either culpability or non-culpability for a prohibited outcome according to whether or not it finds causation on the part of the accused or the defendant. But it is not true, as is sometimes alleged, that the presence of discretion means the concept of causation is without substance and simply a manipulative tool for either attributing or not attributing culpability. Daniel Callahan explains that "the mistake here ... lies in confusing causality and culpability, and in failing to note the way in which human societies have overlaid natural causes with moral rules and interpretations. Causality (by which ... [Callahan] means the direct physical causes of death) and culpability (by which ... [he] means our attribution of moral responsibility to human actions) are confused ... [in some] circumstances."[150] It could well be, however, that the legal concept of causation sometimes exhibits confusion.

Drawing lines that are allegedly artificial or semantic distinctions is often used as an argument against those who oppose euthanasia, but not the right to refuse treatment. Some people say, for example, that there are only artificial differences between legally actionable omissions and non-actionable ones that result in death; whether or not a duty is present remains a matter of discretion and value judgment, which has only a facade of objectivity. Likewise, they argue, distinctions between suicide and euthanasia will not bear moral weight and should not be of legal importance. These lines, though sometimes fine, are both real and important. They correspond not only to logic, I suggest, but also to collective wisdom, precedent, and deeply rooted intuitive, moral, and emotional responses. These "other ways of knowing" must be given space within which to function and must be taken into account. And even the critics of drawing lines, who are usually pro-choice on euthanasia, need to draw lines between acceptable and unacceptable instances of euthanasia – a distinction that usually depends on circumstances, purpose, and consent in relation to the act causing death.[151] In summary, unless all acts of euthanasia were to be allowed, which has never been proposed, the drawing of lines is unavoidable. Although they draw lines allowing respect for refusals of treatment and provision of necessary treatment for the relief of pain and other symptoms of serious physical distress (even if this could shorten life), but prohibit euthanasia, this line-drawing should not be a basis for objection to the case of those who oppose euthanasia. All participants in the euthanasia debate draw lines. But advocates and opponents draw different lines.

The report puts forward another interesting argument: "Doctors, after all, have no religious scruples about interfering with predestined death in formerly fatal illnesses which they can now cure. In what circumstances, then, is a doctor ever ethically justified in assisting death?" We have accepted "playing God" with respect to curing, in effect, so why not accept it with respect to killing? The implication is that interfering in the natural order to cure helps to justify interfering to kill. Do we need to justify interfering in either case? I suggest that we do. In the past, when the purpose of medical intervention was to cure, or at least to provide therapy, the presumption was that interfering in the natural order was justified. In more recent times, however, when we worry about respect for rights and freedoms or about overuse of medical technology and its potential to do harm as well as good, that presumption might no longer be made. This change could be indicated by the fact that we have evolved principles requiring informed consent to medical interventions. And we have always required that the anticipated benefits outweigh anticipated harms and risks. Consequently, the presumption that one is justified in interfering in the natural order to cure could be a partial but inadequate justification for proceeding with a medical intervention aimed at cure. Without necessarily identifying it as such, whether through presumption or proof, we do justify interfering in the natural order to cure. Likewise, we would have to justify interfering in it to kill. The latter cannot be justified simply by arguing that we interfere in the natural order to cure, as if the acceptability of this kind of intervention in itself justifies interfering to kill when it is, to quote the report, "ethically justified."

The report probably addresses here an argument against euthanasia: that hastening death interferes in the natural order and that such interference is wrong. True, this is not necessarily a strong argument. But whether it is depends on circumstance, the way in which we interfere, and the consequences of doing so. To repeat, we must justifiy our interferences and, in this respect, there is a great difference between interfering to cure and doing so to kill. Consequently, contrary to what is implied in the report, allowing the former provides no automatic justification for the latter. Again, this does not necessarily mean that interference to kill cannot be justified; it just cannot be justified in this way.

A more subtle argument along the same lines is that medicine itself creates "an obligation to honour requests for euthanasia. When life-prolonging technology has led to what the patient believes is a life not worth living ... does this create a special responsibility for the medical profession in general and the patient's doctor in particular to consider sympathetically sustained requests for active voluntary euthanasia?"[152] Here is one possible interpretation of the rationale that underlies this question: when we have prolonged someone's life by interfering in the natural order, that life can be stopped by euthanasia without offence to the natural order. If it were not for the initial interference, after all, the person would be dead. A wide application of this reasoning and the precedent it could establish would be terrifying. Anyone whose life was probably saved by antibiotics or surgery for appendicitis, for example, would come within its parameters.

In the context of the language of euthanasia, it is worth noting the description of what the report sees as being at issue, namely, "the useless prolongation of miserable life." According to the report, "a doctor's duty to prolong life is not concerned with all forms of life, but only human life of a quality that the person concerned wishes to have prolonged." One would need to ask here what counts as "quality human life," as compared with a "form of life," because these conditions are contrasted. First, it is noteworthy that "human" is left out in the first mention of life, although that would seem to be the topic. Physicians, as such, are not concerned with other forms of life. Second, there is now a state of high activity in modern, Western societies with respect to the quality-of-life principle. It was developed largely to found a claim to health care. It is now being used, as in the report, as a justification for denying health care.[153] Many other well-known questions are raised here. Who judges quality of life? Many people judge their own quality of life to be better than health-care professionals, who assess them, judge it to be. Can people understand a reduced quality of life, in relation to

themselves, before actually experiencing it? Should it be judged in relation to the cost of maintaining their lives? Moreover, what would we do
for those who either do not have or never had the capacity for wishes? Is
there no duty to prolong their lives?

The report is unclear in this respect. It is "concerned solely with occasions when assisted death is requested – not the related issues of ending the lives of infants, or of patients who are unconscious or unable to
make a valid request." But, later, it states that, "with a patient who cannot express a wish, the doctor's duty is to prolong life only if it can be
assumed to be such that this would be the patient's wish, or if, as in the
case of infants or mentally handicapped patients, there is nothing to
contradict the presumption in favour of prolonging life." Although
the report relies on a presumption in favour of life, it clearly assumes
that this presumption can be rebutted in the case of those who are not,
and possibly never have been, competent. The conditions for a rebuttal are entirely unstated. Moreover, the difference in nuance between
saying that the doctor has a "duty ... to prolong life only if" (which is
how the report puts it) and the doctor has a "duty to prolong life unless" (which more accurately reflects the law) is significant. The former
is a suspensive condition; the duty to prolong life arises only when conditions are fulfilled. The latter is a resolutive condition; the duty arises
unless conditions negating it occur. Opposing basic presumptions
underlie these two approaches. Unlike the former, the latter protects
life in circumstances of equal doubt as to whether life should be
prolonged.

The report concludes that, "if ... relief is not possible, distress is severe, and the patient asks to have his life ended, the circumstances are
analogous to those of the soldier's wounded comrade, the soldier's gun
being replaced by the doctor's syringe ... the balance of the moral argument ... shift[s] towards asking why death should *not* be assisted. The
greater the unrelieved pain and distress, the more ethical a doctor's decision to assist death if the patient desires it." This argument changes
the basic presumption from one that opposes euthanasia to one that
supports it. Also, it raises the question of whether there are degrees of
"ethicality" in relation to euthanasia. If so, at what point can euthanasia
be characterized as ethical or, more important, unethical? Or does this
proposed approach imply that decisions to terminate life in the circumstances described are never unethical – but that some are more ethical
than others? Finally, the military analogy is seldom encountered in the
literature on euthanasia. If it were true – and it is horrible to think that
it might be – that soldiers shoot their wounded comrades, would that
act be morally and legally acceptable? Would that behaviour be relevant
to the arguments for and against euthanasia? This example brings

home the message that not only pacifists should agree that we need constantly to rethink our attitudes to war, including our justifications for engaging in it, and, if we do, the rules governing conduct in armed conflict. It is also noteworthy that, according to this report, patients need not be terminally ill to justify providing them with euthanasia; they need have only an incurable disease. Are we meant to interpret this approach as similar to that of the wounded soldier who is not dying but who, for various reasons, cannot be taken to safety?

More extreme examples of language that promotes suicide by terminally ill people and euthanasia can be found in a text I have already mentioned: *Final Exit* by Derek Humphry. Here are a few examples. The hospice movement and the pro-choice on euthanasia movement are presented as consistent and compatible with each other: "Quality of life, personal dignity, self-control, and above all, choice, are what both hospice and the euthanasia movement are concerned with."[154] But even though many people (possibly most) in the hospice movement agree with these aims in general, they would strongly disagree with euthanasia as a means of achieving them.

There are efforts to normalize the carrying out of euthanasia. Humphry writes that, "if you are unfortunately obliged to end your life in a hospital or motel, it is gracious to leave a note apologizing for the shock and inconvenience to the staff. I have also heard of an individual leaving a generous tip to a motel staff."[155] This statement could imply that a hospital offers nothing more to a dying person than a motel and that committing suicide in a motel is nothing more than a serious inconvenience to the staff, for which, at least in some measure, they can be compensated by a tip. Other examples of language that normalizes euthanasia include references to spousal love and devotion: "A surprising number of people, particularly devoted couples, want to handle the process themselves. It is their final act of love together."[156] Although Humphry claims that his book is intended only as a guide to suicide for terminally ill people, he imagines its use by non-terminally ill people in double suicides with their terminally ill spouses.[157]

One of Humphry's most highly recommended methods of suicide is that of the plastic bag and "either a large rubber band or a ribbon," plus "sufficient sleeping pills to ensure two hours sleep."[158] This method could be seen as a way of normalizing self-willed death, including euthanasia. It reduces repugnance or horror in several ways. First, part of the equipment suggested – "a ribbon" – can be associated with events such as tying up a little girl's hair or wrapping a present – warm, caring, gratifying, and life-affirming activities.[159] One may surely ask if the word was chosen to elicit these associations, to normalize suicide and, by association, euthanasia. And what about the suggestion that people should undertake trial runs of both the sleeping pills and the plastic bag? A trial run of the plastic bag so impressed the author that he performed it for "his Hemlock Chapter meeting a week or so later. Everyone was both amused and impressed." He "urged them to go home and try it on for themselves in order to get more comfortable with the whole concept." The final decision, Humphry says, is on whether to "use a clear plastic bag or an opaque one. That is a matter of taste. Loving the world as I do, I will opt for a clear one if I have to."[160] At one level, this statement indicates some sense of unreality, some hint of fantasy, of disbelief that death – the final exit – will result. The story of Barnum and Bailey's circus comes to mind. When the sideshow tent (with the most tattooed man, the two-headed serpent, the giant woman, and so on) became too crowded, a man would walk around the tent ringing a bell and displaying a board on which was written, "This way to the egress." People would follow him, thinking they were being led towards some other, even more exotic, exhibit – often imagining it would be a rare bird – only to find they had been led out of the tent. When they exclaimed that they had not finished looking at the exhibits, they were told they could re-enter the tent after paying another admission fee. With euthanasia, however, re-entry is not an option – except for those who believe in reincarnation or entry into another life after death.

STRUCTURING THE ANALYSIS

Euthanasia, like almost all other situations that raise important ethical questions, should not be dealt with in isolation. To do so would place us at risk of making ethical errors and setting harmful precedents. Euthanasia must be viewed, first, in the context of other medical interventions and non-interventions at the end of life and, second, in a broader context. These contexts can be sketched here only in very broad and superficial terms.

Placing Euthanasia in the End-of-Life Decision-Making Context

The medical interventions and non-interventions at the end of life can be described as a continuum that includes refusal of treatment; withdrawal from "life support" (for example, respiratory support); withdrawal from artificial nutrition and hydration;[161] provision of necessary treatment for the relief of pain or other symptoms of serious physical distress (even that which could shorten life); suicide; assisted suicide; and euthanasia.

I suggest there is a difference in kind, not merely in degree, between euthanasia and interventions in all the other "categories" except assisted suicide. This comment raises the question of where assisted suicide – in particular, physician-assisted suicide – fits. Opinion is divided as to whether it should be classified with euthanasia, with suicide, or even as some *sui generis* category. If we emphasize the fact that assisted suicide involves the act of people with respect to themselves, it could be treated as suicide – a private act. But if we emphasize that assistance is required, we have "concerted communal action" and, therefore, a public act that should not be legitimated and institutionalized.[162] When physicians are knowingly involved, moreover, the profession of medicine itself is implicated. It is a public enterprise, which means that the involvement of physicians is not, essentially, a private matter.[163]

Some incidents of "assisted suicide" belong in the category of suicide: a patient uses medication not prescribed for this purpose to commit suicide. Others belong in the category of euthanasia: the act of a physician is morally equivalent to euthanasia and legally equivalent to it as well – except for the absence of causation, because the patient's act in killing himself is held to be a *novus actus interveniens*, cutting the chain of causation between the physician's act and the infliction of death. Likewise, the physician provides a patient with the means to commit suicide and has the intention[164] of helping her to do so. In general, the term "physician-assisted suicide" is used only to describe the latter types of intervention – those that are characterized here as being equivalent to euthanasia – not the former. Sometimes the term is extended to include euthanasia that involves lethal injection by a physician. Again, consider the use of language. The term "physician-assisted death" tends to replace or include physician-assisted suicide, and then be interpreted to include euthanasia. The language of physician-assisted death, rather than that of euthanasia, is almost certainly used to avoid the disapproval and win the support of those who oppose euthanasia but not suicide, or, in some cases, physicians assisting in suicide.[165]

Philosopher Margaret Battin reports that, in Germany, physician-assisted suicide is not tolerated, but assistance by non-physicians is accepted. Compare this approach with that of most Canadians and Americans who promote physician-assisted death. They propose that an exception to the crime of assisting suicide should be allowed, but only for physicians. In the Netherlands only physicians have had legal immunity for carrying out euthanasia and the new euthanasia legislation continues this approach. Clearly, important cultural and historical facts influence attitudes. So do individual and societal attitudes to physicians and the medical profession. It is very important to be aware of these differences because they can shake us out of arrogance or complacency – the idea that our way of viewing a situation is the only way – and provide crucial insights into whichever position we choose.

From a legal point of view, the Canadian case of *Rodriguez* v. *Attorney General of British Columbia and Attorney General of Canada*[166] is unique with respect to the claim that the plaintiff sought to enforce. The plaintiff, Sue Rodriguez, suffered from amyotrophic lateral sclerosis (Lou Gehrig's disease, or ALS), a degenerative neuromuscular condition that affects breathing and swallowing, among other physiological functions. She sought a ruling from the court that the prohibition on aiding and abetting suicide in section 241 of the Canadian Criminal Code[167] was invalid, on the grounds that it contravened the Canadian Charter of Rights and Freedoms[168] (in particular, section 7, which protects "the right to life, liberty and security of the person"; section 12, which protects "the right not to be subjected to any cruel and unusual treatment or punishment"; and section 15, which provides for equality before and under the law, and equal protection and equal benefit of the law without discrimination, in particular, on the basis of physical disability). The case was ruled on, ultimately, by the Supreme Court of Canada, but the reasoning at each level of hearing provides insights.

In a detailed judgment, the trial court, the Supreme Court of British Columbia, acknowledged that "the state's interference through criminal law when a person's life or health may be in danger may violate an individual's right under s. 7 to security of the person."[169] But section 7 is not violated by the prohibition on assisting suicide because, in the absence of this prohibition, the plaintiff would still have no right to assistance in committing suicide; therefore, no right protected by the Charter is affected by the prohibition. The court recognized that sections 7 through 14 of the Charter are placed under the heading "Legal Rights." Relying on this characterization and a judgment of the Supreme Court of Canada as authority, the court adopted a narrow interpretation of the rights protected by section 7. In summary, the court held that the restrictions on liberty and security of the person, against which section 7 protects, are only "those that occur as a result of an individual's interaction with the justice system and its administration."[170] The court found that the plaintiff was not involved in any of these interactions; therefore, section 7 was inapplicable. Moreover, the cause of the plaintiff's inability to carry out her decision to commit suicide would not be any restriction on her rights. Rather, as her health deteriorated, the cause would be her illness, and this "does not amount to an infringement of a right to life, liberty or security of the person by the state."

The Supreme Court of British Columbia held that the right against cruel and unusual treatment or punishment was limited to "state-imposed punishment in the context of criminal law regarding a person brought into the legal system" and, consequently, was not applicable to the plaintiff's case. Likewise, the prohibition on assisting suicide did not offend the prohibition in section 15 on discrimination on the basis of physical or mental disability; the prohibition "is designed to protect, not discriminate, regardless of the condition of patients or the cause of any vulnerability which may result in them expressing a desire to terminate their lives."[171] Moreover, the court held that even if rights and freedoms guaranteed by the Charter were violated by the prohibition on assisting suicide, the restriction would be demonstrably justified in a free and democratic society; therefore, it would fall within the "saving provision" of section 1 of the Charter and be constitutionally valid.

The case was appealed to the Court of Appeal of British Columbia,[172] which split in the judgments handed down – two judges dismissed the appeal and one, the chief justice, upheld it, finding for the plaintiff. Each judgment considers how section 7 of the Charter should be interpreted, in the "legislative, social and philosophical context of our society,"[173] when it comes to prohibiting or allowing physician-assisted suicide for terminally ill patients (especially competent ones who are unable to commit suicide without assistance). The Court of Appeal focused on establishing the breadth of the right to security of the person in section 7 of the Charter and on what constitutes a justifiable infringement of it – one that is "in accordance with the principles of fundamental justice." Chief Justice McEachern, in dissent, found that the prohibition on assisted suicide in section 241(b) of the Criminal Code was action by the state that deprived Rodriguez of her right to security of the person. Moreover, this deprivation was "not in accordance with principles of fundamental justice" or saved by being a limitation on a guaranteed freedom that could be demonstrably justified in a free and democratic society, as provided by section 1 of the Charter. The chief justice held "that any provision [of law] which imposes an indeterminate period of senseless physical and psychological suffering upon someone who is shortly to die anyway, cannot conform with any principle of fundamental justice."[174]

Like the chief justice, Justice Hollinrake held that the prohibition on assisted suicide in section 241(b) of the Criminal Code deprived Rodriguez of her section 7 right to security of the person. Unlike the chief justice, though, he held that this deprivation was in accordance with the principles of fundamental justice and, therefore, that section 241(b) was not unconstitutional.

Justice Proudfoot took a much narrower interpretation of the section 7 right, at least in relation to the facts of the case before her. Like the court of first instance, indeed, she might view the scope of protection given to security of the person by section 7 as limited to the "criminal context." Regardless of how her judgment should be interpreted in this respect, she expressly limited the scope of rights in section 7 with the statement that "obviously death is the antithesis of the s. 7 guarantee of 'life, liberty and security of the person.'"[175] This observation raises a complex matter that can be only mentioned here. There could be conflict between respecting someone's right to liberty and security of the person and that same person's life, if the former rights are broadly interpreted to include respect for the exercise of "positive content" rights to autonomy. One way to resolve the conflict is to recognize that a right to life is just that – a right, not an obligation – and that, moreover, rights can be waived. An alternative response is that the rights in section 7 must be interpreted consistently with each other. Consequently, rights to liberty and security of the person may not be used to detract from respect for someone's life. This position can be supported by relying on a doctrine of "abuse of rights." It can be argued that, for people to use their right to liberty or security of the person in a way that contravenes respect for their lives, would be to abuse these rights (that is, to use them for a purpose exactly the contrary to that for which they were intended). And an "abusive" use is an invalid exercise of those rights.[176]

Justice Proudfoot did not, however, base her judgment on section 7 of the Charter. Rather, she held that there was no *lis pendens*, no justiciable issue – that is, one that could be litigated – before the court. Rodriguez had sought a declaration stating that if a physician were willing to help her commit suicide, the unnamed physician would be exempt from future criminal liability. Justice Proudfoot concluded that "there can be no doubt that this is a hard case but it ought not, in my opinion, be allowed to influence the court to make bad law. I would regard as bad law a precedent which would pave the way for persons not defendants in either civil or criminal proceedings to seek and obtain immunity from liability for unknown persons for offences not yet committed and which may never be committed."[177]

The case was appealed to the Supreme Court of Canada.[178] All nine judges held that section 241(b) of the Criminal Code, in preventing Rodriguez from obtaining assistance in committing suicide, infringed her constitutionally protected right to security of her person under section 7 of the Charter. The five judges in the majority ruled that, taking into account the interests of society in prohibiting assistance in committing suicide, this infringement of her right was in accordance with the principles of fundamental justice. Therefore, section 241(b) was constitutionally valid. A plurality of four judges in dissent focused, much more exclusively than the majority, on individual rights to autonomy and gave little weight to claims that the protection of society required the prohibition of assistance in committing suicide. They held that the infringement of Rodriguez's rights to security of her person and, in the case of two judges, her constitutional right not to be subject to wrongful discrimination on the basis of physical handicap were infringed by section 241(b). These infringements could not be justified under the saving provisions in section 7 (that the infringement of a section 7 right was in accordance with the principles of fundamental justice) or section 1 (that the infringement was prescribed by law and is a reasonable limit that can be demonstrably justified in a free and democratic society) of the Charter; therefore, the dissenting judges held that section 241(b) of the Criminal Code was unconstitutional.

At each level in *Rodriguez*, the courts addressed two important questions: first, their proper role in dealing with a matter such as the legalization of euthanasia; and, second, when faced with a case requiring them to decide on legalization, the basis on which they should decide. As the judge at first instance stated, "in the case at bar this court is asked to move ... beyond the judicial domain and into the realm of general public policy."[179] Justice Hollinrake, in the Court of Appeal, recognized that courts could be seen as "shying away from the full force of the power entrusted to them under the Charter ... [in saying that] it is the function of Parliament to legislate [on these matters]."[180] And Chief Justice Lamer of the Supreme Court of Canada stated that the court must decide on the "right to choose suicide ... without reference to the philosophical and theological considerations fuelling the debate on the morality of suicide or euthanasia. It should consider the question before it from a legal perspective."[181] Ultimately, it will almost certainly be for the legislature to decide whether to continue prohibiting physicians from assisting patients in committing suicide.[182]

I return now to the descriptive categorization of interventions at the end of life. Overlying this breakdown is another analysis that can be applied to classify these interventions and establish whether there is, first, an obligation to treat; second, no such obligation; or, third, an obligation not to treat. This analysis depends on distinguishing between prolonging life and prolonging dying. The former might or might not be required. For example, prolonging life is not required when there is valid refusal of life-support treatment by a competent adult. Prolonging dying is never required (except, possibly, if a competent adult requests treatment that could have this effect and is able to give informed consent).[183] Concepts relevant to not prolonging dying include those of "futility"[184] (which recognizes that there is no obligation to provide medically futile or useless treatment) and "proportionality" (which recognizes that there can be overuse, underuse, and proper use of medical treatment, especially when it involves technology).

A proportionality principle postulates that, when the burden of treatment – harm and suffering inflicted by treatment – is out of proportion to any hoped-for benefit, there is no obligation to provide it. There are, of course, very personal and deep value judgments involved in judging the harms and benefits. Consequently, although the principle is easy to state in theory, it is not always easy to apply in practice. In fact, it is often very difficult. And the principle has come under increasing criticism as being an unacceptable shield for physicians imposing their value judgments about treatment on patients. One way in which the principle becomes easier to apply, in some cases, is through the mechanism of "advance directives" – legal devices such as the "living will" and "durable power of attorney" – because these directives implement as far as possible the patient's own value judgments regarding harms and benefits.

These legal mechanisms mean that the right to self-determination can bridge "the incompetence gap." Patients' wishes can govern even after they are no longer competent to express them. These mechanisms are based on and implement a principle of respect for people and their rights to self-determination and autonomy. A secondary effect, however, could be to benefit others. Withdrawing treatment, according to the wishes of patients, has beneficial symbolism. It promotes respect for people and for their wishes concerning themselves. Also, it saves the community or family the agony of deciding, the guilt that can be associated with any decision, and the cost of treatment. This process can be compared with withdrawing treatment on the basis of someone else's decision, one that can have harmful symbolism. It can sometimes say, in effect, that the lives of these people are not worth living and, therefore, not worth the cost of maintaining.

I will not discuss here the rapidly evolving use of "advance directives" in decision-making at the end of life, though this general area of decision-making forms the "surroundings" of euthanasia. I argue that there is a difference in kind between euthanasia and these other situations. Nevertheless, what happens in one of these areas can influence what happens in the others.

Identifying Basic or Initial Presumptions

The analysis of euthanasia can begin with four possible *prima facie* presumptions: first, "no" (euthanasia should be absolutely prohibited); second, "no, unless" (there is a basic presumption against euthanasia unless conditions are fulfilled, but it should be allowed in some circumstances); third, "yes, but" (euthanasia should be allowed in general, but prohibited in some circumstances); and, fourth, "yes" (euthanasia should be allowed).

Choosing the first or last presumption clearly reflects a major difference. The second and third are closer to each other, but the choice between them is not neutral. The symbolism of "no, unless" is closer to
the traditional symbolism against euthanasia, whereas the symbolism
of "yes, but" is characteristic of a society that accepts euthanasia. Moreover, the basic presumption will govern in situations of equal doubt as
to whether or not conditions for an exception are fulfilled. Therefore,
"no, unless" would rule against euthanasia in conditions of doubt, and
"yes, but" for euthanasia under the same conditions. Further, anyone
relying on an exception normally has the burden of proving that it applies. Therefore, someone carrying out euthanasia under "no, unless"
would have the burden of proving that euthanasia is justified in those
particular circumstances. In contrast, someone opposing euthanasia
would have the burden of showing that euthanasia is unjustified under
"yes, but."

It is interesting to analyse the Dutch situation in terms of these presumptions. Prior to the new legislation legalizing euthanasia, the
Dutch had adopted a "no" *prima facie* presumption in theory and a
"yes, but" presumption in practice – or, possibly, a "no, unless" *prima
facie* presumption, because, as I have already noted, the legal justification for euthanasia was that the defence of "force majeure" – in the
sense of conflicting duties – applied to excuse something that would
otherwise be prohibited. But the practical effect of the procedural
guidelines for prosecuting allegedly unjustified euthanasia which were
previously in place was that the burden of proving lack of justification
was on those who wanted to prosecute, not on those who performed
euthanasia. This situation reflects "yes, but." The new legislation
clearly enacts a "yes, but" presumption.

Probably, and paradoxically, the most basic presumption relevant to
euthanasia is that in favour of life. This presumption can differ from
sanctity of life, in that the former, though primary, can be rebutted; the
latter is often said to be absolute. The presumption in favour of life operates as a fundamental principle in both legal and ethical systems. The
questions raised by this principle in the context of euthanasia include
the following: When would quality-of-life considerations, if ever, displace it? Could a doctrine of necessity ever apply in such a way that it
justifies overriding the presumption in favour of life? One example is
pain-relief treatment that is necessary, but could shorten life. Could respect for people and their rights to autonomy and self-determination
displace the presumption in favour of life? One example is respect for
the informed refusals of treatment by competent people. Can claims of
the community – such as saving money – ever displace it? Is respect for
the person a reason that is different in kind from other reasons for

displacing the presumption in favour of life? Is respect for the person a preferable reason because it is less of an affront (or at least a less direct affront) to the sanctity of life value – which is similarly based, arguably, on respect for the person? But is sanctity of life primarily aimed at ensuring respect for the person or is its main purpose to protect the community, by protecting the person for the sake of the community? If so, it has a function similar to that of early criminal law. The aim was not so much to protect individuals for their own sake but to protect them for the sake of their society. Also worth considering is the question of whether detracting from an important value, such as sanctity of life, is latent or overt. We are much more tolerant of latent detractions from important values than overt ones, because the former do not threaten society and its symbolism as the latter do. Legalizing euthanasia would be an overt threat to the value of sanctity of life.

Moreover, not only ends are important. So are means, which include the principles used and the reasoning applied in justifying a course of conduct. For example, death resulting from respect for a competent person's refusal of treatment does not cause damage to the value of the sanctity of life to the same extent as euthanasia. Moreover, there can be a vast difference in terms of the precedent set by different lines of reasoning, although the conduct and outcome in the case that sets the precedent would be the same whichever line of reasoning were used. For instance, there is a great difference between regarding respect for refusal of treatment as being necessary in order to respect the person and classifying this as euthanasia – that is, regarding withdrawal of treatment in these circumstances as a precedent for euthanasia. Although ends or results can both set precedents, the stronger precedent-setting force is often the reasoning used to justify and the means used to attain those ends or results. Death itself cannot set a precedent, because all of us ultimately face death. And if death itself were to set a precedent, it could mean an end to restrictions on the way in which death could be inflicted. The important precedents are how death may and must not be allowed to occur and the reasons on which these conclusions are based.

Proponents of euthanasia argue for a presumption in favour of it on the grounds that it is a rational response. But rationality, itself, is not a justification for euthanasia or any other conduct. We need to consult also our moral intuition and even our emotions. In some cases, for some people, compassion could make euthanasia "feel right." But I suggest that it does not (or, at least, should not) "feel right" as one of the fundamental principles on which to base our society. Although feelings can sometimes be misleading in terms of ascertaining what is and is not acceptable conduct (as indeed can rationality, which we have sometimes found to our sorrow), we ignore feelings at our peril. We need to take into account "examined emotions" as well as cognitively based analysis in deciding whether or not euthanasia is acceptable at the societal level.[185] Feelings can act as important warnings that, although, rationally, two situations might seem the same, there might be additional factors.[186]

Which basic presumption should govern, initially, with respect to intervention by the state in decisions regarding treatment at the end of life? If the decision is a purely private one, the presumption is that the state should not intervene; if it has public aspects, though, this is not the case. Whether there is an initial presumption either for or against state intervention in someone's decision does not make a great deal of difference for competent adults in relation to decisions falling within a range of conduct that is not considered contrary to "public policy" in common law systems or to "public order and good morals" in civilian legal systems. This is true because – whether respecting personal decisions is regarded as a basic presumption or an exception and, likewise, but alternatively, the claim of the state to intervene – the personal decision will govern. The choice of presumption is determinative when incompetent people are involved, however, because the initial presumption cannot be displaced and will govern.

In *Cruzan*[187] a majority of the United States Supreme Court used a basic presumption that the state has a right to govern decisions concerning medical treatment unless someone's decision in this regard falls within specific parameters. Similarly, in *Quinlan,* the court held that "the state's right to protect life weakens and the right to privacy strengthens as the prognosis dims."[188] In contrast, the dissent in *Cruzan* used a presumption that people have a right to decide for themselves on medical treatment unless their decisions fall outside specific parameters (when the state may intervene).

We need to investigate these presumptions because a presumption against state intervention in personal decisions, desirable in the case of refusing treatment, is also being used to support claims to euthanasia on the grounds that, likewise, the state should not interfere in these decisions.[189] One relevant distinction between these two situations concerns the definition of medical treatment. I suggest it is incorrect to classify euthanasia in that category. Therefore, a precedent that governs personal decisions concerning medical treatment does not necessarily apply to euthanasia. This is not, in itself, an argument against euthanasia. It is an argument against legitimating euthanasia by analogy with the right to, or the right to refuse, medical treatment, and against this right being used as a legal precedent for legitimating euthanasia. It is clear in the public debate that this route to legitimating euthanasia has become a major strategy of those who are pro-choice on euthanasia.

Some people argue that the state has no legitimate role in relation to decisions concerning euthanasia because euthanasia is a private decision and, in a pluralistic society, the state has no moral justification for invading private decisions. Although it is true that dying is, in many senses, an intensely private event, the involvement of third persons – which, by definition, is the case in euthanasia – means the decision is not only a private one. If euthanasia were institutionalized, moreover, which it would necessarily be by the passage of law allowing it, it could not remain a private decision: It would have a major public aspect.

Seeking Insights: The Difference between Being Anti-euthanasia and Being Pro-life

There are two differences between being anti-euthanasia and being pro-life. The first is that not all or, possibly, most of those people who oppose euthanasia would regard themselves as pro-life – on abortion in particular. Nor are their objections to euthanasia religiously based, which can be true (or at least is often assumed to be true) for people who are pro-life on abortion. Moreover, non-pro-life, anti-euthanasia people, unlike some pro-life people, advocate the provision of necessary treatment for the relief of pain and other symptoms of serious physical distress, respect for valid refusals of treatment, and withdrawal of futile or "disproportional" treatment even when any of these actions could or would shorten life. The second difference is that some anti-euthanasia people (who might or might not be pro-life on abortion) would allow capital punishment. That is, they do not oppose all killing of other people; they are anti-euthanasia (and pro-life on abortion), but not uniformly pro-life.

What can one learn by comparing euthanasia and capital punishment, a form of killing that is – disgracefully, in my opinion – legalized in some jurisdictions? People can adopt one of four possible positions: first, against capital punishment and against euthanasia; second, for capital punishment but against euthanasia; third, for capital punishment and for euthanasia; or fourth, against capital punishment but for euthanasia. What underlying philosophy would each of these positions represent? The first is a true pro-life position. It demonstrates a moral belief that all killing (except, usually, as a last resort in self-defence) is wrong. The second position represents the view of some religious fundamentalists. To uphold the sanctity of life requires the prohibition of euthanasia; capital punishment, in contrast, is justified on the grounds that this punishment is deserved and just according to God's law. The third position is that of some neo-conservatives: capital punishment is a fitting penalty – one must forfeit one's life after committing a very serious crime – but taking one's own life in the form of euthanasia, too, is acceptable. The fourth view is that of some civil libertarians: one may consent to the taking of one's own life, but one must not take that of anyone else.

One can see where the various groups agree and disagree with each other. The true pro-lifers and the fundamentalists agree with each other in being against euthanasia, and some conservatives and civil libertarians agree with each other in supporting its availability. On the other hand, the true pro-life and civil libertarians join in their views in opposing capital punishment, whereas the fundamentalists and some conservatives agree in supporting it. In short, with respect to the issue involved here, the taking of one person's life by another, various groups can coalesce and agree in some instances, but be radically divergent in others. We need to be aware of these possibilities in assessing the political realities, public policy stances, and analyses relevant to euthanasia.

Seeking Further Insights:
Anti-Anti-euthanasia and Anti-Pro-euthanasia

Although the aim is the same, and although the various arguments in both cases overlap, there can be a difference in the content of the arguments of the pro-euthanasia position and those used to argue against the anti-euthanasia position. The same is true with respect to arguing against the pro-euthanasia position and arguing for the anti-euthanasia one.

Arguments against the Anti-euthanasia Position
The arguments against the anti-euthanasia position call into play powerful emotions and morally challenging rhetoric. They ask us to place ourselves in the shoes of suffering people who want euthanasia.

SUFFERING AND MERCY   Euthanasia is advocated as something that reduces suffering. Therefore, those who are anti-euthanasia can be perceived as being pro-suffering. No humane person advocates suffering, but everyone does not see unavoidable suffering as entirely negative. Some cultures or religions attribute value to suffering. Suffering is not always the greatest evil. Acts aimed at relieving it, including euthanasia, are not necessarily a lesser evil and might, therefore, be unacceptable. Not ending life is characterized as the infliction of suffering, not an example of our inability to relieve suffering. We need to ask whether this attitude is yet another example of the "do something" syndrome. Not being able to act with the aim of improving a very distressing situation (even when we recognize that our efforts will be futile) makes us highly anxious. We do not accept that there are some situations in which we cannot or ought not to do something. We assume that doing something is better than doing nothing and that doing something will improve the situation in moral or practical or even political terms.

Physicians can experience and display an especially powerful version of the do something phenomenon. They can be very uncomfortable, even highly anxious, if they feel unable to improve a patient's situation, especially if the patient is seriously ill – as all terminally ill patients are. One response to these patients can be to more-or-less abandon them – to visit them less often than other patients and to spend little time with them. Another response is, as Daniel Callahan says, "the great temptation of modern medicine, not always resisted ... to move beyond the promotion and preservation of health into the boundless realm of general human happiness and well-being." Although physicians can do much good in trying to achieve these objectives, not all ways of doing so are acceptable or do more good than harm. In particular, "it would be terrible for physicians to think that in a swift, lethal injection, medicine has found its own answer to the riddle of life. It would be a false answer; given by the wrong people."[190]

Some people regard being anti-euthanasia as a non-merciful stance. It is difficult to argue against those who see themselves as merciful and their opponents as unmerciful. Proponents of euthanasia argue that it is unethical not to provide euthanasia, because this stand is unmerciful. Prohibiting euthanasia is not only non-beneficent, for them, but also maleficent. There is a stronger moral obligation not to do harm than to do good, although distinguishing between the two can sometimes be difficult. To argue that failure to provide euthanasia is unmerciful and that this is maleficent, consequently, is a stronger argument in favour of euthanasia than simply arguing that to provide it is to confer a benefit. But it is also argued that euthanasia is compassionate and beneficent, and that it benefits the patient, the family, health-care professionals, and society.

"REASONABLY WELL OR DEAD" Some people argue, as well, that not prohibiting euthanasia contravenes the aim that people be either "reasonably well or dead." It is true that, largely as a result of modern medical technology, we can now be very sick and live for a considerable time; the "wellness curve," rather than gradually declining, can be "squared" by euthanasia. In other words, euthanasia allows one to go directly from being reasonably well to being dead. It is possible to "square" the morbidity curve by good palliative care and pain relief treatment, however, rather than euthanasia. Wellness, or at least a sense of well being, does not necessarily depend on the absence of disease.[191] Stated another way, in the vast majority of cases, euthanasia would be unnecessary (in the sense of being the only way of avoiding serious suffering) if good palliative care – including adequate pain-relief treatment – is provided.

LIBERTY Some people argue that euthanasia should be available as a matter of respect for personal liberty. Therefore, those who oppose euthanasia fail to respect important liberty rights. We need to be careful, however, before equating "wanting to die," in the sense of feeling ready for death and even welcoming it, and "wanting to be killed." Many (probably most) people at the end of their lives are "ready to die," but this does not mean that they "want to be killed."

Further, as I have already noted, the availability of euthanasia is not one-sided in its impact on liberty. Although it can be regarded as extending the range of choice over how and when to die, its availability can also create pressure to request or agree to euthanasia – which restricts liberty.[192] There is also a more subtle way in which the availability of euthanasia could interfere with liberty. At a 1992 conference on medicine, ethics, and law, Denise Ross, from the Dana Farber Cancer Institute, described a conversation she had with a young, terminally ill patient about pain management. He mentioned assisted suicide and euthanasia. She discussed these interventions with him, but felt obliged to inform him that she would not assist him in these ways. He replied rhetorically: "Of course not. Do you think that I would feel comfortable talking to you about this if you would."[193] It is possible that we need to have a trusted and trustworthy institutional forum in which to explore these matters without fear of being subjected to them. The forum used to be organized religion, but for many people, now, medicine has replaced it. A liberty interest would be breached by not retaining this new forum – which is one argument why, even if euthanasia were to be legalized, it should not become part of medical practice.

Arguments against the Pro-euthanasia Position

These arguments focus on the unavoidable harm that legalizing euthanasia would cause to our collective "human spirit," and to the integrity of two of our most important societal institutions – medicine and the law – and their practitioners.

PRECEDENT   At an individual, or micro, level, people of "good conscience" can believe that euthanasia is morally acceptable in some circumstances, especially those of intense, unrelievable suffering. But some people argue that euthanasia is unacceptable, even if one accepts the morality of this restricted use, because of the precedent that allowing it would set at the societal level. In this respect, it can be argued that prohibiting euthanasia is even more important in a secularized world than in a religiously based one. In the former, after all, worldly acts are the only source of our values. And what would happen in a secularized world with a shortage of health-care resources? Would people be graded on a scale of "useless" to "highly useful," and resources allocated or euthanasia provided accordingly? Would this classification give rise to a continuum ranging from less ethically acceptable acts of euthanasia to more ethically acceptable ones? This continuum could be compared with the law's "digital" approach. Unless all acts of euthanasia were allowed, the law would require that a line be drawn across the range of acts, dividing them into two groups. One group would be legally acceptable and the other legally unacceptable – although the acts that make up each group would not be equally acceptable or unacceptable from other perspectives, including the ethical one. Where would the law draw a line on the euthanasia continuum? Would some instances of euthanasia that most people consider ethically dubious, or even unethical, be characterized as legal?

OTHER ARGUMENTS   I will summarize arguments against the pro-euthanasia position that have been explored by others, especially by Peter Singer and Mark Siegler,[194] Susan Wolf,[195] Daniel Callahan,[196] and Alexander Capron.[197] These arguments include perversions of the proper aims of medicine, if physicians are the ones who carry out euthanasia. Physicians' involvement in euthanasia would turn medicine from its goal of healing and caring to one of eliminating those who need care. Euthanasia would extend into *all* physician-patient interactions, not only those directly involving euthanasia.[198] Euthanasia can desensitize and brutalize those who carry it out. This is a particularly disturbing possibility, because those same people are our healers and caregivers – physicians and other health-care professionals. Moreover, this outcome would reverse the separation of the two roles of the witch doctor (the modern physician's ancient predecessor): that of healer and of death inflictor. (The most influential and important articulation of this separation is to be found in the 2,000-year-old Hippocratic Oath.) As physician and ethicist Leon Kass so powerfully states, "the deepest ethical principle restraining the physician's power is not the autonomy or freedom of the patient; neither is it his own compassion or good intention. Rather it is the dignity and mysterious power of life itself."[199] Euthanasia puts the "very soul of medicine" on trial.[200]

As I have said at various points throughout this chapter, the symbolism of euthanasia is unacceptable even if it is carried out for the most humane reasons. It constitutes the most serious derogation from the sanctity of life. It has been well said that sanctity of life has been unduly identified with and confined to the religious commandment. But there are secular reasons – moral, rational, and medical – for respecting the sanctity of life and rejecting euthanasia.[201]

To allow euthanasia would inflict suffering and have potentially dangerous effects on already vulnerable groups, such as disabled or chronically ill people. The same grounds put forward to justify carrying out euthanasia on terminally ill people are often true for these other people throughout their lives. Even if they were not at risk of being subjected to euthanasia, their lives would be devalued by the fact that others in a similar position were subjected to it.[202] For these reasons, since the advent of the current movement to legalize euthanasia, disabled people have formed groups that work to prevent this change from occurring. In Canada, the Council of Canadians with Disabilities has been very active and effective in presenting its case and critiquing the pro-euthanasia one. One similar group in the United States has the quirky – but arresting – name of Not Dead Yet.

Some say there would be a greater danger of abuse if euthanasia were legalized than if it were not. Even if this contention cannot be established, those advocating euthanasia should at least have the burden of proving the contrary. Potential abuses include the possibility that euthanasia could be involuntary; it could be carried out secretly even though – indeed, because – it would be legal (because legalization would encourage people to consider it ethically acceptable and to use it in situations that otherwise would be considered unacceptable by everyone); people would be encouraged to seek euthanasia; it could take the form of "surrogate euthanasia" (with someone other than the one being euthanized authorizing the procedure); or it could be applied in a discriminatory way in terms of those subjected to it.[203] As Singer and Siegler state, these risks are especially serious in an era of "cost containment, social injustice and ethical relativism."[204]

The availability of euthanasia could detract from developing better care for dying people; it would be quicker and easier than research to develop and improve care. If euthanasia had been available, would we have developed the sophisticated palliative care techniques that we have today?[205] It would be interesting to examine the Dutch situation in this respect. What about the availability of palliative-care resources and hospices there? Was euthanasia the solution to their unavailability or inaccessibility? Also, legalizing euthanasia could create pressure to accept or to request it to relieve burdens on family and society. Euthanasia would probably interfere with current legal approaches to the refusal of treatment. As Wolf[206] points out, the courts would be reluctant to stay out of decisions at the end of life if euthanasia were one option. Moreover, we might not have developed mechanisms such as "advance directives" if euthanasia had been an option.

 Most contentiously, perhaps, one can argue that euthanasia interferes with the final stage of human development: dealing with death. As a solution to the difficulties of death, euthanasia is short-term, simple, easy in some senses, and appealing to some people. But we need long-term perspectives on death. These could be more complex and difficult in many respects. Through them, however, we are more likely to work out the mystery and complexity of our dying or even living, because the latter is necessarily related to the former.

Finally, euthanasia would set a precedent of universal application. At some point, each of us must face death. This universality can be regarded as beneficial in the sense of strong personal identification with the possibility that, if euthanasia were legalized, it could be applied to us. That should make us think very seriously about whether we agree with the precedent that legalizing euthanasia would set. At some stage, each of us would be the person on the other side of "the veil of ignorance" to whom the euthanasia decision could apply. John Rawls suggests we should make difficult decisions behind this veil, because we do not know, at the time of decision, which actors we will be when the decision is implemented.[207] The universality of a euthanasia precedent is immensely frightening in the potential extent of its use. There are some fine lines we should never cross. One of these, I propose, is that separating euthanasia from other interventions or non-interventions at the end of life.

CONCLUSION

We are not only logical and rational. We are also emotional, intuitive, and spiritual (which is not necessarily the same as religious). Our "ways of knowing" are complex, diverse, and vast.

Some arguments for euthanasia are logical and rational (for example, that there is no difference between actively killing and allowing to die), but they can be instinctive and emotional as well (that we are obliged to be merciful and to relieve suffering). The arguments against euthanasia are logical and rational (the "slippery slope"), but also instinctive and emotional (the sanctity of human life). For some people, the arguments are also religious or possibly just spiritual.

Euthanasia should be seen as different in kind, not merely degree, from other acts or omissions that could or would shorten life. One crosses a great divide in undertaking intentional killing. Although pain and other symptoms of serious physical distress should be relieved, it must always be the pain or other symptoms that one seeks to eliminate, and not the person with the pain or symptoms. Even if euthanasia were justified in a few individual cases, moreover, the effect on society of legalizing it would be unacceptable.

When we disagree, it is important to delve below the level of disagreement and to try to find a deeper consensus. To start from consensus and move to disagreement is not the same as starting from disagreement. The two poles of the euthanasia argument are clear: pro-choice on euthanasia (no interventions aimed at reducing or eliminating suffering, including the infliction of death, should be prohibited) and pro-life (all interventions that could or would shorten life should be prohibited). It is much more difficult to be in the middle of this debate and draw a line somewhere in the grey (or "purple-pink"[208]) zone between the poles – that is, to argue that some acts that shorten or fail to prolong life should be prohibited and others, even those with the same outcome as prohibited acts, should be allowed. We can all agree that none of us is "pro-suffering," and none of us is anti-death when "its time has come." Where we disagree is the means that may be used to reduce suffering, cause death, or allow death to occur.

The euthanasia debate is immensely important. It is one of the most important current issues in setting the legal and ethical tone as we embark on our journey into the twenty-first century. Is prohibition of euthanasia an example of sacrificing the individual (who wants it) for the good of the community (which would be harmed by it)? Is euthanasia the final act of love of caring individuals and a caring society? Or is it an isolation ritual whereby the individual is expelled from the collective, the members of which bond to each other through shared guilt?[209] To answer these questions will take wisdom, compassion, courage, and hope. Taken together, these qualities are the opposite of despair, which so often is (but often need not be) present in situations that give rise to calls for euthanasia. How we deal with euthanasia is likely to be one of the most important mirrors of ourselves, our society, and our relationships – both as intimates and as strangers. We need to take great care in fashioning the lyrics of the songs that we sing about it, because our lyrics will play a crucial role in creating the reality about euthanasia that gives rise to these reflections. Moreover, our decisions and actions will create not only immediate reflections but also themes and echoes of enormous importance for those who come after us – especially those who will live in the distant future. We need to sing "the song of life: the lyrics of love." This music includes the song of death as an inevitable part of life – but not the lyrics of euthanasia.

4 "Death Talk" in Canada: The *Rodriguez* Case

In both literal and metaphorical senses, euthanasia is an end-of-a-millennium controversy. Some of the most complex and serious decisions we will face as individuals, families, communities, and society will be determined by how we approach, structure, analyze, and resolve the euthanasia debate. This debate can be regarded as the tip of an iceberg, an image that brings to mind the fact that the vast majority of the matters affected by the debate are submerged and hidden,[1] and the possibility that legalization of euthanasia could prove to be an icy (slippery) slope. Legalizing euthanasia can be seen also as a stone thrown into a pond; the stone represents euthanasia and the pond, society. It is not enough to examine only the stone itself; there is also much work that needs to be done in identifying every resulting ripple and its impact.[2]

To do so, we must establish a "questioning framework" built on a transdisciplinary, transcultural, and transsectoral base that can accommodate input from members of the community and people with expertise, formal and experiential learning, thinking and feeling, secular and religious beliefs, and qualitative and quantitative perspectives – to name just some of the diverse contributions that are needed. We must recognize also that this debate goes to the very heart of what it means to be human, and to the basis and nature of human community and society.

In entering into this momentous debate, we need to strive for honesty and integrity in ourselves and to start from a presumption that our "opponents" are operating on the same basis. In short, our disagreements must be focused on euthanasia and questions raised by it, not on a lack of respect for those with whom we disagree. It is within this broad and deep context that the judgment of the Supreme Court of Canada in *Rodriguez* v. *Canada (Attorney General)*[3] must be considered. It is also within this context that political action on euthanasia must be viewed.

Acceptance of the approach outlined above means recognizing that, although the death of each of us is an intensely personal and unique event, we are not dealing with just the death of any individual – for instance, Sue Rodriguez – in the euthanasia debate. In deciding whether euthanasia (physician-assisted suicide)[4] is or should be legal, as Rodriguez was arguing, we are reflecting, and reflecting on, matters basic to the world view that gives meaning to the life of everyone and to communal life. Seeing euthanasia in this context raises many questions. To cite a few of them:

- Do we believe that we are nothing more than highly complex thinking, feeling, and living machines? Or do we believe that human life transcends the purely mechanistic realm and that there is a mystery beyond ourselves that we cannot ever fully contemplate – "the mystery of the unknown" (and perhaps unknowable) – but that we should respect or even revere?
- Are we fearful of mystery? Do we convert mysteries – including that of death – into problems in order to feel more control over them? Does euthanasia represent a response that is generated by converting the *mystery* of death into the *problem* of death?
- Why are we engaged in the euthanasia debate now, when the basic conditions giving rise to the circumstances that elicit calls for euthanasia – pain, suffering, and terminal illness – have always been part of the human condition, and we have always been able to kill each other?
- What impact would legalizing euthanasia have on people who are sick, old, or unable to "control the use of their bodies,"[5] including the impact on their perceptions of themselves and our perceptions of them?
- Are there reasons, other than the obvious ones of expertise, for "medicalizing" euthanasia and delegating it to physicians?
- Why do we call many instances of euthanasia "physician-assisted suicide," not "euthanasia" or "homicide"?[6]
- Are we manipulated in the euthanasia debate by the use of special rhetoric (that is, language designed to persuade or impress with respect to a position)? Are we even aware of the rhetoric?
- Who should have the burden of proof to show that legalizing euthanasia would not be seriously harmful to society?[7]

- Can we justifiably distinguish between euthanasia and withholding or withdrawal of treatment that results in death? What is the moral and ethical divide in relation to decisions and actions that result in death? Is it between the voluntary decision-making of competent people and surrogate decision-making? That is, should we focus on the decisions involved and their ethical acceptability? Or is this divide between killing (euthanasia) and allowing to die (withholding or withdrawal of treatment)? That is, should we focus on the acts involved and their ethical acceptability? Should the legal divide be the same as the moral divide?
- Should those who advocate the legalization of euthanasia bear the burden of proof and be required to show, before the event, that legalization would cause no serious harm?
- By legalizing euthanasia, would we be in danger of "deforming" fundamental concepts important to the operation of criminal law in general? These concepts include those of intention; the non-relevance, in general, of motive to culpability; the doctrine of causation; the distinction between homicide and suicide; or the role of consent of the victim (or, more accurately, the absence of a role) in criminal liability for homicide.
- Should the euthanasia debate be conducted primarily through the courts and the lens of the Canadian Charter of Rights and Freedoms,[8] as in *Rodriguez?*
- Is "rights talk" the most appropriate framework within which to structure the euthanasia debate?
- How should the Parliament of a postmodern democracy deal with euthanasia? That is, on what basis should members of parliament decide how to vote? By consulting their electorate? On the basis of their own consciences?
- What balance should be struck in dealing with the conflict between individual rights and societal claims that is generated by euthanasia?
- Is the demand for euthanasia the result of liberalism, in the form of intense individualism, gone wild? Or is it a rational response of caring individuals and a caring community?
- Does the demand for euthanasia reflect a loss of community? Death used to bring the community together. But if there is no community to come together, and if death is experienced in isolation not only by those who die but also by those who are bereaved, euthanasia can be predicted as a likely response.
- How can we represent the interests of society in a public debate carried out largely in the mass media? Seeing the courage and tragedy of people such as Sue Rodriguez rightly elicits our deepest

compassion and empathy. But doing so creates an imbalance because there can be no comparable image of society.

- Does this debate reflect the fact that we are a death-denying but also death-obsessed society that has lost its main forum – namely, organized religion – for death talk?
- Could the euthanasia debate reflect a society that is suicidal, homicidal, and very fearful as a result? Would legalizing euthanasia allow us to believe that we have both individual and societal death under control – tamed, that is, and civilized?
- Is euthanasia yet another expression of turn-of-the-century nihilism, in the sense that we define ourselves collectively by what we are not – as postmodern, post-patriarchal, and even post-antibiotic – instead of what we are? In particular, does euthanasia reflect that we are a post-sacred society – one that has lost all sense of the sacred (which is not necessarily connected with either the presence or loss of organized religion)?
- Is the way in which we die primarily a socially or culturally structured event, like marriage? Just as we have institutionalized divorce, should we likewise institutionalize euthanasia so that we can "divorce" life?
- Is euthanasia a response to an almost total loss of death rituals in secular, postmodern Western societies? Does it function as a ritual or as a substitute for it?
- How would legalizing euthanasia in Canada affect the global community? Would it set a precedent?[9] Canada is often regarded, and sometimes promotes itself, as a model for other societies in terms of showing respect for people, human rights, and human ethics. Would Canadians want to be emulated in regard to legalizing euthanasia?[10] Would legitimating euthanasia open the door to serious and frequent abuse of the right to life in some societies – especially those with a history of such abuse – and lead them to attempt legitimation of their conduct on the basis of a Canadian example?
- How do we want our children and grandchildren to die?[11]
- What type of society do we want to pass on to future generations? What effect would legalizing euthanasia have on the values and symbols of a future Canadian society, on its memes (the units of cultural information that we pass on from generation to generation, the inherited cultural norms of society)?

Those are some of the questions we are dealing with when we engage in the euthanasia debate. Often they are incommensurable, for euthanasia can be as much a matter of religion as it is health and illness, of literature as it is law, of aesthetics as it is ethics.[12] I would like to comment briefly now, with reference to *Rodriguez*, on three matters that relate to some of these questions.

EMOTION AND COGNITION

In the euthanasia debate, what should be the respective roles of cognitively based and emotionally based judgment?

We have a peculiar sensation, possibly of cognitive dissonance,[13] in reading the judgments of the Supreme Court of Canada in *Rodriguez*. Why? This intensely personal and emotional debate is about something of great societal importance: when and how each of us dies. Yet the court, of necessity, handled this case almost entirely through the lens of classic legal analysis – in particular, Charter analysis. The limitations imposed by a predominantly legal approach to euthanasia, however, can result in both benefits and risks or harms.

One benefit of legal analysis is that it can allow us to identify those parts of an argument that are rationally, or cognitively, based and those parts that are emotionally based. To deal with euthanasia, we need to have and to explore both types of reaction and to be aware of when we are using one or the other. This statement might seem to imply that cognitive and emotional processes can be clearly divided. They cannot, but the emphasis can be more on one than the other. Moreover, the starting point of analysis, on a continuum from pure reason to pure emotion, can alter its end point and, therefore, a decision regarding the matter analyzed. Despite this continuity between cognitive and emotional processes, we often purport to separate them in practice. One weakness of doing so appears if we act on the basis of this separation – that is, if we form our response by using only one or the other. Another weakness occurs when we examine only the dominantly emotional or dominantly cognitive aspect of each side of an issue (especially if we do not examine the same aspect with respect to each side). There are important cognitive and emotional aspects on both sides of the euthanasia debate, all of which should be taken into account.[14]

This proposal does not ignore the dangers of taking into account the emotional and intuitive responses (including, on occasion, those based on moral intuition) to euthanasia. Rather, it recognizes that there are at least equal dangers in *not* doing so. Although emotional responses must be allowed to play a role in the euthanasia debate, safeguards are needed. For instance, the intense compassion and empathy that Rodriguez elicited through her public statements and appearances, particularly on television,[15] need to be balanced by cognitively based arguments – especially with respect to the impact that legalizing euthanasia would have on society – on what can be called "the ethical and legal tone" of society. The old saying that hard cases make bad law sums up the danger of relying on emotional responses to the exclusion of cognitive ones.

Most often in law, we tend to be concerned, usually with good cause, about the cognitive overwhelming the emotional. Judges rarely, if ever, talk in their judgments about exercising moral intuition, yet we expect them to do so and more or less assume that they do. Could it be, however, that a highly rational, cognitive approach to euthanasia might indicate the absence of moral intuition? As is probably true of justice,[16] we might notice only its absence, not its presence. We ignore our feelings, particularly when they involve moral intuition, at our peril.

In this respect, it is interesting to note the results of a survey carried out on a group of American physicians. Although they knew that there was no ethical or legal difference between justified withholding and withdrawal of life-support treatment, they felt a major difference and had much greater difficulty with withdrawing treatment than withholding it.[17] This example might provide a useful warning. In general, with-holding-of-treatment cases are much more ethically and morally clear-cut than withdrawal ones. It might be a safeguard of both us and those affected by our actions that we find it more difficult to act in the latter case than the former. Arguably, our long-standing approach of prohib-iting euthanasia, but accepting refusals of treatment, indicates that most people sense a difference between giving lethal injections and ac-cepting decisions to refuse life-support treatment. It is a strong feature of all the dissenting judgments in *Rodriguez* (and an essential one to each dissenting judge's recognition of Rodriguez's right to assistance in ending her life) that there are no morally significant reasons to dis-tinguish between euthanasia and accepting refusals of life-support treatment and that there should be no difference in the way in which the law deals with each situation. Is this an example of a cognitive approach displacing necessary emotional responses?

Perhaps the most surprising statement in *Rodriguez*, that of Chief Jus-tice Antonio Lamer that Canadians have a "right to *choose* suicide,"[18] might reflect yet another variation of the relation between cognitive and emotional responses in making legal decisions. In this instance, a cognitive approach might be masking a primarily emotional one. Presumably, "a right to choose suicide" means a right to commit sui-cide; there would be no point in having the right to choose a course of action that one has no right to undertake.[19] I will not discuss here the wider implications of recognizing this right,[20] but it is important to understand why the chief justice recognized it, a right for which there is no precedent (not that the Supreme Court needs one). He discussed access to euthanasia through the lens of discrimination under section 15 of the Charter. He held that the law, in prohibiting Rodriguez from being given assistance to commit suicide, unlawfully discriminated against her (as a handicapped person unable to commit suicide without help) with regard to her right to choose suicide. This particular use of the discrimination provisions in the Charter is unusual, resting, as it does, on a right that had never before been articulated. Does it reflect a reality in which the chief justice was acting on feelings of compassion and mercy towards Rodriguez? Was he using sophisticated, technical, legal reasoning to fashion a ruling that would allow these feelings to be implemented in practice? In short, there is a sense that cognitive tools – the law as set out in the Charter – have been used to articulate and act on a deeply felt emotional response.

In post-modern, secular Canadian society the courts (especially the Supreme Court of Canada) and Parliament have become the highest cathedrals. It is not surprising, therefore, that – as is often true in religious experiences – non-cognitive factors could strongly influence the approach taken by the judges on euthanasia.

BALANCING INDIVIDUAL AND SOCIETAL INTERESTS

In the euthanasia debate, what weight should be given to societal interests – especially in upholding the concept of the sanctity of life – when these interests are in conflict with individual ones?

Probably the most important difference between the majority and the dissenting judges in *Rodriguez* is the weight each group gives to the interests of society. The dissenting judges clearly did not consider that any interest of society would outweigh the interests of terminally ill, competent patients. These judges considered it necessary to respect people's rights to autonomy, self-determination, dignity, control, and choice in relation to determining for themselves the manner, time, and place of death. In contrast, the majority held that the interests of society (or possibly the interests of vulnerable people, who might be persuaded to commit suicide, and societal interests in protecting them[21]) outweigh these interests of the individual.

The majority stated that, in deciding on the constitutionality of prohibiting assisted suicide in subsection 241(b) of the Criminal Code,[22] although "liberty and security of the person interests are engaged," a consideration of these interests cannot be divorced from the sanctity of life, which is one of the three Charter values protected by section 7.

None of these values prevail a priori over the others. All must be taken into account. The majority recognized that "security of the person is intrinsically concerned with the well-being of the living person." It referred to human life as "sacred or inviolable (which terms ... [are used] in the non-religious sense ...)." That is, human life has "a deep, intrinsic value of its own." And it articulates one question of fundamental importance as "the degree to which our conception of the sanctity of life includes notions of quality of life as well."[23] This statement is interesting, because, almost invariably, the concepts of sanctity of life and quality of life are seen as being in opposition to each other (although, logically, they need not be). Certainly, the former is not usually treated as including the latter; rather, sanctity of life is used as a counter-argument to propositions that someone's quality of life is so low as to be not worth preserving, especially if that would require the use of scarce or expensive health-care resources.

Does sanctity of life differ from respect for life? And, if so, in which ways? As noted above and on other occasions in its judgment, the majority explicitly or implicitly referred to the value of sanctity of life.[24] In comparison, Justice McLachlin in dissent, with Justice L'Heureux-Dubé concurring, referred to "the state interest in protecting life."[25] Justice Cory, likewise in dissent, refers to the "basic position ... that human life is fundamentally important to our democratic society."[26] Whether the judge was indicating that respect for human life depends on democracy or vice versa, or both, is not clear. In any case, we need to ask whether the content of all or any of these or similar terms used by the various justices in *Rodriguez* is the same. If not, might these terms represent a continuum from greater to lesser degrees of protection of life? For instance, although a concept of respect for life could have identical content to one of sanctity of life, it might not. And it is of much less certain content than the latter. Where is the cutoff point on the continuum with respect to decisions based on the law's fundamental presumption in favour of life? That is, how broad would the range of decisions that are regarded as legally acceptable be on the continuum described?[27] How flexible is this cutoff point? How flexible should it be?

The majority in *Rodriguez* linked the protection of vulnerable people with the protection of life:

Section 241(b) has as its purpose the protection of the vulnerable who might be induced in moments of weakness to commit suicide. This purpose is grounded in the state interest in protecting life and reflects the policy of the state that human life should not be depreciated by allowing life to be taken. This policy finds expression not only in the provisions of our Criminal Code which prohibit murder and other violent acts against others *notwithstanding the consent* of the victim, but also in the policy against capital punishment and, until its repeal, attempted suicide. This is not only a policy of the state, however, but is part of our fundamental conception of the sanctity of human life.[28]

This passage presents another contrast between the majority and the dissenting decisions. The majority recognized that consent to being killed neither alters the legality of the act nor ought to, even when the killing is in the context of euthanasia. The dissenting judges, in holding that physician-assisted suicide should be allowed, placed heavy emphasis on the consent of competent patients who want assistance to die as the necessary safeguard to prevent any misuse of such assistance.

The majority mentioned the sanctity of human life in relation to its preservation – but recognized that the use of this principle for that purpose might "be subject to certain limitations and qualifications reflective of personal autonomy and dignity."[29] Life-sustaining medical treatment may be refused by competent persons or where there is "compelling evidence that withdrawal of treatment was in fact what the patient would have requested had she been competent."[30] This understanding, in turn, is to recognize that it can be consistent to espouse the sanctity of life and yet try neither to prolong life nor to avoid death in some circumstances. If the occurrence of death detracts from upholding this principle, then the principle is meaningless: all of us die, and, therefore, life could never be regarded as sacred. It is *how* death occurs, not *if* it occurs, that has an impact on the sanctity-of-life principle. Respect for the latter does not mean preservation or prolongation of life at all costs. Rather, it governs what we must not do to interfere with life and what we must do to protect it, because to do or not do so, respectively, would detract from respect for its sanctity.

This discussion raises an important and difficult question: Are accepting refusals of life-support treatment and providing pain-relief treatment (that could shorten life, but is necessary to relieve pain) exceptions to the principle of sanctity of life? If so, are they serious threats to maintaining the principle? It can be argued that these interventions do not constitute exceptions because they do not involve a primary purpose of shortening life. Therefore, they are beyond the principle's scope. If this argument is incorrect, however, I propose that these interventions are justified exceptions. Although they derogate from the principle, they do not threaten or harm it.[31] Just because this outcome is true of some exceptions does not mean it is true of all. Indeed, if all or even some particular kinds of exception could be justified, no principle would remain. In my view, euthanasia would be this kind of exception; to regard it as justified would, in fact, have the effect of eliminating the principle of the sanctity of life.

Not all threats to important societal values are of the same nature and, depending on their nature, the destructiveness of their impact can vary. Overt threats to maintaining important societal values, such as the sanctity of life, are much more dangerous than latent ones. Euthanasia presents an overt threat. Only a latent threat, if any, is posed by respect for refusals of treatment or provision of necessary pain-relief treatment that could shorten life. In other words, even if it were true that these interventions and euthanasia all constitute threats to the sanctity-of-life principle, euthanasia is a vastly more serious threat.

Canadian society accepts many withdrawals or withholdings of life-sustaining treatment, or providing pain-relief treatment even if it could shorten life. One consequence is that advocates of euthanasia increasingly argue that this acceptance establishes a precedent for a "right to die" through euthanasia.[32] To respect competent people's refusals of life-support treatment that result in death is to recognize that the principle of sanctity of life is not absolute. Therefore, they argue, the following questions are ones not of principle but of degree: What exceptions to the principle of sanctity of life should be allowed? Where should the line be drawn with respect to euthanasia?

If this argument were correct, then the basis for any recognized exception would be important in connection with the types of intervention that ought to, or would, be authorized as a consequence. If refusals of treatment are respected on the basis of respecting a right to autonomy, then, unless one limits the scope of exercising this right – for instance, through a doctrine of "abuse of rights," or through legislation (which is currently the case with the prohibition on assisted suicide in the Criminal Code[33]) – it is arguable that euthanasia is simply another exercise of the right to personal autonomy. In that case, it ought to be allowed, in the same way that refusals of life-sustaining treatment are allowed, as just one more autonomy-based exception to the principle of sanctity of life. But if the basis for respecting refusals of treatment is respect for a right to inviolability (the right not be touched without consent), which is a more limited version, or subcategory, of the right to autonomy,[34] it would set no precedent that could be used to legitimate euthanasia.

It is true that a value judgment is involved in arguing that refusals of treatment should be respected and that pain-relief treatment, even treatment that could shorten life, should be provided – but that euthanasia should be prohibited. But it is not an arbitrary judgment. There is a difference, even if one does not regard it as a morally significant difference, between not prolonging a life and giving a lethal injection. The nature of the act of giving a lethal injection is and feels different from the act(s) involved in not prolonging a life. And having a primary intention to kill is different from not having it, even though, in not prolonging a lie, it is recognized that death could or would ensue as a consequence of the intervention or non-intervention.

Is the sanctity of life a concept that is fundamental to the paradigm that governs a secular society as compared with a religious one? We need to be very careful. Concepts that have traditionally been associated with religion, such as the sanctity of life, should not be thrown out simply on the basis of this connection. Although, in the past, concepts of this kind have been fundamental values by virtue of being religious norms, they can be crucial also in establishing the foundation for a secular society. When we did not need to look beyond religion for authority for our values, we could use religion to establish them. This association does not necessarily mean that the same concepts and values cannot be used, and are not needed, if religion is unavailable to authenticate them. There are good reasons, other than religious ones, to uphold the sanctity of life. We should be careful also not to reject concepts that have become associated with certain ideological or political stances merely because of these ties.

The majority in *Rodriguez* implicitly referred to the sanctity of life in articulating the grounds on which both the House of Lords[35] and the Law Reform Commission of Canada,[36] to paraphrase the majority's ruling, have not been prepared to recognize the legality of providing active assistance to people in carrying out the desire to end their lives.

First, the active participation by one individual in the death of another is intrinsically morally and legally wrong, and secondly, there is no certainty that abuses can be prevented by anything less than a complete prohibition. Creating an exception for the terminally ill might therefore frustrate the purpose of the legislation of protecting the vulnerable because adequate guidelines to control abuse are difficult or impossible to develop.[37]

This passage raises two related questions. Does the majority adopt the principle that euthanasia is intrinsically morally and legally wrong, or simply say that the House of Lords and the Law Reform Commission of Canada have adopted this principle? And would exceptions allowing euthanasia for terminally ill people be acceptable if both they and the people to whom they were applied could be safeguarded?

On reading the judgment of the majority as a whole, one is left with the strong impression that, although it relied on both of the bases described, either one or the other would have been sufficient for its holding that physician-assisted suicide should not be legalized (at least on the basis of upholding a Charter challenge to legislation prohibiting euthanasia or physician-assisted suicide).[38] It is noteworthy, however, that in dissent, Justice McLachlin, who spent considerable time in her judgment dealing with that of the majority, mentioned only the danger of abuse as the reason on which the majority based its holding. Moreover, she would further restrict the basis of the majority's ruling by limiting the type of abuse that she believed had worried the majority. According to her, the majority saw the limitation on the right to security of the person, constituted by the prohibition on assisted suicide, as "necessary to prevent deaths which *may not truly be consented to.*"[39] This interpretation would mean that, if consent to physician-assisted suicide could be safeguarded, it would be allowed by the majority (or, more precisely, that it would be unconstitutional to interfere with a person's obtaining such assistance). I think that the majority's fears are much more broadly based than this concern and clearly include not only the impact on individuals of allowing euthanasia but also the impact on society. As the majority says:

Overall, then, it appears that a blanket prohibition on assisted suicide similar to that in s. 241 is the norm among Western democracies, and such a prohibition has never been adjudged to be unconstitutional or contrary to fundamental human rights ... [S]ocietal concern with preserving life and protecting the vulnerable rendered the blanket prohibition preferable to a law which might not adequately prevent abuse.[40]

Finally, one major difference between the majority and the dissenting justices (in relation to balancing conflicting societal and individual interests) lay in the choice of a basic presumption from which each group started its analysis. Those in the majority spoke of "balancing ... the interest of the state and the individual."[41] Though not explicitly, they analyse from a basic presumption of the sanctity of life.

Sanctity of life, as we will see, has been understood historically as excluding freedom of choice in the self-infliction of death, and certainly the involvement of others in carrying out that choice. At the very least, no new consensus has emerged in society opposing the right of the state to regulate the involvement of others in exercising power over individuals ending their lives.[42]

In contrast, the dissenting justices began from a basic presumption of the individual's right to autonomy.[43] This difference can be captured by comparing the statements in the judgment of the majority and in those of the dissenting judges concerning which principles are not absolute. These statements, in identifying a principle as not absolute, implicitly indicate that it is fundamental. The majority recognized that the sanctity of life is "not absolute."[44] Dissenting judges – for instance, the chief justice – recognized that the scope of a person's right to autonomy and self-determination "is never absolute."[45] Basic presumptions are not neutral; they determine the outcome in cases of equal doubt as to whether or not a burden of proof has been fulfilled.[46] If the basic presumption is the sanctity of life, it will govern unless displaced by proof, at least on the balance of probabilities, that it should not apply. The same reasoning is true with respect to a basic presumption favouring the principle of a person's right to autonomy (in this case, to choose death by euthanasia). The outcome, in a situation of equal doubt, when the former presumption is regarded as fundamental would be the polar opposite of the outcome when the latter presumption is so regarded – although, to state the obvious, each analysis deals with the same degree of doubt about the same matters. I do not suggest that the majority and the dissenting justices reached their decisions principally as a result of some procedural effect, but we should always be aware, in using the law, that legal forms are never mere formalities.

CONCEPTS AND LANGUAGE

How does our choice of concepts, especially the language in which we choose to express these concepts, influence the debate over euthanasia? To begin with, the case we are discussing has been largely referred to as the "*Sue Rodriguez* case" and not the "*Rodriguez* case," which would be the more common legal shorthand. The use of the plaintiff's first name undoubtedly reflects many factors, including our emotional reaction to Sue Rodriguez, our personal identification with her and her plight (in view of the fact that we all inevitably face death), and the nature of the issue being litigated: our right to claim relief from suffering – or at least not to be inhibited in seeking it in whatever ways we, as individuals, find acceptable.

Words that appear with unusual frequency in the judgments of both the majority and the dissenting justices – even for a case that raises important questions about the breadth of individual freedom protected by the right to security of the person under section 7 of the Charter – are *autonomy, self-determination, dignity, choice,* and *control.* There is much that needs to be explored with regard to the Supreme Court's use, in the *Rodriguez* case, of the concepts these words represent. We need to consider matters such as the impact of our choice of language in formulating concepts[47] (language is not neutral, as I often say, especially in relation to matters such as euthanasia and when used by our highest court); the scope of possible definitions of each concept;[48] what these definitions reflect about our attitudes, values, and beliefs as individuals and as a society; and the impact exclusive emphasis on each one would have on important societal and cultural symbols – including those that support or detract from our seeing ourselves as a community and from the responsibilities and privileges this sense entails.

Likewise, we need to recognize the two-edged sword that concepts such as euthanasia can provide. Depending on the content attributed to them (which depends partly on the language in which they are formulated) and the way in which they are used, their effects can vary radically. Quoting Lawrence Tribe, the majority recognized this threat when it stated that "legalising euthanasia, rather than respecting people, may endanger personhood." In the same vein, the majority noted that "the principles of fundamental justice leave a great deal of scope for personal judgment, and the Court must be careful that they do not become principles which are of fundamental justice in the eye of the beholder *only*."[49] The latter part of this statement focuses on one possible meaning of the concept of dignity. I point out elsewhere that dignity can be an extrinsic characteristic; people are dignified, from this perspective, according to whether we attribute dignity to them. In other words, dignity exists only in the eye of the beholder. But dignity can be an intrinsic characteristic, too; people are dignified *whether or not* others attribute it to them.[50]

In view of the emphasis placed on dignity in all judgments of the Supreme Court in *Rodriguez*, it is important to explore this concept. Was an intrinsic or extrinsic definition of dignity used in relation to euthanasia? One problem with an extrinsic definition is that it opens up the possibility that people would need additional characteristics – other than simply being people – to be respected on the basis of having dignity. It is much safer to require the presence only of a universally shared intrinsic characteristic in order to be owed respect on the basis of having dignity, to respect people simply because they are persons, or, even more protectively, simply because they are human. We should recognize, to cite the majority in *Rodriguez*, "the *intrinsic value* of human life and ... the *inherent dignity* of every human being."[51]

CONCLUSION

This is a period of intense activity with respect to moulding a new societal and cultural paradigm (the story that informs us as a society and necessarily has an impact on us as individuals). Euthanasia itself is already an important part of our story; its prohibition makes it so.

Should we rewrite the story? Should we legalize euthanasia? Should we change what is arguably the most fundamental principle on which our society is based – that we must not kill each other – to one that allows us to kill in some circumstances for reasons of mercy and compassion? Would legalizing euthanasia help or hinder us, both as individuals and as a society, to find meaning in (human) life?

5 The Definition of Euthanasia: A Paradoxical Partnership

A paradoxical partnership has emerged concerning the definition of euthanasia. Both the pro-choice side (the death with dignity movements – those who believe that euthanasia should be available) and the anti-euthanasia side (which includes the pro-life movement) use a similarly broad definition, but with the aim of achieving exactly opposite effects. This very broad definition includes the following claims to rights: to refuse life-support treatment; to give "advance directives" while competent, in anticipation of incompetence, refusing such treatment through documents such as a "living will" or a durable power of attorney (which allows a person to choose a substitute decision-maker, or representative, should the person become incompetent); to refuse artificial hydration and nutrition, either personally (at the time or in advance, through a living will) or through a substitute decision-maker; to be offered necessary pain-relief treatment (even if it could shorten life); to non-interference in the commission of suicide if one is a terminally ill person; to have assistance, if that is required, in committing suicide; and, finally, to be provided with euthanasia itself (an intervention intended to kill).

Pro-choice groups – those in favour of allowing euthanasia – argue that all these measures come within the definition of euthanasia because they all assist in achieving the goal of a "good death" (which is the meaning of "euthanasia"). At least some of the pro-life groups agree that all these measures constitute euthanasia, but they argue that none of them should be allowed, because all of them constitute an unacceptable affront to the supreme value of the sanctity of life. In short, both sides would classify all these interventions as euthanasia. The difference is that pro-choice groups use this wide definition to argue that all the interventions listed are equally acceptable and pro-life groups to argue that all of them are equally unacceptable.

In my view, both sides are wrong; the dividing line between acceptable and unacceptable measures lies somewhere in the middle. Competent adults must have the right to refuse treatment, in particular, life-support treatment, including artificial hydration and nutrition. They have the right to be offered any treatment necessary to relieve pain, moreover, even if it could shorten life. A dividing line should be drawn between recognition of these rights and acceptance – in particular, legalization – of assisted suicide and euthanasia. The latter – assisted suicide and euthanasia – should not be allowed. The word "euthanasia" is used here to mean the intentional infliction of death by one person on another, in a situation of terminal illness, for the purpose of relieving suffering.

Ironically, by including within the definition of euthanasia all the types of intervention referred to above, pro-life groups could be promoting the legalization of euthanasia and physician-assisted suicide – or at least could be failing to make a contribution that would reduce the likelihood of legalization (which they might have done if physician-assisted suicide and euthanasia had been addressed separately). Consequently, I propose that much more carefully and clearly defined terminology must be used in this extraordinarily important debate.

It is noteworthy that legislative proposals to legalize physician-assisted suicide and euthanasia are almost always included in bills that cover the full range of interventions and non-interventions at the end of life. This scope is no accident; the approach is likely to assist in achieving legalization. Many people reading this legislation might not be aware of what "physician-assisted death" means, when allowing physicians to help their patients commit suicide or to provide euthanasia – that is, to kill them – are included among a full range of provisions that also cover the right to refuse treatment, "living wills," durable powers of attorney, and the right to pain-relief treatment. The dilemma is compounded when one must vote either for or against a total package of these types of intervention. The language is very gentle on the pro-euthanasia side of this debate. It is hard to reject the total package, even for people who do not believe in euthanasia. I strongly advocate that physician-assisted suicide and euthanasia be addressed expressly, clearly, and separately from other decisions concerning treatment at the end of life. Measures to deal with those decisions, such as recognition of the right to refuse treatment and the right to adequate pain-relief treatment, have been implemented in law and subjected to considerable testing in the courts, especially in Canada and the United States. They are of great importance and, in my view, must not be abandoned either in theory or in practice. But people should not be placed in the position of having to decide either for or against those measures, on the basis of whether they are for or against euthanasia.

Unlikely partnerships, such as the one described here between the pro-choice and pro-life groups in relation to the definition of euthanasia, are not unique to that context. For example, in the past, an unlikely partnership emerged between some feminists and members of the pro-life movement. Both groups, though for different reasons, oppose all forms of reproductive technology and consistently aim for a permanent moratorium on the development and use of such technology. The feminists want to prevent what they see as the exploitation and control of women, along with harm and risk to them and to children born through the use of this technology. Members of pro-life groups object also to new technologies for those reasons, but their primary objection is that it constitutes an unacceptable form of control or interference in reproduction and, as such, an affront to the sanctity of human life. Where the groups divide is with respect to abortion. The feminists see that as necessary to avoid the exploitation of women, but members of the pro-life groups object to it as unacceptable interference with the sanctity of life. The disagreement over abortion has, to a large extent, been kept separate, however, from the agreement with respect to reproductive technology. That division allows the two groups to become allies on one battleground, but to remain opponents on the other.

How should suicide – in contrast to assisted-suicide – be viewed in the context of the euthanasia debate? Suicide is not illegal in many countries. It was decriminalized because its criminalization had caused more harm than good. Assisting suicide – aiding and abetting, and counselling – is often a criminal offence. One justification for the different legal treatment of suicide and assisted suicide is that suicide is essentially a private act and should be judged according to one's own morality. Only in connection with a public act – or a private one with public consequences (when legal intervention to prevent the consequences is likely to do more good than harm) – should the law step in. If one regards the assistance of others, whether they are physicians or not – or perhaps especially if they are physicians – as converting a private act of suicide to a public act, then it is appropriate and necessary for the law to be involved. In my view, the law should prohibit assistance. Even if one accepts the importance of the fact that some people regard physician-assisted suicide and euthanasia as moral – indeed, as ethically required in view of the argument that "to refuse euthanasia is unmerciful and as such unethical" – the precedent that legalizing these measures would establish would be highly dangerous.

It bears repeating that euthanasia should be distinguished from the provision of necessary pain-relief treatment – including, when necessary, treatment that could or would shorten life. That is not euthanasia. Nor is the justified withdrawal of treatment euthanasia. Further, the distinction between morality and law should be kept in mind. Not all matters regarded as immoral should be illegal. Even if some people consider refusal of life-support treatment immoral, this does not necessarily mean that it should be illegal as well.

I conclude with one example that should provide a warning and a lesson for those who oppose euthanasia. Nancy Cruzan, whose case was brought to the United States Supreme Court, was in a permanently comatose state. Hysteria centred around this case to the effect that withdrawing hydration and nutrition from Nancy Cruzan – even when doing so would accord with her wishes – constituted euthanasia and, as such, should be prohibited. This line of argument has caused much damage to efforts at convincing people to prohibit euthanasia. It might, indeed, have promoted pro-euthanasia sentiment. I do not propose that people should not argue against withdrawal of hydration and nutrition in these circumstances; as a matter of personal morality, integrity, and honesty, one might feel compelled to take this position. The point is that this problem must be handled separately from euthanasia. Not to do so is to risk the most serious confusion and the most unacceptable outcome, whether one is for or against euthanasia: it would be allowed or prohibited on the basis of allowing or prohibiting other measures, which are different in kind, not just in degree, from euthanasia.

6 Legalizing Euthanasia: Why Now?

Until very recently, all countries prohibited euthanasia, although it had been legally tolerated – not legalized, but not prosecuted, provided it complied with various conditions – since the early 1970s in the much studied and cited case of the Netherlands, where it has just been formally legalized.[1] Many countries are now experiencing an unprecedented rise in calls to legalize euthanasia.[2] Some of these demands come from within the profession of medicine.[3] Oregon law[4] now authorizes physicians to prescribe lethal doses of medication for their patients.[5] And the United States Second Circuit Court of Appeals[6] and Ninth Circuit Court of Appeals[7] struck down prohibitions on assisting in suicide[8] as constitutionally invalid, although these decisions were later overturned by the United States Supreme Court. In a then-unique example, the Northern Territory of Australia enacted a bill in 1995 to legalize euthanasia.[9] This legislation was subsequently overruled by the Australian Commonwealth Parliament.

The euthanasia debate is a momentous one. It involves problems that range from the nature and meaning of human life to the most fundamental principles on which societies are based. This debate involves our individual and collective *past* (the ethical, legal, and cultural norms that have been handed down to us as members of families, groups, and societies); the *present* (whether we will change those norms); and the *future* (the impact that any such change would have on those who come after us).

As a result, we must consider the impact of legalizing euthanasia not only at an individual level (which, in the mass media, and therefore in the general public forum, has been the focus of debate) but also at institutional, governmental, and societal levels. And not only in the present but also for the future. We need to consider factual realities, such as the possibilities for abuse that legalizing euthanasia would open up, as well as the effect that doing so would have on the important values and symbols that make up the intangible fabric that constitutes our society and on some of our most important societal institutions.

DEFINITION

Whatever one's personal position on the acceptability of euthanasia, it is essential to know what we mean by that word. I discuss the definition elsewhere in more detail, thus a brief definition will suffice: "Euthanasia is a deliberate act that causes death undertaken by one person with the primary intention of ending the life of another person, in order to relieve that person's suffering."[10] Refusals of treatment – including life-support treatment or artificial hydration and nutrition – and provision of necessary treatment for the relief of pain or other symptoms of serious physical distress are not euthanasia, even if they do shorten life.[11] In the latter case, the primary intention is to respect the right to inviolability – the right not to be touched without consent – or to relieve pain, not to inflict death (as it is in the former case).

The term "physician-assisted suicide" is often used to describe what is really euthanasia. The physician carries out the act that causes death. In physician-assisted suicide, properly so-called, physicians would give patients the means to kill themselves with the intent that patients would so use them. Legally, there is a difference between physician-assisted suicide and euthanasia. The latter is homicide, not suicide. It is either murder or manslaughter under the criminal law in the United Kingdom, Australia (except in the Northern Territory before the repeal of its euthanasia law), Canada, and each state of the United States. Criminal liability for physician-assisted suicide would lie in aiding, abetting, or counselling another person to commit suicide. The use of terms such as "physician-assisted suicide" – or the even more ambiguous "physician-assisted death" – to mean euthanasia leads to confusion. But although these interventions are legally distinct crimes (and, some believe, morally distinguishable), at a societal level many of the worries that legalizing them would present would be the same. From this perspective, they can be discussed together.[12] Unless some distinction must be made, therefore, in this chapter I use the word *euthanasia* to include physician-assisted suicide.

It is necessary, and only honest, to state at the outset where one stands. I am against legalization. I cannot argue against euthanasia from an empirical base, however. Carrying out euthanasia constitutes a very serious criminal offence in the vast majority of jurisdictions; consequently, research may not be undertaken to produce "hard" evidence of the impact that legalizing it would have. Opponents of legalization are therefore open to the criticism and challenge that their arguments are purely speculative and lacking in scientific rigour. This difficulty has become manifest in another way. The burden of proof has somehow shifted from those who promote legalization to those who oppose it – a lamentable situation. ⌐How ironic that the norm that we must not kill must now be defended more vigorously than its opposite.⌐

The problem of producing evidence is not as severe for those who are pro-euthanasia because they base their case on respect for individual autonomy, the failure of palliative care to relieve all suffering, and the allegation, often, that physicians are secretly practising euthanasia anyway. They can use polls and surveys – which have the appearance, at least, of producing "hard" data – to show that many people believe they should have a right of access to euthanasia, that the suffering of some terminally ill patients cannot be relieved, and that some physicians admit to carrying out euthanasia. The fact that it is easier to establish the case for legalization than against it, moreover, could distort the process of making a decision about legalizing euthanasia and, consequently, the ultimate decision. Other factors could have the same effect. It would be an interesting research project to compare the number of pro- and of anti-euthanasia articles in leading medical journals and to examine the reasons for any discrepancies found between these numbers. I predict that a substantial majority would be pro-euthanasia. If so, we would need to take care that the popularity of that position does not unjustifiably influence the decision.

A NECESSARY QUESTION: WHY NOW?

Why are we considering legalizing euthanasia now, after our society has prohibited it for almost two millennia?[13] It is true that the population is aging; modern medicine has extended our life span, with the result that it is more likely now than in the past that we will die of chronic degenerative diseases, not acute ones. It is also true that many countries lack adequate palliative care, and some physicians are ignorant about treatments for the relief of pain and suffering, while others either fail or refuse to provide them. Medical practice, too, has also changed. A lifetime relationship with "the family doctor" is largely a relic of the past, and the feeling of isolation that people can experience in seeking help from health-care professionals is probably a reflection of the wider isolation that individuals and families experience. But the capacity to relieve pain and suffering has improved remarkably. Not one of the bottom-line conditions usually seen as linked with the call for euthanasia – that terminally ill people want to die and that we can kill them – is new. These factors have been part of the human condition for as long as humans have existed. Why, then, are we considering such a radically different response to this situation?

Societal and Cultural Causes

I suggest that the principal cause is not a change in the situation of individuals who seek euthanasia; rather, it is profound changes in our postmodern, secular, Western, democratic societies. Some of these changes involve trends that have been emerging since the eighteenth century, but only recently have they all co-existed and each has overwhelmingly dominated its opposite, or countervailing, trend. The factors I single out here do not constitute a comprehensive list. They are not all of the same nature, so they are not all treated in the same way or depth. Indeed, I mention some very briefly. In any case, each requires a much more thorough examination. And my conclusions about their strength, causal link to euthanasia, or impact are clearly open to challenge. My aim is to provide a rough map – a somewhat impressionistic overview – of the societal and cultural factors giving rise to and influencing the movement to legalize euthanasia. There are, moreover, still strong forces that resist the legalization of euthanasia, most notably the Catholic Church, evangelical Christian churches, Orthodox Judaism, and Islam.

Individualism

Our society is based on "intense individualism," even in connection with death and bereavement – possibly, individualism to the exclusion of any real sense of community. If this highly individualistic approach is applied to euthanasia, especially in a society that gives pre-eminence to personal autonomy and self-determination, it is likely to result in the belief that euthanasia is acceptable.[14] There seems to be either a total lack of consciousness or a denial that this kind of individualism can undermine the intangible infrastructure on which society rests, the communal and cultural fabric. Individualism untempered by concern and recognition of a duty to protect and promote community will inevitably result in destruction of the community. Thus, although legalizing euthanasia is a result of unbridled individualism, the former would also promote the latter, at least in terms of tipping the balance between the individual and the community further towards the individual.

Almost all the justifications for legalizing euthanasia focus primarily on the dying person who wants it. Indeed, it is usually considered unacceptable to promote the case for euthanasia by arguing that it would benefit others or society, except possibly as a secondary gain. Here are two examples of such a secondary gain. People would be relieved of the burden of caring for terminally ill people. And countries with publicly funded health-care systems (such as those in the United Kingdom, Canada, and Australia), and Medicare and Medicaid in the United States – all countries in which the legalization of euthanasia has recently been a focus of controversy – would save limited health-care resources for allegedly more beneficial uses. This reticence to mention benefits to others or society might be changing, however. In the American case of *Lee* v. *Oregon*,[15] the trial court noted that the defendant's argument in support of the constitutional validity of the Oregon Death with Dignity Act[16] allowing physician-assisted suicide would reduce the financial burdens caused by terminal illness.

There is yet another sense in which intense individualism might give rise to calls for euthanasia. In postmodern Western societies, death is largely a medical event that takes place in a hospital or other institution and is perceived as occurring in great isolation – patients are alone, separated from those they love and the surroundings with which they are familiar. Death has been institutionalized, depersonalized, and dehumanized. Intense individualism and seeking to take control, especially through euthanasia, are predictable and even reasonable responses to the circumstances. To avoid legalizing euthanasia, therefore, we must give death a more human scale and face.[17]

Mass Media

At first, we created our collective story in each other's physical presence. Later on, we had books and print media, which meant we could do so at a physical distance from each other. Now, for the first time, we can do so through film or television and, consequently, at a physical distance from – but still in sight of – each other no matter where we live on the planet. We do not know how this shift will affect the stories we tell each other to create our shared story, our societal and cultural paradigm – the store of values, attitudes, beliefs, commitments, and myths – that informs our collective life and, through that, our individual lives, and helps to give them meaning. Creating a shared story through the mass media could alter the balance between the various components that make it up. In particular, we might engage in too much "death talk" and too little "life talk." We can be most attracted to that we most fear, and the mass media provide an almost infinite number of opportunities to indulge our fear of, and attraction to, death.

Failure to take into account societal- and cultural-level issues related to euthanasia is connected with "mediatization" of our societal dialogues in general and the one about euthanasia in particular. We see the stories that make up these dialogues only as they are presented by the mass media, an avenue that introduces additional ethical issues – those of "media ethics." It makes dramatic and emotionally gripping television to feature an articulate, courageous, forty-two-year-old divorced woman who is dying of amyotrophic lateral sclerosis, begging to have euthanasia made available and threatening to commit suicide while she is still able – thus leaving her eight-year-old son even sooner – if she is refused access. This scenario describes Sue Rodriguez, who became a national figure in taking her case for euthanasia to the Supreme Court of Canada. In 1993 the court denied her that right by a majority of five to four, with a plurality of dissenting judgments.[18]

The arguments against euthanasia, based on the harm it would do to society in both the present and the future, are much more difficult to present in the mass media than arguments for euthanasia. Anti-euthanasia arguments do not make dramatic and compelling television. Visual images are difficult to find. Viewers do not personally identify with these arguments, which come across as abstractions or ideas, in the same way they do with those of dying people who seek euthanasia. Society cannot be interviewed on television and become a familiar, empathy-evoking figure to the viewing public. Only if euthanasia were legalized and there were obvious abuses – such as proposals to use it on those who want to continue living – could we create comparably riveting and gripping images to communicate the case against euthanasia. Consider *The Children of Men* by P.D. James, set in the year 2025.[19] The novel's first chapter features a scene in which many elderly people die through mass euthanasia. That description evokes a powerful anti-euthanasia response in readers.

The vast exposure to death we are subjected to in both current affairs and entertainment programs might have overwhelmed our sensitivity to the awesomeness of death and, likewise, of inflicting it. Gwynne Dyer has described research showing that human beings have an innate resistance to killing each other, and that this resistance is operative even among soldiers in battle – unless they have been desensitized in order to overcome it. Frighteningly, children are subjected to the techniques developed to achieve this desensitization through their exposure to violence in the mass media.[20] Reports from the 1990s on violent crime in major American cities have shown a drop in the crime rate. But "youth crimes – particularly violent crimes by the young [the super-predators] – are increasing and will continue to increase."[21]

Ironically, the most powerful way in which the case against euthanasia has been presented on television is probably through Dr Jack Kevorkian's efforts to promote euthanasia and the revulsion they evoked in many viewers, including those who support euthanasia. A documentary film about a Dutch physician providing euthanasia to a terminally ill patient who requested it has a similar impact.[22] The film, telecast on prime-time television in Canada and the United States, elicited a chill in many viewers,[23] and condemnation for exploiting both the patient and euthanasia itself.[24] If capital punishment were televised, viewers might be horrified enough to demand its abolition. But the opposite could also occur. People might be as fascinated as they once were by public executions. This personal closeness to, or distance from, the infliction of death is an important difference between euthanasia and physician-assisted suicide. Everyone, including the physician, is more distant from the infliction of death in the latter case than in the former. In the Northern Territory of Australia, where euthanasia was legalized briefly,[25] a computer-activated "suicide machine" that could be triggered by the terminally ill person was developed and used for carrying out the first death.[26] We distance ourselves from inflicting death even when doing so is legal.

When it comes to euthanasia, it could be argued, people react one way in theory and another in practice. It is much easier to approve of euthanasia in theory than in practice, which probably reflects moral anxiety about euthanasia and an ethical intuition as to its dangers. That reaction should send a deep warning, which should be heeded. The difference might also partly explain why polls on euthanasia show that, even when over 75 per cent of those polled say that they approve of it, under 50 per cent of those same people actually vote for it[27] – except in the case of the Oregon Death with Dignity Act of 1994. Maybe these people like "death talk"[28] more than "death practice." It is also possible that the survey instruments used in these polls are not well designed and, therefore, give rise to confused or ambiguous results.[29]

Denial and Control of Death and Death Talk

As I say several times in this book, ours is a death-denying, death-obsessed society.[30] Those who no longer adhere to the practice of institutionalized religion, at any rate, have lost their main forum for engaging in death talk. As humans, we need to engage in it if we are to accommodate the inevitable reality of death into the living of our lives. And we must do that if we are to live fully and well. Arguably, our extensive discussion of euthanasia in the mass media is an example of contemporary death talk. Instead of being confined to an identifiable location and an hour a week, it has spilled out into our lives in general. This exposure makes it more difficult to maintain the denial of death, because it makes the fear of death more present and "real." One way to deal with this fear is to believe that we have death under control. The availability of euthanasia could support that belief. Euthanasia moves us from chance to choice concerning death. (The same movement can also be seen at the beginning of human life, when it results from the use of new reproductive and genetic technologies at conception or shortly thereafter.[31]) Although we cannot make death optional, we can create an illusion that it is by making its timing, and the conditions and ways in which it occurs, a matter of choice.[32]

Fear

We are frightened not only as individuals, however, but also as a society. Collectively, we express the fear of crime in our streets. But that fear, though factually based, might also be a manifestation of a powerful and free-floating fear of death in general. Calling for the legalization of euthanasia could be a way of symbolically taming and civilizing death – reducing our fear of its random infliction through crime. If euthanasia were experienced as a way of converting death by chance to death by choice, it would offer a feeling of increased control over death and, therefore, decreased fear. We tend to use law as a response to fear, often in the misguided belief that the law will increase our control over the things that frighten us and so augment our safety.

Legalism

It is not surprising that we have, to varying degrees, become a legalistic society. The reasons are complex and include the use of law as a means of ordering and governing a society of strangers, as compared with one of intimates.[33] Matters such as euthanasia, which would once have been the topic of moral or religious discourse, are now explored in courts and legislatures, especially through concepts of individual human rights, civil rights, and constitutional rights. Man-made law (legal positivism), as compared with divinely ordained law or natural law, has a very dominant role in establishing the values and symbols of a secular society. In the euthanasia debate, it does so through the judgments and legislation that result from the "death talk" that takes place in "secular cathedrals" – courts and legislatures. It is to be expected that those trying to change society's values and symbols would see this debate as an opportunity to further their aims and, consequently, seek the legalization of euthanasia.

Materialism and Consumerism

Another factor, which I can mention only in passing, is that our society is highly materialistic and consumeristic. It has lost any sense of the sacred, even of the "secular sacred"[34] (although some scholars in the field of religious studies, such as Paul Nathanson, put forward an interesting case for the vitality of "secular religion"[35]). The result favours a pro-euthanasia position, because a loss of the sacred fosters the idea that wornout people may be equated with wornout products; both can then be seen primarily as "disposal" problems.

Mystery

Our society is intolerant of mystery. We convert mysteries into problems. If we convert the mystery of death into the problem of death, euthanasia (or, even more basically, a lethal injection) can be seen as a solution. As can be seen in descriptions of death by euthanasia – for instance, that of a young man dying of AIDS[36] – euthanasia can function as a substitute for the loss of death rituals, which we have abandoned at least partly to avoid any sense of mystery. A sense of mystery might be required also to "preserve ... room for hope."[37] And euthanasia could be a response "based on a loss of faith in what life may still have in store for us. Perhaps, what is needed ... is a different kind of faith in life and in the community of caregivers."[38] This need is especially acute in situations of serious illness. If the interactions I have just outlined are occuring, I postulate a complex relation between some degree of comfort with a sense of mystery and being able to elicit in others and experience ourselves hope and trust. This leads to a question: Could the loss of mystery – and of hope, faith, and trust – be generating nihilism in both individuals and society? And could calls for the legalization of euthanasia be one expression of it?

The loss of mystery has been accompanied by a loss of wonder and awe, both of which we need in some form as humans. Also lost is the sense that we, as humans, are sacred in any meaning of this word (that we are, at least, "secular sacred").[39] These losses are connected in both their nature and their causes, but they might not be inseparable. We might be able to retain some of these senses (for instance, a sense of the sacred) and not others (a sense of awe, at least in the form of traditional taboos used to elicit awe).

Impact of Scientific Advances

Among the most important causes of our loss of the sacred is extraordinary scientific progress, especially because science and religion are viewed as antithetical.[40] New genetic discoveries and new reproductive technologies have given us a sense that we understand the origin and nature of human life and that therefore we may manipulate – or even "create" – life. Transferring these sentiments to the other end of life would support the view that euthanasia is acceptable. Euthanasia would be seen as a correlative and consistent development with the new genetics; its acceptance would be expected. According to this view, as I have noted elsewhere, it is no accident that we are currently concerned with both eugenics (good genetics – good at birth) and euthanasia (good death – good at death, of no trouble to anyone else). Yet another connection between genetics and euthanasia could arise from a new sense of our ability to ensure genetic immortality – seeing ourselves as an immortal gene – and, as a result, some reduction of anxiety about the annihilation presented by death.

The paradigms used to structure knowledge in general have been influenced by genetic theory. These paradigms have already been the bases for new schools of thought in areas well beyond genetics. They can challenge traditional concepts of what it means to be human and what is required to respect human life. For instance, evolutionary psychology, a subcategory of sociobiology, sees the characteristics usually identified as unique markers of being human – our most intimate, humane, altruistic, and moral impulses – as the product of our genes and their evolution.[41] At a macrogenetic level, deep concern about overpopulation (as compared with earlier fears of extinction due to underpopulation) might, likewise, have diminished a sense of sacredness in relation to human life.

But countervailing trends, such as the environmental protection movement, are beginning to emerge. A powerful recognition of innate dependence on the ecological health of our planet has resurrected a sense of the "secular sacred" by reidentifying the absolute necessity of respectful human-Earth relations.[42] Moreover, science can be linked with the sacred; it just depends on how we view it. Rather than assuming that the new genetics is a totally comprehensive explanation of life, for example, we can experience it as a way of deepening our sense of awe and wonder at what we now know – but even more powerfully at what, as a result of this new knowledge, we now know we do *not* know.[43] We can, in other words, see the new genetics and other sciences as only some of the lenses through which we are able to search for "the truth."

Competing World Views

Though immensely important in itself, the debate over euthanasia might be a surrogate for yet another, even deeper, one. Which of two irreconcilable world views will form the basis of our societal and cultural paradigm? As discussed in a previous chapter, there is also a third world view – the "pure mystery" view. It rejects euthanasia on the ground that it is prohibited by religious commandment. Important as such commandments are to their adherents, in secular societies they cannot be used directly as the basis for public policy on euthanasia. Consequently, this view is not discussed further here.

According to one of the other two world views, we are highly complex, biological machines whose most valuable features are our rational, logical, cognitive functions. This world view is in itself a mechanistic approach to human life. Its proponents support euthanasia as being, in appropriate circumstances, a logical and rational response to problems at the end of life. (Being anti-euthanasia can, of course, be just as logical and rational a response.[44])

I hesitate to refer to Nazi atrocities because they can readily be distinguished from situations in which the use of euthanasia is currently being proposed. It is easy to argue that those horrific abuses were different in kind from any that would occur if euthanasia were to be legalized in our society. But consider the question about the Nazi doctors that George Annas and Michael Grodin describe as "among the most profound questions in medical ethics": "How could physician healers turn into murderers?"[45] David Thomasma, citing the work of Robert Proctor,[46] states that the primary answer is that "society, itself, was primed to develop a *biological basis for its political platforms.*"[47] I propose that current efforts to legalize euthanasia might reflect a connection of these same two factors, but in the reverse order. Those who are pro-euthanasia are, at one level, seeking a political platform for a solely or predominantly biological view of human life – especially in terms of having it form an important element in any new societal paradigm. As I have noted elsewhere, this view can be called the "gene machine" or "pure science" position.[48] Its far-reaching impact and consequences should, at the least, cause us to think carefully before taking any steps to legalize euthanasia.

The other world view (which for some people is expressed through religion, but can be, and possibly is for most people, held independently of religion, at least in a traditional or institutional sense) is that human life consists of more than its biological component, wondrous as that is. It involves a mystery – at least the "mystery of the unknown" – of which we have a sense through intuitions, especially moral ones. Again, as I have already proposed, this world view includes a sense of a "space for (human) spirit" and the "secular sacred." It sees death as part of the mystery of life, which means that, to respect life, we must respect death. Although we might be under no obligation to prolong the lives of dying people, we do have an obligation not to shorten their lives deliberately. There are some fine, but immensely important, distinctions to be made when it comes to grey areas of decision-making at the end of life. Giving pain-relief treatment that is necessary to relieve pain, but that could or would shorten life, would be morally, ethically, and legally different from giving a lethal injection to end life deliberately. This view may be called the "science-spirit" position.[49]

IMPACT ON MEDICINE

We need to consider how the legalization of euthanasia could affect the profession of medicine and its practitioners. Euthanasia takes both beyond their fundamental roles of caring, healing, and curing whenever possible. It involves them, no matter how compassionate their motives, in the infliction of death on those for whom they provide care and treatment. It can be described as "a merciful act of clinical care"[50] and, therefore, it can seem appropriate for physicians to administer. But the same act is accurately described as "killing," too. This means that euthanasia places "the very soul of medicine on trial."[51] We need to be concerned about the impact that legalization would have on the institution of medicine – not only in the interests of protecting it for its own sake but also because of the harm to society that damage to the profession would cause.

With the decline of organized religion in many postmodern, secular, pluralistic societies, it is difficult to find consensus on the fundamental values that create society and establish its ethical and legal "tone" – those that provide the "existential glue" that holds society together. Many people do not personally identify with the majority of societal institutions. There are very few institutions, if any, with which everyone identifies except for those – such as medicine – that make up the health-care system. These, therefore, are important when it comes to carrying values, creating them, and forming consensus around them. We must take great care not to harm their capacities in these regards and, consequently, must ask whether legalizing euthanasia would run a high risk of causing this type of harm.

ᶜCan we imagine teaching medical students how to administer euthanasia – how to kill their patients?ᶜ A fundamental value and attitude that we reinforce in medical students, interns, and residents is an absolute repugnance to killing patients.[52] If physicians were authorized to administer euthanasia it would no longer be possible to teach that repugnance. Maintaining this repugnance and, arguably, the intuitive recognition of a need for it, are demonstrated in the outraged reactions against physicians carrying out capital punishment when laws provide for them to do so.[53] We do not consider their involvement acceptable – not even for those physicians who personally are in favour of capital punishment. We, as a society, need to say powerfully, consistently, and unambiguously that killing each other is wrong. Physicians are very important carriers of this message, partly because they have opportunities (not open to members of society in general) to kill people.

It is sometimes pointed out that many societies justify one form of killing by physicians: abortion. This procedure was justified, traditionally, on the grounds that it was necessary to save the life of the mother. We now have liberalized abortion laws, which reflect a justification that hinges on the belief that the fetus is not yet a person in a moral or legal sense. In justifying abortion, attention is focused on the woman's right to control her body; access to abortion is considered necessary to respect this right. Besides, it is argued, abortion is aimed primarily not at destroying the fetus but at respecting women's reproductive autonomy. Indeed, when destroying the fetus is the primary aim – as it is in sex selection – even those who agree with abortion on demand often regard it as morally unacceptable. And the rarity of third-trimester abortions in most countries shows that, once we view the fetus as a "person," we do not find killing it acceptable.[54] Consequently, legalized euthanasia would be unique in that the killing involved could not be justified on the grounds either that it is necessary to protect the life of another (which, as well as being the justification for some abortions, is also that for the other examples of legally sanctioned killing – self-defence, "just" war, and, in theory and in part, capital punishment) or that it does not involve taking the life of a person (the justification used for some abortions). Euthanasia would seem likely to affect physicians' attitudes and values, therefore, in ways that, arguably, abortion does not.

We need to consider whether patients' and society's trust in their treating physicians and the profession of medicine depends in large part on this absolute rejection by physicians of intentionally inflicting death. Moreover, we cannot afford to underestimate the desensitization and brutalization that carrying out euthanasia would have on physicians. Keep in mind that the same might be true of abortion. We should remain open-minded about this possibility – even if we believe women should have a right of access to safe, legal abortion. Sometimes, dealing with new ethical issues can cause us to review ones we believe have already been settled ethically. It could be that rightful concerns about the impact on physicians of their being involved in euthanasia would cause us to reconsider the effect of abortion on physicians involved in it. In short, one problem with the position of those who promote abortion on demand is that it threatens to continue undermining the link between medicine and respect for life. Some will argue in response that abortion is "different." But that is another debate, which I will not explore here.

It is sometimes remarked that physicians have difficulty in accepting death, especially the deaths of their patients. This attitude raises the question of whether, in inculcating a total repugnance to *killing*, we have evoked a repugnance to *death* as well. In short, there might be confusion between inflicting death and death itself. We know that failure to accept death, when allowing death to occur would be appropriate, can lead to overzealous and harmful measures to sustain life. We are most likely to elicit a repugnance to killing while fostering an acceptance of death – and we are most likely to avoid confusion between a repugnance to killing and a failure to accept death – if we speak of and seek to convey a repugnance to *killing*, when that is the appropriate word (although it is an emotionally powerful one), instead of death. Achieving these aims would be very difficult in the context of legalized euthanasia.

The Art of Medicine

Finally, I propose that it is a very important part of the art of medicine to sense and respect the mystery of life and death, to hold this mystery in trust, and to hand it on to future generations – especially future generations of physicians. We need to consider deeply whether legalizing euthanasia would threaten this art, this trust, and this legacy.

CONCLUSION

Every country will need to decide whether to legalize euthanasia. Making this choice will be, and will require, a complex process. It is crucial that all of us in each of our roles – whether as concerned citizens, professional organizations, or policy-makers – engage in the euthanasia debate.

This debate will involve many questions about euthanasia at both the individual and societal levels, but three of the most important are the following. First, would legalization be most likely to help us in our search for meaning in our individual and collective lives? Second, how do we want our grandchildren and great-grandchildren to die? And third, in relation to human death, what memes (fundamental units of cultural information that are inherited by being passed from generation to generation) do we want to pass on?

7 Euthanasia by Confusion

"There's glory for you!"
"I don't know what you mean by 'glory,'" Alice said.
"I meant, 'there's a nice knock-down argument for you!'"
"But 'glory' doesn't mean 'a nice knock-down argument,'"
Alice objected.
"When I use a word," Humpty Dumpty said in a rather scornful
tone, "it means just what I choose it to mean – neither more
nor less."

Lewis Carroll, *Through the Looking-Glass*, chapter 6

The euthanasia debate is beset by confusion – a condition caused both by accident and by design. One important way to promote the legalization of euthanasia is through various types of confusion. First, the examples of such confusion span the domain of semantics: confusion in definition; confusion created by choice of language; and confusion of association and analogy. Second, they span important areas of ethical and legal analysis: confusion of means and ends; confusion in the use of the legal concepts of intent and causation; and confusion in interpreting common-law precedents. We need to examine, understand, and, where possible, dispel these confusions.

CONFUSION IN SEMANTICS

Confusion in Definition

The definition of euthanasia, as of physician-assisted suicide, is highly confused. For the sake of clarity, as proposed elsewhere, euthanasia should be defined as "a deliberate act or omission that causes death, undertaken by one person with the primary intention of ending the life of another person, in order to relieve that person's suffering."[1] The paradigm case of euthanasia is the giving of a lethal injection[2] to a suffering, terminally ill person who requests it and gives informed consent. Yet neither a requirement for informed consent nor that the person be terminally ill is an element of the definition given above. This definition, therefore, includes both non-voluntary euthanasia (the patient is incompetent to give or withhold consent) and involuntary euthanasia (the patient is competent, but euthanasia is administered without asking for consent). In the Netherlands, by contrast, the guidelines previously governing the country's *de facto* legalization of euthanasia defined it as requiring "explicit consent."[3] And that country's new legislation governing euthanasia and physician-assisted suicide[4] spells out the requirements for due care on the physician's part, which include that the patient's request for euthanasia must be voluntary, well considered, and lasting. As a result, non-voluntary and involuntary interventions aimed at ending life are not regarded as euthanasia, although, in practice, some Dutch doctors seem unaware of this distinction.[5]

Another way in which confusion arises is that many people who support euthanasia lump together, under the global category of "medical decisions at the end of life," decisions concerning palliative care, pain-relief treatment, refusals of treatment (including of life-support treatment and especially of artificial hydration and nutrition), and physician-assisted suicide and euthanasia. They argue that all these decisions, aimed at trying to ensure that patients experience a "good death," but that could or would shorten their lives, involve euthanasia. Although this is true in a broad etymological sense, this definition of euthanasia can give rise to serious confusion.

Physicians and nurses who accept such a broad definition, and who are asked in surveys whether they have ever been involved in euthanasia, are likely to state that they have. These statistics can be used as evidence that many health-care professionals are carrying out euthanasia secretly and that it would be safer for individuals and society to legalize euthanasia, bringing it out into the open and ensuring that it is not used abusively. This line of reasoning is sometimes taken further, to imply that people who oppose legalization should reconsider their position because legalization would result in fewer cases of euthanasia being performed than if euthanasia were to remain prohibited. Quite apart from the fact that there is no evidence to indicate that any reduction would occur – indeed, the results of over twenty-five years of *de facto* legalization in the Netherlands would suggest the contrary[5] – this argument entirely misses the point. The primary objection of many who oppose euthanasia is that to kill another person is inherently wrong. The fear of the abusive use of euthanasia, if it were to be legalized and even if it were not, is a secondary, though important, objection. If the basic objection to physician-assisted suicide and euthanasia is that they are different in kind, not just degree, from other decisions about medical treatment at the end of life, then lumping all these procedures together assumes what must be proved: that physician-assisted suicide and euthanasia are morally and ethically the same as other forms of end-of-life medical care that could or would shorten life. If physician-assisted suicide and euthanasia are to be justified, it must be on their own merits, and not by false association with other interventions that are considered ethically and legally acceptable.[6]

Definitional confusion is also generated by describing all decision-making relating to medical care and treatment at the end of life as "medical decisions." This term is a misnomer; many of these decisions are not medical decisions at all. They have foundations, aspects, and effects far beyond medicine and are better referred to as "decisions at the end of life in a medical context." These characterizations are important because they alert us to the wide range of considerations beyond medicine that must be taken into account and also to people other than health-care professionals who should be involved.

Within a narrower context, the term "physician-assisted suicide" is also confusingly used. Often it refers to euthanasia – physicians intervene on patients with a primary intention of killing them, most often by giving lethal injections – which is homicide, not suicide. As I have discussed elsewhere, this term is sometimes changed to "physician-assisted death," which can mean euthanasia or physician-assisted suicide, but also connotes a broad range of procedures that physicians undertake – indeed, that they have ethical and legal obligations to undertake – to help dying people. We all want physicians to assist us in those ways,[7] but we do not necessarily mean in stating this wish that we agree with physician-assisted suicide and euthanasia.

The euthanasia debate is too important to carry out on the basis of confusion over what does and does not constitute euthanasia. The most honest and clear approach would begin with a debate over whether we agree that the law should be changed to allow physicians to give lethal injections to terminally ill, competent adults who request and give their free and informed consent. This is not the only question we need to answer about euthanasia. Others are, for example, if we reject euthanasia, should we allow physician-assisted suicide? Or, if we allow euthanasia, should it be available in the case of some incompetent people? But we need to deal first with a situation in which we all agree that euthanasia is involved. We should start with the most straightforward one, that of physicians giving lethal injections to competent, suffering, terminally ill people who request and consent to it. This restriction of the analysis should help us to eliminate from the debate the confusion over the definition and what flows from it – such confusion is bad for all of us, whether we are for or against euthanasia.

Confusion in Language

A matter related to confusion in definition is the confusion that can occur from our choice of descriptive language. A vastly different impression is made, or emotional reaction evoked, or behaviour elicited by describing euthanasia as "a merciful act of clinical care"[8] or as "killing."[9] In this respect, an interview I conducted with Roger Hunt, an Australian palliative-care physician who was influential in the legalization of euthanasia in the Northern Territory of Australia, is instructive.

When I asked Dr Hunt, "Tell me why you think doctors should be allowed to kill dying patients who want this?" he objected to my use of the word "kill." He said he "prefer[red] to be specific about terms that we use in medicine" and that we should talk of "voluntary euthanasia, rather than … killing. Kill is a broad word that includes murder, manslaughter, and various other types of killing. We're [people who are pro-euthanasia] talking specifically about VAE [voluntary active euthanasia]. Now if doctors are involved in VAE, I think most people expect it of doctors not to turn their back on someone who is dying and suffering, and walk away."[10] Not only most people, as Hunt states, but probably everyone expects doctors not to walk away from suffering, dying patients. But do they expect most doctors also to provide euthanasia? Moreover, is this approach likely to cause confusion? Something with which we all agree – the primary obligation of personal care that physicians owe to their patients – is inextricably linked with euthanasia through language and sentence structure. This link is created by the word "it," which refers both to doctors not walking away and to voluntary active euthanasia.

The term itself and the fact that it has been reduced to an acronym (VAE) are noteworthy. Does the acronym make euthanasia seem less threatening, more familiar, and ordinary? The terms "passive euthanasia" and, less often, "voluntary passive euthanasia" are used by people who are pro-euthanasia to describe withdrawals or refusals of treatment that result in death. They argue that if these procedures are morally and legally acceptable – as most people who are against euthanasia agree they are, provided various conditions are fulfilled – these same people should agree that euthanasia is acceptable. In other words, they contend that all these interventions constitute euthanasia and that it should make no ethical or legal difference whether it is done by passive or by active means. In contrast, those who are anti-euthanasia base their case on the proposition that there are long-established, well-understood, profound, and important differences between allowing people to die and making them die – putting them to death.[11] To be consistent with this position, and to avoid confusion as to what is and what is not euthanasia, they oppose the use of the term "passive euthanasia" to describe justified withdrawals of treatment that will result in death.

Then, too, there can be confusion about what dying people mean to communicate by their language. Many people, at some stage of terminal illness, express the wish to die. Indeed, accepting death could be an important part of the dying process. This acceptance is very different from wanting to be killed. We need to keep this distinction in mind when assessing whether people are really asking for euthanasia. Even if they are, we need to be certain that this is not a way of asking some other question or of seeking reassurance and comfort. Some people worry, for example, about being unbearable burdens on caregivers or about being abandoned.[12]

A striking example of different interpretations of what dying patients communicate has been the focus of considerable controversy. In an article published in the *Journal of the American Medical Association*, Dr Herbert Hendin and his colleagues[13] comment on a Dutch study of euthanasia carried out by Dr Gerrit van der Wal and others[14] (of which a summary account was published in the *New England Journal of Medicine*).[15] Hendin and his co-authors point out that, in 1995, there were more than 1,500 Dutch cases of doctors administering lethal doses of opiates to patients with the intention of killing them. In the vast majority of these cases, "no request for death was made by the patient," although some patients were mentally competent and could have made known their desires. In a press interview,[16] van der Wal confirmed that "no request for death was made by the patient in these cases," though he added that "doctors had received previous approval to administer opiates." Requests to do whatever was necessary to ease pain had been made by the patients at some point. In short, the best reading of this situation, from the point of view of the physicians involved, was that they interpreted a request for pain-relief treatment as these patients' consent to being killed. The alternative is that these physicians simply decided, despite the Dutch guidelines that applied at the time, that the patients' consent to euthanasia was irrelevant.

Interpreting patients' requests for pain-relief treatment as requests for euthanasia has a worrying flip-side that could augment one effect of the legalization of euthanasia: it can cause patients to refuse opiates they desperately need for the relief of pain because they are frightened of being killed.[17] This outcome reportedly happened[18] after the legalization of euthanasia in the Northern Territory of Australia.[19] It could raise similar concerns for people who live in jurisdictions where euthanasia is still prohibited. Consequently, even those who are pro-euthanasia should oppose the use of pain-relief medication as a way of carrying out euthanasia because the latter can deliver a message that results in terminally ill people, who are frightened of being subjected to euthanasia or who are morally opposed to it, depriving themselves of essential pain-relief treatment.

Confusion in Association

Describing euthanasia as simply the "final stage of good palliative care,"[20] and thereby associating it with this kind of care, can affect our impression of euthanasia and our reaction to it. Although not everyone agrees on all aspects of what constitutes the best palliative care, it would be surprising to find disagreement with its underlying objectives: the relief of pain and suffering and the provision of humane and compassionate care for dying people. If, then, as the pro-euthanasia argument goes, euthanasia is simply another example of good palliative care, why would anyone oppose it?

Proposing that euthanasia is just one part of good palliative care is an example of putting a "medical cloak" on euthanasia. Doing so makes euthanasia a medical issue concerning primarily individual patients, their families, and their physicians. We bury or ignore the fact that euthanasia is equally important as a philosophical and societal issue. One way to identify the effects of this medical-cloak confusion is to ask, as has been proposed, whether we should have a specially trained group of lawyers, rather than physicians, carry out euthanasia.[21] This process would make us disconnect assumptions about euthanasia from those about physicians and the medical context. In general, we say that physicians seek to do no harm; medical treatment is involved when physicians intervene; and the medical context is an ethical and safe forum. These assumptions about physicians, when applied to physicians carrying out euthanasia, can make euthanasia seem acceptable. I have observed, anecdotally, that some of the same people who strongly object to describing euthanasia as killing also object to the suggestion that lawyers be authorized to administer euthanasia; it would be unacceptable, they argue, to permit lawyers to kill people. It could be that what we decide about euthanasia would be the same whether we make the decision within or beyond the medical context – as, primarily, a medical or a non-medical matter. The point is, however, that we cannot afford simply to assume that this result will be the case.

Another confusion of association arises in some survey instruments in which the questions asked inextricably link euthanasia and the provision of adequate pain-relief treatment. People are asked whether they agree that a terminally ill person in great pain and suffering should be allowed to request a lethal injection. There are at least three problems here. First, respondents' emotional responses to the thought of leaving people in pain can colour their responses to euthanasia and make them more favourable to it than they would otherwise be. Second, the only response provided for in some questionnaires is either to agree or to disagree with both euthanasia and pain-relief treatment that will shorten life. There is no way to record agreement with pain-relief treatment but to reject euthanasia; respondents must accept or reject "the package." Third, this approach confuses euthanasia with pain-relief treatment that will shorten life; it can be an example of such treatment being defined as euthanasia.

Yet another source of confusion is the association between religion and opposition to euthanasia. An argument often used by those who are pro-euthanasia is that those who oppose it do so essentially on religious grounds. Although it is true that some people do oppose euthanasia because of their religious beliefs, there seems to be a reluctance to admit that there are good secular reasons to oppose euthanasia. Less frequently, confusion can also be caused by automatically associating being pro-euthanasia with being anti-religion. In some religious denominations, even members of the clergy are pro-euthanasia.[22] I do not intend to deny that people's religious stance can influence their views on euthanasia, but we should be careful before assuming so. Even more important, we should avoid devaluing or dismissing views just because they are associated with religious beliefs. We are usually sensitive, today, to religious bigotry, but we are not always as sensitive to anti-religious bigotry.

Still another confusion of association is that between individualism and a sense of personal identity. We could need a sense of personal identity most when we are dying. It would help to give us a sense that our lives have had meaning, which we probably need to die peacefully. Currently, many people seek a sense of personal identity through "intense individualism," especially through its dominant feature of providing a sense of being in control. Euthanasia shares this feature with intense individualism; it is a very powerful expression of seeking control. Most people, however, probably cannot find a sense of personal identity in intense individualism. They need to find it in a structure of complex human relationships, including those that can be created only by feeling that one is a member of a community. As Isaiah Berlin says, "I am [at least in some important respects] what I see of myself reflected in the eyes of other people."[23] In short, paradoxically, we might be able to find full individual identity only by participating in communities – by immersing individuality in the greater whole. This need for community to be fully human individuals brings us face to face with a major problem in many contemporary Western societies: the loss of a sense of community.

Loss of community might also be a causal factor in the emergence of the euthanasia debate. Death no longer occurs in the community. It is no longer surrounded by tradition, ritual, and ceremony. Dying people are often isolated, even to the extent that they can suffer intense "pre-mortem loneliness," to repeat Jay Katz's arresting description.[24] Death is often sterilized, deritualized, and dehumanized. Euthanasia might be a complex response to this postmodern social reality. It accommodates an approach to death that is highly individualistic but, at the same time, surrounded by ritual explicitly associated with this way of dying.[25]

CONFUSION IN ETHICAL AND LEGAL ANALYSIS

Confusion of Means and Ends

There is also confusion between the ethical and legal acceptability of some outcomes and of the means used to achieve them. The strongest version of the pro-euthanasia argument, in this respect, is the following: if death is inevitable and imminent for someone who wants and consents to euthanasia, then providing it is no different from withdrawing life-support treatment from someone who refuses it and dies as a result. In both cases, the argument goes, death is the outcome; the means used to achieve it are not morally distinguishable and should not be legally distinguished; it is inconsistent, they continue, to support the ethical and legal acceptability of some withdrawals of treatment that result in death, but not euthanasia by lethal injection. To summarize: there is no ethical or moral difference between death resulting from a refusal of treatment and death resulting from a lethal injection, and there ought to be no legal difference. Applied to physician-assisted suicide, properly so-called, this argument becomes the following: in refusing treatment that results in death, a person commits suicide; there is no moral or ethical reason to distinguish this process from physician-assisted suicide; therefore, these two situations should be treated in the same way by the law.[26]

In contrast, those who are anti-euthanasia argue that there really is a moral and ethical difference between accepting refusals of treatment, even if doing so results in death, and giving lethal injections or assisting people in committing suicide; therefore, the legal difference between these situations should be maintained.[27] They argue that the way in which death occurs is a morally relevant issue: the law should continue to reflect that some of these means are morally and ethically acceptable, but others – euthanasia and physician-assisted suicide – are not.

One example of the confusion of means and ends being used in support of euthanasia can be found in the article "Slow Euthanasia," by physicians J.A. Billings and S.D. Block.[28] They state that physicians frequently "hasten death slowly with a morphine drip," which they describe as "slow euthanasia." They argue that it would be better for everyone – patients, families, and physicians – and more honest to accept "rapid euthanasia." To reach this conclusion, they downplay the relevance of intention in giving treatment that could or even would shorten life. For instance, they equate pain-relief treatment that could have this effect, but which is given with the primary intention of relieving pain, and injections given with the primary intention of killing. They do so by characterizing the means used in both situations as humane and ethical treatment of dying patients (that is, in such a way that they are the same) and point out that the same end – the deaths of patients – results in both situations. As part of this approach they define euthanasia to include necessary pain-relief treatment that will shorten life, and reject the doctrine of "double effect as an unconvincing justification for [this form of] euthanasia."[29]

This article elicited several responses.[30] According to these comments, Billings and Block have failed to appreciate important ethical and legal distinctions that inform not only the law on euthanasia but also the law in general – especially the criminal law. For instance, if doctors hang morphine drips with the primary intention of killing patients, not with the primary intention of relieving their pain, this act would be euthanasia and it would be prohibited as such. But if the drips are needed to relieve pain and the primary intention is "to kill the pain, not the patient,"[31] the law would not regard it as euthanasia. Necessary pain relief treatment that shortens life would be justified under the *doctrine of double effect*. This legal doctrine requires, first, that the act resulting in a bad consequence, the shortening of life, is morally neutral. Providing pain-relief treatment would qualify. Second, the pain relief must not be achieved by shortening life – that is, through a bad consequence. Third, the bad consequence, the shortening of life, must not be primarily intended as either an end or a means; rather, the primary intent must be the legitimate aim of relieving pain. And, fourth, there must be no other reasonable way of achieving the pain relief without involving the undesired effect of shortening life; the proportionality of good and bad consequences required to justify the bad ones must be present.[32] As Bernard Dickens says, Billings and Block "apply an outcome oriented test that simply links a physician's use of medications with their inevitable effect regardless of immediate intent. However, intent is at the centre of ethical and legal judgments in this area, not a secondary or marginal concern unworthy of regard in ethical [or legal] analysis as the authors mildly acknowledge."[33]

To summarize, some of the confusion between euthanasia and pain-relief treatment or refusals of treatment that could or would shorten life is caused by focusing on the outcome, death, and arguing that if someone is terminally ill, it is morally and ethically irrelevant – and should be legally irrelevant – how this outcome occurs. The central issue in the euthanasia debate is not the outcome – death; it is not if we will die, because we all eventually die, but how we die and whether some ways of dying – physician-assisted suicide and euthanasia – ought to remain legally prohibited. To respond, we must examine in greater detail the role that physicians' intentions play in drawing the line between acceptable and unacceptable medical interventions that could or would shorten life.

Confusion of Intent

A fundamental principle in criminal law is that a crime requires both a criminal act, an *actus reus* – conduct that the definition of the crime requires to have occurred[34] – and an accompanying criminal mind, a *mens rea*. In general, the latter is constituted by having an intention to cause the prohibited outcome. Classically, someone is held to have intended an outcome that results from his or her conduct in either of two situations: the outcome is a certain, or almost certain, result of the conduct in question, and the person knows this connection; or the outcome is less certain, but the person wants it to occur. In general, motive is irrelevant in deciding whether *mens rea* is present, though there are exceptions to this rule.[35] Recently, some courts have taken a more straightforward approach. They have held that, in criminal law, intention bears its ordinary meaning of aim or purpose; foresight of even certain consequences is, at best, merely evidence from which purpose might – or might not – be inferred by the jury.[36]

But even in jurisdictions in which courts use the more stringent, classical approach to intent, when the motive is to relieve pain and not to kill, a *mens rea* of intention to kill is not taken into account by the criminal law, even though it would otherwise be present in giving necessary pain-relief treatment that would shorten life.[37] These cases fall within the exception to the classical rule that motive is irrelevant to intent. Because there is no motive to kill the patient, there is no criminal *mens rea*. Giving pain-relief treatment is not the *actus reus* of a culpable homicide, moreover, because it is not an *unlawful* act causing death, as required for that crime.[38] Likewise, one way in which the law justifies the legality of withdrawing treatment that results in death, as compared with the illegality of physician-assisted suicide or euthanasia, is through a distinction with respect to intention. In physician-assisted suicide and euthanasia, the primary intent is to cause death. In withdrawing life-support treatment that patients have refused, the primary intent[39] is not to cause death but to respect the *right to inviolability*, the right of patients not to be touched without their consent. That includes the right not to have treatment applied to them without their informed consent. Indeed, it would be a criminal assault to continue treatment that patients have refused.

But if life-support treatment were withdrawn from incompetent patients who had not previously refused it (or whose substitute decision-maker had not validly done so), there is a potential for criminal liability. Once again, intent would be relevant in deciding whether this liability would be imposed. If the treatment were withdrawn because it was medically futile, there would be no criminal liability; if it were not medically futile and was withdrawn with the primary intent of killing, this act would constitute the crime of homicide. And that, depending on the circumstances and the definition of euthanasia used, might or might not be classified also as euthanasia.[40] In short, a primary *intent to kill* is never legally acceptable. An intent of allowing to die might or might not be legally acceptable, depending on all the circumstances.

Legal immunity for administering necessary pain-relief treatment, given with the primary intention of relieving pain but with the knowledge that it could or would shorten life, is implemented through the doctrine of double effect. One way of viewing this doctrine is that it allows motive or primary intent to negate a *mens rea* of intention to kill, which would otherwise be present. The doctrine of double effect could be regarded as functioning also as the law's way of building into the requirements of the *actus reus* the absence of elements that otherwise could function as a defence of necessity. In the context of providing necessary pain-relief treatment that would shorten life, this defence can be articulated as follows: the necessity of using some means to relieve pain justifies the use of these means even though the undesired result of doing so would be the shortening of life. Transferred into the context of *actus reus*, the elements of this defence are as follows: the *actus reus* of a culpable homicide is absent if the act causing death was the administration of treatment necessary to relieve pain. This is a strained analysis. Why does the law not just apply necessity as a defence?

I can think of at least two reasons. First, there could be an important aim of not raising the spectre of criminal liability in the context of providing fully adequate pain-relief treatment; fear of attracting criminal liability could make physicians reluctant to treat pain. As a true defence, necessity operates by way of "confession and avoidance," which means that it raises the possibility of criminal liability. The actor confesses to an act that attracts criminal liability and then avoids liability for it by proving all the essential elements for a defence of necessity. Second, there is probably concern not to open up the defence of necessity in the context of medical treatment at the end of life for fear that it could be extended to apply to euthanasia. That can be achieved by using the absence of "necessity" as a necessary element of the *actus reus* of any crime associated with the giving of pain-relief treatment[41] rather than by using necessity as a defence in these circumstances. Indeed, those who are pro-euthanasia do argue that a defence of necessity should apply to the provision of euthanasia, as the Dutch courts have held.[42]

Responses to this proposition by those opposed to euthanasia are of two kinds. First, they argue that a defence of necessity has never been applied to allow the taking of human life except when that could be justified on the grounds that it was necessary to save one's own life (that is, as self-defence) or to protect the lives of others. Second, they point out, difficult as it can be to accept, that we cannot eliminate all suffering, that we should not seek to eliminate it by inflicting death, and that euthanasia is unnecessary for the relief of pain. In extreme cases, pain relief can be achieved in ways that do not involve killing patients. Total sedation is one. This option makes it very unlikely that a court would hold that a defence of necessity would apply to justify euthanasia as a way of relieving pain.

The use of total sedation in the case of dying patients is yet another issue that raises complex moral, ethical, and legal problems. These issues cannot be explored here, but, as the Canadian Parliament's Special Senate Committee on Euthanasia and Assisted Suicide[43] recommended, they indicate a need for in-depth research. In a few rare cases, when patients are receiving good palliative care, but all other measures to relieve pain or other symptoms of unbearable physical suffering have failed, total sedation could be the treatment of choice – one that is ethically and legally acceptable. There should be serious concern, however, if the number of these cases in a given unit were more than a very few. It would be a strong indication that the treatment was, in fact, being used as a form of slow euthanasia, properly so-called.[44] Moreover, as in other areas of the euthanasia debate, choice of language can have a profound effect on the way we view total sedation. Some people who are pro-euthanasia have decried their opponents' willingness to approve of people dying in a state of "pharmacological stupor," while being unwilling to permit lethal injections. Although we might not agree with the substance of the arguments that these criticisms reflect, they contain a valid warning of the need for all of us, including those who are anti-euthanasia, to question constantly the essential nature, moral and ethical integrity, and consistency of our actions, values, and beliefs concerning end-of-life decision-making.

Returning to intent, there is probably no *mens rea* of intention when pain-relief treatment that only might shorten life is given, because the outcome might not be certain enough to be intended and death is not a desired outcome. Alternatively, there might be a *mens rea* of reckless-ness – conscious, unjustified risk-taking – that would support a charge of manslaughter and even, in some circumstances in some jurisdic-tions, murder. But when the risk-taking with respect to shortening life is the only way to relieve pain, it is most unlikely to be considered unjustified; therefore, there would be no *mens rea* of recklessness.

Those who are pro-euthanasia argue that it is impossible in many cases to know whether the primary intent is to relieve pain or to kill pa-tients – or, indeed, that both aims could be present concurrently.[45] It might not seem possible to know in some cases. But keep in mind that juries in criminal trials are asked to make these determinations with re-spect to intent every day. Even if the task proves difficult in some cases, it does not lessen the importance of making a distinction between these different primary intents and recognising the impact beyond in-dividual cases that changing this approach would have. The criminal law is an important value-forming, value-upholding institution. Chang-ing it, therefore, would have important effects on values. The present legal approach to giving treatment that is necessary to relieve pain, but could or would shorten life, distinguishes a primary intent to relieve pain from a primary intent to kill and imposes criminal liability only when the latter is present. This means that society can maintain its most important fundamental norm – that we must not kill each other – while still allowing physicians to relieve pain. It is essential that we do both, which we could not do if we legalize euthanasia.

Confusion of Causation

Physicians often describe themselves as being deeply confused by the law's approach to the presence or absence of causation with respect to death resulting from a withdrawal of life support treatment, for exam-ple, as compared with the administration of a lethal injection. This confusion is not surprising. Causation is a complex, technical, and nu-anced area of legal theory. It can be confusing even for lawyers. The le-gal concept of causation and its application to decision-making at the end of life in a medical context is explored in this section.

Some confusion in understanding the law's approach to causation when death occurs as a result of a refusal of treatment, as compared with a lethal injection, has been introduced by those in favour of eu-thanasia. They argue that distinctions made between these two situa-tions are artificial with respect to causation. They contend that, in both cases, the "but for" test – the law's test for causation-in-fact – shows that the physician's act was responsible for the patient's death. But for the withdrawal of treatment, the patient would not have died; therefore, withdrawal of treatment was the cause of death. But for the lethal injection, the patient would not have died; therefore, the lethal injection was the cause of death. This approach contains confusion of at least two kinds.

First, an analysis of causation becomes relevant in criminal law only when there is conduct that could constitute a crime, accompanied by the required *mens rea*. The question is, then, whether that conduct caused the prohibited outcome. In the case of a patient's refusal of treatment and the withdrawal of treatment after that refusal, there is no illegal act of which a causal link to the outcome must be established in order to impose criminal liability. But when a physician gives a lethal injection (which, in itself, constitutes the *actus reus* of a crime) and agrees that this action was accompanied by an intention to kill (the required *mens rea*), it is relevant to ask whether this lethal injection was the cause of death. But for the lethal injection, would the patient have died at that time? Only if it is proved beyond a reasonable doubt that the injection was the cause of death is the physician criminally liable. To find criminal liability, in other words, causation is an essential requirement that must be established as part of the *actus reus* and in addition to *mens rea*. It is not a factor that, standing alone, gives rise to liability. Hence the argument that a physician "caused" a patient's death either in turning off a respirator following the refusal of treatment or in giving a lethal injection – and, therefore, that both cases should be treated alike in terms of criminal responsibility – fails to understand or to apply some of the most basic tenets of criminal law.

The second confusion is that those who are pro-euthanasia assume that the "but for" test must always be applied. The law sometimes recognizes causal connections without this test being satisfied, however, and it ignores some connections that would be established under it.[46] Moreover, in the case of a refusal of treatment that results in death, the "but for" test is complicated because there is not a sole cause of death. There are two causes: the patient's underlying condition and the removal of life support. If the "but for" question were framed simply in relation to the patient's condition that gives rise to the need for life support – "But for the underlying condition, would the patient have died when taken off the life support?" – and the answer is no (as it is when people are dependent on life support), then it is the patient's underlying condition (natural causes) that caused death, for *the purposes of the law*, not removal of the respirator. But when should the question be framed in this way?

When many causes are present, a value judgment is involved in choosing which formulation of the "but for" test predominates in establishing causation-in-fact,[47] and which of the causal factors – one, more than one, or all of them (each of which could attract legal liability) – count in establishing criminal liability. When one has a duty not to continue treating patients with artificial life support, because they have refused it or because it is medically futile, then it is inappropriate to formulate the test of causation (even if it were relevant to assess causation itself, which it is not if the act of withdrawing treatment is legal) in terms of whether death was caused by the withdrawal of treatment. Physicians cannot have a legal obligation both to withdraw treatment and not to withdraw it. We must choose which of these duties predominates in each situation. If the former, then the relevant test for the cause of death is this: But for the underlying condition, would the patient have died? If the latter, it is this: But for turning off the respirator, would the patient have died?

Yet another approach is to recognize that the withdrawal of life-support treatment such as repiratory support involves a situation of multiple causation in which one cause (respiratory failure) is, in itself, sufficient to cause death; the other cause (turning off the respirator) is not sufficient in the absence of respiratory failure. Although the courts could still hold the latter to be a cause for the purposes of the law (a contributing cause) – and would do so when turning off the respirator constitutes an illegal act – they do not do so when the act of turning it off is legal. Although causation is irrelevant in the latter circumstance, paradoxically, at first glance, the courts have often taken pains to justify their decisions not to impose criminal liability in these cases, *from the point of view of causation*; they hold that, from the law's perspective, turning off the respirator was not the cause of death. We could speculate on the psychological reasons that make judges feel compelled to offer this explanation. Most probably, however, the courts have found it necessary to rule that death results from natural causes in respirator cases for two reasons: to distinguish these cases from lethal-injection cases; and to avoid any possibility that they could be seen as setting a precedent to the effect that lethal injections would be legally acceptable.

It is clear in tort cases that cause-in-fact (the test for which in single-cause cases is most often "but for") does not, by itself, establish causation for the purposes of legal liability. Cause-in-law, *causa causans*, is required as well.[48] It is sometimes referred to as the "essential" cause or causes, if any, among the causes-in-fact, that will be regarded as the cause by the law. Although this second aspect of causation, "causation as a question of law,"[49] is relevant in criminal law, it is seldom openly discussed in that context. When it is, the courts and commentators recognize the hesitancy and uncertainty that surround its definition and application.[50] These difficulties are probably associated with fear that open use of the doctrine could give the impression that a finding of causation, and hence of criminal liability, is discretionary on the part of the judge. The same fear is absent, at least to the same degree, in imposing civil liability in tort cases; in this context, the concept is constantly identified and used. Indeed, on occasion, criminal law judges have turned to tort law cases to clarify and explain cause-in-law.[51] Consequently, it is worth examining how this concept functions in that area.

In the law of civil responsibility – tort law – the tests for causation-in-law are of varying degrees of stringency. The test that most favours liability is that causation-in-law will be present for those consequences whose risk of occurence would not be unforeseeable to reasonable people in the same circumstances. The Privy Council described what constituted this kind of foreseeable risk as "one which would occur to the mind of a reasonable man in the [same] position ... which he would not brush aside as far-fetched."[52] A test that favours liability less is that causation-in-law will be present only for those consequences whose risk of occcurence a reasonable person in the same circumstances would have reasonably foreseen.[53] The two tests can give different results because a risk that is not reasonably foreseeable (causation-in-law would be absent under the latter test) might not be unforeseeable (causation-in-law would be present under the former test). A causal test of directness, too – how directly the resulting harm is linked with the wrongful conduct – though no longer a sufficient test of causation-in-law, can play a role in assessing this element.[54]

In the context of criminal law, the test of causation that most favours the accused would be used, as there is a presumption in the law against imposing criminal liability.[55] Consequently, an accused person must have subjectively foreseen the outcome of the conduct that gives rise to criminal liability, or the risk of this occurring (though not the exact way in which this outcome results), in order to be held causally responsible for that outcome. Subjective foreseeability of the consequences, rather than objective foreseeability (as in civil law), is necessary because, as discussed previously, *mens rea* is an essential element in imposing criminal liability. Indeed, the requirements of *mens rea* mean that some elements necessary to establish causation overlap with those necessary for intention. Moreover, when the prohibited outcome results from crystallization of a risk, the likelihood of occurrence of that risk (in practice though not in theory) must probably be higher in criminal law than in civil law for it to be characterized as reasonably foreseeable within the context of proving causation. Again, this is because there is a presumption of innocence in favour of accused people, which means that all doubt must be resolved in their favour.

In the context of criminal law, Colvin summarizes the situation relating to causation as follows:

In the common law, two different general tests have been used in handling questions of causal responsibility. They will here be called the "substantial cause" test and the "reasonable foreseeability" test. The "substantial cause" test is a retrospective test. It involves looking backwards from a result in order to determine whether, in the light of all that happened, a particular causal factor has played a substantial role in bringing about that result. In contrast, the "reasonable foreseeability" test is a prospective test. It involves adopting the position of the person who was alleged to have caused the result and then looking forward from the conduct towards the result. The question is asked whether or not the conduct made the result a reasonably foreseeable consequence, in the sense that it was within the normal range of expected outcomes ... Each of these tests carries a good deal of judicial support. In most instances they yield the same outcomes but divergences are possible. Unfortunately the courts have avoided confronting the differences between the tests. Cases are handled by reference to one or the other, with the alternative usually being ignored. If the alternative is recognized at all, the choice which has been made is usually not defended.[56]

We can apply these tests of causal responsibility to death resulting either from the withdrawal of life-support treatment that the patient has refused or from the administration of a lethal injection. Death is a *reasonably foreseeable* result of withdrawing the treatment, but the courts have consistently held that consented-to withdrawals are not the *substantial cause* of death. Death is a *reasonably foreseeable* – in fact, certain – result of lethal injection, too. But one could not imagine a court holding, when there is proof beyond a reasonable doubt that death resulted from the injection, that it was not the *substantial cause* of death.

In tort cases, in deciding whether causation-in-law is present, judges sometimes talk about needing to determine the proximity or remoteness of the damage from the cause. This requirement can be regarded simply as another way of expressing the foreseeability-of-consequences test of causation or as an additional test that must be fulfilled to establish causation-in-law. The words "proximity" or "remoteness" accurately connote that, to a greater or lesser extent, this test involves an exercise of judicial discretion in making a finding as to causation. The test can be regarded as a device that allows a judge to factor into the decision-making a determination as to moral blameworthiness. It allows a judge to find that, even though causation-in-fact is established, causation is absent in a particular case if blameworthiness is low or absent. The words "proximity" and "remoteness" are seldom used by courts in ruling on causation in criminal-law cases.[57] This judicial reservation is probably, again, due to these words – and any concepts they represent – strongly implying a discretionary component in the decision about causation; the identified exercise of discretion is much more carefully constrained in the context of criminal culpability than of civil liability.

It is important to note how the tests of remoteness or proximity interact with the causation-in-fact or "but for" test. "What is meant by 'proximate' is that because of convenience, of public policy, or a rough sense of justice, the law arbitrarily declines to trace a series of events beyond a certain point. This is not logic. It is practical politics."[58] In summary, even if "but for" the act the outcome would not have occurred, the court can still find that, in the eyes of the law, there is no causal link between that act and that outcome. We can speculate on whether the concepts of remoteness and proximity could help to explain the different findings on causation in relation to death resulting from the refusal of life support treatment and that resulting from a lethal injection. What role does the absence of moral blameworthiness play in finding that the withdrawal of life support does not cause death? Or does the presence of natural causes and the fact that death would not result in the absence of these causes make death from a refusal of treatment remote from, not proximate enough to, the withdrawal of that treatment? The same analysis would not apply to death from a lethal injection.

Public policy, another test that involves an exercise of discretion, may also be used in tort law to justify a finding that causation is absent, although judges have classically been reluctant to use it because of its perceived nature as "an unruly horse."[59] This test is sometimes articulated as an element in assessing cause-in-law or as a part of the test for proximity or remoteness, but it is best viewed as an additional test. It is used to find that, for reasons of public policy, causation is absent. But it is not used to find the contrary – that for reasons of public policy, causation is present. In other words, when called into play as an element of the doctrine of causation, public policy operates only to provide immunity from legal liability, not to impose it. Once again we can speculate whether there is an element of public policy at play in finding that causation is absent when death results from withdrawal of treatment following a patient's request, but this same element is not operative when death results from a lethal injection.

It is worth noting here that, outside the context of causation, the notion of public policy plays a special role in criminal law when it is used to characterize acts to which the consent of those affected by them may or may not function as a defence. For instance, the intentional infliction of bodily harm, beyond a very limited degree, is held to be contrary to public policy. Therefore, in the common law, the consent of those suffering from that harm is not a defence.[60] In contrast, consent to an act of minimal harm that is not deemed contrary to public policy protects the person inflicting the harm from a charge of criminal assault.

In this respect, we can compare an act of turning off a respirator on which someone depends for life support with that of giving a lethal injection. Turning off a respirator is not, in itself, contrary to public policy. Therefore, one way to justify it is with the patient's consent at that time or in advance, or, if the patient is incompetent and has not left advance directives, with the consent of a legally valid substitute decision-maker. But giving a lethal injection is, in itself, contrary to public policy. Therefore, consent is irrelevant to criminal liability. This scenario raises the question of how necessary pain-relief treatment, given with the primary intention of relieving pain but with the possibility or expectation of shortening life, should be *prima facie* characterized from a public policy perspective. Just as the intent to relieve pain and not to kill justifies, through the doctrine of double effect, the administration of treatment, this same intent legitimates it from a public policy perspective. Therefore, it can be given with the patient's consent. Indeed, *not* doing so should be considered contrary to public policy.

This discussion, as a whole, raises the sometimes vexed question of judicial discretion and the role it should play in determining legal liability. Views differ, depending on how the exercise of that discretion is characterized. There is a major difference between identifying it as an example of purely arbitrary decision-making on the part of the judge and characterizing it as the judge's use not only of pure reason but also of additional "ways of knowing." Judges in both the Supreme Court of Canada and United States Supreme Court, for example, found that a legislative ban on assisted suicide, which includes physician-assisted suicide, was not unconstitutional. To support their ruling, they looked to the history of their respective countries, including their legal and legislative histories – that is, to human memory as a "way of knowing." Memory was used to balance a strictly reasoned argument that there was no moral, and ought to be no legal, difference "between letting a patient die and making that patient die,"[61] allowing the courts to find that there were important, profound, and well-established differences.

Confusion of Case Law

I turn now to an article published in the *Lancet* – yet another argument, based on confusion, for the legalization of euthanasia. J.K. Mason and D. Mulligan propose that euthanasia be introduced by stages.[62] It should be made available first, they say, for people suffering from specific conditions.[63] The two conditions they suggest are permanent vegetative state and progressive neurological disease. In making this proposal, the two authors decry the fact that "the rhetoric of euthanasia is blurred," and then proceed to add confusion. In this instance, the confusion resides in their interpretation of two Canadian judgments. They argue that the courts, in these cases, were moving towards support for euthanasia. One of these cases, *Nancy B*,[64] involved a refusal of treatment that resulted in death. In the other, *Rodriguez*,[65] as discussed in previous chapters, the Supreme Court of Canada was faced with a claim that the Canadian Criminal Code's prohibition of assisting a person to commit suicide,[66] which includes physician-assisted suicide, contravenes constitutional rights to liberty and security of the person. In other words, this latter case involved the court adjudicating a claim that terminally ill people have a constitutionally protected right to the assistance of physicians in committing suicide.

Mason and Mulligan first recognize that medically futile treatment may be withheld or withdrawn from patients in a permanent vegetative state. I have already mentioned in passing the terms "medically futile treatment" and "futile treatment," which are sometimes used interchangeably, are difficult to define, and whose identification often involves value judgments. There is no ethical or legal obligation to continue giving medically useless treatment. Indeed, at least in publicly funded health-care systems, there is an ethical obligation *not* to waste scarce health-care resources, which such treatment would involve. Therefore, we must not avoid the need to make decisions as to when treatment becomes medically futile.[67] Provided that care is taken to limit strictly the definition of what constitutes medically futile treatment in any given case, most people who are anti-euthanasia would agree that treatment may be withdrawn. They would not agree, however, that this constitutes either euthanasia or, as Mason and Mulligan propose, a basis for its approval.

There is another way in which confusion between the withholding or withdrawal of treatment and euthanasia can arise. It involves cases in which either withholding or withdrawing treatment would constitute euthanasia. For instance, to withhold or withdraw life-support treatment from someone who had always been mentally incompetent, with the primary intention of inflicting death, rather than on the basis that any reasonable physician would agree that the treatment was medically futile, would be, at best, euthanasia.[68] As this example demonstrates, and as I have already noted, it is not only what we do but also our reasons for doing so that are important in defining whether conduct constitutes euthanasia. Moreover, it is these reasons, and not simply the outcome of any given decision, that will set the precedents for what is legally allowed or prohibited.

Mason and Mulligan base their case for introducing "euthanasia by stages" on their finding "strong indications that courts and law enforcement authorities outside the United Kingdom are coming to accept the practice [of euthanasia and physician-assisted suicide]."[69] As I have said, they cite as authority for this proposition two relatively recent Canadian cases, the decisions of the Superior Court of Quebec in *Nancy B*[70] and the Supreme Court of Canada in *Rodriguez*.[71] *Nancy B* involved withdrawal of life support. It is important to understand the legal basis on which the court allowed withdrawal of medical treatment, therefore, in order to know whether the court was, as Mason and Mulligan assert, in fact tending towards support for euthanasia or, more accurately, physician-assisted suicide. *Rodriguez* involved a claim that prohibiting physician-assisted suicide contravened individual rights protected under the Canadian Constitution. For the same reasons, it is important to understand the law on which this claim was founded, and that on which the judgments handed down in the Supreme Court of Canada were based.

Nancy B required the court to apply the Civil Code of Quebec (private law in Quebec is governed under a civilian juridical regime, as in France). The Civil Code provides that "the human person is inviolable," that is, not allowed to be touched without the person's consent.[72] The code expressly provides, in addition, that medical care or treatment must not be given to a competent person without that person's free and informed consent.[73] Nancy B had suffered irreversible respiratory paralysis as a result of Guillain-Barré syndrome and was dependent on a respirator. She asked for this life-support treatment to be discontinued. The court affirmed Nancy B's right to refuse treatment, even though doing so would result in her death.

The court held that the duty to respect a refusal of treatment is almost absolute in the case of a competent adult person.[74] It found that Nancy B wanted "the respiratory support treatment being given to her to cease so that nature can take its course."[75] It ruled that this "may not properly be viewed as an attempt to commit suicide ... [because] death ... would be the result, primarily, of the underlying disease, and not the result of a self-inflicted injury."[76] In particular, the court found that turning off the respirator would not offend any provisions of the

Canadian Criminal Code[77] (which is based on the common law), because it would involve no act that would constitute homicide or assistance with suicide. The judge concluded "that homicide and suicide are not natural deaths whereas in the present case, if the plaintiff's [Nancy B's] death take place after the respiratory support treatment is stopped at her request, it would be the result of nature taking its course."[78]

In *Rodriguez*, all judges of the Supreme Court of Canada strongly upheld the right to refuse treatment – in particular, on the basis of respect for the person's right to inviolability – but, just as strongly, a majority differentiated this ruling from any right to have assistance in committing suicide or access to euthanasia. The technical legal basis of the majority's judgment was that the prohibition on assisting in suicide in subsection 241(b) of the Criminal Code was constitutionally valid; assistance could be interdicted by Parliament through the criminal law. In coming to this conclusion, the majority analyzed the relevant sections of the Canadian Charter of Rights and Freedoms,[79] that part of Canadian constitutional law that allows people to challenge the validity of legislation on the grounds that it contravenes the individual's constitutionally protected rights. To support their decision, though, the majority extensively explored the history of prohibitions on assisting in suicide, the approaches of other jurisdictions, and the common law governing medical decisions at the end of life.[80]

Of the four dissenting judges in *Rodriguez* who held that the prohibition on physician-assisted suicide was constitutionally invalid, the judgment of the chief justice of Canada was the most unprecedented. Chief Justice Lamer ruled that there is a "right to choose suicide"[81] enshrined within Canadian constitutional law; a failure to provide assistance in committing suicide to patients who are physically unable to carry it out themselves contravenes constitutional rights against discrimination on the basis of physical handicap legislated in section 15 of the Canadian Charter of Rights and Freedoms. It was essential to Chief Justice Lamer's ruling that the prohibition of assisted suicide in the Criminal Code was unconstitutional. In order to find that, he had to find a right of the plaintiff with respect to having assistance to commit suicide; that this right was infringed as a result of discrimination; and that this discrimination flowed from the prohibition on assisting someone to commit suicide. The chief justice found that under the Charter and in the common law, the rights of the individual to self-determination and autonomy give rise to a *right to choose, in accordance with the law,*[82] *how to conduct one's own life.*[83] Moreover, in view of the fact that Parliament had repealed the legislation making suicide a crime – which, the chief justice said, made suicide legal – he ruled that this right to choose extended to a right to choose suicide. There is no necessary reason to suppose that this "right to choose suicide" would be limited to people who are terminally ill, as Chief Justice Lamer himself recognises,[84] or even to people who are ill. In fact, the contrary could be argued, since the chief justice based this right to choose suicide on the general rights of all individuals to self-determination and autonomy. This reasoning also raises the question of whether providing emergency medical care for patients who have attempted suicide and are unconscious or incompetent, or those who refuse medical treatment to ameliorate the consequences of their attempts (which raises difficult and complex ethical and legal questions), could contravene this right were a majority to recognize its existence.

This brief mention of some complex questions raised in the long judgment of the Supreme Court of Canada in *Rodriguez* can be contrasted with Mason and Mulligan's use of the case to support their proposal for legalizing physician-assisted suicide. They state that "the arguments [by which they seem to mean the reasons of the majority of the Supreme Court of Canada, in upholding the constitutional validity of the crime of assisted suicide] were ... based very largely on Canadian constitutional law and the dissenting opinions [which would have allowed physician-assisted suicide and included the judgment of the Chief Justice] were of more general application."[85] If anything, the contrary is true. A "right to choose suicide" has never been articulated in common law, and I think it highly unlikely that it could be established except on a constitutional law foundation. Indeed, it was because the prohibition on assisted suicide in the Criminal Code breached Sue Rodriguez's rights to autonomy and self-determination, and because these rights were protected under *her right to security of the person* in section 7 of the Charter, that the Chief Justice held the prohibition unconstitutional and, therefore, ruled that it should be struck down. Interestingly, he did not rely on the section 7 *right to liberty*. Nor did he discuss the interaction of the section 7 *right to life* with the section 7 *right to security of the person*, when the rights to self-determination and autonomy, which this latter right encompasses, are used to choose suicide. Moreover, the ratio of his judgment is that the prohibition on assisted suicide in the Canadian Criminal Code constitutes prohibited discrimination within the anti-discrimination provisions of section 15(1) of the Charter. In other words, constitutional law was essential and central to the chief justice's finding that Rodriguez had a right to the assistance of a physician in committing suicide – that she had a right, in fact, to euthanasia.

In *Rodriguez*, one of the main arguments presented in support of physician-assisted suicide was one I outlined previously: that Canadian law recognizes patients' rights to refuse treatment even when this refusal could or would result in death; that this is to recognize a right to die; and that it should make no difference legally whether this right is exercised through passive means (refusal of treatment) or active means (physician assistance in committing suicide or euthanasia). It is important, therefore, to understand the juridical basis of the right to refuse treatment. This basis can vary, and the extent to which a right to refuse treatment can be used to ground an argument for the legalization of euthanasia varies accordingly. This can be seen by comparing the situation in Canada with that in the United States

In Canada, the right to refuse treatment has been consistently interpreted by the courts, with the exception of some dissenting judges in *Rodriguez* (who articulated a broader base for this right), as founded on the right to inviolability – that is, the right not to be touched without one's consent. This right is of only negative content and legally cannot be used to found a positive content right to assistance in committing suicide or of access to euthanasia. But in the United States, the courts have interpreted the penumbra right of privacy (which the United States Supreme Court has found surrounds that country's Constitution[86]) as including a right to personal autonomy. This right has been held to have both negative-content and positive-content limbs; it encompasses not only a right to refuse treatment[87] but also a positive-content right to decide what happens to oneself. The latter includes rights to be free from state interference in the form of law in deciding what should happen to one's body.[88] This right was interpreted by the United States Ninth Circuit Court of Appeals[89] and the Second Circuit Court of Appeals[90] as giving rise to a constitutional right not to be prevented from seeking physician assistance in committing suicide. These cases were appealed to the United States Supreme Court, which reserved the courts of appeal, ruling that state laws prohibiting assistance in suicide are constitutionally valid.[91] But the constitutional validity of state laws that would allow euthanasia or physician-assisted suicide (in countries such as the United States and Australia, which have federal constitutions that give jurisdiction over criminal law to the states) remains an open question.[92] This issue is very likely to be tested in the near future.

CONCLUSION

The euthanasia debate is a momentous one. As pointed out elsewhere, it involves our past (the norms and values we have inherited), our present (whether we will change these values), and our future (the impact that a decision, now, either for or against euthanasia, will have on our descendants both as individuals and a society).[93] The outcome will set the "death tone" of the society in which we live and die. It will have a major impact on the societal and cultural paradigm – the shared story – on which society will be based.[94] Consequently, we need to engage in this debate not only with great honesty, integrity, and courage but also with clarity rather than confusion. This clarity must extend to recognizing that there are many important points relating to decision-making at the end of life on which we all agree, whether we are for or against euthanasia. We must then start from agreement, not disagreement. Doing so would change the debate's tone. And that, in turn, could change its outcome.

Almost everyone agrees that competent people should be able to refuse treatment – when necessary through advance directives (living wills or durable powers of attorney) – and that, when it is impossible to know someone's wishes, there is no legal or moral obligation to continue medically futile treatment. Likewise, almost everyone agrees that people have the right to adequate pain-relief treatment, even if it could or would shorten life, if this is necessary to relieve pain. Where we disagree is whether physician-assisted suicide and euthanasia should be legalized. This decision must be faced head-on and not dealt with by confusing it, whether accidentally or intentionally, with rights to refuse treatment or the provision of adequate pain-relief treatment. To do so is to pre-empt the question that needs to be addressed – whether there ought to continue to be a legal difference between refusals of treatment and the provision of adequate pain-relief treatment on the one hand and physician-assisted suicide and euthanasia on the other.

In answering these questions, we should recognize the harm that can be done to the law, in general, by the facile use of legal concepts – whether those of intention, causation, or "precedent" in the form of case analysis. It should be a matter of serious concern, especially to lawyers, when those using these concepts to promote the legalisation of euthanasia distort them, whether intentionally or because they have only a poor understanding of them from a legal point of view. Moreover, the question is not only a matter of our rightful, profound sympathy for people experiencing serious suffering, and whether, as Mason and Mulligan suggest, there are dreadful diseases or conditions for which we believe euthanasia is appropriate, but also whether allowing physicians to intervene with a primary intention of inflicting death is inherently acceptable as a foundational principle and basic value. We must not answer this question through confusion or in "stages." Rather, we must answer it openly, honestly, directly, and – I hope – wisely.

8 (a) Guidelines for Legalized Euthanasia in Canada: A Proposal

TORSTEN O. NIELSEN

SUMMARY

Arguments for liberty, mercy, and dignity support the legalization of euthanasia, but the possibility of undesirable social consequences present a problem. Accordingly, proposals for legalization must include suggestions to prevent involuntary euthanasia, to prevent unconscious coercion of the terminally ill to request euthanasia, to protect and enshrine the availability of first-class palliative care, to ensure documentation for purposes of enforcement and study, and to spell out enforceable consequences for violations.

Guidelines set by the Royal Dutch Medical Association for legalizing euthanasia have largely failed to meet these requirements. In North America, proposals for legalization, such as Oregon's Measure 16 and the minority opinion in Canada's Rodriguez case, are also flawed in meeting these criteria. Legislation in the Northern Territory of Australia came closest to meeting the requirements outlined, but was overruled after a brief period in effect.

In Canada, any attempts at legalization must be preceded by a comprehensive survey of current euthanasia practices and the improved availability of palliative care. This article makes a specific proposal for ethics committees operating at a regional health board level to approve legal euthanasia within careful guidelines. Composition, procedures, and mandate are described. If a set of guidelines, balancing any right there is "to die with dignity" with a responsibility to protect the weakest in society, is proposed first by the medical community, Parliament may have the courage to enact legislation.

INTRODUCTION

While many arguments have been raised in favour of legalized euthanasia, the most compelling are easy to understand. The principles of liberty and autonomy over one's body are in themselves justification enough for active voluntary euthanasia, as long as no significant harm is caused to others. The principle of beneficence supports merciful relief of suffering as a duty for all to consider, and there are cases where hastening death is the quickest and most effective way to relieve such agony. Finally, "death with dignity" in a chosen manner, surrounded by loved ones, is an attractive idea, providing terminal patients with a comforting sense of control over their fate. Not surprisingly, a significant body of public and medical opinion favours the liberalization of euthanasia laws.[1]

SOCIAL CONSEQUENCES OF LEGALIZED EUTHANASIA

Arguments opposing euthanasia often depend on predictions of wider social consequences that, while of lesser importance to the patient in question, may be more important to society. Primary among these worrisome consequences is the contention that legalization might erode the value of life and create a "duty to die."[2] An insidious but realistic scenario is suggested: for the terminal patient, euthanasia would not just bring about the relief of suffering; the request would also bring the closer attention of intimate care-givers, and minimize costs and stress for both loved ones and the health-care system.[3] The formerly independent patient, now wholly reliant on care-giver support, would be acutely aware of the burden this condition places on others, and would realize that an ultimately hopeless fight for life is a drain on everyone's resources. Death would become the noble and honourable choice. The slippery slope to unconscious coercion presents a strong argument against euthanasia because it suggests that, in respecting the autonomy of one individual, we compromise the autonomy of others and of future generations. The dying would want to play their appointed role and be killed; nevertheless, the new social order would have coerced this decision. For patients who might want to hold on to their lives and to their fundamental right of existence, their liberty would be compromised.

Legalized euthanasia could also lead to an erosion in palliative care.[4] In particular, palliative care focuses on pain control, treatment for depression, and social support. Indeed, these three factors can, if resolved, reverse a patient's wish to die in an impressive 85 per cent of cases.[5] Treatment of pain and depression, in spite of the availability of effective interventions, is often suboptimal.[6] If euthanasia becomes accepted or even preferable, partly because of medical convenience and cost, and this trend becomes reflected in an erosion of palliative-care skills, the choice not to die becomes more difficult.

While proponents usually intend euthanasia to be limited to competent patients, the possibility remains for a slippery slope to the involuntary euthanasia of incompetent patients. By this argument, if we permit "physician-assisted suicide," where the patient self-administers a lethal prescription, we are then also likely to allow a doctor to push the syringe (voluntary active euthanasia). If so, then an advance directive should be accepted as representing a now-incompetent patient's wish to die by active euthanasia. It is but a short step to allow a proxy decision-maker who knows the patient well to request euthanasia. Precedents will then leave open the possibility in other cases where it is unclear whether the patient would have wanted to die.

GUIDELINES FOR LEGALIZED EUTHANASIA

If euthanasia is to be legalized, it must be done under legal or professional guidelines that counter the slippery-slope arguments which are identified in table 1.

Worldwide Attempts to Legalize Euthanasia

In 1973, a Dutch physician assisted in her mother's suicide; she received a suspended sentence and inspired a pro-euthanasia movement. Books were written suggesting guidelines for legalizing euthanasia. When a lay volunteer who assisted an elderly patient's suicide also received a suspended sentence, the court implied that it would not have convicted the woman had she more closely adhered to similar guidelines. In response, the Royal Dutch Medical Association (RDMA) designed a series of euthanasia guidelines for physicians. This quasi-legal framework, which was written by doctors, has been accepted by Dutch society. Since its 1984 publication, while euthanasia remains technically illegal, no doctor adhering to these guidelines has been prosecuted.[7] [Editorial note: These guidelines have now been replaced by legislation that is consistent with them.]

Table 1
Criteria for Legalization of Euthanasia

- Prevent involuntary euthanasia of incompetent patients
- Prevent unconscious coercion (a "duty to die")
- Protect and enshrine palliative care
- Ensure documentation for enforcement and study
- Provide for enforcement of legal sanctions

To guard against involuntary euthanasia, the RDMA guidelines reserve euthanasia for competent patients or those leaving a clear advance directive. To reduce the likelihood of unconscious coercion, the treating physician must speak with the patient alone and be convinced that the decision is entirely the patient's own choice. The physician must be sure that the patient expresses a "lasting longing for death" and that the decision results from neither impulse nor depression. A second medical opinion must confirm these impressions. The patient must be experiencing "perpetual, unbearable, and helpless" suffering, and, in an effort to ensure that palliative care has been attempted, the patient must also have considered alternatives to death. Physicians are expected to write a case report, showing that the criteria have been met, which is reviewed by health and legal authorities. Methods of enforcement and legal sanctions are not defined. By these means, the Dutch have attempted to meet criteria 1 through 4 from table 1.

The Netherlands had had over a decade of experience with the *de facto* legalization of euthanasia, when the government commissioned an investigation into its consequences (the 1990 Remmelink study). Among physicians, 85 to 90 per cent still support the policy. Each year, more than 25,000 patients discuss euthanasia with their doctor, 9,000 make a formal request, and 3,000 die by this means, usually administered as an overdose of intravenous thiopental.[8] Over 50 per cent of Dutch doctors have performed euthanasia.[9] Patients' motivations for seeking euthanasia were also surveyed; roughly 60 per cent cite a loss of dignity, 50 per cent intolerable pain, 30 per cent humiliating dependency, and 20 per cent claimed to be "tired of life." While 2.9 per cent of all deaths occurred by euthanasia and fell within the guidelines, an additional 0.8 per cent of total deaths (1,000 persons/year) were by euthanasia of incompetent patients who did not leave a clear advance directive.[10] Half of these requests were initiated by the family and half by the doctor, the usual justification being that the action was in the patient's "best interests." In an estimated 50 per cent of euthanasia cases, no official report was made, apparently because doctors still fear legal repercussions.

Since there has been no enforcement of adherence to the guidelines (criterion 5, table 1), the obligation for documentation has failed and the slippery slope towards involuntary euthanasia has materialized in Holland. Whether a slippery slope towards unconscious coercion is developing is difficult to study, as it depends on a subtle shift in social attitudes. There has been no public outcry; indeed, the Dutch in general are proud of their tolerant attitude towards euthanasia. The RDMA has modified the guidelines, requiring the second medical opinion to be from a doctor with no relationship to the patient or the primary physician, and encouraging assisted suicide instead of doctor-perpetrated euthanasia where possible. Since we lack studies establishing how much involuntary or coerced euthanasia occurred before the introduction of the RDMA guidelines, it is difficult to ascertain whether there has been an increase.[11] The guidelines do not guarantee that palliative-care options must be exhausted before proceeding to euthanasia. Thus, there is reason to believe that the three most worrisome slippery-slope arguments against legalized euthanasia are indeed manifesting themselves in Holland.

Nevertheless, advocacy groups around the world have been inspired by the Dutch model to propose their own guidelines for legalized euthanasia. In Oregon, a voter-sponsored ballot initiative, The Oregon Death with Dignity Act (Measure 16), was narrowly approved in 1994. Intended as a law rather than a set of guidelines, it is more specific than RMDA position papers.[12] To prevent cases of involuntary euthanasia, the bill permits only assisted suicide, and two medical doctors must confirm the patient's competence. To ensure that patients are acting of their own free uncoerced will, the request must be witnessed by two persons, one of whom has no family relationship to the patient and will gain no inheritance. Requests can only be acted on for patients whose medical prognosis is for death within six months. Psychiatric consultation is optional. No provision to ensure palliative care is included, other than compulsory disclosure of its availability. A written standard request form is required, as is reporting to the health department, which is responsible for compiling statistics. Assisting suicide outside these boundaries remains a class A felony. A court decision to suspend this legislation[13] was reversed on appeal, and the U.S. Supreme Court has chosen not to review that decision, meaning that, since October 1997, Measure 16 has been in effect.

In Washington and New York, attempts to strike down the laws banning assisted suicide on constitutional grounds were defeated on appeal. In June 1997, the U.S. Supreme Court ruled that assisted suicide is not a fundamental right and that it is out-weighed by the state's interest in preserving life, preventing coerced decisions to give up life, and protecting current standards of medical ethics.[14] Meanwhile, different arms of the federal government are making conflicting statements on the mandate and ability of the Drug Enforcement Agency to sanction doctors who write lethal prescriptions.

The Canadian Supreme Court ruled (1993) in the case of Sue Rodriguez, a forty-two-year-old mother suffering from amyotrophic lateral sclerosis who held that her disease would render her physically unable to take her own life before progressing to the point where she would wish to die. Because others with a hopeless prognosis, miserable existence, but no paralysis are able to kill themselves, she petitioned the court for access to physician-assisted suicide. The majority, in a 5–4 decision, rejected her claim, noting that the Canadian Charter of Rights and Freedoms guarantees liberty in the same sentence that also guarantees rights to life and the security of the person.[15]

The dissenting judges, including the chief justice, argued that the risk of abuse does not necessarily override the principle of liberty and suggested strict guidelines under which assisted suicide could be safely legalized. Patients' competence would have to be certified by both the attending physician and an independent psychiatrist, who must also certify that the patient's decision was not the result of any known coercion. The treating physician and the regional coroner were to attend the suicide, and the enforcement of guidelines was ensured by requiring court approval of each case. These safeguards provide guarantees that criteria 1, 4, and 5 of table 1 are met. The individual court approval clause offers protection against action from unconscious coercion, if only by making the process prohibitively difficult for all but the most motivated patients. The main flaw is in the protection of palliative care; the minority opinion considers sufficient grounds "a terminal state of suffering but for medication," a condition still amenable to palliative therapy. In the wake of the Supreme Court's ruling, euthanasia will remain illegal under Canadian law until Parliament proposes new legislation. The most recent private member's bill trying to revive the issue was defeated in March 1998.

In the face of widespread public support for euthanasia,[16] legislation has been tabled in several Australian jurisdictions. The Northern Territory Rights of the Terminally Ill Act 1995 was intended to legalize euthanasia at the request of competent patients, and to provide procedural safeguards against abuse of human rights resulting from this change.[17] To guard against involuntary euthanasia, this act required the patient to be judged mentally competent by two medical practitioners as well as a psychiatrist, and doctors were required to certify that the patient's decision was free from known coercion. Palliative care was well protected in this legislation: a physician certified in palliative care had to provide the patient with information, and the treating physician could not proceed to euthanasia if any reasonable palliative-care option remained untried. The coroner had to be informed and statistics maintained. Finally, penalties for violations were clear: $10,000 if anyone tried to bribe or similarly influence a doctor, $20,000 or four years' imprisonment for coercing a patient's request, and $10,000 or two years' imprisonment if the physician failed to adhere to the documentation requirements. In March 1997, however, the federal Australian Senate narrowly passed a bill to override the Northern Territory Act, and physician-assisted suicide and active euthanasia are again illegal in all Australian jurisdictions.

Guidelines for Legalized Euthanasia in Canada

I propose a new set of guidelines that, because it involves an ethics committee, differs from any of the models already described. Before legalization of euthanasia in Canada can proceed, however, change must occur on two fronts. First, there must be a comprehensive survey of the prevalence of assisted suicide, voluntary euthanasia, and doctor- or family-initiated euthanasia of incompetent patients, to assess whether subsequent legislation is causing a slippery slope.[18] Second, there must be improved availability of palliative care,[19] so that euthanasia is not used where more suitable and desirable means exist to satisfy the needs of the terminally ill. Meeting this prerequisite requires the design and dissemination of palliative-care standards, a survey to determine whether these standards have been met, and action to ensure the availability of palliative care to all Canadians.

The new regulatory level I propose is a regional euthanasia ethics committee, to ensure that regulations are met and to document each case in a publicly accountable manner. The committee, composed of nine members, would be chaired by a medical ethicist. Physicians on the committee would include a palliative-care specialist, a psychiatrist experienced in dealing with the terminally ill, and, on a rotating basis, a medical specialist relevant to the case in question. There would also be a social service worker, a lawyer, and an appointee from the coroner's office. To ensure accountability, the last two spots would be reserved for lay representatives from pro- and anti-euthanasia non-governmental organizations. Approval of a request would require a two-thirds majority.

To prevent a slippery slope to involuntary euthanasia, requests would only be taken from patients of the legal age of majority, and not by proxy, nor even by advance directives that might suffice for withdrawal of life-sustaining therapy. Competence must be certified by the attending physician and by an independent psychiatrist, who must rule out clinical depression. The physician must be present at the time of death. To screen out patients acting mainly from socially motivated unconscious coercion, the patient (and never the physician or family) must initiate the request. The attending physician must certify that the patient is in an incurable terminal state and, with the psychiatrist, confirm that the patient has reached an independent and firm decision. It is important that the ethics committee understand the patient's motivating circumstances before it permits euthanasia, since its primary mission includes the safeguarding of "the interests of those at risk of attempting suicide for other reasons."[20] To protect palliative care, consultation is obligatory to assess whether there is any correctable pain, depression, or isolation contributing to the request. The ethics committee is bound to reject any application where reasonable palliative-care options remain untried; unbearable suffering despite the best available palliation is a prerequisite for euthanasia.

For the ethics committee to consider a case, it must receive documentation including a standard request form, a witnessed signature for informed consent, and a full case report showing how the patient meets the criteria for competence, free will, and an incurable terminal state with no remaining palliative-care options. Furthermore, the patient must be available by telephone to answer questions from committee members. The coroner's representative would ensure that euthanasia statistics are maintained and made publicly available, along with general facts surrounding approved cases.

Legal provision is made for contracts and insurance, so that the death is treated as though it were caused by the underlying disease. Once the ethics committee's approval comes through, the treating physician is immune from professional or legal sanction for acting on the patient's request. Acting without such approval remains a criminal offence, but since courts have often given suspended sentences to doctors who were trying to act in their patients' best interests, and since inadequate sanction would undermine the ethics committees, violations would bring a minimum six-month suspension of a medical practitioner's licence. Minimum three-month suspensions would be imposed for distorting medical reports to facilitate approval.

This proposal pre-empts less careful legislation pushed forward by populist opinion, or the possibility that courts, in striking down a law against assisted suicide on the merits of one case, will leave a vacuum in regulation. Sober reflection on each case from an emotional distance is retained; an ethics committee would have more experience in this task than would a court. Physicians would know where they stand with regard to the law and their profession, would accept a public responsibility to be the providers of euthanasia, and would be able to conduct research into improved methods. With the requirement for a comprehensive survey of (illegal) euthanasia practices before a law is passed, comparative study can occur to assess whether slippery slopes are developing and to allow guidelines to be modified. The require- ment for good palliative care would create an impetus for its improve- ment rather than its erosion. Allowance is made for the severe, clear cases that cause the most concern, but not for other scenarios. This precaution is consistent with public surveys that show 65 per cent sup- port for allowing euthanasia in cases of terminal patients with severe pain, but only 35 per cent for elderly and disabled patients who feel like a burden, 25 per cent for those with chronic treatment-resistant depression, and 15 per cent for those with chronic ailments who are unhappy with life.[21]

The Canadian Medical Association warns that "consideration should be given to whether any proposed legislation can restrict euthanasia and assisted suicide to the indications intended."[22] With three doctors and a committee to oversee decisions, mistakes in assessment of com- petence become unlikely. The mandatory professional sanctions mean that violations would have to occur in secrecy, as they do already. Follow-up surveys should help assess whether such violations would in- crease once cases are legitimized. Finally, political pressure to relax regulations would be limited because the guidelines are designed to allow euthanasia in the most tragic cases.

Objections may be raised against this proposal's exclusion of incom- petent patients, regardless of whether they leave an advance directive. The cost of holding the line against a slippery slope to involuntary euthanasia means the usual methods for dealing with incompetent patients cannot be accepted. For ethical approval, the patient's compe- tent wishes must be directly expressed to the physician, psychiatrist, palliative-care specialist, and ethics committee. A patient can make a request, while competent, when degeneration is certain and compe- tence may be lost in the future; an approved request could be acted upon weeks later. Withdrawal of all life support remains an option;[23] the argument that this course entails more suffering than euthanasia is of insufficient weight to counter concerns about a slippery slope to involuntary euthanasia.

Finally, this proposal entails the creation of a new bureaucracy, which is cumbersome, costly, and will cause delays. The regulations are burdensome but necessary; euthanasia is a privilege extended by a compassionate society in limited conditions. The cost can be justified if there is enough public will. Opponents of euthanasia fear a slippery slope should they yield any ground; supporters grudgingly propose weak guidelines only after prospective legislation is struck down by courts, since they discount the possibility of a slippery slope and believe liberty overrides all. With this proposal, proponents of euthanasia will find that in obvious cases of intractable suffering, euthanasia is legalized. Opponents get clear legislation now, before courts strike down laws and leave a vacuum in regulation, or before cases become publicized where prosecutors refuse to press charges.

This proposal allows society to provide a compassionate service, mainly through established institutions. It respects the principle of liberty, yet provides safeguards against consequences that compromise the life and liberty of others. It fulfills the "moral obligation to suggest a mechanism for protecting the interests of those at risk of suicide as a result of temporary depression or unhappiness."[24] In placing restrictions on euthanasia, this proposal balances any right there is "to die with dignity" with a responsibility to guard against abuse of the weakest in society.

8 (b) Guidelines for Legalized Euthanasia in Canada: A Rejection of Nielsen's Proposal

The article by Torsten Nielsen, "Guidelines for Legalised Euthanasia in Canada,"[1] can be challenged on many bases, nine of which I will identify here.

First, good ethics depend on good facts. Good ethical and legal "facts" start with primary sources that are up to date and accurate. The 1990 Remmelink study, on which Dr Nielsen relies, was repeated in 1995 with different results in relevant and important respects.[2]

Second, the Australian studies on which Nielsen relies were part of a concurrent effort to support the legalization initiatives that were being considered by Australian state or territorial legislatures, most notably that of the Northern Territory – which did legalize euthanasia. (This legislation was subsequently overridden by the Australian Commonwealth, not merely by the Australian Parliamentary Senate, as Nielsen states.) The findings in several of these articles, however, can be challenged. For instance, health-care professionals, particularly physicians, who were asked whether they had participated in euthanasia might wrongly have thought they had done so. They might have thought they had carried out euthanasia if they had accepted refusals of treatment from their patients' or their patients' legal representatives which resulted in death when withdrawn; or if they had given treatment that was needed to relieve pain but could have shortened life. They might have responded to the survey accordingly. Neither situation, though, involves euthanasia.

Third, in commenting on the Royal Dutch Medical Association's (RDMA) guidelines, Nielsen cites as his authority the work of two of Australia's most well-known "euthanasia advocates," academics Helga Kuhse and Peter Singer. It is probably not surprising, therefore, that Nielsen fails to mention that the reason the RDMA advocated these guidelines – to quote Nielsen, "encouraging assisted suicide instead of doctor-perpetrated euthanasia where possible" – was their concern about the harmful emotional impact on physicians who were carrying out euthanasia.

Fourth, Nielsen's analysis of *Rodriguez*[3] could be misleading. It is impossible to examine each of the complex and legally nuanced judgments of this case here, but Nielsen makes fundamental errors such as referring to the dissenting judges as though there was one dissenting judgment in which they all concurred. In fact, there were three dissenting judgments that differed markedly in their reasoning. And the judges did not, as Nielsen states they did, rely on the constitutional right to liberty. Rather, they relied on the right to security of the person – the right to decide for oneself what should happen to one's body.

Fifth, Nielsen's suggestion for "regional euthanasia ethics committees," which would be required to approve euthanasia in individual cases before it could be carried out, is reminiscent of the previous requirement in section 251 of the Canadian Criminal Code for therapeutic-abortion committees. To comply with the law, all abortions had to be approved by committees. It was this requirement that was struck down by the Supreme Court of Canada in *Morgentaler*[4] on the basis that it interfered with a woman's right to security of her person as protected in section 7 of the Canadian Charter of Rights and Freedoms. (The Supreme Court judges who ruled in this way did so on the basis that the Criminal Code provision was arbitrary in its operation, and situations could arise where a woman needed an abortion to protect her life or health and a committee would be inaccessible or refuse its approval.) If, as Nielsen suggests, the right to euthanasia is also based on liberty and security of the person (autonomy), then interference with these latter rights by a committee such as he proposes would likely be constitutionally invalid for the same reason.

Moreover, the basis of Chief Justice Lamer's dissenting decision in *Rodriguez*, on which Nielsen seems partly to base his suggestion for euthanasia ethics committees, was that Sue Rodriguez was a physically handicapped person who could not commit suicide without aid. Thus, Chief Justice Lamer held, the Criminal Code prohibition on providing assistance in suicide wrongfully discriminated against her as a disabled person and, consequently, was constitutionally invalid pursuant to section 15 of the Canadian Charter. The same reasoning would likely apply to any law that required dying patients to "be available by telephone to answer questions from committee members" before they could have access to euthanasia. What proportion of dying people would be well enough to comply?

Sixth, there is a fundamental inconsistency in Nielsen's approach. He relies on authorities that advocate the right to euthanasia and physician-assisted suicide as flowing from people's rights to liberty, autonomy, and self-determination; yet, at the same time, he advocates a system that would leave the ultimate decision about euthanasia in the hands of someone other than the person who wants it. One of the analytical difficulties for people who support euthanasia is that, although they argue that it is based on a right to personal autonomy, the need to limit this right is unavoidable.

For instance, if a heart-broken sixteen year old whose first love affair has just ended wants to commit suicide, nobody thinks that she should be allowed to do so – and certainly not that she should be assisted in carrying out her wishes. Yet her decision to commit suicide is an exercise of her right to autonomy. When asked how that limitation could be justified, Professor Judith Jarvis-Thompson (a philosopher who signed the brief that was presented to the United States Supreme Court in the case that Nielsen refers to, *Vacco* v. *Quill*[5]) argued that if people would probably be grateful later on that you had prevented them from committing suicide, you would be justified in interfering with their exercise of autonomy. This shows that whether we are pro-euthanasia or anti-euthanasia, we will all limit people's right to autonomy. Consequently, the difference between the pro-euthanasia and anti-euthanasia stances on autonomy is where the line should be drawn, not, as is argued by many who support the legalization of euthanasia, that respect for personal autonomy should be more or less absolute (that is almost absolute), with respect to decisions about physician-assisted suicide or euthanasia.

Seventh, Nielsen's suggestion of euthanasia-ethics committees that would be available across Canada is reminiscent of Dr Jack Kevorkian's proposal for regional suicide centres throughout the United States. Kevorkian added to his proposal a recommendation for the development of a new medical speciality – obiatry. Obiatrists would be physicians specially trained to carry out euthanasia.

Eighth, Nielsen seems to misunderstand the basis on which many people who oppose euthanasia actually do so. It is not simply because they "fear a slippery slope should they yield any ground" and, thus, would accept a scheme under which euthanasia would be better regulated than it is, because, he alleges, it is being carried out secretly. Many people who are against euthanasia believe that it is wrong to kill another human being; to legalize such killing, especially to institutionalize it in the medical profession, is to set destructive values for our society

Finally, I note the language that Nielsen uses. He says, for example, that his "proposal allows society to provide a compassionate service." Although it is true that people advocating euthanasia are doing so for compassionate reasons, we need to be aware of how our choice of language influences our decisions as to what we see as ethically acceptable.[6] Putting a medical cloak on euthanasia – for instance, having a physician carry it out and describing it as the final act of good palliative care, and associating it with compassionate motives of which we all approve – can cause us to lose sensitivity to the fact that, at its base, it involves one person (usually a member of the healing profession of medicine) killing another person who has sought care from that healer.

This text was sent to the author of the article, and his reply follows.

---

8 (c) Guidelines for Legalized Euthanasia in Canada: A Response to Somerville's Rejection

TORSTEN O. NIELSEN

Dr Somerville's "Point of View" article raises several issues, perhaps the most important of which are the constitutionality of a euthanasia-committee approach, the underlying reasons motivating those who oppose euthanasia, and the fundamental conflicts inherent in arguments based on patients' autonomy.

First, however, I am compelled to respond to Somerville's attacks on my sources, interpretations, and choice of language. Although her last paragraph makes it seem as though I describe euthanasia as "the final act of good palliative care," at no point do these words appear in my article.

I was aware of the 1995 sequel to the Remmelink study on euthanasia in the Netherlands,[1] but reference to it was deleted for the sake of brevity. Somerville holds, without elaborating, that it had "different results in relevant and important respects," whereas I agree with the editors of the *New England Journal of Medicine* that this study "shows that practices in 1995 were not much different from those in 1990."[2] Somerville may be referring to a moderate increase in voluntary euthanasia cases, falling within the Dutch guidelines (partially explained by changing demographics). Regardless, the conclusion that the three most worrisome slippery-slope arguments against legalized euthanasia are manifesting themselves in Holland remains unchanged.

As for the minority opinion in the *Rodriguez* case, while two primary lines of reasoning (unfair discrimination and unwarranted limitation of patients' autonomy) are invoked by four dissenting justices,[3] their three written opinions overlap, each discussing both these issues. All reach the same conclusion in favour of Ms Rodriguez's application for assisted suicide and its constitutionality in some circumstances.

Somerville draws an analogy between the proposed regional euthanasia committees and the therapeutic abortion committees found to be unconstitutional in the *Morgentaler* case. Although this approach represented a similar attempt at an ethical compromise, embryos lack legal standing and, consequently, the embryo's rights could not justify, in law, limits on a woman's autonomy. In contrast, the law recognizes the rights of persons who have become incapacitated, and the protection of these rights has already frequently been used as a legal justification for limiting patients' autonomy in euthanasia requests, potentially making euthanasia committees constitutionally valid. Another way around this problem is the implementation of guidelines and enforcement on a professional level. If doctors agree on a formal framework under which euthanasia is acceptable, recent history suggests that no one would be prosecuted if adhering to specific and reasonable medical guidelines.

Somerville argues that, in addition to concerns about a slippery slope, most who reject euthanasia are motivated by a fundamental belief that medicalized killing is inherently wrong. I agree that this is a common belief among those opposed to euthanasia, and I respect those who consistently apply such a value system. This moral absolute, however, is not held by all, and imposing a euthanasia ban on those with different values requires justification by other means, the most powerful of which are the slippery-slope arguments I tried to confront.

My proposal does not hold personal autonomy to be "more or less absolute," and by invoking patients' liberty as a justification for euthanasia in some circumstances, yet limiting it with strict guidelines, I am accused of "a fundamental inconsistency." Others would call it striking a balance. Both the ban on medical killing advocated by Somerville, and the pure libertarian approach with which she takes issue, hold the advantage of consistency (which, to lawyers, may be more important than anything else). Nevertheless, both regimes lead to unnecessary suffering by some, and preventing such suffering is worth the cost of burying the goal of consistency in a more complicated regime. There is a way to allow limited exceptions to the bans on assisted suicide and medicalized killing that will help in these cases of misery and suffering, with minimal costs to society.

8 (d) Guidelines for Legalized Euthanasia in Canada: A Response to Nielsen's Response

Even if it is true that the 1995 Remmelink study "shows that practices in 1995 are not much different from those in 1990," it is relevant to know that fact. But the 1995 study also provides additional important information about the practice of euthanasia in the Netherlands and, as outlined in chapter 7, has been the focus of in-depth and broad-based discussion and disagreement. The later study provides evidence of serious abuses of euthanasia, such as carrying it out on incompetent people and on competent people without obtaining their consent to its being administered to them.

Second, Nielsen is incorrect that the four dissenting judges in the *Rodriguez* case all discussed wrongful (what he calls unfair) discrimination. On the contrary, two of the dissenting judges, Madame Justice L'Heureux-Dubé and Madame Justice McLachlin (as she then was), ruled expressly that section 15 of the Charter – the anti-discrimination provision – had no application in that case. Their reasons were that the case was not about discrimination and that to treat it as such could deflect the equality jurisprudence relating to section 15 from the true focus of that section.

Third, in the *Morgentaler* case, the majority in the Supreme Court of Canada (in a plurality of judgments) held that the therapeutic abortion committees established under the Criminal Code were unconstitutional because they infringed on a woman's right to security of her person under section 7 of the Canadian Charter of Rights and Freedoms. A woman could need an abortion to preserve her life or health and might be unable to obtain it legally because she did not have access to a therapeutic abortion committee. The court's ruling that the fetus had no legal rights under the Charter was only indirectly relevant to its ruling regarding the unconstitutionality of these therapeutic abortion committees. It meant that the court did not have to balance any rights of the fetus against the woman's right to security of her person in reaching its conclusion to uphold her right. It is puzzling, therefore, that Nielsen bases his argument for the constitutional validity of the euthanasia committees he proposes on a distinction between "embryos" (fetuses) having no constitutional rights and people wanting euthanasia having such rights. In the cases of both abortion and euthanasia, the persons with constitutional rights – the pregnant woman or the dying person – would be the ones challenging the constitutional validity of needing a committee's approval before they may exercise their right to decide for themselves (assuming, for the sake of discussion, that such a right exists in both cases) to undergo the relevant procedure. It was just such a requirement that was held to be constitutionally invalid in the *Morgentaler* case and, as I previously suggested, for the same reasons could be invalid with respect to the proposed euthanasia committees.

Fourth, Nielsen fails to understand that "doctors agree[ing] on a framework under which euthanasia is acceptable" does not of itself set a legal standard. Courts have been at pains to point out that even if all members of the medical profession agree to a certain standard, this does not bind the court to accepting that standard.

Finally, with or without the safeguards that Nielsen suggests, legally authorizing "assisted suicide and medicalized killing" could never be implemented, as he claims, with "minimal costs to society."

9 Executing Euthanasia: A Review Essay

The book called *Physician-Assisted Death*[1], edited by James M. Humber, Robert F. Almeder, and Gregg A. Kasting, would be more accurately entitled "The Case for Physician-Assisted Death." And even that title could be questioned because the term "physician-assisted death" can be misleading. We all hope for physician assistance, in the sense of humane medical care, when we are dying. The term, however, has become a euphemism for physician-assisted suicide and euthanasia, the topics dealt with in this book. The title might have reflected, as well, that the text is almost exclusively confined to a discussion of these topics in a United States context.

The book begins with a review of the literature on doctors' attitudes and experiences with physician-assisted death. This overview is followed by chapters on the non-necessity of euthanasia, the constitutionality of the right to die, and the case for legalizing both physician-assisted suicide and euthanasia for "competent patients suffering from terminal illnesses who autonomously choose to end their lives."[2] By far the best chapter in the book, on the ethics of physician-assisted suicide, is by David Thomasma. A concluding chapter – the only one that might possibly have an anti-euthanasia stance – analyses the bizarre case of Thomas Donaldson, who applied to a court for an order to permit him to be assisted with cryogenic suspension as a way to end his "present living" so that he could be revived at a later date. That case adds little to the euthanasia debate.

There is a great deal to be said about the arguments and analyses in this book, but only a few randomly chosen examples can be mentioned here. It was incorrect to say at the time the book was published, as it is in the preface, that "the Netherlands passed a law permitting physician-assisted death." (This same mistake is repeated by Gregg Kasting on page 37.) Rather, at that time in the Netherlands, if some conditions were complied with – in particular, reporting requirements – physicians who carried out euthanasia were not prosecuted. Nevertheless, Dutch criminal law, like that of other jurisdictions, does prohibit one person from killing another, although this prohibition no longer applies to a physician carrying out euthanasia in compliance with the requirements of the new Dutch legislation authorizing it.[3] The previous distinction between legalization and non-prosecution of euthanasia, which the new legislation has abolished, was important. There is a difference in the impact on symbolism and, probably, on societal values between legalizing euthanasia and not prosecuting it.[4] There can be a difference in practice, too. Under Dutch law, prior to the new legislation, prosecution for homicide for carrying out euthanasia had occurred.[5] Although such prosecutions are still possible under the new legislation for euthanasia carried out other than in accordance with the act's requirements, it remains to be seen whether they will result.

Diane Meier believes that the morality of euthanasia hinges on whether or not someone is competent and actually requests euthanasia: "Involuntary euthanasia – the act of killing someone without his or her explicit request – is clearly immoral and is fundamentally different from the problem raised by patients with intact mental capacity who request assistance in dying."[6]

Not all those who advocate euthanasia would agree with limiting its availability to competent people; and many of those who oppose euthanasia would not agree that its morality and ethical applicability hinges on the consent of a competent person. Despite opposition to making euthanasia available to incompetent people, Meier's justifications for euthanasia include "that death is in the best interest of the patient ... and the physician's compassionate obligation to relieve suffering."[7] These justifications would apply equally to incompetent people. Consequently, if euthanasia were to be legalized, compelling cases would probably be argued for its being made available to some incompetent people.

Kasting addresses the argument that euthanasia is unnecessary. He challenges the claim "that pain is manageable in 'virtually all,' or at least with 'most' patients with terminal illness"[8] and concludes that "one may still argue that voluntary euthanasia and assisted suicide should remain impermissible for other reasons, but the argument that these acts are unnecessary simply does not hold up."[9]

In reaching this conclusion, Kasting rejects total sedation as an option. He would require, for a treatment to be judged effective in relieving pain and suffering, that "the patients' symptoms truly can be relieved, and are not merely blotted out by drug-induced somnolence or coma."[10] He does not expound further on why he finds total sedation unacceptable. In contrast, the Special Senate Committee on Euthanasia and Assisted Suicide of the Parliament of Canada recommended the development of guidelines to govern the administration of total sedation.[11] Although we might find the idea of total sedation disturbing, we should consider whether it is preferable to euthanasia for terminally ill people experiencing severe, otherwise unrelievable, pain and suffering. Both interventions render patients unaware – they are either unconscious or dead – and, in this sense, the results do not differ. The harmful impact of euthanasia on societal values and symbols is avoided, however, if total sedation is used instead.

Some people will condemn this distinction as sophistry and argue that euthanasia is the approach that manifests greater integrity and honesty. Moreover, they find the idea of rendering patients unconscious while they die much more morally, ethically, and emotionally disturbing than euthanasia. But we should stress the importance of preserving important symbols and values, something we fail at times to do. Total sedation, unlike euthanasia, makes this preservation possible without denying the patient's right to treatment for the relief of pain in those rare cases where it is the only option other than euthanasia.

Kasting states also "that to 'relieve' a symptom – be it pain, dyspnea, or whatever – the patient's quality of life must be improved, not merely obliterated."[12] This definition of relief can be challenged, especially if, as is the case here, it is proposed as an argument against total sedation and for euthanasia. Euthanasia involves the obliteration of life itself. Consequently, it eliminates the question of quality. The relation between quality of life and euthanasia, too, merits careful investigation. As I say elsewhere, the concept of quality of life was initially formulated as a basis on which to found claims to a minimally adequate standard of health care – that is, a right to the health-care resources needed for a minimally adequate quality of life. The concept has been used more recently to achieve the opposite. This result occurs if people are denied access to health-care resources on the grounds that their quality of life is so low that the expenditure is not believed to be merited.[13]

In a chapter entitled "The Constitutionality of Elective and Physician-Assisted Death," Steven Neely argues that the "specific right of the individual to control her/his own destiny ... lies at the foundation of democracy."[14] He notes that the courts have "specifically declined to invoke constitutional privacy"[15] as the basis for "right to die" decisions but have used the narrower liberty interest. This approach has enabled courts to avoid the positive-autonomy aspects of the right to privacy;

that is, they have eschewed privacy in the sense of "rights to" something – euthanasia, for instance, or assistance in committing suicide – that must be provided if the right to privacy is to be respected. In contrast, the liberty interest establishes "rights against" or a "freedom from." An example would be the right against the imposition of treatment that someone refuses.

Neely argues that the right of privacy should be applied to protect "the decision whether or not to continue living"[16] because this decision is "profoundly personal and relate[s] … integrally to the basic freedom of the individual to shape and define her/his own destiny."[17] According to him, this decision is a personal choice that will harm no one else. Again, as is frequently the case with advocates of euthanasia, Neely fails to consider the impact at the societal level.[18] To legalize euthanasia would be to change what is arguably the most fundamental norm on which our society is based – that we must not kill each other – to one that, in some circumstances, we may.[19] As I point out in another chapter of this book, there is some difficulty with using this argument against the legalization of euthanasia in jurisdictions that have legalized capital punishment. Ironically, some of those most in favour of capital punishment – for example, the "far right" – are most opposed to euthanasia. If we examine the legally recognized exceptions to the prohibition on killing – self-defence, capital punishment, and just war – their availability as a justification depends in all cases, at least in theory, on the killing being necessary to protect the lives of those who would otherwise be innocent victims. In contrast with these situations, the unique feature of euthanasia is that its justification is not based on the belief that killing is necessary to protect lives.

Neely argues as well for the recognition of "suicide as a fundamental human right under the [United States] constitution."[20] The latter protects a right to life; in effect, he argues, it protects a right to death, too (which, it should be noted, is more extensive than a right to die). Neely does not consider some of the implications of a right to suicide. There would be a correlative duty on persons in emergency rooms, for example, not to treat those who were admitted after attempting suicide. That would be to interfere with their exercise of this right.

As is true for many other authors who promote euthanasia,[21] Neely characterizes recognition by the courts of the right to refuse medical treatment as a "right to die" and argues that, once this right is recognized, the way in which death is brought about is morally and ethically irrelevant; therefore, he argues, it ought to be legally irrelevant. Following this line of reasoning, recognition of the ethical and legal acceptability of the right to refuse treatment implies recognition of the ethical and legal acceptability of physician-assisted suicide and euthanasia. In other words, intentionally shortening life is seen as the moral and ethical equivalent of not prolonging life after a refusal of treatment and, it is argued, all of these actions should be treated in the same way by the law.

The choice of language is crucial not only to the formulation of arguments for and against euthanasia but also to persuasiveness. Compare Neely's "sanctity of personal choice"[22] with "sanctity of life" (used by those who oppose euthanasia). Or consider Neely's promotion of the acceptability and benefits of euthanasia in the following passage: "Dr. Jack Kevorkian has convincingly argued that medicine should recognize a new speciality designed to derive human benefit from death and dying." Obitiatrists "could accordingly lend a comforting hand to those slipping into death, and extract knowledge from the dying to help those left behind ... Planned death would also offer the possible benefits of organ and tissue donation as well as advances in medical research."[23] Whether or not Neely achieves his aim of making the case for euthanasia depends on the reader's reaction to these propositions.

Neely's statement is horribly resonant with the current concern over the sale, by China, of organs from executed criminals – the most extreme example of a "planned death."[24] The donation of organs by those whose deaths are *unplanned* is an act of a different kind from that suggested by Neely. The only analogy that comes to mind is a comparison between surrogate motherhood and an unplanned pregnancy that results in an adoption. But even though surrogate motherhood – planned motherhood for the purpose of giving up children – is ethically and morally contentious, these issues are of a different order and of much less serious concern than the possible scenarios arising from the uses of euthanasia – or at least its advantages – proposed here by Neely.

Likewise, the language of Franklin Miller and John Fletcher, who "recommend legalizing both physician-assisted suicide and physician performed euthanasia for competent patients suffering from terminal illness who autonomously choose to end their lives,"[25] merits consideration. They suggest "careful experiments with prevailing moral policy about when and how to die. Ordinary dying in the United States is no longer a natural event, something that simply happens to us ... '[N]egotiated dying' or 'death by decision' in a clinical context has evolved into the mainstream American way of dying."[26] They speak of "public opinion favouring physician aid in dying ... [as] a favourable sign of the timeliness of moral experimentation."[27] They propose that "strict limits are ethically required where *licensed healers* are responsible for assisting suicide or administering lethal doses of medication. The *medical exit* from life should be open only for competent patients who are dying ... [T]he limitation of permissible euthanasia to voluntary requests of competent, terminally ill patients respects the *right* of patients *not to be killed, except* by their autonomous choice."[28]

This last statement converts the right to life into a right not to be killed. An exception to this right can then be articulated in the same terms as the right to be killed – that is, the right to euthanasia. It is not nearly as easy to formulate an exception to the right to life. I note here references to "licensed healers" instead of "physicians" (presumably the ones to whom reference is made) and to "medical exit," which sounds like *Final Exit*, the title of a self-help suicide text.[29] As I point out on many occasions elsewhere, the use of language on both sides of the euthanasia debate is certainly not neutral, and we should be acutely aware of how our positions are influenced by rhetoric of one kind or another – that is, special language designed to persuade or to change the substance of arguments in often subtle, but sometimes major, ways.[30]

Miller and Fletcher compare safeguarding euthanasia with safeguarding medical research, suggesting that it can be accomplished with a "euthanasia committee."[31] This proposal assumes that euthanasia is, in principle, morally and ethically acceptable and that the issue is simply one of safeguarding its use. One way to promote the acceptance of euthanasia is to normalize it, to make it seem similar to conduct that we find acceptable and uncontroversial. Equating euthanasia with medical research could accomplish this goal by implying that it is morally and ethically equivalent to medical research on human subjects. Both euthanasia and medical research could then be seen simply as special medical acts that require additional safeguards to protect against their misuse and to protect vulnerable people from abuse – which is, in fact, what Miller and Fletcher propose.[32]

I have already said that the best chapter, by far, is by David Thomasma on the ethics of physician-assisted suicide. Although Thomasma favours euthanasia, he presents arguments not only for it but against it. Thomasma points out the dangers of legalized euthanasia to the medical profession and the risks in terms of their impact on physicians' attitudes, values, beliefs, and conduct.[33] As he says, "it is ironic that at the very time the movements towards patients' rights and patient autonomy have sought to curtail physician infringement and control over individuals, society might permit such physicians to have the ultimate power of life and death in their hands."[34] We have recognized that we cannot trust physicians to comply with patients' decisions regarding medical treatment and that decision-making in a medical context should not be left to the discretion of physicians. Legislation to ensure that physicians respect competent patients' refusals of treatment and legislation on informed consent reflect these insights. At the same time, we are considering giving physicians the power to kill their patients. Physicians need a clear line that powerfully manifests to them, their patients, and society that they do not inflict death; both their patients and the public need to know with absolute certainty – and be able to trust – that this is the case. Anything that would blur the line, damage that trust, or make physicians less sensitive to their primary obligations to protect life is unacceptable. Legalizing euthanasia would do all of these things.

An important point made by Thomasma is that there are powerful political forces in the United States on both sides of the euthanasia debate.[35] This is true also in other countries debating euthanasia. Why is that the case? The euthanasia debate might be a surrogate for an even deeper one over which of two conflicting, irreconcilable, world views will inform the emerging paradigm on which societies of the twenty-first century will be based. As I have noted elsewhere, one world view sees us as highly complex, logical, rational beings, but nothing more; this world view supports euthanasia. The other world view, while recognizing the importance of our cognitive functioning, also recognizes that there is a mystery about human life (even if it is only "the mystery of the unknown"). It incorporates a sense of the sacredness of human life (a sense of the sacred that is not necessarily defined in traditionally religious terms). This world view opposes euthanasia.[36]

Inevitably, the euthanasia debate engages some of our deepest feelings and beliefs. Consequently, some aspects of our lives provide useful information to others engaged in the debate. The list of contributors included in *Physician-Assisted Death* should have identified the professional background of each author. That way, readers could have contextualised their arguments.

In the euthanasia debate, it is necessary – and required by honesty – to disclose one's position. As is undoubtedly evident by now, I am against euthanasia. I hold this view principally because of the immense harm that I believe euthanasia would cause to our sense of the mystery of human life and to very important societal values and symbols. Consequently, I disagree with much in *Physician-Assisted Death*, in particular its almost exclusively utilitarian analysis of euthanasia. That approach centres on risks of abuse and whether these risks can be adequately protected against. With the exception of Thomasma's chapter, the question of whether euthanasia is morally and ethically right or wrong is not explored. Again with this exception, the text is largely ahistorical, as though euthanasia were a problem that has arisen for the first time. We need a historical perspective.[37] We need to ask why we are considering legalizing euthanasia now, when none of the conditions usually cited for the necessity and the possibility of euthanasia –

namely, terminally ill people are suffering, they want to die, and we are able to kill them – is new. I propose that the cause is not to be found in the situations of those who seek euthanasia but in the characteristics of secular Western democracies at the turn of the millennium.[38] We need long and deep thinking on the question of whether or not to legalize euthanasia – accompanied by intense and sensitive monitoring of our own feelings about it.

10 Why Aren't Physicians Interested in the Ethics and Law of Euthanasia? A Conference Report

At the Twentieth International Congress of Chemotherapy (in Sydney, Australia in 1997), a session on physician-assisted suicide and euthanasia was included under the ambiguous title, "To Assist or Not to Assist? That Is the Question." As I say elsewhere (for instance, in chapter 7 on "Euthanasia by Confusion"), speaking euphemistically of euthanasia as "physician-assisted death" causes serious confusion. Most of us want the assistance of physicians when we are dying, but that does not necessarily mean that we want physician-assisted suicide or euthanasia. The content of the session was well advertised on site, with a feature article in the congress report of the previous day entitled "The Physician and End-of-Life Issues: A World-wide Dilemma."

Because the conference was held in Australia, the inclusion of euthanasia (a word used here to include physician-assisted suicide), as a topic for discussion, was particularly apropriate. The Northern Territory of Australia, for the first time in the modern world apart from the Nazi regime, had passed legislation, The Rights of the Terminally Ill Act 1995, legalizing euthanasia carried out by physicians. Many people (including physicians) mistakenly believed that euthanasia had been legal in the Netherlands for twenty-five years. In fact, at that time it was still prohibited by Dutch criminal law. Provided that some conditions were complied with, however, Dutch physicians were not prosecuted for carrying out euthanasia. In other words, there was only a *de facto* legalization of euthanasia, not a change in Dutch law; in strict legal theory, the latter was still prohibiting euthanasia. It was only early in 2001 that euthanasia was legalized in the Netherlands. Just three months before the conference, the Australian Commonwealth Parliament passed the Euthanasia Laws Act 1997 (Cwth) overriding the Northern Territory legislation. But the controversy was heated at that time, as it still is, both in Australia and elsewhere – especially in the United States and Canada.

There were over 4,000 registrants at the conference, of whom approximately thirty attended the "euthanasia session" in an auditorium with a capacity of at least 2,000 people. We were told by a member of the conference's organizing committee that there had been dissension over whether to include a session on end-of-life issues, especially euthanasia. Could the committee have worried that including euthanasia on the program of a conference devoted to chemotherapy would link euthanasia with chemotherapy, and that this association might cause fear on the part of those who need chemotherapy and, perhaps as a result, a refusal of this treatment? If the committee worried that people would not be interested in the topic, the attendance numbers proved them correct. But that lack of interest raises serious questions of another kind.

Euthanasia is a major medical-ethical-legal issue in the countries of many attending the conference. Many physicians present – especially those involved in oncology and the care of patients with AIDS – face the difficult problems presented by end-of-life decision-making in their daily work. Why were they not sufficiently interested to attend the session? Why were they not interested in at least the ethical and legal aspects of pain-relief treatment that could or even would shorten life? Were they unaware of current debates? Did they believe, in most cases incorrectly,[1] that they had the required knowledge? Did they not care about not knowing? Did they believe that this was not a necessary or legitimate part of their area of medical expertise? Or did they have "euthanasia fatigue," "euthanasia burn out"? Was their absence a warning that many physicians, who should know how to care for and treat dying patients, are tragically and wrongfully ignorant about palliative medicine – including pain-relief treatment – and the ethical and legal issues associated with it? If so, this is a frightening scenario for all of us. We will place our trust in these physicians, after all, at the most vulnerable stage of our lives – when we are dying.

We should examine the impact that legalizing euthanasia would have on medical professionals too and on medicine itself (see chapter 6, "Legalising Euthanasia: Why Now?"). Protection of the ethos and ethics of medicine is important not only for its own sake but because – especially, again, in postmodern, secular, Western democracies – medicine is a very important value-carrying institution for society as a whole. Harm to medicine harms society. Questions raised in this context include the following: What would be the effect on medical students and physicians-in-training of role models who carry out euthanasia? Would medical students be taught how to perform euthanasia? Why are they, on average, receiving very little teaching about pain-relief treatment and often no introduction to palliative medicine? Dealing with pain and terminally ill people will, inevitably, be a situation faced by all physicians. Our best intentions to "do good" in theorizing about pain-relief treatment will be useless unless we can persuade physicians that, in practice, they have much to learn in this respect. If the Sydney conference is truly a warning sign about physicians' attitudes to end-of-life decision-making about medical treatment, especially pain-relief treatment and euthanasia – they do not want to hear or learn about these matters – it is grounds for genuine concern.

PART THREE

Untreated Pain and Euthanasia

11 Pain and Suffering at Interfaces of Medicine and Law[1]

Traditionally, consideration of "pain and suffering" by the law has been as a specific basis for recovery of damages under the general rubric of awards of damages for non-pecuniary loss. It is from this traditional perspective, the subject of the first part of this chapter, that a wider exploration of the law's response to pain and suffering will be opened up. The second part deals with a more controversial, though by no means novel, problem – that of legal liability arising in relation to pain-relief treatment. Liability can be both civil and criminal. It can concern the contrasting situations of either the unreasonable failure to relieve pain or the relief of pain when that action might entail the shortening of life. The third part moves into the territory behind law and medicine in search of a goal common to both. This goal, I suggest, is the relief of suffering. I hope to show that some legal mechanisms, such as the doctrine of informed consent, will, like many medical treatments, play a role in reducing suffering.

The connecting theme among the three parts of this text can be described in another way, too. Each part involves two considerations: questions raised by honouring or not honouring the value of "quality of life," and the range of actual and potential responses of the law to these situations. In short, one way of describing traditional awards of damages for "pain and suffering" (discussed in the first part) is as compensation for reduction in the plaintiff's quality of life. Legal liability for negligent failure to relieve pain (discussed in the second part) could be established by proving failure to take reasonable care in offering necessary pain-relief treatment either to improve quality of life or to prevent avoidable deterioration. Here, I address the question of whether quality of life can ever be so poor, owing to pain, that life-shortening measures should be allowed. The third part involves an example of the way in which the law could operate as a mechanism to reduce suffering – that is, as a mechanism to maintain or improve quality of life.

Before pursuing this discussion, we should consider whether there is any distinction between the concepts of pain and suffering. The two words are often used interchangeably, especially in relation to psychological pain, whether connected with physical pain or not. The *Oxford English Dictionary* supports that usage. But there might be analytical advantages of greater certainty and precision if the word "pain" is used for physical sensations and "suffering" for psychological and broader phenomena. Suffering would include, but would not be limited to, both purely mental pain and the psychological aspects of experiencing physical pain. People can be said to experience suffering when they perceive themselves as threatened with either loss of control or disintegration of their very person.[2] Furthermore, all people faced with these situations suffer, although the intensity differs and depends on the presence of inherent or acquired coping mechanisms. Such mechanisms are intrinsic and can also be extrinsic. For example, while much of the suffering, in the sense defined, of a high-level quadriplegic person dependent on a life-support system cannot be alleviated, some suffering-reduction mechanisms may be available. Providing a switch-off button, which the person can use to arrest the system, may reduce the person's suffering, even if the button is never used, because it allows the person to control whether he or she continues living.[3]

It is interesting to consider whether the law distinguishes between pain and suffering. These words have always been used conjunctively – for instance, in describing an award of damages for non-pecuniary loss – without distinguishing between them or abandoning either of them. It could be argued, therefore, on the basis of the usual legal rules of construction, that the use of both words, rather than just one or the other, is not redundant. There is some distinction, consequently, at least for legal purposes.[4]

NON-PECUNIARY LOSS: DAMAGES FOR PAIN AND SUFFERING

I will not pursue here the question of what type of injury or combination of injuries constitutes damage for the purposes of tort law,[5] so as to give rise to a cause of action in tort. I will assume that the injury giving rise to non-pecuniary loss is compensable and will explore how the law assesses the amount of these damages. This area is controversial and difficult for many jurisdictions, where not all the problems have yet been resolved. The case law and doctrine on this topic manifest, at best, and only in recent times, competing organizing and informing principles as to how the amount of damages for non-pecuniary loss ought to be assessed. At worst, and more commonly in the past, no principles have been recognized or applied; the task of assessing damages is abandoned, more or less entirely, to the exercise of discretion on the part of judges. With this situation in mind, readers might consider whether the concept of quality of life could function as a possible unifying and organizing principle underlying all the approaches taken to the recognition and quantification of damages for non-pecuniary loss – including pain and suffering. The concept of quantity of life, too, is relevant in assessing these damages, but plays a less important role; it would function only when reduction of life span, rather than just pain and suffering, is a factor. But the two concepts, quality of life and quantity of life, can be directly connected. To the extent that perception of a curtailed quantity of life causes present emotional suffering, it is about the quality of life as well. The question of how to assess the damages to be awarded for non-pecuniary loss then becomes two other questions: how are loss of quality and quantity of life to be assessed, and on what basis are they to be compensated?

Damages for non-pecuniary loss tend to be awarded under such headings as "pain and suffering," "loss of amenities of life," "loss of enjoyment of life,"[6] and "loss of expectation of life."[7] Categories such as "inconvenience" and "aesthetic prejudice" can either be considered separate headings[8] or be included under a more general rubric such as "pain and suffering."[9] One difficulty in making awards of damages under these headings is their overlap. For example, under "loss of expectation of life," a court might award an amount for the objective loss suffered when normal life expectancy is shortened. But it might award damages also for subjective awareness of that loss under the heading of damages for "pain and suffering."

Some jurisdictions might treat these headings simply as guides to the exercise of a court's general discretion in assessing and awarding damages for non-pecuniary loss; others might regard them as definitive and exclusive. In some of these jurisdictions the courts have established, by judicial "fiat," limits on the amount that may be awarded under headings such as "loss of expectation of life."[10] In other jurisdictions, courts might place limits on the total sum that may be awarded for non-pecuniary loss as a whole. For example, the Supreme Court of Canada has ruled that, except in very unusual circumstances, the maximum awarded must not exceed $100,000, adjusted for inflation.[11]

All these considerations can be summed up in a few questions. Are damages for non-pecuniary loss potentially available in a jurisdiction? If so, should there be any maximum amount that may be awarded? If the response to the first question is positive, regardless of the response to the second, another question arises: On what basis are these damages to be assessed?

It is impossible to compensate for non-pecuniary loss in the sense of achieving *restitutio in integrum* because, unlike pecuniary loss, this type of damage is not directly translatable into monetary terms. These damages can be regarded as not really compensatory, in fact, because "there is no medium of exchange for happiness. There is no market for expectation of life. The monetary evaluation of non-pecuniary losses is a philosophical and policy exercise more than a legal or logical one."[12] However, some basis must be established for estimating the amount. It is possible to take either a subjective or an objective approach. And it is possible to take either different approaches in relation to different headings of non-pecuniary loss or one overall approach. In the former case, damages for pain and suffering could be assessed on a subjective basis, and those for loss of amenities of life on an objective one. With that approach, the amount awarded for pain and suffering could be calculated from the point of view of what amount is needed over and above what would be awarded to a reasonable plaintiff for loss of amenities to compensate this particular plaintiff properly for "out-of-the-norm" pain and suffering.[13]

Whether assessment is in relation to a subcategory of loss or to overall damages, three fundamental approaches have been suggested: the functional approach, the conceptual approach, and the personal approach.[14] They reflect three different bases for the assessment of damages for non-pecuniary loss (and vary in their objective and subjective elements, or their combination of these elements, and, consequently, may be regarded as cutting across the objective/subjective analysis.

Using the *functional approach*, a court assesses damages by estimating what it would cost to provide the injured person with "a reasonable solace for his misfortunes."[15] In other words, what is the cost of a pleasure to substitute for the plaintiff's lost pleasures or to counterbalance the pain and suffering endured and to be endured? For example, someone who previously enjoyed physical activities, but whose injuries now prevent participation in sport, may be awarded the amount it would cost to install an expensive sound system at home if this alternative would provide a substitute pleasure.

Using the *conceptual approach*, damages for non-pecuniary loss are estimated on the objective basis of what a reasonable person's reaction to the loss would be in terms of pain and suffering experienced. This amount of pain and suffering would then be translated into the amount of monetary compensation awarded to the plaintiff. This approach values each heading of non-pecuniary loss – for example, freedom from pain and suffering – as a personal asset of equal value to all people. In other words, a "proprietary right" or property type basis is used to assess damages, which are awarded for injury to this objective right.[16] The conceptual approach leaves out of the assessment any consideration of the claimant's hypersensitivity or non-sensitivity to a particular situation in terms of pain and suffering. An extreme reaction in terms of mental suffering to facial scarring would not give rise to a larger award of damages, for example, but neither would the plaintiff's unawareness of loss reduce damages.

The *personal approach*, in comparison, means that a court takes into account the plaintiff's subjective reaction to loss and pain and suffering. It tries to estimate in monetary terms what that pain and suffering merit as damages for "past, present and future loss of pleasure and happiness."[17]

In legal systems with neither a global limit on the amount of damages that can be awarded for non-pecuniary loss nor individual limits on any subcategory of these damages, the amount of compensation given is entirely at the discretion of the court. The greater flexibility this discretion confers means that the choice of basis for the assessment of damages might be less important than in systems using a fixed limit. This can be true because difficulties arise in systems where there is a global limit on damages for non-pecuniary loss, as in the common law Canadian provinces. Should the maximum be reserved for the most severe cases of loss, and other cases judged in relation to these and a proportionate amount awarded? Or, if the loss merits the full award, even though it is not the most severe that could be envisaged, should the maximum be given? This difficulty is particularly severe when an objective, conceptual basis for assessing damages is adopted. With a functional or a more subjective approach, it is easier to justify awards of the maximum for pain and suffering arising from apparently less severe physical injuries.[18] Lesser awards for objectively more serious injuries are also possible under such approaches. This is true when a functional approach is used because the cost of an appropriate substitute function is not directly related to the seriousness of the injury.

The Ontario case of *Mulroy* v. *Aqua Scene et al.*[19] is interesting because it illustrates the dilemma of how to assess a plaintiff's subjective reaction. The plaintiff was injured in a motor-vehicle accident with the defendant, who admitted liability. The trial judge appeared to hold that the plaintiff's pain and suffering due to facial scarring was, in fact, more severe than the plaintiff was overtly admitting and awarded damages accordingly. Alternatively, the judge might have been assessing damages on the basis of what a reasonable man's reaction would have been in terms of pain and suffering. The Court of Appeal of Ontario cut down the award. It held that "reading between the lines" was not allowed; the award for non-pecuniary loss "must bear a relationship to the evidence given as to the present realities and future possibilities"[20] concerning pain and suffering. Furthermore, the amount was not to be determined on the basis that the global limit on damages for non-pecuniary loss "set a scale or tariff against which all claims … involving injuries of a lesser nature are to be measured."[21] What the court means, I suggest, is that damages for non-pecuniary loss are not to be assessed objectively, simply in relation to the seriousness of the plaintiff's physical injury in comparison with that of the plaintiffs in the Supreme Court cases that established the global limit on damages for non-pecuniary loss. Rather, the assessment must be subjectively based "to meet the specific circumstances of the individual cases."[22]

Alternatively, the Ontario Court of Appeal might be indicating that the Supreme Court's limit on damages is simply a cut-off point, affecting only the maximum amount that can be recovered for non-pecuniary loss and not the assessment of these damages. According to this approach, the maximum amount could be recovered for loss that was not of the most serious degree.[23] Finally, the Court of Appeal of Ontario held that there should not be large differences "in awards to individuals who do not differ greatly in their age, sex or personal characteristics and reactions."[24] With respect, it might not always be easy to apply these rules simultaneously. There might be problems in deciding what degree of subjectivity or objectivity (or combination of these) is to be used in assessing damages for non-pecuniary loss. In both the functional and subjective approaches, moreover, damages are assessed from subjective standpoints – but from different ones. In the subjective approach (as in the conceptual approach), a monetary value is attached to the plaintiff's pain and suffering. In the functional approach, a subjective assessment is made as to what would function as a substitute pleasure, and its cost is awarded (provided it is not higher than the upper limit). Because subjective assessments are involved in both the subjective and the functional approaches, it might occasionally be difficult to identify which one a court is using.

In summary, it is often difficult to predict what a court will do with regard to awarding maximum damages for non-pecuniary loss in a "fixed total" system. Likewise, it might be difficult to ascertain the basis that a court has used in assessing the amount of non-pecuniary damages to be awarded. It is not uncommon to find all three approaches – functional, conceptual, and personal – being cumulatively considered in arriving at a final assessment.

Finally, the relation between pecuniary and non-pecuniary loss should be considered. A relevant question in this respect is whether damages for non-pecuniary loss fulfill a function other than their immediately apparent and overtly proclaimed one. Because of highly unstable economic circumstances in many countries, which can include unprecedented rates of inflation, it is becoming increasingly obvious that awards for pecuniary loss (past and future losses that can be translated directly into economic terms) prove inadequate when they purport to cover any long-term situation. It has been suggested that damages for non-pecuniary loss are one way of compensating for the inadequacy of pecuniary damages. For this reason, it is inappropriate to set a ceiling on the global amount.[25] A valid challenge to this argument is that the remedy is not to allow large or unlimited awards for non-pecuniary loss but, rather, to modify the assessment of pecuniary loss, making it more appropriate to real compensation needs. This approach would require modifying the system to allow any assessment to be continually updated to reflect true loss as it continues over a lifetime. The distinction between injury and loss is relevant in this context. The latter is compensated by both pecuniary and non-pecuniary damages. The injury does not change; the loss might. But even when the possibility of change and the entailed problems are disregarded, it is much more difficult to assess loss than injury – particularly when doing so involves projection into the future. Modifications that might be required could include abandoning lump-sum awards and substituting structured settlements such as periodic payments.[26]

The relation between awards for pecuniary and non-pecuniary loss raises another question. One reason the Supreme Court of Canada used to justify limiting the award for non-pecuniary loss was that part of this loss had already been compensated by the pecuniary-loss award. Had the plaintiff not been injured, some portion of his earnings would have been available for amenities; his loss of earnings, and hence of some amenities, was already compensated.[27] This reasoning provokes a correlative query: Should damages for non-pecuniary loss be adjusted because the award for pecuniary loss was inadequate to compensate for loss of amenities? The argument would be that the award for pecuniary loss would not provide a justification for limiting or reducing damages for non-pecuniary loss; on the contrary, because of its inadequacy, it would favour increasing the latter and leaving it unrestricted as to the total amount that a court may award.

This brief survey of the traditional approach of the law to awarding damages for pain and suffering is intended as an introduction to what follows: legal liability for pain-relief treatment. I suggest that legal liability and awards of damages for pain and suffering should be extended beyond the traditional range of situations just described, be used as a regulatory device, and be made available as a compensatory mechanism within the context of medical situations involving unreasonable failure to provide pain-relief treatment.

LEGAL LIABILITY IN RELATION TO PAIN RELIEF TREATMENT

The often-inadequate treatment of pain in hospitals has been increasingly well documented in medical literature since the early 1980s.[28] These situations raise two related legal questions, which are examples of pain and suffering at the interface of law and medicine.[29] First, should failure to provide adequate, reasonably available pain-relief treatment constitute medical negligence or malpractice? Second, should it be lawful to give pain-relief treatment when doing so could or even would, probably, shorten life?

These two questions are related because one cannot legally create a duty to give pain-relief treatment and impose private-law liability in tort for unreasonable failure to do so and, at the same time, threaten criminal liability for administering it. That could happen when the treatment indicated as necessary could, or even would probably, shorten life. The solution is to limit the scope of the proposed tort duty within the parameters of conduct established as legitimate by the criminal law. Thus, if treatment could not be given without attracting potential criminal liability, it not only need not or may not, but also *must not*, be given. Consequently, criminal law is important in establishing the scope of a private-law duty to provide pain-relief treatment.

A Differential-Rules Approach

A combination of criminal- and private-law obligations applicable in this area gives rise to three possible rules: that physicians have a duty to take reasonable steps to make pain-relief treatment available; that they have no duty in this respect but may provide it (that is, they have a discretion); or that they have a duty not to provide it. I propose that a *proportionality principle* should be used to decide which of these rules to apply in any given situation. A harm-avoided-benefit-conferred/harm-inflicted-benefit-lost assessment of each possible course of conduct must be undertaken. And there must be a positive balance in favour of benefit. But a quantitative assessment in favour of benefit would not be enough; qualitative factors, too, would have to be taken into account. The nature of the benefit conferred in terms of relief or avoidance of suffering would, in itself, have to justify the type of harm that would be inflicted by conferral of the benefit. In other words, a totally relative or "situational" analysis is not necessarily sufficient. We should take into account absolute factors, too, although people might disagree as to what they are.

Important variables, which should always be considered in assessing the risk/benefit calculus, are related to the medical prognosis. These factors include whether the patient suffers from a terminal illness,[30] whether the pain is chronic or likely to be short-lived, and whether the pain is moderate or severe. The variables relating to the patient must be combined with one relating primarily to the nature of the pain-relief treatment: whether it could or would shorten life. There is no inherent legal difficulty in giving treatment that will *not* shorten life, but liability should be able to be imposed in some circumstances for failing to make it available. There can be legal problems, though, in providing pain-relief treatment that could shorten life.

All these variables should be applied concurrently to decide what conduct is medically, legally, and ethically acceptable. This "balancing approach" is not novel. Until relatively recently, though, physicians would not have considered it acceptable as a guide to making decisions about pain-relief treatment. There are historical reasons for that.[31] Before modern anaesthetics, physicians had to inflict pain to have a chance of saving lives. Also, there was a tradition in some cultures, for instance, in American medicine before 1850, that relieving suffering was much less important than saving life and acceptable only when it posed no danger to life. When these factors are taken into account, the attitudes of some contemporary physicians to pain, though not to be encouraged, are not as surprising as they might otherwise be – especially when one remembers that medicine can be strongly influenced by tradition. Furthermore, their attitudes are not formed in isolation; they often reflect, though sometimes in magnified form, opinions shared by the wider cultural group to which they belong. Thus, it is relevant to know that "midcentury America also witnessed the growth of a masculine cult of toughness and callousness. This anti-sentimental glorification of insensitivity took two very different forms: one, a reaffirmation of the traditional manly ability to endure pain; and the second, a newer, more mechanical form of indifference to suffering."[32] But these attitudes changed later in the nineteenth century and "it may be hard to imagine the extent to which the calculus of suffering constituted a major revolution in the techniques of professional decision-making in medicine."[33] In short, physicians' attitudes must not be ignored in considering whether pain-relief treatment – especially that which might shorten life – should be allowed or even required to be offered to patients. This point raises additional questions: How can those attitudes best be modified if they are in conflict with implementing some ethically required approach? How closely do physicians' attitudes to pain-relief treatment reflect those of the community? And what is the true basis of the community's attitude?

Variables Relating to Patients

TERMINALLY ILL PATIENTS Using the type of analysis just described, I submit that, when terminally ill patients require pain-relief treatment that could or would probably shorten life, and when there are no reasonable alternatives in terms of safety and efficacy, it should not constitute a potential criminal offence (such as murder, manslaughter, or aiding or abetting suicide) to give this treatment with the consent of competent patients (or the consent of incompetent patients' legal representatives); *not* doing so, in contrast, might be a breach of a tort duty sounding in negligence. I will discuss this situation in greater depth later on.

NON-TERMINALLY ILL PATIENTS When patients are *not* terminally ill, it is probably always unacceptable, and should be prohibited, to take a significant risk of shortening life by giving pain-relief treatment – especially when the pain is likely to be of only short duration. All other necessary pain-relief treatment must be offered to the patient.

NON-TERMINALLY ILL PATIENTS WITH SEVERE CHRONIC PAIN A more difficult question is whether treatment that might shorten life should be made available to non-terminally ill people in severe chronic pain. May these patients validly demand it? This query concerns rights *to* health care. May or should such treatment be offered to them? This inquiry raises the more common question of rights and duties *in* health care. As I say, from a legal point of view, the answers depend on an analysis of criminal- and private-law provisions and their interaction. Canadian criminal law, for example, provides that people may not consent to have death inflicted on themselves, and consent does not affect the criminal responsibility of anyone who inflicts it.[34] Thus, although there are probably no limits (apart from statutes that authorize compulsory treatment) to competent patients' right to refuse treatment,[35] there are limits to the treatment they may demand and to which they may validly give consent.[36] I have suggested that limits on the right to demand and consent to treatment should not apply to terminally ill patients with respect to necessary pain-relief treatment. I can think of cases, also, in which such treatment should be available to non-terminally ill patients. For instance, someone at serious risk of committing suicide because of intractable, chronic severe pain should be allowed to choose a pain-relief treatment – even if it might shorten life – if there is no other reasonable alternative.

Consent to Pain Relief Treatment

In short, there are legal restrictions on patients' rights of self-determination and autonomy – or, stated another way, on the effectiveness of consent as a mechanism for legitimating medical interventions. When, if ever, would these restrictions be lifted or relaxed? Regardless of the answer to that question, but within the valid scope of exercising these rights, the will of patients must be respected. In terms of this discussion, these requirements mean that the patients' informed consent to pain-relief treatment that may be given legally (giving it is not prohibited by the criminal law) is required. Correlatively, a patient's informed refusal of such treatment must be respected.

A discussion of consent always raises the question of how to deal with situations in which patients are incompetent to consent. The relevant test of competency should be functional – related to the purpose for which competency is being assessed (to obtain informed consent) and based on to factual, rather than legal, competence. Thus, if patients can understand the nature and consequences of what is being proposed and the nature and consequences of giving or withholding consent, they should be considered competent.[37] Otherwise, one or more other people must make decisions on their behalf. Because pain relief is a therapeutic intervention, these decisions would fall within the valid scope of third-party authorization ("proxy" consent) and should be subject to the same rules as those outlined above with respect to competent patients. The only caveat is that great care should be taken to avoid conflict of interest, especially when decisions that might shorten life are involved. Further, we need to be constantly sensitive to the fact that our decisions on behalf of others, either for or against pain-relief treatment, might not be the same as those we would make for ourselves. There is no way to avoid this dilemma, but it is important to be conscious of it.

An objection can be raised that there are many nuances and grey areas in the "differential rules" approach being suggested here. But, as is often the case with decision-making in a medical context, it is unavoidable. A blanket rule covering all situations would be totally inappropriate. It would fail to take due account of various degrees of pain and suffering in various circumstances – when the differences should be legally significant and are ethnically relevant. In short, the law must be both sensitive and responsive to these factors.

I turn now to an analysis of the law relating to pain-relief treatment from the perspective of its probability of shortening life.

Variables Relating to Pain-Relief Treatment

PAIN RELIEF TREATMENT WITH NO REAL RISK OF SHORTEN-
ING LIFE When there is no real risk of shortening life, the failure to treat pain as a reasonably competent physician would in the same circumstances, including a failure to refer the patient to a pain specialist or clinic when appropriate, should be treated as a tort – as a breach of a legal duty of care, which could found a cause of action in negligence.[38] This duty might be novel in content, but it is not novel in form. It parallels all the other legal duties imposed or assumed when a physician-patient relationship is established. In particular, it parallels the liability that could arise for negligently given pain-relief treatment – for example, an overdose of an analgesic – and could be regarded as an extension of that duty. It is related even more closely to liability arising from negligence in withdrawing pain-relief treatment. Liability could be incurred, for instance, because a patient commits suicide owing to the abrupt cessation of treatment, when no reasonably competent physician would have terminated the treatment in that manner. The obligation suggested would mean that a failure to take reasonable care to treat pain would amount to malpractice, just as would the failure to take reasonable care to treat any other medical condition for which treatment is indicated.

One possible argument against this imposition of legal liability would be that experiencing pain does not constitute, in and of itself, legally cognizable damage. I have already mentioned the tendency of the law to give damages for pain and suffering only when it is associated with physical injury. But there are precedents in the law showing modification of that approach – for example, those allowing recovery for negligently inflicted "pure" nervous shock. These precedents recognize that mental injury unrelated to physical injury can sometimes be legally compensable damage. This recognition can be used, in turn, to support the view that pain arising from a physical condition that was not negligently inflicted by the defendant (and, therefore, is not connected with compensable physical injury), but where there was an unreasonable failure to relieve it, constitutes compensable damage. Calculation of damages would be along the lines, outlined earlier, of those for non-pecuniary loss.

It could be that awarding damages for being left in pain might be seen as more appropriate if the damage suffered by the plaintiff-patient was characterized as a reduction in quality of life, or a failure to maintain it, due to an unreasonable failure by the physician to provide adequate pain-relief treatment, rather than simply as pain and suffering. It could then be proposed that, just as physical injury detracts from quality of life, so does mental injury in the form of pain and suffering. This type of analysis might cause these two types of injury – physical and mental injury – to be seen as more analogous and, consequently, as equally worthy of compensation. Although this proposition might be regarded as simply a matter of semantics, it is important to remember here that our choice of language is not neutral and, further, that depending on how it is used, language can be more or less persuasive.

Although the intention of characterizing damages for pain and suffering as damages for loss of quality of life is to increase the probability of damages being awarded, it could have the opposite effect in some circumstances. This result would occur if a court were to hold that a plaintiff's subjective perception of the deterioration in quality of life were needed before compensation would be granted. However, it is likely that subjective perception of pain and suffering is required before damages will be awarded pursuant to this characterization of the compensable injury.[39] Consequently, although introducing a quality-of-life approach to assessing damages for pain and suffering would not automatically ensure the awarding of damages, in particular, for a negligent failure to treat pain, it is unlikely to cause a denial of these damages when they would otherwise be available. And it might cause an award to be given when it would not otherwise, or even result in a larger award.

It is also relevant, in deciding how to use the law to ensure adequate pain-relief treatment, to ask the cause of inadequate treatment for pain in hospitalized patients. Causes might include the fact

that no one member of the medical team is actually responsible for relieving pain. Staff are caught up in recording physical signs, scheduling and performing the tests and procedures required in the medical workup, enumerating and documenting drugs dispensed and supplies consumed, and so forth – all tasks not directly concerned with how the patient feels. [Fagerhaugh and

Strauss] ... also note the way in which interactive processes (which they term "political"), such as persuading, threatening, bargaining, and cajoling, are used to compel patients to conform to the organisational needs of the ward, to tolerate the discomforts of the workup, and even to deny the side effects of their therapies.[40]

The proposed duty might help to redress this situation. Furthermore, hospitals that fail to take reasonable steps to set up systems that allow patients reasonable access to pain-relief treatment could be liable for negligence in the nature of "systems negligence."[41] That is, a hospital could breach its own duty of care (to establish non-negligent organizational structures) and be directly liable for its own negligence to patients left without adequate pain-relief treatment. This way of holding the hospital liable can be contrasted with the form of liability that has traditionally been imposed on a hospital, when it has been held vicariously liable for the fault of some person who is its employee, or, more recently, who forms part of its organization.

The duty to provide reasonable access to pain-relief treatment that does not carry any real risk of shortening life would be owed to all patients. But it is likely to be particularly important for terminally ill ones, because its recognition could create an added awareness that, even when cure is not possible, duties to treat and care continue. Terminally ill patients can be at particular risk of receiving inadequate pain-relief treatment. Among the reasons are that, when cared for outside specialized palliative care units, they often have less contact with physicians than those who can be cured. Physicians might simply be unaware of their pain. Furthermore, senior physicians might have less contact with terminally ill patients than with those who can be cured, and junior physicians might feel reluctant to order the large but necessary doses of narcotics or other analgesics. The nursing staff would probably be in close and regular contact with terminally ill patients and perceive their pain, but nurses might be unable either to prescribe the necessary pain-relief treatment (because of drug-control laws) or to give frequent or large enough doses of a prescribed drug (because of the way in which it has been ordered). Clearly, stringent rules are needed to govern the prescription and administration of narcotic and other addictive drugs, but these restrictions can cause harm. We should "fine tune" the rules to take account of situations in which these drugs are needed and health care professionals have ethical and legal obligations to fulfil those needs.

In particular, we would do well to consider approaches such as hospitalized patients administering their own pain-relief treatment.[42] That can give patients a sense of control over what happens to them –

which, in itself, might be important in relieving suffering.[43] But would patients abuse self-administered pain-relief treatment? And, if so, would health-care professionals be legally liable? There are risks in any scheme. It is important to recognize this possibility, and also to recognize what risks arise in specific situations. The goal must be to minimize the risks, as far as possible, while still trying to achieve the benefits sought by running them. I suggest that the overall benefits of allowing patients to administer their own pain-relief treatment (when they want to do so and there are no contra-indications such as obvious suicidal tendencies) outweigh the risks. Furthermore, health-care professionals should not incur legal liability for supplying patients with pain-relief drugs for self-administration provided that reasonable steps are taken to minimize the risk of abuse. They should supply only a reasonable quantity of drugs at any one time, for instance, and act as reasonably competent health-care professionals would in the same circumstances.

Within the same context, we should consider whether the total prohibition of some pain-relief drugs – for example, heroin in some countries[44] – is justified. If heroin is a superior analgesic for pain associated with some forms of terminal cancer, as has been claimed, it might be unjust that law-abiding citizens who need it for this purpose cannot get it, even though it can be bought *illegally* for "recreational" use.

One difficulty in the creation of a duty to take reasonable steps to relieve pain is that it might be difficult to prove that its breach caused the patient to suffer pain – that is, to prove causation within the legal meaning of that word. It could be argued that there is no proof, apart from patients' assertions, that they, in fact, experienced the pain, or the degree of pain, alleged. But this is true whenever the damage to be compensated is pain and suffering. Alternatively, it could be argued that there is no proof on the balance of probabilities that the pain would have been relieved even if the duty had been fulfilled, and, consequently, no proof that the breach caused the damage. It could be argued even that patients are responsible for contributory negligence for failing to relieve their own pain. A remote possibility in this respect would be that patients, when given the opportunity, negligently fail to develop an "ability to learn to turn on … [their] own inner pain-control circuits."[45]

Some of these arguments could be defeated by imposing liability on physicians for causing patients to lose chances of avoiding pain rather than for causing them to suffer pain or be left in a state of pain. With that reasoning, losing the chance to avoid pain, rather than the suffering of pain, constitutes the damage. Therefore, the causal link between a physician's breach of duty and the resulting pain need not be established.[46] An alternative analysis of this "loss of a chance" approach, which does not eliminate causation as a factor, is to regard the situation as one in which proof of breach of duty and causation are established by proof of the same event. Even when it is alleged that patients suffered pain because of an inability to use their "own inner pain-control circuits," the "loss of a chance" doctrine is potentially applicable. Previously I suggested that this inability of the patient could found a defence, based on contributory negligence, to the plaintiff-patient's claim for failure to relieve pain. In contrast, application of the "loss of a chance" doctrine means that this inability of the patient could become a source of liability for the defendant. The chance lost would be that of learning "to reduce or eliminate chronic pain through a self-management program taught in a classroom setting,"[47] when that program was, or ought to have been, reasonably available, but was not offered. To propose that a program ought to be available raises the very difficult, and increasingly pertinent, question of how to allocate scarce medical resources. In this respect, we might eventually have to consider not only whether resources should be allocated preferentially to prevention or cure, but also whether claims to pain-relief treatment take priority over some other forms of medical care. A final and more traditional alternative approach would be to hold that causation with respect to failure to offer pain-relief treatment is established by the plaintiff on showing that the physician's tortious omission "materially increased the risk" that the plaintiff would suffer pain.[48]

Another factor in imposing liability for failure to take reasonable steps to offer pain-relief treatment is that an omission, not an act, is the cause of the plaintiff-patient's damage. An omission constitutes fault, for which legal liability can be imposed, only when there is a pre-existing relationship between the parties – one that gives rise to a duty to act. This relationship exists between health-care professionals and patients. Therefore, the former can be liable for their omissions.[49] It is interesting to consider that psychological reasons could explain the common law's traditionally greater reluctance to impose liability for omissions than for acts, in that the law might reflect the emotional reality that people have a greater degree of personal detachment from their omissions than from their acts.[50]

There might also be problems in convincing a judge or jury that substantial damages should be awarded for unreasonable failure to offer pain-relief treatment. "Pain memory," even in those who suffer it, tends to be of limited duration. Thus, the pain experienced might be undervalued. To recovered patients, the pain might be seen as the price of recovery. Dead patients cannot be compensated personally, and it may seem unjustifiable to give damages to the estate because that could be simply a windfall for the heirs. Further, the amount of damages likely to be awarded for negligent failure to offer pain-relief treatment, especially when these claims stand alone, might not be enough to encourage the plaintiffs or their lawyers to undertake litigation. This reluctance would be especially likely if there were any real risk of losing the case. Despite these drawbacks, the possibility of imposing negligence liability should be available. At the very least, it would educate and alert people to the need for sensitivity to obligations to offer adequate pain-relief treatment.[51]

Finally, an award of substantial damages for failure to take reasonable steps to relieve pain might be more readily seen as justifiable if the damage to the plaintiff-patient is analyzed more closely, probably causing it to be defined more broadly. The damage should be regarded not simply as the pain itself and what it is "worth" in terms of monetary compensation, but also as recognition that failure to offer patients reasonable ways of avoiding pain constitutes an affront to human dignity in much the same way that discrimination on the basis of race or defamation does. Substantial damages are awarded in those cases, which, by analogy, could be used as precedents for augmenting the damages awarded for unreasonable failure to offer pain-relief treatment beyond the "value" of the pain itself.[52]

PAIN RELIEF TREATMENT THAT MIGHT SHORTEN LIFE The most common situation in which pain-relief treatment that might shorten life arises is that of terminal illness, and the following discussion will be limited to those cases.[53] Consider the relation between euthanasia and pain-relief treatment given to terminally ill patients. In both cases there is a desire to relieve suffering. The difference is that the primary aim of euthanasia is to do so by inflicting death, whereas that of pain-relief treatment is simply to relieve pain, not to shorten life or cause death (although either might be a secondary effect). One can envisage a continuum. At one end is giving pain-relief treatment that certainly would *not* shorten life. In the middle is a possible double effect – that of relieving pain (which is the primary intention) and that of possibly shortening life (which is not desired). At the other end is a situation of certain double effect – pain-relief treatment that necessarily *would* shorten life. This last case has some characteristics of active euthanasia, but differs from it in that the motive is not to shorten life. Motive is seldom relevant as a differentiating factor that allows criminal liability in one case, but not in the other, with respect to conduct that is otherwise identical and is carried out by someone who has subjective knowledge of its consequences and risks.[54] Consequently, this conduct could be prosecuted as murder or manslaughter, as has been demonstrated in an American case.[55] Euthanasia should not be legitimated or legalized, but the problem presented here must be dealt with. I propose that, to the strictly limited extent that treatment is necessary to relieve the pain experienced by terminally ill people, the criminal law should be interpreted to recognize it as legitimate – even if some people argue that this treatment constitutes euthanasia (an argument that I believe is mistaken).[56] Such an approach has now been taken in practice.

It should be noted in this respect that the Law Reform Commission of Canada proposed that the Canadian Criminal Code[57] be amended to the effect that "Nothing in sections 14, 45, 198 and 199 of the Criminal Code shall be interpreted as preventing a physician from undertaking or ceasing to administer palliative care and measures intended to eliminate or to relieve the suffering of a person for the sole reason that such care or measures are likely to shorten the life expectancy of this person."[58] So far, no such amendment has been enacted in legislation.

The President's Commission in the United States came to the same conclusion, but adopted a different method. It interpreted the law, as it stood, as allowing necessary pain-relief treatment that could or even would shorten life.[59] Therefore, amendment of the law was not suggested: "Health care professionals ought to realize that they are already authorized and obligated to use such means with a patient's or surrogate's consent, even if an earlier death is likely to result. The Commission endorses allowing physicians and patients to select treatments known to risk death in order to relieve suffering as well as to pursue a return to health."[60] The decision to adopt this approach could well have been political; because criminal law is a state jurisdiction in the United States (in contrast to Canada, where it is a federal matter), amendment of the law would require each state to take action and could result in important differences among states. The advantage of the American approach is that it does not open up, as the one proposed by the Law Reform Commission of Canada does, the possibility of interpreting a change in the law as moving towards the legalization of euthanasia or even intending to implement it.

The distinction between pain and suffering might be relevant also in justifying the distinction between euthanasia and pain-relief treatment that could shorten life. Euthanasia can be regarded as shortening life in order to prevent suffering, which is to be distinguished from steps directed primarily at relieving pain (although these, too, would reduce suffering).

Within this context, the possibility of espousing one principle overtly (for instance, a belief in the sanctity of life) and a contradictory principle latently (for instance, derogations from sanctity of life as an absolute value) should be mentioned. We tolerate hidden derogations from values that we consider overriding, or derogations that appear to occur by chance, much more readily than frontal attacks on them. Thus, we might emphasize the necessity of giving pain-relief treatment to seriously disabled new-born babies, for instance, and characterize our interventions as such – de-emphasizing (or even failing to articulate) the life-shortening effect. Moreover, we might "confuse" life-shortening and death-inflicting pain-relief treatment in these circumstances. This confusion can have important ramifications, because the former might be justifiable and the latter not. Pain-relief treatment can be characterized as life-shortening, rather than death-inflicting, when the situation involved is one in which death is inevitable within a relatively short time, no matter what procedures are undertaken, and it is the only reasonably effective way available to relieve pain. In contrast, some pain-relief treatment could be regarded as death-inflicting. Suppose it were given to a child with Down's syndrome to relieve discomfort or pain associated with an operable condition such as duodenal atresia, which would prove fatal without an operation. The decision not to operate on the child would be made more palatable if the pain were relieved. An even clearer case of death-inflicting pain-relief treatment is when the rules of a hospital nursery provide for feeding of infants only on demand; sedation in the guise of pain-relief treatment is given to babies with spina bifida to prevent them from waking and demanding nourishment, with the result that they die of starvation.[61]

INFORMED CONSENT AS A MECHANISM FOR AVOIDING SUFFERING

The notion of "patient as person" promoted by Paul Ramsay has been a catch phrase of the rise of interest in medical-ethical-legal matters since the late 1960s.[62] Its importance cannot be overemphasized. There is some interesting historical material on the concept of the person, which is relevant to understanding what constitutes pain and suffering and, I suggest, to understanding a possible role for the legal doctrine of informed consent in reducing suffering.[63] This material is about the origin and effect of mind/body dualism.

Cassel has proposed that "the split between mind and body that has so deeply influenced our approach to medical care was proposed by Descartes to resolve certain philosophical issues. Moreover, Cartesian dualism made it possible for science to escape the control of the church by assigning the noncorporeal, spiritual realm to the church, leaving the physical world as the domain of science. In that religious age, 'person,' synonymous with 'mind,' was necessarily off limits to science."[64] The concept of person has a different meaning today, when it tends to refer more to the totality of the person. Cassel continues that "the mind body dichotomy ... depersonalizes the sick patient ... An anachronistic division of the human condition into what is medical (having to do with the body) and what is non-medical (the remainder) has given medicine too narrow a notion of its calling. Because of this division, physicians may, in concentrating on the cure of bodily disease, do things that cause the patient as a person to suffer."[65]

In short, suffering is something that people feel emotionally. It is something more than simply an unpleasant and distressing bodily sensation, which, I have suggested earlier, can be distinguished as pain.[66]

The philosophical concept just noted is obviously relevant to medicine and its goal of relieving suffering. It might, however, seem far removed from the practical realities that health-care professionals face each day, and largely irrelevant to any legal discussion. But perhaps not – not if we see the ultimate aim of both medicine and law as being to relieve not just pain but the suffering of people within the wider meaning of that concept. With this thought in mind, I will examine some aspects of the doctrine of informed consent, which is applied daily in medical practice.

The functions of informed consent have often been considered. They include preservation of autonomy, self-determination, inviolability, privacy, and respect for the person.[67] By pursuing the approach taken by Cassel, we can develop another possibility, which might be a unifying factor underlying the values articulated here. Informed consent might actually be aimed at, and a mechanism for, the prevention of suffering. Further, it might prevent suffering at the expense of experiencing pain.

To the extent that suffering occurs, as Cassel suggests, when "persons perceive ... a threat ... to their integrity as persons,"[68] and because they have no power to control the situation, informed consent might help to redress the balance. This correction would occur if adherence to the requirements of the doctrine of informed consent were to have the effect of affirming the personhood of patients and giving them some measure of control. The process of obtaining informed consent has the potential to produce these results because of its requirements for interaction in terms of both verbal and non-verbal communication, the delivery of information, "apparent understanding" of the information by patients, and eliciting a decision from them.[69] To state the same idea in another way, the requirement of informed consent might help health-care professionals to see each patient as an individual rather than as a member of a homogeneous group. Making a patient the reference point of what is required for informed consent helps to emphasize the uniqueness of all patients, along with the necessity to articulate their unique needs as they perceive them and their desires.[70] Some people have pointed out the risks of emphasizing this doctrine and worry that "our preoccupation with 'autonomy' as an absolute has become an obsession reaching pathological proportions, allowing us to substitute the idea of a rational, independent mind of a Cartesian sort for the painful realities of being sick, dependent, and in need of help."[71] This warning should be kept in mind. There is no "best of all possible worlds," so requiring respect for personal autonomy carries some risks of harm. It can result in failure to confer a benefit when doing so would constitute an overwhelming advantage to the person whose autonomy is being respected. And insisting that people exercise their autonomy can cause them stress or conflict. Efforts must be made to minimize these harms. But more harm is done almost always by not recognizing people's right to autonomy.

According to some critics, it is merely theory that many proclaimed aims of informed consent can be achieved. In practice, they say, these aims are either impossible to attain[72] or seldom realized as well as they might be. Despite that argument, on the whole, there is a consensus in the medical profession that physicians should try to obtain informed consent. But this consensus might be apparent, not real. It might have arisen not from true accord, but because disagreement is considered unacceptable. This distinction between real and apparent consensus can have important practical implications: depending on whether participation in the consensus is real or apparent, physicians might act very differently in practice. When their participation in the consensus is only apparent, the process of obtaining informed consent might be honoured in form rather than substance. The contrary is likely to be true when they really participate in the consensus. The idea that informed consent might be a mechanism for reducing suffering is important, because it might promote genuine consensus among members of the medical profession as to the necessity of informed consent in substance and lead to that being an aim more often in practice. A real consensus becomes much more likely when the goal of seeking informed consent is seen as being not merely to uphold some civil libertarian values (to which not everyone subscribes) but also to reduce suffering (a value which is more widespread, even universal).

The view that an aim of informed consent is to reduce suffering causes informed refusal of treatment to take on a different perspective than if requirements of the doctrine are seen merely as formal ones. An informed refusal of treatment – which inflicts pain on patients from the physicians' point of view – might, at the same time, reduce suffering from the patients' point of view. This consideration could make some refusals more acceptable to those who currently disagree with, or have doubts about, honouring them.

There are additional ramifications resulting from regarding informed consent as a mechanism for suffering reduction. The exception to requiring informed consent, known as "therapeutic privilege," would have to be narrowly construed. According to this doctrine, physicians need not disclose information to their patients, which the law would otherwise require, if disclosure would, in itself, mentally or physically harm the patients.[73] In short, therapeutic privilege is aimed at reducing patients' suffering. But if disclosure and the process of obtaining informed consent reduce suffering, the availability of therapeutic privilege as a justification for non-disclosure of information will be more limited than it would otherwise be. The suffering-reduction effect of informed consent means that even when all the other conditions precedent to the application of therapeutic privilege are present, the latter doctrine will not be available unless the suffering avoided by applying it at least outweighs that resulting from the failure to obtain informed consent. Therapeutic privilege must incorporate a requirement that its use result in a negative net balance of suffering being inflicted before it is potentially available to justify a non-disclosure of information in the context of informed consent. This approach should lead to more precise and in-depth analysis of therapeutic privilege than in the past.

Perceiving informed consent as a suffering-reduction mechanism presents yet another matter. All elements of the doctrine of informed consent – the requirements of competence, information, and voluntariness that form part of its fundamental basis,[74] the purposes that it is generally understood to serve, and the way in which it is applied in practice – tend to focus (if not exclusively, then almost exclusively) on cognitive functions. Dealing with competent adults, one assumes that the expression of their will generated by the exercise of their cognitive functions corresponds to what they want – that is, to their feelings.[75] But what about people whose cognitive functions are impaired to the extent that they are incompetent to give or withhold consent? There might be a brutal disregard for, and contravention of, the feelings of those who cannot think but can still feel – that is, those who can experience emotionally.

On the whole, we do not yet have any identified mechanism that protects the feelings of incompetent people and, as far as possible, honours and implements decisions that respect their feelings. There are instances, however, in which that approach has been adopted. One recommendation of the Law Reform Commission of Canada, in its working paper on the sterilization of mentally incompetent people,[76] is that the wishes of incompetent people must be taken into account in deciding for or against non-therapeutic sterilization.[77] And courts faced with decisions on whether to order the initiation or prolongation of treatment on mentally incompetent people, or faced with their refusals of treatment in the psychiatric context, have often referred in their decisions to the necessity of taking into account their feelings – whether these have been expressed in the past or are currently being articulated.[78] Consequently, these feelings should be taken into account by substitute decision-makers. Anecdotally, I have been told by surgeons that they have not operated on incompetent patients who have refused mutilating treatment, such as the amputation of a limb, when they believed that their patients, despite incompetence, had three characteristics: a strong sense of bodily integrity, clearly opposed interference with it, and would experience severe suffering if their feelings were not respected. A careful use of this approach should be encouraged. As the law now stands, however, physicians run some legal risk in acting on the refusals of incompetent patients – just as they would in acting on their consent. It is difficult to suggest how the law could be modified. Clearly, feelings should not always be the decisive factors in deciding whether to give or withhold treatment. If they were, there would be no need to assess competence at all; the sole issue would be discerning a patient's feelings either for or against medical treatment. This issue arises within a discussion of pain and suffering, perhaps, because its solution lies to some degree within the same context.

The feelings of incompetent people concerning medical procedures should be taken into account in assessing the overall pain and suffering that would be inflicted on them by imposing or not imposing procedures. The course of conduct likely to offer the least suffering (which must be assessed taking into account that caused by contravention of feelings) should probably be the one adopted. The danger is that this approach is open to abuse. It could become a screen used to justify failure to treat incompetent patients. But the fact that some approaches are open to abuse is not always a good enough reason to reject them. When proper substantive and procedural rules and safeguards are established, the feelings of incompetent people regarding proposed medical treatment could be taken into account as a relevant factor in deciding on that treatment without creating undue risk by so doing.

In short, viewing informed consent as being a way to reduce suffering would create an added awareness of the need to develop mechanisms to aid in reducing emotional suffering, which might be inflicted by the doctrine of informed consent itself if it operates from a theoretical basis related only to cognitive functions. For instance, rules governing substitute decision-making might be developed and formulated with this consideration in mind.

Finally, informed consent might have a role to play in reducing the suffering of physicians, at least in the form of malpractice suits. Patients might have unrealistic hopes because physicians fail to provide information about the risks of the treatment and its outcome. When physicians terminate relationships with patients, the latter might feel abandoned and

then a malpractice suit becomes the mechanism by which to force the "abandoning" physician to share both the responsibility for the outcome and – less obviously – the experience of distress and rage occasioned by suffering ... Ideally, the clinical utility of informed consent lies in bridging the gap between either of the two fantasies – helpless ignorance or omnipotent certainty – and a more complicated reality ... The real clinical opportunity offered by informed consent is that of transforming uncertainty from a threat to the doctor-patient alliance into the very basis on which an alliance can be formed. This is particularly important, since a sense of working together with the doctor may be one of the major elements in avoiding negative reactions to treatment ... [Informed consent] can be a focal point in establishing a therapeutic alliance. Seen as a dialogue in which both the cognitive and affective implications of uncertainty are acknowledged and shared, informed consent is a powerful clinical tool. Through its use, helplessness is replaced by a degree of control as the patient becomes a coexperimenter rather than a passive object of experimentation. Hopelessness is replaced by a degree of hope as the patient comes to see that uncertainty does not imply irrationality, defeat, or abandonment. Finally, the alliance between the patient and physician, instead of being undermined by the specious denial of uncertainty, is strengthened by the mutuality of its acceptance.[79]

Thus, there might be reciprocity in suffering-reduction: reducing it for either the patient or the physician might reduce it for the other as well. Likewise, augmentation of suffering could be reciprocal.

CONCLUSION

One matter most people agree about is that, to the extent that we are able, we should aim to reduce and, if possible, to alleviate pain and suffering. That demands recognizing what constitutes pain and suffering; identifying the causes; and trying to devise mechanisms that would counteract them. I have written a preliminary exploration of the role of law in its interaction with medicine in achieving these aims.

There is an interesting precedent for the theory that the interaction of law and medicine might give rise to humanistic developments in both disciplines. The teaching of psychiatry was first introduced into the curricula of medical schools as part of medical jurisprudence. Later, developments in the field of psychiatry greatly influenced the law to adopt a more humanistic approach. Thus, the cross-fertilization of medicine and law could generate vitally necessary and compassionate developments in both professions and, possibly, in wider spheres.

More general repercussions of this interaction could result, because the disciplines of law and medicine have not only practical but also symbolic functions. Among the latter are those of affirming the worth of every person and establishing profound respect for life. Adopting and implementing the goal of relieving suffering has a direct value in itself, but it also performs this symbolic function. Indeed, recognition of its symbolic function might be important in understanding the full scope of the operation of law and medicine in practice. For example, it has been suggested that the major increase in health-care costs in the United States, despite maximum efforts to contain them, might be generated by desire to acknowledge and reaffirm the worth of the individual, because recognition of this value has been seriously eroded in other areas of human activity owing to "the rise in depersonalization and alienation imposed on the individual by post–World War II industrial and economic development."[80] In fact, if one fears for the survival of a sense of the uniqueness of the individual, there would be no more disturbing evidence to support this fear than the failure of society to react to individual pain and suffering with personal empathy and with attempts to alleviate it. And this fear would be magnified if those failing to respond were health-care professionals, because the public quickly and correctly identifies their lack of empathy as hypocrisy – a serious problem in those who have an overt and professed commitment to relieving pain and suffering.

Finally, it might be that recognizing a common goal for law and medicine would help to shift the focus away from what is often perceived as a purely adversarial relationship between the two professions. No more worthy common goal than relief of suffering could be chosen for what I hope are still two of the "helping professions." This is not a paternalistic, "do-gooder" pursuit. And it must never become an exercise of power or a cover for arrogant intermeddling, even if disguised as compassion. Conduct aimed at relieving suffering should develop from and encompass a genuine care and concern for others, a perception of the many ways in which harm and suffering can be inflicted, and, perhaps, the ways not considered before in which it could be ameliorated.

12 Ethics, Law, and Palliative Treatment and Care: The Dying Elderly Person

Every word in the title of a working paper by the Law Reform Commission of Canada, *Euthanasia, Aiding Suicide and Cessation of Treatment,*[1] has a negative content – that of aiming to reduce suffering by eliminating suffering people or treatments that prolong their lives (and hence their suffering). One example of the latter would be when a competent patient has given an informed refusal of further treatment aimed at prolonging life. There is also an important correlative positive principle that pertains in these situations, however, and it must be clearly stated, understood, and applied. This principle is not new, but it bears emphasizing and repeating. The fact that we have no useful, active treatments, the fact that we cannot cure or prolong the lives of patients, and the fact that active treatment is contra-indicated in terms of the suffering that it would inflict in comparison with the benefit that it could possibly achieve – none of these facts means that we can do nothing. In short, the duty to care – what is sometimes termed the duty of palliative care – continues to the extent that patients need care and for as long as they do. Anyone who is dying is highly vulnerable. But dying old people can be among the most vulnerable in terms of receiving the treatment and care they need.

PALLIATIVE CARE AND TREATMENT

It is worth considering whether we should refer to palliative treatment rather than palliative care, or whether we should use both terms. Yet once again, we must keep in mind that language is never neutral.[2] To the degree that the term "palliative care" has a neutral, non-active, non-obligatory connotation, its use would be undesirable. Still, it is important to establish the duty to care and not only to treat. Furthermore, it could be important to recognize that all members of the health-care team treat and care for patients. Often, only physicians are regarded as treating – and not as having the duty to care; other members are seen as caring only.[3] Recognition that all members of the team both treat and care is important in two respects. First, it emphasizes that all health-care professionals have the duty to care. Second, it helps to avoid a situation in which the administration of treatment is given a higher status than care and, therefore, appears to be a more desirable course of conduct to pursue.

We need to identify the hoped-for palliative effect of any therapy given with this aim. Frequently, one finds what could be termed "internal inconsistencies" in palliative-treatment programs. For example, a decision might be properly made that all further treatment aimed at cure or prolonging life is contra-indicated – not only medically but also ethically and legally. As a result, haemodialysis might be stopped; respiratory support, however, is continued. Who is being treated by the respiratory support? Despite the decision to discontinue treatment, a decision to treat the patient has been made, although it is not beneficial. Is the treatment intended for the benefit of the patient's family or for members of the health-care team? Treating these "others" is not always unjustified.[4] However, we should be aware of what we are doing and should carefully analyze whether doing so is justified in any given circumstances.

Some interventions that might be necessary for palliative treatment could have the secondary effect of prolonging life. For example, it might be consistent to accept a patient's decision not to have surgery or cardiopulmonary resuscitation in the event of a cardiac arrest and, at the same time, recommend a blood transfusion aimed at providing greater comfort to the patient. The transfusion would constitute inconsistent treatment only if it had no palliative purpose.

There might be other situations in which decisions concerning life-prolonging treatment appear at first glance to be inconsistent with each other but, on closer examination, prove justified. Some life-prolonging treatment might be indicated as inappropriate (for instance, cardiopulmonary resuscitation), but that does not automatically mean that all treatments of this kind would be inappropriate. In multiple-systems disease, some aspects of morbidity can be cured and others stabilized, but other aspects remain irreversible and progressive. A classic example would be someone with terminal cancer who contracts pneumonia. The patient must be treated as a whole person, not as a collection of separate maladies. The judgment as to what is required is difficult, particularly for physicians who have been trained only in a reductionist way and are used to making decisions on the basis of reactions to identified disease syndromes rather than to a complex, complicated, whole person.[5] There are no formulaic answers to these problems. However, perhaps most important, when decisions must be made concerning the discontinuance of treatment aimed at prolonging life and in relation to palliative treatment, one must be sensitive to the intricate and delicate nuances involved.

The matter of the consistency of the components of the total program undertaken as palliative treatment and care raises predominantly medical questions, although they have legal and ethical ramifications. But the discussion of two questions about palliative treatment, to which I now turn, begins primarily from a legal basis, although it has major implications in the context of medical decision-making and practice. Consider the first of these questions: Should failure to provide adequate, reasonably available pain-relief treatment constitute medical negligence or malpractice? Now, consider the second: Is it, or should it be, lawful to give pain-relief treatment when doing so might shorten life? As discussed in chapter 11, these two questions are related because a private-law obligation to provide adequate pain-relief treatment cannot be created if, in fulfilling the obligation, there would be a risk of incurring criminal liability for shortening life. Below, I summarize the conclusions reached in chapter 11.

The first inquiry must be the following: When does potential criminal liability arise from administering pain-relief treatment? Relevant variables include whether the patient is or is not terminally ill, and the nature of the proposed pain-relief treatment in terms of whether it is most likely or unlikely to shorten life. Pain-relief treatment cannot be classified into two alternative categories, that likely to shorten life or that not likely to do so. These descriptions represent the two end points on a continuum of danger to life arising from pain-relief treatment. Likewise, it has been said that life is a terminal illness, and the difficulty of defining when a patient can be characterized as terminally ill should not be overlooked. Again, a continuum, rather than alternative categories, is involved.

A wide range of possible questions can arise in situations displaying various degrees of intensity of these two variables of danger to life from pain-relief treatment and whether the patient is terminally ill or not, but, as we saw in chapter 11, the two raised above are particularly important. First, is there any legal obligation to take reasonable steps to provide pain-relief treatment for patients who need it? Second, what are the legal problems associated with pain-relief treatment when it might shorten life? The first question is important in relation to elderly people, because they can be afraid of seeming demanding of physicians and, therefore, reticent to request treatment. They are also likely to hold physicians more in awe than do younger people, a respect that contributes to the same outcome. The second question is particularly important in relation to terminally ill people, many of whom are elderly.

A DUTY TO PROVIDE PAIN RELIEF TREATMENT

Failure to give adequate pain-relief treatment is well documented. I explore the reasons elsewhere,[6] and they are complex and varied. They include the failure of patients to communicate with those who can relieve the pain; desensitization of health-care professionals to the pain that they see all around them; the fact that patients might have the most contact with people who are unable to order pain-relief treatment and might have little contact with those who are able; and inadequate education of health-care professionals regarding pain-relief regimes.

Furthermore, there are social, ethnic, and even biological and genetic factors involved in how we perceive our own pain or that of others. Then, too, there are factors such as fear of the law and even moral inhibitions on relieving pain. For example, some people might want to avoid causing what they, most often mistakenly, perceive as addiction to pain-relief drugs.

When the variety and diversity of these compounding factors are taken into account, it might not seem surprising that the law has not imposed liability on health-care professionals for unreasonable failure to relieve pain. But, as I propose in chapter 11, there should be liability in some circumstances.

The failure to treat pain as a reasonably competent health-care professional in the same circumstances would do (including a failure to refer patients to pain-treatment specialists or pain-treatment clinics) should be considered a breach of a legal duty – one that could give rise to a cause of action based in negligence. This duty would mean that not taking reasonable care to treat pain would amount to malpractice, just as would the failure to take reasonable care in treating any other medical condition. It should be noted that the duty suggested would not be limited to physicians. However, the content of the duty imposed would not be the same for all health-care professionals. A physician would be required to take the steps that any reasonably competent physician in the same circumstances would take (a nurse, those that a reasonably competent nurse would take, and so on).

Many problems might be involved in creating this potential liability in negligence. The question, however, is whether the benefits of this approach would likely outweigh any harm caused – which might be the case if it renews sensitivity to the need for relieving pain and causes health-care professionals to respond to patients in need.

PAIN RELIEF TREATMENT
THAT COULD SHORTEN LIFE

The second major question to be considered involves pain-relief treatment that could shorten life. It has been proposed that there should be a private-law duty to take reasonable steps to relieve pain. But what if the only reasonably effective treatment could, or would, shorten life? Is any duty to provide pain relief abrogated in that circumstance? Furthermore, rather than being liable for not giving pain-relief treatment, or being in a neutral situation of having no duty to give or not to give it, could there by legal liability for doing so?

As explained previously, the answers depend, first, on analysis of the criminal law. The Canadian Criminal Code[7] establishes that people may not kill others with impunity;[8] aiding and abetting suicide is a crime;[9] and people may not consent to have death inflicted on themselves.[10] In applying these criminal-law provisions to the medical context, though, two distinctions are relevant: between terminally ill and non-terminally ill patients; and between pain that is acute (of short duration) and that which is chronic – and, in the latter case, between severe and not-so-severe pain.

In the case of non-terminally ill patients in whom the pain is likely to be acute, pain-relief treatment that could shorten life is almost certainly never justified. In similar patients with severe chronic pain, it could be justified. This would be the case, for example, when patients might commit suicide if treatment were not given and there are no safer alternatives.

More often, in practice, it is terminally ill patients in chronic and severe pain who require pain-relief treatment that could shorten life. These cases are germane to the relation between euthanasia and pain-relief treatment. As explained elsewhere, in both cases there is an effort to relieve suffering. The difference is that the primary aim of euthanasia is to do so by inflicting death, whereas the primary aim of pain-relief treatment is simply to relieve pain – not to shorten life or cause death (although either might be a secondary effect). One can envision a continuum. At one end is pain-relief treatment that would not shorten life. In the middle is treatment with a possible double effect – that of relieving pain (which is its primary intention) and that of possibly shortening life (which is not desired). At the other end is treatment with a certain double effect (pain is relieved, but life is necessarily shortened). This last case has some characteristics of active euthanasia, but it differs in that the motive is not to shorten life. Although motive is seldom relevant as a differentiating factor in deciding that criminal liability should be imposed in one case but not another for conduct that is otherwise identical, a primary motive to relieve pain should exempt the health-care professional providing the pain-relief treatment from criminal liability for doing so.

As soon as it is established that there is no criminal offence involved in making pain-relief treatment that could shorten life available to patients who want and need it, there would be no reason for the suggested private-law obligation (taking reasonable steps to make pain-relief treatment available) not to apply to this treatment as well. The only exception might be for physicians who believe it contrary to their conscientious beliefs. Two positions could be taken with regard to that situation. One would be to accommodate their beliefs by not requiring them to give the treatment, but, at the same time, requiring them either to call in other physicians who would do so or refer their patients to other physicians.[11] The latter alternative would not always be an acceptable approach to take to terminally ill patients. For example, it would be unacceptable if it would cause psychological trauma to patients owing to unreasonable disruptions of the physician-patient relationship on which patients are emotionally dependent.

The other position is not to allow conscientious objection by physicians. Then, failure to make treatment available could result in private-law liability of the physician sounding in damages. That approach should be adopted when no other physician willing to give necessary pain-relief treatment is accessible.

CONCLUSION

Because we cannot treat in the sense of cure does not mean that we have no obligation to treat in the sense of care. Among the most important obligations towards dying elderly people is that of adequate and effective pain-relief treatment. Unfortunately, this obligation has often been neglected in the past. However, there appears to be a new awareness of and sensitivity to the need to fulfill it. To the extent that the law has been an impediment, it must be changed. Most of us would probably apply to ourselves, to our loved ones, and to the people whom we care for in a professional capacity a sentiment expressed by my father. At one stage, when he was terminally ill, because of inadequate pain-relief treatment, his life consisted of nothing but trying to cope with pain. He said, "I want to live as long as I can, but I don't want to go on if it means enduring this excruciating pain." His pain was relieved after protest to the physicians caring for him, and he lived another nine months. He asked me to try to ensure that other old, dying people were not left, as he had been, without adequate pain-relief treatment. We must all try to ensure that for everyone.

13 The Relief of Suffering: Human Rights and Medicine

This title refers to three major areas that have been a focus of conceptual and practical developments in late-twentieth-century societies: human rights, medicine, and the relief of suffering. What are our obligations in each of these contexts, and what is the relation among them?

THE RELATION BETWEEN HUMAN RIGHTS AND MEDICINE

What is the relation between contemporary concepts of human rights[1] and medicine? One way to explore this question is to ask three others: What is the relevance of human rights to governmental decision-making regarding medicine? What is the relevance of human rights in the context of decision-making by medical institutions? And what is the relevance of human rights in relation to decision-making by or for those who find themselves in the medical system? To answer each of these questions requires the articulation of human rights and the procedures for their implementation. But although description is necessary, it is not sufficient. The implementation of human rights requires willingness to act. In the medical context, moreover, it necessarily involves ethics and law. In this context, human rights, ethics, and law are intimately linked.

There is a common thread linking respect for persons, including respect for their human rights, medicine, ethics, and law. Each one, whether a value, activity, undertaking, or discipline, involves trying to

relieve human suffering in one way or another – or to avoid its infliction in the first place. We should be constantly aware of that, whether
dealing with politicians at the governmental level, hospital administrators at the institutional level, or physicians or patients at the individual
level. We are all, in our various ways and through our different contributions of expertise, commitment, integrity, and involvement, trying
to reduce suffering to the greatest possible extent.

There is an old saying that the physician heals the body, the priest
heals the soul, and the lawyer heals society. Recognition of human
rights in medicine relates to the protection of bodies, souls, and societies. This dictum recognizes the existence of a commonality among
medicine, ethics, and law (including human rights) by linking physicians, priests, and lawyers. It is noteworthy, in this regard, that the common word establishing this interlinking is "healing." This commonality
indicates that it is not only relief of suffering but also healing that we
are involved in when we link medicine, ethics, and human rights – especially, one hopes, when these rights are expressed as laws. Indeed,
viewing law as a healing instrument has opened up a new field of law
called therapeutic jurisprudence.

If we examine some of the fundamental concepts of bioethics, we
could conclude that it is a specialized area of human rights in medicine. Bioethics and human rights both encompass respect for the person – for instance, through respect for rights to autonomy and self-
determination, non-maleficence (do not harm others), beneficence
(do good whenever possible), and justice (distribute equitably and respond to legitimate claims and needs).

Non-maleficence (*primum non nocere*; first, do no harm) is a primary
concept in both human rights and medicine. It has an important expression in the obligation not to inflict suffering and, whenever possible, to relieve it. Beneficence (if possible, do some good) is certainly a
goal in medicine, but it might not be as clearly a goal of human rights.
The latter tend to be of negative, rather than positive, content. That is,
the rights involved are usually *rights against* something being done to
one, rather than *rights to* something. This tendency should be reas-
sessed in the context of human rights in medicine.

Elsewhere, Andrew Orkin and I have identified and compared three
"generations" of human rights.[2] The first encompasses political and
civil rights. They include the rights to liberty and security; equality before and under the law; freedom of expression, conscience, religion,
and mobility; and freedom from mistreatment and arbitrary detention.
These rights are reflected in Articles 2–21 of the Universal Declaration
of Human Rights (1945),[3] and were incorporated into the International Covenant on Civil and Political Rights (1976).[4] The second

"generation" comprises economic, social, and cultural rights. They include rights to economic and social security, work, an adequate standard of living, health, education, and leisure (as outlined in Articles 22–27 of the Universal Declaration and incorporated into the International Covenant).[5] The third and most controversial "generation" is a result of developing countries' demands for a more equitable social and economic order. It includes collective rights to development, humanitarian assistance, information, and environmental well-being. Its origin can be found in Article 28 of the Universal Declaration: "Everyone is entitled to a social and international order in which the rights set forth in this declaration can be fully realised."[6] Clearly, many of these rights are important in the health and health care context. Observe the progression from rights of negative content (rights against) to rights of positive content (rights to). The latter are much less often recognized and implemented, especially in practice, often because the economic means necessary to do so are not made available.

This discussion is not to imply that negative-content rights are unimportant. For instance, it is essential to have a right against medical treatment in order to refuse and, thereby, avoid unwanted treatment. It is especially important when the treatment involved would constitute officious inter-meddling. For example, someone who is terminally ill refuses life-support treatment to avoid becoming dependent on a machine. From both the medical and human-rights standpoints, these rights are fundamental.

But a right to refuse treatment is not much help if one wants to be admitted to an emergency room for life-saving care and no beds are available. What is needed is a positive-content human right, one that establishes at some fundamental level the right of access to at least a minimal standard of health care. On the whole, in Canada and the United States, there are no legislated, positive-content rights to medical care, although some rights have been established through case law for emergency situations. Quebec is an exception. Under the Quebec Charter of Human Rights and Freedoms,[7] by virtue of the general right to assistance if one's life is in peril, one could claim a right to some medical care. Section 5 of Quebec's Health and Social Services Act[8] establishes a legal right to "adequate" medical care. This right gives rise to a correlative duty on the part of "establishments" – which include hospitals and nursing homes – to provide care. But section 5 does not establish an absolute right to this care; the right is limited to a level of care that is consistent with the organization and resources of the "establishment." That is the level of care set by governmental bodies and institutions. They have discretion to decide how resources should be allocated, both to and within medicine. A "section 5 right" to care and treatment could, therefore, depending on the nature of the treatment, be contentless despite the fact that it is drafted in positive-content terms. Allocation of and access to medical resources involve many fundamental human rights, as well as ethical and legal issues at multiple levels.

SUFFERING

If there are human rights against having suffering inflicted, or to have suffering relieved, we must know precisely what they are – precisely what it is that there are rights against or to. As pointed out in chapter 11, suffering can be defined as losing control over what happens to one and, concurrently, experiencing a sense of one's own disintegration.[9] These two aspects of suffering are related, in that suffering is an absence of any power to control or to influence, in any meaningful way, a perceived process of one's own disintegration. One might not be able to stop the process of disintegration. Terminally ill people, for example, might be – or at least might experience themselves as being – in that state. But they are likely to suffer less if they have some control. We can help them in that respect. For instance, we can allow them to choose their treatment or regulate its modality – such as the dose of pain-relief therapy.

Respect for human rights can often result in enhancing the control people have over their own persons, especially in a medical context. Consider the rights to privacy, to physical and mental integrity, to freedom of speech, to freedom of association, and to life, liberty, and security of one's person; these rights give people control over what they may do, what they may say, with whom they may associate, where they may go, and what may be done to them. Such rights can be most important when we are sick and most vulnerable. These rights are also, correlatively, safeguards against coercion. They prevent people from being forced to stay in hospitals, for instance, when they want to leave.

These fundamental human rights are articulated, explicitly or impliedly, in legal instruments. The most important in Canada are the Canadian Charter of Rights and Freedoms[10] and, following that, the provincial codes of human rights. One way to characterize them would be as legally implemented suffering-reduction mechanisms. That is obvious when one thinks about the reasons for respecting human rights – especially the aim of ensuring respect for people through respect for their human rights. But their deeper aim, reducing suffering, is seldom identified explicitly. The same insight is provided by considering prohibitions of wrongful discrimination. Avoiding wrongful discrimination is a central theme in the human-rights context and a frequent one in the medical context. Its occurrence is often a source of intense suffering.

In short, human rights, medicine, and the relief of suffering are strongly linked. The last is a common goal of the first two. This connection could mean that the application of human rights in medicine (that is, the combination of human rights and medicine) is a powerful way to relieve some forms of suffering, much more so than seeking this goal through each "context" alone. It could offer the possibility of a multiplied or synergistic relief of suffering – an augmented effect beyond the sum of the separate parts.

THE RELATION BETWEEN LAW AND SUFFERING

The relation between law and suffering is seldom considered explicitly. Law, in itself, can either inflict suffering or reduce it. Law can be used as well to implement measures that would avoid or relieve suffering. In these cases, the law can be regarded as an instrument external to, or "once removed" from, the relief of suffering itself. But some legal instruments, such as the Charter,[11] can be viewed as direct suffering-avoidance mechanisms – especially suffering caused by the law itself. The Charter ensures that law – for instance, legislation – does not inflict unnecessary or unjustified suffering. To be constitutionally valid, legislation that infringes on Charter rights or freedoms must conform to "the principles of fundamental justice"[12] and the limits imposed must be reasonable and such as can be demonstrably justified in a free and democratic society.[13] Other requirements of the Charter, such as fairness and equality before the law,[14] can have a similar function.

It could be argued that the Charter and similar legal instruments are legal implementations of fundamental ethical principles. This link can be characterized as an example of ethics "informing" law, rather than vice versa (which has usually been the case). Such a view of the Charter is reinforced by regarding it as a suffering-reduction instrument, since a primary function of the application of ethics is to avoid or reduce suffering when reasonably possible.

Possibly the most dramatic example of the Charter being used to strike down legislation, expressly on the basis that it unjustifiably inflicts suffering, is to be found in one of the plurality of judgments of the majority of the Supreme Court of Canada in the *Morgentaler* case.[15] Chief Justice Dickson and Justice Lamer (as he then was) held that section 251 of the Criminal Code[16] (now section 287), the Canadian "abortion law," was constitutionally invalid, *inter alia*, because it infringed a woman's right to security of her person under section 7 of the Charter. These judges reasoned that the very existence of the section's procedural requirements for performing a legal abortion – in particular, that a "therapeutic abortion committee" must certify the woman's medical need for one – meant that a pregnant woman who needed an abortion to protect her life or to avoid a serious threat to her health could not be certain of obtaining one. What if, for example, a therapeutic abortion committee had not been established in her hospital or region? These judges reasoned that a woman's knowledge that she might not be able to obtain a legal abortion, when clearly therapeutically necessary (especially when her life could be threatened by not having one), would be a source of severe psychological suffering. The mere existence of these legislative provisions, they ruled, infringed women's constitutional right to security of their persons.

A further consideration in relation to law, human rights, and suffering is potential conflict between respect for individual human rights and communal claims, especially the protection of collective rights, if they do or should exist (which is open to debate). Some communal claims to the protection of public health can conflict with individual rights to autonomy, confidentiality, and privacy. How can we resolve this conflict? I propose that this is now a crucial and fundamental question in relation to the future development of human rights – especially in the medical context. It is probably in the latter context, I suggest, that this issue will be most fully explored first, new approaches tried first, and new responses – though probably not solutions – developed first. Responses will need to be subject to continuing review and adjustment.

Concepts of human rights, as developed in Western European and Anglo-American legal traditions, focus strongly on individuals as individuals. This focus has been essential to win adequate recognition of their rights. But individuals do not exist as isolated units; they live in a complex series of relationships with other individuals, institutions, governments, and society as a whole. Further developments in human rights will have to take all these relationships into account. It will almost certainly require more sophisticated and nuanced concepts than the current ones.

We will need to explore the difference between protecting the group for its own sake (because it wants, and has a right, to survive as a group) and protecting it for the sake of the individual (to maximize respect for the human rights of all individuals). Much work is required to understand what is needed and how best to fulfill these needs if we are to protect human rights in a broader context than one focused exclusively on the individual. One problem that we might face is that the individualistic human-rights concepts are often inadequate in terms of taking into account the full reality and complexity of a modern medical context. I do not suggest that the pendulum has swung too far towards individual rights and is swinging away from these rights and back to communal concerns. We could, rather, imagine these two sets of claims as being "parallel rights."[17] The best image is that of a double helix; we are returning to communal concerns, bringing with us a sensitivity to individual human rights.

Is it possible to establish some kind of system or structure that would allow both individual and collective claims, needs, or even rights to be taken into account concurrently? We often face this need in connection with HIV infection and AIDS. Solutions are easy when one person is right and the other wrong; it is not so easy when they are both right (both have valid claims, but they are in conflict). In these cases, a "no harm" answer is almost always unavailable. Choosing between competing claims means choosing between harms. How we do this and what we choose will set far-reaching human-rights and other precedents. And that, in turn, will have a major impact in setting the ethical and legal tone of our society.

FACTORS CAUSING INQUIRY INTO HUMAN RIGHTS IN MEDICINE

A range of factors, some of which relate to medicine directly, have stimulated inquiry into the role and function of human rights in medicine and medicine in human rights. It is no accident that there has been a remarkable increase in the exploration of human rights in the medical arena.

The Changing Role of Organized Religion

One of the factors precipitating this interest is a change in the role of organized religion in the public square and, in some societies, a decline in adherence. There is a major cascade of causes and effects of this phenomenon. For instance, it has been suggested that sexuality has replaced religion in our lives.[18] Another effect is that humanistic concerns that are epitomized and institutionalized in human-rights principles and law have, to some extent, replaced religious ones; the focus is more on this world than the next. These humanistic concerns require a secular forum in which to be expressed and implemented through value creation, value articulation, value carrying, and value exploration, by both individuals and society. One forum that plays a major role in these respects is that of medicine.

Medicine as a "Safe Forum"

Medicine was chosen by default. Although trust in many, or most, professions and institutions has been shaken, there might still be more trust in medicine than in most other institutions – especially political ones. Areas that present human-rights dilemmas in the context of medicine include euthanasia, reproductive technology, AIDS, and health care for an aging population. These issues might be considered too dangerous, on the whole, to be dealt with in an unsafeguarded forum. Medicine carries the values of caring, healing, "first do no harm," relief of suffering, and humaneness; most other institutions carry few, or even none, of these values. As a result, medicine appears to be a safer forum in which to "try out" approaches to potentially dangerous problems. If the results were to prove unacceptably harmful, these approaches might be able to be confined and abandoned. Dangerous precedents that could be used broadly outside medicine might be established, but it could be easier in a medical context than in other ones to confine these dangerous precedents or to eliminate them. Even acceptable precedents within that context (such as the intentional wounding that occurs in every surgical operation) would be unacceptable outside it and, therefore, not transferable to others. It is worth noting, finally, that these characteristics – non-precedent setting, non-transferability – might not be true for most non-medical contexts. This factor reinforces the appropriateness of medicine as the forum in which some difficult ethical and human-rights issues should be handled initially.

Breaches of Values in Medicine

Worth articulating here is the correlative form of the proposition that medicine carries and establishes important values for society as a whole. If caring, humaneness, and relief of suffering are breached in the medical context, they are breached not only for medicine but also for society as a whole. Because medicine carries the symbolism that we are caring individuals and a caring society, for instance, it also carries the value of not caring – if this is, in fact, what we do. This latter possibility explains some of the uproar in the general community caused by something done in the medical context – in hospitals, for example – although the health-care professionals involved are astonished, because they view their conduct as perfectly reasonable in the health-care context. Very often, the uproar does not relate to the immediate and direct effect of the act performed, especially if it is judged solely within the medical context. It relates to the wider implications of what was done and what it means in terms of precedent-setting for society as a whole. Deciding not to treat a very premature new-born child might seem an entirely appropriate decision to a neonatoligist, for instance, but could be regarded as unacceptable by members of the general public.

*Personal Identification with Breaches of Human Rights
in Medicine*

All people can relate personally to breaches of human rights in the medical context, because, at some time, they or their loved ones have been threatened by illness or death, have needed medicine to respond to their needs, would perceive a non-response as a breach of fundamental human rights, and know how they personally would feel (not only what they would think) under similar circumstances. This personal, emotional identification with breaches of human rights in medicine provides a rare opportunity to raise the level of sensitivity to breaches of human rights in general. As citizens of Western democracies, we do not relate to many other breaches of human rights – political imprisonment, say, or even racial discrimination – in the same way that we would, for example, to denying medical care to a desperately ill child. This universal personal identification might provide a unique opportunity to educate people about human rights more generally. The sensitivity to human rights that can be raised by their breaches in the medical context might be able to be generalized to raise sensitivity to breaches occurring outside this context. Fortunately, many of us have not been personally threatened by non-medical breaches of human rights. We do not personally identify ourselves with them, therefore, or those who suffer them. Although we think that these breaches are wrong, we do not necessarily feel the pain involved. But we could learn to transfer to these other breaches of human rights the sensitivity that we experience in relation to breaches of human rights in medicine.

Because breaches of human rights in medicine are usually non-violent, they often arise from indifference to patients and are perpetrated in the name of doing good. Investigation of such breaches could be particularly valuable for insights about other breaches. In the medical context, indifference, the opposite of both love and hate, can be particularly cruel – indeed, a cause of immense suffering – to patients. The purpose of "doing good" can obscure sensitivity even to the fact of breaching human rights. It has been said that nowhere are human rights more threatened than when they are breached in the name of conferring benefit. Also, it is more difficult to identify and deal with those who breach human rights when they purport to do good than when they do not.

THE JUXTAPOSITION OF MEDICINE, HUMAN RIGHTS, AND SUFFERING

Finally, what insights could the juxtaposition of medicine, human rights, and suffering provide? There are many "high tech, modern, medical miracle" situations that could be examined in response to this question, but I want to address some issues and situations that arise every day in every hospital with this question in mind. It might be more difficult both to identify and to deal with breaches of human rights when they occur within everyday life, or, at least, we might be much less sensitive to them.

Informed Consent

The relation between informed consent and respect for human rights is clearest when one articulates the principles underlying requirements for informed consent. Informed consent is one way of respecting people's rights to autonomy and inviolability, both fundamental human rights.

Informed consent has been much talked about in ethics and law, but, as discussed in chapter 11, not usually in relation to reducing suffering. If suffering is loss of control over what happens to oneself, and if requiring that physicians have informed consent to treatment is a way of giving control to patients, then informed consent is a way of reducing suffering.[19]

We may feel differently about an outcome that involves suffering when we have chosen it, as compared with when it has been imposed on us, even though the outcome is the same. Choice can reduce suffering. Consider the treatment of breast cancer. A woman might feel very different, and suffer less, when she has chosen to have a mastectomy after a range of alternative treatments, with their benefits and risks, has been explained and offered to her, than she would if she felt that this same treatment had been imposed on her.

If the doctrine of informed consent is viewed and required as a way of reducing suffering, physicians would be more likely to accept it and honour it in practice, and not only in theory. Furthermore, some very difficult problems could be analyzed differently. I return, again, to a case we have discussed previously. At a conference held for the opening of the International Year of the Handicapped, a question was raised regarding quadriplegic people. One woman said, "I work at a unit for persons with high level spinal injury, such that the only thing that these patients can do, voluntarily, is to blow breath." She said that in any other place in the world, at that time, every one of these patients would have been dead; they could be kept alive at this unit, though. A board with buttons on it, which responded to blowing, had been designed. Paralyzed patients could cause books to be brought down and pages turned, providing they blew on the appropriate buttons. These people were all on respirators. The question was, "Is it ethical and legal to include a button, which the person would be able to blow on, to turn off the respirator?" The woman explained that this button would not be able to be activated for the first six months, because they wanted the people on respirators to "settle down." If we see this choice as a way of reducing suffering, in that it allows patients control over their treatment and provides a way to refuse treatment – a right that is enjoyed by all people, but that paralyzed people need a special way to exercise – we might view it differently than if it is characterized as, for example, a means to commit suicide. We cannot alter the fact that these people are quadriplegic, which causes them much suffering. But they might feel differently about living in this state if they have chosen to live. Indeed, they might choose to live provided they have a right to refuse the treatment that keeps them alive. The doctrine of informed consent is meaningless unless it includes, as it does, the right to refuse treatment: the right of "informed refusal."[20] In some circumstances, such as those described above, this can translate to a right to be allowed to die free of officious intermeddling. And that could be the most basic of human rights.

Pain-Relief Treatment

As discussed on many occasions in this book, adequate pain-relief treatment has not always been readily enough available, particularly for dying people. To remedy this failure to relieve intense, avoidable suffering, we must carefully consider our attitudes and conduct. To label people with pain "complainers," to express fear that they might become addicts, to provide pain-relief treatment on a set schedule and not according to need – all of these things are unethical and should, in cases that cause serious harm, be legally actionable.[21] We need thorough education about pain-relief treatment, especially in hospitals. It should be based on acceptance of the principle that people have a right to it, or, even more exactingly that it is a fundamental human right. Pain-relief treatment that could or even would shorten life raises the most problems. If necessary to relieve pain, it should be made available with the patient's informed consent, prior authorization through a "living will," or with the informed consent of a legal representative or substitute decision-maker appointed through a "durable power of attorney." Intentional or negligent failure to provide adequate pain-relief treatment should be a potential source of legal liability – indeed, of medical-malpractice liability. In other words, there should be a legal obligation on physicians to make treatment available. This obligation is particularly easy to justify if access to needed pain-relief treatment is regarded as a basic human right.

We also need to become sensitized beyond our own personal zones of activity. For instance, we should be sensitive to the fact, as has been reported in *The Lancet*,[22] that over 30 per cent of people die with inadequate or no pain-relief treatment, especially in developing countries. Surely this is a situation with which anyone can personally identify; it is a horrifying statistic. According to one explanation, many developing countries are reluctant to make available the cheapest, effective drug for relief of serious pain – heroin – because they are afraid it will be diverted into "recreational" use. But that does not justify allowing the situation to continue. And neither does it justify developed countries attaching as a condition of their aid to developing countries that the latter must take steps that result in making narcotic drugs unavailable to their citizens who need these for pain relief. When thinking about the necessity for relieving pain, we should free-associate with "cruel and unusual treatment or punishment" and torture – and how they are dealt with in the context of human rights. Failure to provide pain-relief treatment can be compared. Nothing is more dehumanising, destructive, or degrading than to be in serious pain – especially when someone who is, or should be, able to relieve it refuses to do so.

Confidentiality, Human Rights, and the Relief of Suffering

Failure to respect medical confidentiality can be a breach of human rights and a cause of suffering when it is experienced directly as a form of depersonalization. It can be a cause of suffering more indirectly, too, when lack of control results from the breach of confidentiality. That can result in stigmatization and wrongful discrimination. Think of AIDS patients, for whom not enough is done to protect confidentiality. As a result, people who have neither the need nor the right to know the patients' diagnosis can become aware of it to the serious detriment of patients. People have lost their jobs or been refused continuance of their life or health insurance because their HIV-infected status became known in this way.

People should have a right to control the generation, recording, and dissemination of information concerning themselves. This right means that, as a general principle, all these activities would require informed consent. Any exception should be narrowly construed and clearly justified. Exploration of this principle and its exceptions has been undertaken elsewhere.[23] The problem is urgent and continuing. In summary, I suggest that any breach of confidentiality must conform to the ethical requirement that it is the least restrictive, least invasive alternative reasonably available, and likely to be effective in achieving a justified aim.

Allocation of Resources "to" and "in" Medicine

When it comes to the allocation of, and access to, medical resources (all of which can be regarded as "scarce"), many examples are "high-powered, high technology" ones. But the same problems arise at the everyday level.

Consider a situation that arose in one Montreal teaching hospital. An old lady spent four days in the emergency room because there was no bed for her anywhere else. The emergency room, where she died, was lit, twenty-four hours a day, with glaring lights. She had only curtains around her bed. What were her human rights? What were the human rights of her family and loved ones? What are the obligations of government, institutions, health-care professionals, and each of us? We might not have the right to very sophisticated and expensive medical technology, but surely we do have a right to avoid situations of this kind. Another example would be long delays. Patients are forced to wait for diagnostic tests, or test results, for serious illnesses. This delay is an avoidable form of intense psychological suffering. I suggest that we have a human right to humane and compassionate medical care, which includes a right not to have reasonably avoidable suffering inflicted (as occurred in the old lady's case) and to have unavoidable suffering in the form of pain relieved.

CONCLUSION

Mahatma Gandhi once pointed out an effective political device: when there are serious domestic problems, politicians could avoid, or at least reduce, their negative political impact by causing the population to focus on equally bad or worse events occurring beyond their borders.

We should make sure that our concern with human rights outside our own country does not mask the fact that we should be equally concerned with human rights inside our country. One area in which this is crucial is in the complex, often hidden, seamless web of human rights in medicine, which requires that we fulfill our obligations not to inflict suffering and to relieve or reduce it whenever possible.

14 Death of Pain: Pain, Suffering, and Ethics

The title "Death of Pain" can be interpreted in two ways: either *people die* of pain or the *pain dies*, but not the people who had suffered from it.

Some people die of pain directly, because leaving them in pain could conceivably shorten their lives. All their physical and psychological resources are focused on dealing with the pain, and they become exhausted sooner than would otherwise have occurred. People can die of pain indirectly, too. For instance, they might commit suicide because of it. In one case an elderly man, who had been in chronic pain for a very long time, was refused pain-relief treatment by a *locum tenens* physician on the grounds that he was addicted to the pain-relief drugs that his regular physician had prescribed for him. The old man returned home and committed suicide by hanging himself. His elderly wife found him dead in their woodshed. Physicians often worry that pain-relief treatment might shorten life, but it might never have occurred to this physician that the opposite could happen – that *refusing* to treat the pain could shorten life.

People can die of pain indirectly in another sense too. Fear of being left in pain is one of the major forces giving rise to calls for euthanasia. We need to compare killing people in pain and killing the pain, but not those who suffer from it. In some cases, euthanasia is proposed or used (as it sometimes is in the Netherlands[1]) as a substitute for compassionate and adequate treatment for pain.

If failure to relieve pain can have deathly consequences, why are some patients left in pain? To answer this question, we need to know some facts. We sometimes overlook the importance of having good facts in dealing with ethical issues. This is a serious mistake. *Good facts* (including, if necessary, research to establish them) are essential to *good ethics*, which, in turn, is essential to *good law.*

Also, we need to ask what our obligations are with respect to pain-relief treatment. What ought we to do (what is it our ethical and, I will suggest, legal duty to do)? What ought we not do (what is it our ethical and legal duty not to do)? And what need we not do (what may we or may we not do, because there is no duty present either to act or not to act)?

Having decided on our obligations, what must we do to ensure that they are honoured? One way is through the formulation of concepts that will encourage their fulfilment. Keep in mind that concepts and the language in which we choose to articulate these obligations are neither neutral nor merely descriptive. The concepts that we use for addressing important problems (such as pain and its treatment) both reflect and form us as individuals, institutions, and society; they influence the attitudes, values, beliefs, responses, and actions based on them. This influence is especially important in eliciting our responses to providing pain-relief treatment or euthanasia, in which powerful emotional and value-based factors are at play. I will return to concepts involved in establishing these values, attitudes, and beliefs; after that, I will discuss briefly the relation between pain-relief treatment and euthanasia.

WHY ARE PEOPLE LEFT IN PAIN?

Asking the question why people are left in pain is the necessary first step in establishing an ethical response to people in pain. The questions currently being asked often indicate how we will act in the future; the responses we currently give tend to reflect the past. As with many apparently simple questions, however, the answer(s) to this question reflects a complexity that cannot be explored comprehensively here.

Factors affecting sensitivity or non-sensitivity to the pain of others range from cultural to personal, from historical to self-protective, from psychological (that we lose pain memory) to social. They include the attitudes of health-care professionals to pain-relief treatment and to pain itself along with the influence of culture on these attitudes. They also include the problems of communicating that one is in pain and, therefore, eliciting what can be called a "pain-relief reaction" in health-care professionals; the inability of those in pain to verbalize their pain, especially young children; distancing from those in pain by those who could provide relief; and indifference to pain on the part of those obligated to relieve it.

HEALTH-CARE PROFESSIONALS' ATTITUDES

The attitudes of health-care professionals to pain, pain-relief treatment, and patients – either in general or to particular patients or groups of them – can all affect patients' access to adequate pain-relief treatment.

Attitudes to Pain-Relief Treatment

Sadly, it is still not uncommon to hear health-care professionals state that patients in pain are "just complainers" or that they do not want their patients to become "addicted." I was consulted by a physician who told me the following story. She was on night call at a major hospital, which accommodated many old and chronically ill patients. She was called to see a man who had very advanced metastatic carcinoma of the prostate. He was in severe pain. When she examined his chart, she found that the only pain relief ordered was Tylenol®. She changed the order to morphine, brought his pain under control, and gave instructions that morphine was to be used in a way that would keep the pain under control. She did not work at the hospital the following night. The night after that she was again called to see this same man. He was still in pain. On her way into the room, she commented to the nurse that they obviously needed to increase the dose of morphine. The nurse replied that the man was not on morphine; he was on Tylenol®. The attending physician, during the day, had changed the order, noting in the record that he would not have his patients becoming drug addicts. The physician on night call made a formal complaint to the director of professional services. The latter was aware of this attending physician's attitude, but was having great difficulty persuading him to provide adequate treatment to relieve patients' pain. The physician had argued that it was a matter of his right to professional autonomy to decide what treatment should be given.

This case is shocking as an isolated incident. It is even more shocking to learn of a similar case involving a different attending physician in the same hospital. This incident occurred several weeks later. A man dying of cancer of the larynx suffered from severe abdominal cramps. He had barely slept for three days. He, too, was given only Tylenol® by his attending physician. These cases together bring up the issue of the ethical "tone" of an institution. The tone in this one, if these examples are typical, is unacceptable. A very few people at the highest level of authority set the ethical tone or standards.[2] They have an important obligation to ensure that adequate pain-relief treatment is offered to patients, an obligation they must recognize and fulfill.

Attitudes to Pain

Tradition can still influence attitudes to pain, particularly those of practitioners in tradition-based and tradition-sensitive professions such as medicine. Historically, before the development of modern anaesthetics, physicians had to inflict pain in order to have any chance of curing or helping patients and, in many instances, of saving lives. As pointed out in chapter 11, in American medicine before 1850, the relief of suffering was a secondary consideration at best – saving life was the primary one – and acceptable only when it imposed no danger to life. This tradition could still have strong subliminal effects.[3]

Some physicians might be indifferent to pain, or at least to pain suffered by some groups of people. It is often noted that terminally ill people are, in effect, abandoned by some health-care professionals. This results in what psychiatrist and ethicist Jay Katz has called "intense pre-mortem loneliness."[4] Many patients would rather be dead than unloved, abandoned, and left in pain.[5] As I will discuss shortly, asking for euthanasia is one response that demonstrates this preference.

Physicians' attitudes are not formed in isolation; they reflect the larger culture. In this regard, it is interesting to note, as also mentioned already in chapter 11, that "mid-century America witnessed the growth of a masculine cult of toughness and callousness. This anti-sentimental glorification of insensitivity took two very different forms: one a reaffirmation of the traditional manly ability to endure pain; and the second, a newer more mechanical form of indifference to suffering. [Unless we are aware of these factors] ... it may be hard to imagine the extent to which the calculus of suffering constituted a major revolution in the techniques of decision-making in medicine."[6] In short, physicians have not always seen it as their role to be concerned about pain and suffering. Indeed, some have seen it as not their role. How closely do the attitudes to pain and suffering of contemporary physicians reflect those of the contemporary community? What are these latter attitudes? One way of answering this question is to identify the cultural factors that foster the relief of pain or suffering and their presence or absence in the community.

COMMUNICATION

To elicit the response of relieving pain or suffering requires its communication to those who can relieve it. But the form of communication can influence its effectiveness.

Some unpublished work by sociologist Ellen Corin[7] is interesting in this regard. She found that, in the United States, people who claimed to be in serious pain and suffering were seldom responded to by health-care professionals until they articulated their claims in terms of rights. In France (and some other French-speaking countries), "rights talk" tended to be ignored. But if patients claimed to be suffering and in pain, health-care professionals responded to them. Both responses indicate cultural preferences, or prejudices, and should make us aware of the role these factors can play in promoting or preventing access to treatment for pain.

Those who are unable to verbalize their pain, and therefore to communicate it by describing it in words, are often assumed to be in no pain. Research on the failure to treat or prevent pain in children has demonstrated this attitude. Until very recently we carried out medical interventions on children with little or no pain relief treatment – something that would never happen to adults.[8] Historically, people of low intelligence or even of low socioeconomic status (for instance, slaves) were believed not to have much sensitivity to pain.[9]

It is easier to detach from those who cannot communicate with us, or whose status or position we do not identify with. The result is that we depersonalize them. Sometimes we even deliberately avoid communication with others in order to take advantage of this reaction. Researchers forced to seek informed consent had difficulty carrying out risky or painful experiments; they did not have this same difficulty in the absence of personal communication.[10] One function of ethical and legal requirements relating to informed consent is to act as a counter-measure to this reaction, which places others at risk as well as dehumanizing them. To summarize, dis-identification and depersonalization can be seen as a method of blocking communication. They can be used consciously or unconsciously, especially when the content of the communication is frightening or painful to us – which is often true of the communication of pain.

Communication of pain can be blocked for an additional reason. When we are in serious pain, the pain possesses us; we are the pain. Others might then dis-identify from the pain that is seen as us, rather than identifying with us as people who happen to be in pain. They might do so as a protective mechanism, almost as though the pain could be contagious (or from fear of finding themselves in similar pain). Even health-care professionals can have these reactions. Instead of empathy they seek dis-identification (this is not me and could not be me). As a result, they depersonalize others who are in pain (they are not people like me or even people at all).

The ultimate, most horrible example of this phenomenon is torture. Torturers dehumanize their victims and, in the process, themselves as well.[11] Although torture might seem very far removed from many of the realities in which health-care professionals live and work, we need to be aware of the terrible fact that, in many cases of torture (possibly the majority), physicians are involved.[12] In some contexts the number of cases could be as high as 90 per cent. The involvement of physicians in administering the death penalty (in some states in the United States, for example)[13] is a related problem.

Both the infliction of pain and the infliction of death isolate other people. At one level they are "isolation rituals."[14] These rituals reassure those carrying them out that the same thing could not happen to them. Moreover, they also have the effect of bonding through shared guilt all those carrying out these rituals.

Recognizing how horrible these situations are and that they are far removed from any personal experience of most health-care professionals, could we nevertheless learn from them? Could ignoring pain have some of the same causes and display some of the same characteristics as the infliction of torture? These are tough questions to face, but they must be asked if we are to remedy the situation of patients left in pain. These questions are not fanciful or theoretical. In the *Rodriguez* case, which has been discussed in previous chapters, the Supreme Court of Canada was required to decide whether, in prohibiting physicians from helping patients in severe pain to terminate their lives,[15] the Canadian Criminal Code provision[16] that made assisted suicide and, therefore, physician-assisted suicide an offence was unconstitutional. Among other things, the court considered whether this prohibition constituted cruel and unusual treatment or punishment, acts that are prohibited by the Canadian Constitution. The court split five to four, the majority holding that the section of the Criminal Code prohibiting physician-assisted suicide was constitutional. The constitutional right against being subjected to cruel and unusual treatment or punishment was held not to be contravened by the prohibition on assisting suicide because it did not constitute any "treatment" of the plaintiff by the state (as is required for unconstitutional action under the Canadian Charter of Rights).[17] But the point of note here is that it was argued that leaving patients in unbearable pain could contravene the prohibition on cruel and unusual treatment or punishment – that is, the prohibition of torture.

Yet another barrier to communication of pain can involve the problem of telling the truth in cases of terminal illness. If patients are not told the truth, particularly in cultures that associate the administration of narcotics with fatal illness, adequate pain relief might not be provided; doing so would reveal the truth about terminal illness.

THE LAW AND PAIN AND SUFFERING

The law manifests an ambivalent approach in its response to cases in which pain and suffering are elements. We need to be open-minded, involved, and insightful if we are to find effective ways of using the law to reduce the likelihood that people will be left in pain.

The Law's Response to Pain and Suffering

The law's response to pain and suffering reflects some of the same reticence that are find in medicine. There have long been fears of both fraudulent claims and opening the "floodgates of litigation" by recognizing claims and awarding damages for "pure" mental injury[18] (that is, psychological harm that does not arise directly from physical injury).

Courts also speak of not awarding compensation for the "normal vicissitudes of life." These are almost always defined to include injury in the form of "pure" mental pain. One example would be grief or bereavement in the survivors of those wrongfully killed. Even when damages for pain and suffering can be recovered through a legal action, courts have limited the amount of damages. The Supreme Court of Canada has placed a limit, or "cap," on the total amount of damages that can be awarded for pain and suffering. The court made this decision largely to prevent a trend in Canada, similar to one that can be seen in American cases, towards very large jury awards for damages for pain and suffering. Some of these awards were handed down in medical malpractice cases.[19]

Fear of Legal Liability

Fear of legal liability, too, can inhibit adequate treatment for pain. This reaction is especially likely if the treatment could, or would probably, shorten life. These situations are becoming less likely, however, as more sophisticated treatments emerge.

There are no cases in which legal liability has been imposed for the provision of "reasonably necessary" pain-relief treatment. And authoritative bodies – the President's Commission for the Study of Ethical Problems in Medicine[20] in the United States, the Law Reform Commission of Canada,[21] and the House of Lords[22] in England – have stated that the provision of necessary pain-relief treatment is not a matter of potential legal liability. Nevertheless, many physicians still seem to believe that it is. Is it because what we know and what we feel are sometimes different?

Consider some studies on physicians' attitudes to withholding treatment as compared with withdrawing it.[23] One group of researchers in the United States found that although physicians understood that withholding and withdrawing treatment were governed by the same ethical and legal principles, many of them did not feel convinced. They were much less comfortable with the thought of withdrawing treatment than withholding it. The former was seen as a more difficult decision to justify than the latter, which could translate to a belief that they were at greater risk of legal liability for withdrawal of treatment than withholding it. In one sense they might be correct. Often withholding-of-treatment decisions are more medically clean-cut – it is obvious that treatment will not benefit the patient by prolonging life – and, therefore, are more ethically and legally clean-cut than are withdrawal decisions in which the medical facts are more ambiguous.

In any case, one radical response would be threatening to sue physicians for gross medical malpractice for failing to treat pain.[24] If it is not possible to get across the message that physicians need not fear legal liability for giving necessary pain-relief treatment, in other words, one remedy might be to bring home the message that they need to be concerned about legal liability for not doing so. (I do not advocate suing physicians as a general principle, but leaving patients in pain is such a serious matter that, lacking any other way to ensure relief that patients are offered relief, this approach would be merited.)

Leaving patients in pain can be regarded as not only unethical but also negligent (or even, I am tempted to say, criminally negligent). It should be regarded as unprofessional conduct. In other words, it should constitute a basis for disciplinary action by professional licensing bodies. This approach is not out of line – indeed, it is consistent – with that taken in general on the legal liability of physicians and other health-care professionals and on professional disciplinary action involving them. Leaving patients in pain can be regarded as equivalent to other culpable omissions by physicians such as failure to remove an acutely inflamed appendix, when no competent physician would fail to act. But not only the acts of individuals can be regarded as negligent; systems, too, can be "guilty" of negligence.

Negligent Systems

One example of a negligent system can be seen in the film *Terms of Endearment*. A young woman dying of breast cancer is in terrible pain. Her mother begs the nurse for help. According to her schedule, the nurse replies, there are still thirty minutes before the next morphine injection. This response is horrifying, but common. The system and its rules are considered more important than the patients. Priority is given to the comfort, calm, and security of health-care professionals; with no need to make any decisions, they may simply "follow orders."

An event in a Montreal hospital well illustrates yet another aspect of a negligent system. It involved a young physician attending a young man dying of AIDS. The patient was in terrible pain. At midnight there was no more morphine available in the hospital ward. The physician was told that "the pharmacy does not open again until tomorrow morning at nine o'clock." In desperation, the physician gave a lethal injection of potassium chloride, which, unlike morphine, was available on the ward.

Unreasonable failure to consult a specialist or to seek a second opinion can constitute medical malpractice. I suggest that this standard should be applied also in cases of unreasonable failure to consult on the treatment of pain. And an unreasonable failure to establish a system of reasonable access to pain specialists could constitute "systems negligence."

We should also, as mentioned previously, consider whether approaches to try to prevent the misuse of drugs could constitute an ethically and legally unacceptable system at a macro level – especially in connection with pain relief in developing countries. About 30 per cent of patients there die without any treatment for pain[25] because narcotics are made unavailable. That is a response to demands from developed countries (attached to foreign aid programs) to join "the war on drugs." This requirement probably does little to reduce the illegitimate use of these drugs, but it seriously inhibits their legitimate, indeed required, use.

CONCEPTS

We need to identify the ethical and legal concepts among those we currently recognize and use that could help to ground an obligation to relieve pain. These concepts can be substantive or procedural. Substantive concepts that could support claims of access to pain-relief treatment include the following: trust, human rights, respect for persons, respect for human dignity, relief of suffering, healing (which can be contrasted with curing), and covenant. A procedural concept is the order of analysis, that is, whether it starts from ethics or law.

Trust

Trust is essential to the formation and maintenance of all good human relationships. But not all forms of trust are the same. For example, we can compare paternalistically based trust (blind trust) with trust based on an egalitarian relationship (earned trust).[26] Blind trust is founded on role, status, position, and power. It operates on the basis of a principle that can be summarized as follows: "You should (must) trust me because I know what is best for you and will act only in your best interests." In contrast, earned trust is based on mutuality and reciprocity, a principal that can be stated as follows: "You can trust me because I will show that you can trust me."

The theory of trust that we espouse and use will affect the approaches we take. In a relationship based on blind trust, health-care professionals are likely to control the treatment for pain. If the relationship is based on earned trust, control is shared with or given to the patient. As pointed out elsewhere, suffering occurs when we lose control over what happens to us, accompanied by a sense of our own disintegration.[27] This means that having control can reduce pain and suffering. Therefore, the earned-trust approach, because it augments the patient's sense of control, can help to relieve both. Keep in mind, however, that although we can demand the blind trust of those we leave in pain, we cannot earn their trust. In other words, failure to relieve pain is antithetical to establishing earned trust, which is the essential base of contemporary relationships between health-care professionals and patients.

The change from blind trust to earned trust does not eliminate the need to have confidence in physicians. But physicians must merit this confidence by demonstrating their competence and integrity; in the past, such characteristics were often assumed. One sign of this change is the relatively recent requirement that physicians attend continuing medical-education classes as a condition of renewing their licences to practise medicine. One hopes that instruction about advances in pain-relief treatment will be treated as a core course in these classes.

Human Rights

To leave patients in avoidable pain and suffering should be regarded as a serious breach of fundamental human rights. In recent years there have been challenges to the universality of human rights, often along the lines that this concept is a creation of modern Western democracies and related to their political ideologies (in particular, their emphasis on individualism).[28] In a narrow sense, there is some truth to that position. The difficulty can be overcome, however, if we focus on the spirit of what we seek by promoting human rights and look for ways in which the goals we are trying to achieve can be developed and enhanced in all societies. One way, I suggest, is to focus on respect for all people. In the context of human rights, this objective is implemented through the concept of "respect for persons."

We should recognize the following principles: the informing principle of human rights is one of respect for persons; respect for persons is a universal requirement that, in some societies, we implement through the concept of legal rights; the concept of respect for persons is inextricably linked to that of human ethics, as well as, ideally, to that of legally enforceable human rights;[29] and to leave people in avoidable pain and suffering is to show great disrespect for them and to breach fundamental requirements of human ethics and human rights.

According to the *Oxford English Dictionary*, the word "respect" means to look back, to regard, to consider, a relationship of one person or thing to another, heed, care, attention, to treat with consideration. Compare looking back with looking down. We need to look back on (respect) and relate to others in pain in all of the senses denoted and connoted by the word "respect." But we need to avoid looking down on them, which connotes and denotes the opposite. This approach would do much to remedy the situation of failure to relieve pain. Also, we should look back on, not abandon, those in a form of pain that has its source at a macro level. Think of those who are caught in devastating wars or civil conflicts. We are obliged to do whatever we can to relieve their suffering.

Human Dignity

The term "human dignity" can operate as another expression of respect for people and for their human rights, but it can be misused. This can occur if human dignity is regarded as an extrinsic (attributed) characteristic of some people, not an intrinsic (essential) feature of all people by virtue of being human. The danger of the former usage is that it allows us to argue that some people have no dignity and that, therefore, nothing requires us to respect them.

Relief of Suffering

No more worthy goal can be promoted than the relief of suffering. It is a goal that gives a common aim to medicine, ethics, and law. In the exercise of our various professions, we all are, or should be, trying to relieve suffering (although we do so in different ways).

The aim of relieving suffering is the basis of consensus for "right thinking" people. Starting from consensus rather than disagreement can be very important in setting a constructive tone for and, therefore, in determining the outcomes of analyses and discussions. Starting from consensus, we do not feel the same way about those with whom we disagree as we do when starting with disagreement. In short, the starting point is not neutral with respect to the decisions we make – including those about pain-relief treatment.[30]

Finally, emphasizing the relief of suffering has an important impact on the values, attitudes, and beliefs of both individuals and society and, as well, on symbolism. As a shared value, in particular, it has an important impact in terms of establishing a "high" ethical tone and an appropriate legal tone.

Healing as Distinct from Curing

Too strong an emphasis on curing can cause us to abandon or ignore those who cannot be cured. We need to emphasize that they can still be healed. For example, their pain can be healed. Furthermore, we need to recognize that this is an immensely important task.

Covenant

The relationship between patients and health-care professionals can be characterized as a covenantal or fiduciary one. Both concepts are related to trust. Part of the covenant between a physician and a patient is that the former has an obligation to provide the latter with access to treatment for pain.

Covenant is related to the legal concept of contract, but it has a less materialistic aura. We often speak of it in terms of the "sacred," especially in relation to the nature of the obligations engendered. Consequently, within the context of covenant, one can speak of a "sacred duty" to relieve suffering by providing pain-relief treatment.

Analyzing from Ethics to Law

In contrast to the substantive concepts, procedural concepts way seem unimportant at first. In fact, however, they have profound implications. We should keep in mind that "form is no mere formality": procedural concepts can have profound effects on substance. This procedural concept involves a change in the order of analysis: instead of analyzing from law to ethics, as was most common in the past, we now analyze from ethics to law.

Take the question of whether we should provide pain-relief treatment that could shorten life. In many cases, analyzing from law to ethics has indicated to physicians that providing treatment is not allowed (although they were mistaken is this belief). But analyzing from ethics to law always indicates the opposite; it would require that we act to relieve pain and that the law accommodate us in (and certainly not prohibit us from) doing so. As I have already said, the starting point, the initial or basic presumption, is not neutral in terms of its effect on the outcomes of analyses and, therefore, of decisions. In short, it can matter whether we start from ethics or from law.

FEAR OF PAIN, DECISIONS AT THE END OF LIFE, AND EUTHANASIA

The problems presented by euthanasia are complex and diverse.[31] I discuss them in greater depth in other chapters. But some points regarding the interrelations of euthanasia and relief of pain are particularly relevant to this discussion of attitudes to pain and how to ensure its relief.

Almost everyone fears pain and being left in pain. In some senses, the power of modern medicine to prolong life provokes precisely these fears. The latter are sometimes summed up in statements that have a dramatic impact. People say they would rather be dead than "left to the mercy of doctors and their machines."[32] Some argue that the way to avoid the danger of this happening, and the fear it engenders, is by making euthanasia available. But that, I argue throughout this book, is a dangerous and harmful response.

To the extent that fear of pain or of being left in pain is a contributing factor in provoking calls to legalize euthanasia, it is imperative to change any reality that provides a basis for this fear. We should regard ourselves as having the strongest of ethical obligations to achieve such change. To do so is of the utmost importance to those whose pain would be relieved; to the reality and image of health-care professions and professionals as caring ones (and correlatively avoiding their being and being seen as not caring ones if they do not act to relieve pain); and to society itself, particularly in terms of maintaining some of its most important symbols and values. We must seek ways to relieve suffering and to kill pain, not the people who have pain and suffering.

CONCLUSION

In closing, I would like to explain the origin of my interest in the topic of pain and suffering at the interface between medicine and law. My father was in Australia and dying of widely disseminated prostatic carcinoma. I was telephoned in Canada and told that he had developed brain metastases and would die within a few days. I flew to Australia to find him mentally incoherent and in great pain. I insisted that a pain specialist be called in. His treatment was immediately changed, the pain brought under control, and he became entirely lucid. As I noted previously, he lived almost pain free for another nine months. He said two things to me: that he wanted to live as long as he could – but not if he had to endure such terrible pain; and that I must do something to help others in the same situation. (Probably not many of them had daughters who would "go berserk," as he described me as having done, in order to obtain essential pain-relief treatment.)

Decisions on how to deal with pain and suffering will depend, in part, on what we can do about it. This, in turn, depends on research; appropriate clinical systems; educating health-care professionals about pain-relief treatment; provision of access to health care, including pain-relief treatment; and so on. Both as individuals and as a society we must be courageous, compassionate, and wise in our approach to this topic.

PART FOUR

Respect for Dying People and Euthanasia

15 (a) Death at a New York Hospital

ENGELBERT L. SCHUCKING

The double doors of the critical-care unit in the kidney ward of a prestigious New York hospital stood wide open. Visitors, nurses, and nurses' aides walked in and out of the room, but I hardly noticed this busy traffic.

I stood near the elevator banks, where I had been ordered to wait. In my hands were plastic shopping bags from Gristede's filled with cosmetic and medical paraphernalia, bottled water, and legal papers, but I was unaware of them as I stared at the woman on the raised bed in the northeast corner of the critical-care unit. Intense light illuminated her naked body without a shadow, as if she were onstage, totally vulnerable. She was lying flat on her back, arms by her sides, her breasts standing up, filled with fluid. She had scant pubic hair, her legs were slightly parted, her right foot was turned outward.

Brenda Hewitt, poet and editor, was an Englishwoman of great style and wit who began her career on the *New Statesman* and came to the United States over twenty years ago. When the tragic events I am about to describe were all over, the following obituary appeared in the *New York Times:*

Brenda Hewitt, Editor, 53
With Johnson Publishing

Brenda Hewitt, the former editor of the book division of the Johnson Publishing Company, died of a kidney ailment in a New York hospital last Thursday. She was 53 years old and lived in Greenwich Village.

Miss Hewitt, who was born in London, edited and produced the Johnson Publishing Company's entire output from 1966 to 1973. This included such titles as *Black Power U.S.A.* by Lerone Bennett as well as classics that formed the core of many black studies programs. In the early 1960s, Miss Hewitt edited manuscripts at the University of Chicago Press, including Milton Friedman's *Capitalism and Freedom*. During the last 10 years, although Miss Hewitt was ill, she occasionally edited books for small presses.

I lived with Brenda for more than sixteen years. When her kidneys stopped working and she became a home dialysis patient, I nursed her. In the past six years I never left her alone for more than a few hours at a time, except for two one-day business trips. We loved each other, and her illness had brought us so close together that we could often read each other's thoughts.

But now she and I were back in the kidney ward where, eight years ago, she had received her first emergency dialysis. Dr P, her personal doctor since 1976 and director of dialysis at the hospital, had sent an ambulance to bring Brenda here for treatment of a possible infection. I had come along.

In the ninety minutes since our arrival the hospital staff had only exacerbated her critical condition by doing test after test – as if she were a new patient – without treating her. Dr X, the intern in charge of Brenda's treatment, had shown little interest in what I could tell him about her condition. In fact, he had cut me short and ordered me to wait outside. What I saw from there worried me: her naked body lay absolutely still.

The first-year resident on duty, Dr Y, was standing on Brenda's left side. He picked up her left wrist. He said cheerfully, "How are we, Miss Hewitt?"

There was no answer. I edged towards the open door of the critical-care unit to get a closer look. The doctor dropped her wrist and slapped her face. Her head rolled over lifelessly. He said, "There's no pulse." Dr X put his stethoscope on Brenda's chest. "No heartbeat," he said.

When I came close to Brenda's bed I noticed they still didn't have an airway. I said: "I want this resuscitation stopped. I'm legally authorized to make this decision." A few heads looked up, but that was all.

A long time seemed to elapse and then someone said "Code." Nobody hurried as they do on TV. A nurse rolled in a green steel flask that had been standing outside. She made me step out of the way. It was 5:14 p.m.

A nurse climbed on Brenda's bed and started to thump Brenda's chest. They had begun CPR (cardiopulmonary resuscitation). The nurse was kneeling at Brenda's left side, pushing her sternum rhythmically down with both hands. Meanwhile, Brenda's head was lying flat on the bed, face up. Somehow it had returned to its previous position, before Dr Y had slapped her face, which meant she certainly could not get any air. There was a huddle of personnel near the head of her bed, apparently trying to get a respirator to work. But no one had created an airway.

As millions of Americans know, the ABC of CPR is A (airway opened), B (breathing restored), C (circulation restored), in that sequence. If a person is unconscious, the lower jaw drops down and backward, so that the tongue seats the pharynx. To open the airway–A–you have to tilt the person's head all the way back, lift the neck so that the chin points straight up, remove any dentures, and then, if breathing does not resume spontaneously, start B – mouth-to-mouth resuscitation. But keeping the heart going will not ventilate the lungs, and lack of oxygen for more than four to six minutes results in irreversible brain damage. For a severely anemic patient like Brenda, the critical time might be even shorter.

I began to realize that, unexpectedly, the moment that Brenda had been awaiting for such a long time had finally come: her deliverance from years of almost continuous, unimaginable pain.

After eight years without kidney function, precariously supported in a state of constant severe anemia by a dialysis machine at home, blind in one eye, with severely impaired vision in the other, unable to walk because of a collapsed arch in her right foot, diabetic since youth, and stricken with multiple other afflictions, she was free at last. Death, the Redeemer, had come.

It was the previous summer that Brenda had decided she didn't want to be revived if death came. I had promised her *not* to resuscitate her in that event. No promise I had ever made had been so difficult; it went against all my feelings of wanting to keep Brenda with me as long as possible. Afterwards, I removed vials of epinephrin (adrenalin) and sodium bicarbonate that had been taped to the dialysis machine. Intravenous injection constitutes the last step – D, Definitive (Drugs) – in the ABCD of CPR.

I had also promised to make her wishes known if she could no longer speak. Suddenly a great calm came over me. I knew what I had to do and I was going to do it.

I took the legal papers from the plastic bags I carried. They gave me the power to help Brenda and included a handwritten living will, signed by her and two witnesses the previous September, and the original medical consent and authorization, drawn up with the help of an attorney and signed by Brenda before a notary public. It read:

I, Brenda Margaret Hewitt, residing in the City, County and State of New York, do hereby nominate, designate and appoint Engelbert L. Schucking, with whom I have lived in a close and loving relationship for these past number of years, as the person with full and complete right and authority to make for me any and all necessary and desirable determinations with respect to my health, medical care and/or treatment in the event that I shall, any time, be ill, incapacitated and unable to act on my own behalf or in the event that in the judgment of my physician or health provider it is not in the best interests for me to make such determinations.

I reject the use of artificial life support measures such as electrical or mechanical resuscitation of the heart when it has stopped beating, by mechanical respiration when my brain can no longer sustain my own breathing.

The documents stressed that I knew about Brenda's wishes to decline certain medical treatments, authorized me to receive all information about her, and waived all claims she might have against the medical personnel who followed my instructions.

With these papers in my hand, I tried to enter the critical-care unit to confront the doctors. A short, heavyset nurse's aide stepped in front of me. "You are not allowed in there!" she said gruffly.

"I am legally authorized," I replied, waving the papers.

"You must stay out," she insisted.

"I'm going in."

When I came close to Brenda's bed, I noticed that they still didn't have an airway. "I want this resuscitation stopped immediately!" I said. "Miss Hewitt doesn't want to be resuscitated! I'm legally authorized to make this decision for her. I have here the original of her living will signed by her before witnesses. I've also a notarized medical consent and authorization, signed by her, for me to act on her behalf to consent to or withhold treatment. Using that authority, I want this treatment stopped at once!" These words were said in a loud, clear, and commanding voice. I had the eerie feeling of merely having delivered *her* message while I was helplessly witnessing the inexorable destruction of her brain.

A few heads looked up, but that was all. The chest thumping continued without interruption. Finally a doctor urged me, "We must discuss this matter outside." He gestured for me to follow him. Reluctantly, I went with him into the corridor. He studied the papers, then asked me to wait. He would talk to the doctors inside.

When he had not come out again after about ten minutes, I walked back into the critical-care unit. Brenda was a heart-rending sight. A couple of hoses were stuck into her mouth, presumably ending in a tracheal tube. Her face was grotesquely distorted. There was a deep cut in the inside of her left thigh, and she was lying in a pool of pink arterial blood.

A man in a white hospital smock turned to me and introduced himself: "I am Dr Z, the chief medical resident." I gave him the documents and he read them. When I tried to help with an explanation, he said sharply, "I can read." He handed the papers back to me and added, "You have to step outside." He didn't express any concern about Brenda's wishes, but merely seemed disturbed that I was a witness. I didn't budge.

"What gives you the right to cut her up like a piece of meat against her will?" I asked angrily. Nobody answered. They just went on.

I tried the last argument I had to prevent them from treating Brenda against her will. "If you restore heartbeat, breathing, and electrolytes, but she comes out of this with brain damage, I'll hold each one of you who participates in this and the hospital jointly responsible," I said loudly. "I'll sue you and the hospital for every cent we can get."

"You're raising your voice. You're upset. You're disturbing the patients," said Dr Z.

"I am upset," I answered, "but that doesn't mean I don't know what I'm talking about. I must raise my voice if that's the only way to be heard."

Dr A, a senior staff member of the hospital's kidney centre, then arrived. He told me to come outside with him and we would consult a hospital administrator. He read carefully through the legal papers and listened when I told him some of the reasons for Brenda's decision against any attempt at revival when death came.

Dr A said amicably that the doctors who had disregarded Brenda's instructions were "erring on the side of life." I told him I didn't accept this excuse because doctors are not allowed to operate without informed consent. They were acting against the patient's wishes. We had a civilized discussion without result. He said he would talk to the doctors – Could I wait here for a moment? I said I would.

To reassure myself, I took Brenda's purse from one of the plastic bags I still carried. Next to her driver's licence and credit cards was a slightly crumpled white envelope, unsealed, addressed "To whom it may concern." I read what she had put down in her own hand in even horizonal lines – clear, precise, and unemotional

June 28, 1983

I have reached what appears to me to be the logical end of my life, and this statement is intended to protect me from well-intentioned efforts of the medical profession to restore or support life in me if I should, as a result of accident or design, fall into a state where I am unable to sustain argument on the subject, or to sign waivers.

I therefore state that from now on I would welcome death, and would want to resist any means used to avert it.

If I should become comatose or not fully conscious through the use of pain-killing drugs or any other substance which it might seem appropriate to me to take, no effort should be made to revive me or to use life-support mechanisms to maintain me in such a condition.

I went back to the unit to find Dr A and to try to see what was going on. A tall, burly man in a grey security guard's uniform and armed with a nightstick barred my way. "You can't go in there," he told me.

"My common-law wife is in there, dead or dying," I said. "She has legally authorized me to make all decisions with regard to her treatment. Will you prevent me by force if I go in there to be with her?"

"You can't go in there," he repeated, not moving. When I took a step forward, he assumed a threatening attitude.

I tried to think of another strategy. I needed a lawyer now if anything was to be done to follow Brenda's wishes. Perhaps I had to get a court order even to see her on her deathbed. I had promised her that I would be with her when death finally came. I phoned Brenda's attorney, but she was not at home.

At last Dr A came back. He informed me that Brenda's heartbeat and breathing had been restored. He was careful to point out that her breathing was hand-supported by some sort of bellows, not by an electrically powered automatic respirator. Presumably he remembered that Brenda's living will had explicitly rejected the use of "mechanical respiration."

What could I reply to Dr A? There wasn't the slightest chance her brain was still intact. Angrily I told him I was going to sue them for what they had done to her. I said I had been prevented by threat of force from seeing her. Dr A promised that he would arrange for me to see Brenda for "two minutes."

Dr A had more news. "The doctors have decided they will have to drain fluid from the bag surrounding the heart of Miss Hewitt," he said.

"A pericardiocentesis!" I exclaimed. "They can't do that without consent."

In the sober language of medical experts, a pericardiocentesis is considered a "potentially lethal procedure." It is a terrifying operation. The patient is propped up in a seated position and then approached by the surgeon with a trocar, a hollow dagger, which is connected to a large syringe. The doctor drives the trocar into the pericardium, the double-layered sac that contains the throbbing heart and the beginnings of the major blood vessels. The fluid constricting the heart is then drained off.

What Dr A had announced to me was, in fact, the beginning of a new turn in torture in which Dr X, nine months out of medical school and not yet allowed to treat people outside the hospital, would get the chance to perform an operation that is normally done only by cardiac or thoracic surgeons in a cardiac catheter laboratory. It could only mean agony for Brenda and further mutilation of her body.

I *had* to get a lawyer. Quickly. I tried twenty-four-hour lawyers from the Yellow Pages. I got only answering machines, except that in one case a secretary answered and said her employer would call me at home after midnight. He did – three days later.

Dr A returned to tell me I could now see Brenda for my "two minutes." But I was not prepared for what I saw. Her legs were stretched wide apart and her calves were tied to the sides of the bed. The straps were tight around her lower calves, where she could never bear even to be lightly touched. She was still naked. They had gone into the subclavian vein on the right side of her chest.

She was on a *mechanical* respirator. Either Dr A had lied to me or the medical team had assumed they could do whatever they wanted with her body. The intern, Dr X, stood near the bed.

"You are going to perform a pericardiocentesis," I asked.

"Yes," he said.

"You can't do that without consent," I told him. "You've no right and you know it. She's legally authorized me to act on her behalf. This will be aggravated assault and battery. I'll sue you. Do you think you can cut her up just as it pleases you like a piece of meat? Who gives you the right? Who do you think you are?"

An impatient Dr A motioned me out of the room and told me they had not been able to reach Brenda's personal physician, Dr P, so a hospital administrator had approved the actions of the staff. Brenda's own wishes apparently meant nothing.

I looked past the security guard into the care unit. Brenda's face and most of her body were hidden from my view by a screen. She had been propped up on a high seat behind it and I could see her legs dangling limply out in front. Dr X was facing her with the instruments on a table nearby.

Brenda was blind in her right eye. The lens in her left eye had been extracted to remove a cataract. She had to wear a soft contact lens and glasses to see things nearby. Probably all she could see in front and to her left was a glaring blur. Dr X would be faceless when he stabbed her.

It would be a quiet operation. If Brenda felt the cutting edge of the trocar piercing her heart, there would be no sound from her. A victim who has her mouth taped shut around air hoses and a tube in her windpipe cannot scream.

TUESDAY, 6 A.M.

It had begun as an ordinary nondialysis day. She had been sitting on the side of the bed, as usual, through the small hours of the morning, very tired but unable to sleep because of pain.

To deal with the pain, she massaged her legs, arms, and back with lotion. To pass the time, she often counted to ten thousand and back in a morning, or she would compose long stories in her mind. This morning she had tried to read a few more pages of *Little Men*. There was a mark at chapter 8 of the book she was never to finish.

Itching had also been particularly bad lately. She had scratched herself in a number of places that had become infected. I had put some bacitracin and neomycin on the lesions.

When I got up that day to prepare the assignments for my classes, Brenda was just drifting off to sleep. I woke her at 10: 30 a.m. She didn't like being awakened – it meant forsaking her dreams for the world of pain – but she had to take insulin and eat something.

In her dreams Brenda was still free. She had described this clash between dream and reality in a poem about a dying dolphin:

ESCAPE

All day she nestled by the marble flanks,
One salt-flecked sunwarmed arm across his back,
Her green eyes clear and fathomless with dreams
Of leaping, free and potent, from the seas.

She saw her body soar beside her god,
Bright water in cascades from gleaming skin,
The burst of sunlight on their skywards heads,
The shock of water to their smooth return.

She dreamed of journeys through a friendly sea
To islands, sandbars, reefs, and secret rocks;
Of silent hosts crooning in wordless tongue
Whose gentle strength upheld her failing force.

All day she dreamed. They went to her at dusk,
Urgent for dinner and preprandial drinks.
Her gaze was limpid, but her body cold
The dolphin's marble texture strangely warm.

When I left to teach my class, she was ready to go back to sleep. I put the cordless phone into the wheelchair at her bedside, lowered the blind, and filled the carafe with spring water. I blew her a kiss: "Bye, Peetel," I said, using a nonsensical pet name we had for each other. "Bye, Peetel," she said sleepily. I had not kissed her in years. The slightest touch on most of her body simply meant more pain.

She was still asleep when I returned from my noon class. At 3:30 started a bath. Plain water, even if treated with bath oils, hurt her skin. I ran the bathwater, therefore, through a large carbon filter, which took almost an hour. At 4:30 I woke her and lowered her into the bathtub.

After the bath I wheeled Brenda into the living room to her chair by the TV set. Harpo, her favourite cat, had been waiting all day for her to emerge from the bedroom. I served a Swiss mushroom soup with two slices of buttered toast. When she finished eating, I put the cordless phone, spring water, Demerol, the mail, the wastepaper basket, and a cup of hot tea within reach and left in a hurry to teach my evening class.

When I returned she was sitting in the wheelchair at the threshold of the kitchen, where I kept the spring water. She'd been thirsty and managed to transfer herself into the wheelchair to get more water. For one hour she'd been trying to get the wheelchair over the half-inch-high threshold, but she hadn't had enough strength. I felt guilty because, on the way home, I had stopped at the college bookstore to look at a sale and was ten minutes late.

I helped Brenda back into the chair, fetched her water, and put two stuffed peppers into the oven. I had brought back the weekly harvest of some 250 homework papers. Brenda helped me put them into alphabetical order and related the news: Gary Hart was the apparent favourite in the Connecticut primary.

I drew four units of insulin from the vial and handed her the syringe and an alcohol wipe. She pulled up her long white nightgown and injected the drug into her left thigh. The cat on her armrest jumped off – he couldn't stand the smell of the isopropyl alcohol on the wipe.

I disposed of the syringe and served dinner – a green pepper stuffed with rice in tomato sauce. She balanced the plate on her knees as she ate. We talked about politics. The *New York Times* was lying on the table between us, opened at the book page. She hadn't done the puzzle yet. We'd do that the next day, together, during dialysis.

After dinner, Brenda took a Demerol and a Valium. At 11, just after the TV news had started, she said, "I think I have a fever."

I helped her into the bedroom. Her blood sugar was high. She began to feel nausea, which could have been caused by the high blood sugar. Her pulse was accelerated, normal for a rising fever, but the temperature was not very high: 100.7 degrees Fahrenheit. Her blood pressure seemed all right. Her breathing was normal – twelve times a minute, not too deep, not too shallow, no coughing – I wasn't very worried. If we could get the blood sugar back to normal, she might feel a lot better the next day. The whole episode might just be one of the low-grade fevers she got almost every month and that usually disappeared the next day.

Towards midnight Brenda said, "I feel very ill." And after that, "I think I am dying."

How did she know? I looked at her. She seemed tired, but I did not see a hippocratic [sic] face. I had not noticed the coming of *mal'ak hamaveth*, the Messenger of Death.

WEDNESDAY, 12 MIDNIGHT

I sat by her bedside all night to comfort her. The blood sugar came down in the morning and I gave her some dextrose intravenously very slowly, to forestall an insulin reaction. She was unable to keep down food or orange juice. The nausea and the fever remained. I thought she might have a staph or strep infection that had started with the lesions on her skin.

I called Dr P, her personal physician, at 9 and told him about Brenda's condition. "You'll have to bring her to the hospital, Engelbert," he said. "You know she wouldn't want to go," I told him, "but I'll ask her and call you back."

I woke her. Her condition had not changed in the past nine hours. "Peetel," I said, "I think you have an infection. I've talked to Dr P. He says you'll have to go to the hospital. Are you willing to go?" I gave her a sip of hot water from the thermos bottle. She swallowed slowly and answered, "No, I want to die at home."

"Do you mind if I get a doctor to look at you?" I asked. "Perhaps he can take a blood culture and Dr P might then be willing to prescribe an antibiotic that I can give you on dialysis later." She didn't seem to care. I called Dr P back. He said he was willing to talk to the doctor who would come to see her.

I called one of the housecall services listed in the Yellow Pages. The doctor, a young nephrologist, came two hours later. He looked at Brenda briefly and took her blood pressure. I showed him my home chart and her last blood chemistry. He tried to reach Dr P the phone, but Dr P was out to lunch. He said Dr P could call him through his agency; they would beep him. Then he took me aside: "You have to get her into a hospital."

"She refuses to go," I said. "She's had very bad experiences." He insisted: "She has an infection. If she does not get treated, she can be dead in a few hours." He wouldn't prescribe any antibiotics that I could give Brenda during dialysis or give her any himself without talking to Dr P. I wrote him a check for $40 and he left.

At 2 p.m. I finally reached Dr P and gave him the number of the doctor who had seen Brenda. About twenty minutes later Dr P called back. He had talked to the doctor and they both agreed I had to bring her to the hospital. I said I'd like to give her vancomycin (an antibiotic that we had used for Brenda's infections in the past, but our supply had run out) during dialysis at home and asked if he could phone in a prescription. Dr P said, "No. This infection can be caused by anything. Vancomycin might not be effective."

"She's very weak," I told him. "The stress of transport has to be considered and, as you know, she has refused to go."

"You can wait till she's in a coma and then take her," Dr P said.

"No, I couldn't do that," I replied.

His voice became urgent. "Engelbert, this is an emergency that you can *not* treat at home. I'll phone the kidney ward. They'll have a bed ready for her and I'll send an ambulance."

"Yes," I said.

Dr P hung up. I shall regret that yes till I die.

I packed in a hurry. In a couple of days, I thought, we would be back home.

The doorbell rang. I woke Brenda and said: "Peetel, I'm very sorry. I'm at my wit's end. They won't give you antibiotics unless I take you to the hospital. The ambulance is here. I'm very sorry, Peetel. I don't know what else to do." Brenda was only half awake. She turned away from me to lie on her side. She said nothing. I knew what I was doing was wrong. I had betrayed her.

Brenda's bed wasn't ready when we arrived at the kidney ward. A patient was wheeled out of the critical-care unit and an empty bed was brought in. A tall young man in a white smock introduced himself: "I'm Dr X. I'm in charge of your wife."

"Are you an intern?" I asked.

"Yes," he said.

A shorter young man joined us and said, "I'm Dr Y. I'm the resident in charge of your wife."

"Are you a first-year resident?" I inquired.

"Yes," he said. "Dr X will ask you some questions about the patient."

Dr X asked me, "Is she allergic to penicillin?" I remembered the last time Brenda had been asked this question. "No," she'd said, "just to doctors."

Dr X wanted to know what medication she took. I told him, adding that she was a diabetic and blind in her right eye. I showed him the home chart. He looked at it for only a second. "I see, her blood sugar was never under 100 today."

"No," I said, "not at all. It was 70 this morning."

But he didn't seem to listen. He handed the chart back to me as if all this information could be of no interest to him and said abruptly: "I have to do a few tests. You have to wait outside."

I left reluctantly. If Brenda had been given a single room I wouldn't have budged. But with other women being treated in the critical-care unit, I felt out of place. I realize now I should never have left her.

From the visitors' lounge I saw Dr X with a tray of test tubes filled with blood (the hospital bill listed fifty-two different blood tests – costing a total of more than $1200 – for this evening alone). He said they'd be finished soon with their tests. I was stunned. The only words I could think of came from the field of engineering: "destructive testing."

When I took up my watchpost by the elevator banks, Dr X and Dr Y, flanking their charge, seemed to be discussing something. They didn't look at their patient. Their patient was dead.

THURSDAY, 9 A.M.

Brenda appeared unchanged since the previous night, but her eyelids were moving. Was she trying to convey something? Both eyelids simultaneously went open-shut, open-shut, open-shut. But then I realized this motion was exactly synchronized with the respirator. No message from behind dead pupils – just a reflex. My love had been turned into an obscene puppet.

The pupil of her left eye did not respond to light. She was in a coma. Her beautiful brain had been destroyed.

No sign of Drs X, Y, or Z. I asked whether Dr P had been in to see her. He had not. I left to go talk to him.

"Have you seen Brenda?" I asked.

"No, not yet," he said. "But I've heard. It's very sad."

"I want you to do two things," I announced, looking him straight in the eye. "One, I want her removed immediately from the kidney ward and transferred to another critical-care unit in the hospital."

"I'm afraid that's impossible," said Dr P. "No other critical-care unit in this hospital would take Brenda in her present state."

I was surprised by this flat refusal. I told Dr P: "My second request is, I want the respirator removed."

I reminded him that Brenda had given him a copy of her living will and the medical consent and authorization form, and asked him to attach them to her chart. He had agreed to honour them. I handed him copies of these documents and the letter she had left for her friends and family.

Dr P read all the papers and said: "I'll have to talk to the doctors. I'll be over there later."

I left and went back to the kidney ward. A man suddenly appeared behind me. He said he had heard I was having problems with the doctors attending Miss Hewitt. Perhaps he could help me – he was the "patients' representative." Could we go into the visitors' lounge to discuss the matter?

We did so, but it soon emerged that he was not very interested in learning what had happened yesterday. I became suspicious and asked, "Who are you working for?"

"The patients," he answered.

I tried again: "Who employs you?"

"The hospital," he replied.

Possibly sensing my misgivings, he said: "Let's not get involved in what happened yesterday. Let's talk about today. Perhaps we can make a deal." He handed me his business card. I shuddered, suddenly comprehending: here was the Messenger of Death. A salesman in a business suit suggesting, "Let's make a deal." He made copies of my documents and asked me whether I was agreeable to having a conference with Drs P, X, Y, and him in the doctors' lounge. I said yes.

There were no handshakes when I met the assembled doctors. Dr P was sitting at the conference table with Brenda's medical chart in front of him. Drs X and Y were also there, but barely acknowledged my presence.

"Can you tell me how long her brain was without oxygen?" I asked.

Dr Y answered, "She was without circulation for five minutes, but the blood pressure was so low for twenty minutes that the oxygen supply was quite insufficient during that time."

"Would you then say that she has suffered extensive brain damage?" I asked. "Yes," he said.

"What is your prognosis for her coming out of the coma?"

"Our experience with diabetic dialysis patients who have suffered brain damage is that the damage is usually severe and irreversible," he answered. I wondered whose experience he meant. He looked too young to be speaking so authoritatively from his own.

"Did you take an EEG [electroencephalogram]?" I asked.

"No."

"Her living will," I continued, "states clearly and explicitly that she rejects respiration by machine. I want the respirator removed."

Dr P said, "Yes, we shall do that," and added quickly, "We'll naturally withhold dialysis."

Today the doctors seemed to be more inclined "to err on the side of death." Was that the "deal"? If Brenda could breathe on her own, I thought, I'd take her home. Not one of these doctors would ever touch her again.

I asked how long she might live without artificial respiration. The answer was, "We don't know."

"I have a last request," I said. "I want all restraints taken off her, anything that might make her feel uncomfortable after you have removed the respirator, and then I want to be left alone with her."

The conference was over. Dr P wrote a long statement on Brenda's chart, closed it, and, clutching it tightly, said, "I'll have to go." I smoked a cigarette to calm myself. The first time I read the medical consent and authorization, it had registered in my mind simply as a legal document. Now I began to understand what it meant. It was a letter of ultimate love and trust. What it said, in effect, was: "I am all yours; *you* decide how much I shall suffer; *you* judge what will be done to me. Let me live if you want me to; let me die if you think it is time."

Was it now "a time to die"? Should I let Brenda die by doing nothing? Dr X interrupted my attempt to find an answer by announcing that I could see her now.

They had covered Brenda with a white sheet up to her neck. The tubes to the respirator were gone, but the leads of the EKG were still attached and the sleeve of a blood pressure cuff hung loosely around her left upper arm. Her pulse was strong, her breathing laboured. Her blind eye was closed, her left eye open. Its pupil was large and did not react to changes in light intensity. She was, perhaps, blind now–a fate she had feared more than death. The contact lens, dried hard, was sticking like a splinter of glass into the left corner of her eye. Her upper denture was in place; presumably it had not been noticed. Brenda's face was puffy, almost unrecognizable. Her neck was distended and bruised. I felt a cold fury. I should *never* have brought her here.

I told the nurse I wanted to be left alone with Brenda, and drew the curtain around her bed. Digital pulse data flickered in red on the monitor screen. The numbers were nonsense; the equipment wasn't working.

I didn't pull back the sheet that covered most of her body. I couldn't bear to see the wounds, the bruises, the hurts they had inflicted on her. I was afraid I might discover more than I had already seen.

I spoke many words of love into her ears, all those silly words lovers use to each other, words of closeness, words that jog memories. No sign of recognition. I urged her to lift a finger. There was no response. Perhaps she was deaf now. I pressed her right hand – it remained limp.

Over the next half hour, the frequencies of pulse and breathing were steadily slowing. I told Brenda her pain and suffering would soon cease. I asked her forgiveness for having brought her here. Her breathing became louder. I held her left hand and felt her pulse. I could smell her neighbour's bedpan. I looked at Brenda for a last message, a last nod, a last sign before death came.

Her heartbeats were five seconds apart when something hit me in the back. Someone had come in under the curtain. I said: "Please, leave us alone. She's dying." Something bumped into my back again. Without taking my eyes from Brenda, I said, "Please go!"

Thanatos, the Angel of Death, had arrived and a voice behind me muttered, "I've come to get the TV set."

I turned half around to look into the blank eyes of a nurse's aide. I told her, "Have you no sense of decency left?" She went without a word.

I had just felt the last beat of Brenda's pulse. There was one more breath, so woeful I shall never forget it. The time was 11:40 a.m. I closed her eye. I kissed her lips at last. It would no longer hurt.

---

15 (b) Searching for the Governing Values, Policies, and Attitudes: Commentary on "Death at a New York Hospital"

One statement is made by almost every person who enters my office to discuss a case of medical malpractice: "Even if nothing can be done for me, I want to make sure, as far as I am able, that this doesn't happen to somebody else." There is a good psychological reason for this attitude: converting a negative event, the consequences of which are often irreversible, into some positive value can help us to deal with the feelings of anger, loss, and outrage the event engenders. This transformation is therapeutic for the person. In addition, it might prove therapeutic for a wider group – those who are helped as a result of awareness raised by the publicity surrounding cases of medical malpractice.

Engelbert Schucking's "Death at a New York Hospital"[1] is a particularly forceful and moving example of the phenomenon just described, although the situation Schucking encountered does not necessarily involve medical malpractice in the strict legal sense of that term. The article communicates strongly, at both cognitive and emotional levels, many of the questions that should be asked in these situations.

WHAT ISSUES ARE PRESENTED BY "DEATH AT A NEW YORK HOSPITAL"?

The common factor in debates over the treatment of dying people is recognition of the need to diminish or alleviate human suffering and to promote humane and sensitive medical care. Unfortunately, none of the five physicians mentioned in "Death at a New York Hospital" treated Brenda Hewitt according to the maxim *primum non nocere* (first, do no harm) or applied to her the never-to-be-cast-aside "patient as person" approach.

There is a continuum in the ways that patients can be approached, and its two poles are reflected in Schucking's article. On one hand, Schucking tells the warm, sensitive, personal, caring, loving, respectful, accepting, human, and humane story of Brenda Hewitt, of their relationship, and of her feelings and thoughts about impending death. In particular, the article documents Hewitt's final request for an act of loving relationship – namely, that her life should be allowed to end peacefully, in the way that she wanted, and free from officious meddling. On the other hand, the medical-hospital machine to whose care Hewitt was entrusted is presented as cold, uncaring, mechanistic. It is insensitive, to the point of suggesting that a young physician will be able to practise a difficult medical technique on a dying woman who has expressly refused any interventions. The people who appear in the chorus of this part of the drama-tragedy are like robots.

Schucking possibly gives a somewhat polarized impression and description of the events and people involved in Hewitt's death. Nonetheless, there is real grief and harm present, and we cannot afford to ignore this reality. Moreover, he is not alone, unfortunately, in experiencing the treatment his loved one and he received in a medical context as brutal. A health-care system that evokes the symbolism of a messenger of death – the patient's representative who handed Schucking a business card – should be replaced by one whose representatives appear as messengers of care and concern.

WHAT CAN BE DONE TO PROMOTE CHANGE?

If we want to reduce the chance that situations of this kind will occur, we should look at our values, policies, and attitudes – and the messages they convey not only at a conscious level but also at an unconscious one and in the form of symbolism. Second, we must establish effective means of communication. For every person like Schucking, who has expressed what he experienced in such a direct and moving way, many more people suffer similarly but go unheard. If someone of Schucking's socioeconomic status and educational background could not communicate with the health-care professionals he encountered, how much less likely are most other people to make themselves heard? Moreover, the health-care professionals described made little or no effort to communicate, in the proper sense of that word, with Schucking.

Third, we need to differentiate between communication and consensus. Communication is imperative; consensus is not always possible. Physicians and hospital administrators are not always bound to follow directions such as those given by Schucking (although, in my view, they should have complied with his instructions in the circumstances described and the basic presumption should be that such instructions ought to be followed). Very infrequently, there is a valid reason to ignore the wishes that were expressed, while competent, by now-incompetent patients or by their "designated or significant others." But there should always be adequate communication. It shows respect for others even when their views are justifiably overridden. It puts others on notice that overriding could occur and allows them to take any steps available to avoid it. It represents the minimal abrogation of the normal rules requiring respect for personal rights. And it maintains, to the highest degree possible, recognition of the personhood of those whose wishes are being overridden. The degree and form of communication required to implement these aims were absent in the situation described by Schucking.

WHAT VALUES SHOULD HAVE BEEN RESPECTED?

Respect should have been shown to Hewitt by respecting her values and her right to decide what should happen to her, both before and after she became incompetent, up to the moment of her death. She had long considered the situation that at last arose and had made her wishes clear. She had taken all possible steps to avoid precisely what happened to her. She had communicated her wishes. And she had identified someone, the one most likely to know what she would want and whom she loved and trusted, to make decisions on her behalf. Moreover, she had formalized these steps by making a living will and providing a durable power of attorney.

It is frightening to think that these steps were so ineffective in achieving the outcome Hewitt wanted. There was nothing else that she could have done legally or extra-legally – apart, perhaps, from committing suicide – in order to ensure that she would never be admitted to a hospital in the last stages of her illness and, as a result, run the risk that her wishes would not be respected. Respect for others' rights to autonomy and self-determination is fundamental to human dignity. Most of us would reject outright the idea that it is justifiable to jail or torture people in order to force them to change their political views. It is equally wrong to "force-treat" someone held in "captive" circumstances,[2] because as health-care professionals we regard this treatment as necessary in order to uphold our values or beliefs.

The living will and the durable power of attorney reflect the efforts of some modern legal systems to ensure more in-depth and effective implementation of the rights to autonomy and self-determination. These mechanisms allow wishes to be honoured even after people have become incompetent. They imply that patients' own values should guide decisions made about their medical treatment.

Values are reflected in policies – a statement that leads to the next question.

WHAT WERE THE GOVERNING POLICIES IN THE HOSPITAL DESCRIBED?

Policies can be articulated at various levels: by the government, the judiciary, or institutions. If courts were to recognize "over-treatment" as a form of medical malpractice – where no reasonably competent physician would have either undertaken treatment or continued it – this judicial policy could (and should) modify physicians' behaviour. The physicians involved at the end of Hewitt's life might have behaved differently if they had known that their acts could make them legally liable for "over-treatment." Of course, it is at best undesirable, and at worst destructive, to have to rely on the threat of legal liability to enforce minimal standards of conduct. Legal liability is a second-order remedy; the first-order remedy, and the appropriate one, is to convince people to modify their conduct for positive reasons – primary among which is that they see the change as promoting a "good" and avoiding a "harm."

Institutional policies, too, are important. One cannot help but think, in reading Schucking's article, that the hospital described had no appropriate institutional policy on the treatment of dying people. Did it have any policy at all? If so, what were its form and content? Was the policy explicit or implicit? Written or verbal? Could it have been simply to ignore the wishes of patients or their substitute decision-makers? Any policy like that would require very substantial rethinking, to say the least.

A few people at the top usually set the ethical tone for a whole institution.[3] Most of the physicians Schucking describes were relatively junior.

Were their approaches personal to them, or did they reflect those taken at the institution generally? If the latter, did these young doctors feel coerced, by positive or negative means, to accept the policies that gave rise to those approaches? We need to humanize institutions as well as the people working in them, although the first step towards the former is usually the latter.

FORMATION OF ATTITUDES

Assuming that the appropriate range of values has been identified and articulated, and that adequate policies for implementing them are in place, one still needs to ensure that "patient-friendly attitudes" prevail. This was not the case in the situation Schucking described. One is left with the impression that the patient was "reified,"[4] that all the health-care professionals Hewitt encountered treated her as an object, not a person. The same is true of the treatment Schucking received. He was cast in the role of a depersonalized nuisance, an impediment to getting on with the job of health-care delivery, rather than someone with a valid role to play and an interest in making decisions that should have been respected.

One important way to develop appropriate attitudes involves the education of physicians and other health-care professionals. This theme has been articulated on many occasions, but reading "Death at a New York Hospital" makes one aware that the message bears repeating. We can now do more in the way of medical treatment than we should do, although drawing a line between the "can" and the "should not" (or even the "should") is sometimes difficult. Despite extraordinary progress in medicine, there remains much that we cannot do. We must realize that it might not always be appropriate to undertake all possible interventions. But this does not mean that it is always appropriate to omit to act, in the sense of doing nothing. In short, on occasion we must follow a middle course. We are sometimes required simply to be present – physically, mentally, emotionally, and spiritually – without either acting (in the sense of undertaking invasive medical treatment) or failing to act (being uninvolved). If the physicians described by Schucking had learned to be present in this sense and not acted beyond what was required for that presence, a very different sequence of events might have occurred.

We should consider not only how to develop ethically appropriate attitudes but also how to change attitudes such as those portrayed, explicitly and implicitly, in "Death at a New York Hospital." We seldom begin with a *tabula rasa*. Again, the most effective way to change attitudes is likely to be educating physicians and other health-care professionals. The latter should learn to characterize as medical successes situations in which their efforts have helped people negotiate the end of life with greater comfort, consideration, and dignity. For physicians, in particular, the death of a patient has characteristically been labelled a failure. Obvious as it might be, it seems we still need to remind ourselves that there can be "good deaths" and "bad deaths," and that what could have been a good one with proper professional care sometimes becomes a bad one because of unwarranted professional intervention. That is what happened to Hewitt. Sometimes only the "good" and the "bad" are negotiable, not the "death." In these situations, success, from the point of view of health-care professionals, should depend on whether "good" or "bad" is the appropriate adjective, not on whether the inevitable death occurs.

Our conduct (especially that of medical systems, professional bodies, laws, and institutions) has not only a concrete and immediate impact but also a symbolic function. If symbols deliver messages of not caring about and not respecting other people, if they project images of hospitals as places of fear and even "torture," remedial steps are needed.

In most circumstances, physicians should do all in their power to save lives.[5] But even interventions that physicians perceive as serving this purpose can be out of place in the immediate situation and fail, overall, to save lives. If people believe that they lose control over what happens to them when they enter hospitals, they will avoid physicians and hospitals. Loss of control is a real form of suffering. Suffering breeds fear. And that could keep people away from hospitals when they could benefit by being treated and possibly cured or by receiving palliative care.

In short, over-interventionist and unfeeling approaches could deter people from seeking out the very professionals and institutions whose primary aim is to render assistance. This reaction could result in an overall net loss of life and damage to health. To avoid that outcome, we could develop models that include the possibility of partial responses to situations rather than enshrining a simple stop-go dichotomy. These models must include mechanisms to help health-care professionals deal with their feelings of helplessness when asked to adopt a non-interventionist approach.

TRUST GIVEN AND ACCEPTED

The matter of trust, too, is important. Brenda Hewitt's personal physician had a copy of her living will and of the durable power of attorney she had executed and "had agreed to honour them." This physician's conduct, in the circumstances described, was a breach of trust towards her. Moreover, to the extent that there is a message given that physicians are not to be trusted, this kind of conduct affects the whole medical profession and the community's perceptions of its members. It is no accident that self-regulating professions use a concept of unprofessional conduct to govern their members. Members who act in such a way as to bring the profession itself into disrepute are guilty of unprofessional conduct. In short, medicine, as an institution, has long recognized that the conduct of any one physician can have effects well beyond the immediate situation.

Finally, an important new insight is contained in Schucking's description of the legal documents – the living will and durable power of attorney – that patients can use to govern their treatment during terminal illness. Schucking describes these documents as instruments of love and trust.[6] Our aim should be to widen that circle of love and trust to encompass all the participants in medical situations involving terminal illness. Obviously, the love contemplated here is not of a romantic or even self-sacrificing kind. Rather, it is love in the sense of "treat others in the way in which you would like to be treated if you were in the same position."

I have observed that when physicians choose physicians for themselves, they seek not only highly competent and experienced practitioners but also people with whom they can communicate, to whom they can relate, whom they can trust to keep them informed and to respect their decisions, and whom they believe are kind, caring, and empathetic. Our obligation as professionals is to learn from ourselves as well as from formal and objective sources. We should at least try to offer those who seek our care conditions similar to those we would hope to experience ourselves – or that we would demand. Relationships between health-care professionals and those people who seek their help – especially between physicians and patients – have a unique characteristic. Most relationships can be described as being between intimates (in which case they are governed primarily extra-legally – that is, governed primarily by ethics) or between strangers (in which case they are often governed primarily by law). The physician-patient relationship, however, has some characteristics of both. It might be this duality that sometimes gives rise to confusion and ambivalence in physician-patient relationships and makes them difficult to govern appropriately.

CONCLUSION

I do not want to leave the impression that I think all physicians are cold, careless, uncaring, or cruel. Perhaps a very few do, unfortunately, manifest some of these characteristics. And perhaps health-care systems sometimes make it difficult for those who are not like this to display their more desirable characteristics. Most physicians want to be, as one physician recently expressed it to me, "as good a physician as I am able." This same physician also remarked that he felt very open to constructive criticism that would help him to achieve his goal. Schucking's article is one more contemporary step along the two-thousand-year-old path from Hippocrates towards raising the sensitivity of health-care professionals and systems to the necessity of first doing no harm.

16 (a) Human Dignity and Disease, Disability, Suffering: A Philosophical Contribution to the Euthanasia and Assisted Suicide Debate

SYLVIA D. STOLBERG

"Death with dignity" has become the rallying cry of the assisted suicide and voluntary euthanasia movement. Its proponents assert that there is a right to prevent our dignity from being undermined by disability and suffering. Because the concept of human dignity carries strong rhetorical and moral force, we are obliged to examine any claims that our society is failing to act in accordance with it. This article examines and refutes the claim that human dignity is lost through disability, disease, dependency, or suffering. Human dignity is not a thing that can be lost, and the claim noted above involves an impoverished interpretation of human dignity and its two essential components – autonomy and worth. Morally, we do not require assisted suicide and voluntary euthanasia to save us from the indignity of natural states and processes.

In a recent issue of *Humane Medicine*, Margaret Somerville asks: "Are we being manipulated by the use of special language in the euthanasia debate? ... Are we even aware of this rhetoric?"[1] She notes that "dignity" is one of those words that, along with "autonomy" and "self-determination," needs "to be explored ... especially when they are to be used in relation to matters such as euthanasia and by our highest court."[2] Since I believe that the notion of dignity carries especially strong rhetorical force, this paper will respond to Somerville's challenge by examining the death with dignity language of the assisted suicide and voluntary euthanasia debate.

The phrase "death with dignity" strikes a deep responsive chord in most of us. It does not fall on deaf ears in contemporary, Western society, which is morally conditioned by recent history to be highly sensitive to such appeals. Demands to be accorded human dignity evoke the spectres of the denial of this right – the indignities that haunt our recent past of segregation and disenfranchisement, of cattle cars and death camps. Nevertheless, I believe we should respond cautiously to demands for death with dignity. The frequency with which human dignity is appealed to in newspapers, journals, codes of ethics, political manifestos, and papal encyclicals testifies to its importance, but should not deceive us into thinking that it is a simple, unequivocal notion. By its etymology, the word "dignity" suggests worth, but it does not indicate what kind of worth humans have, why they have it, whether they possess it equally, and what is required in response to it. In addressing these questions, I deny that human dignity is undermined by states of suffering, disability, dependency, and disease. It follows that we do not need to legalize assisted suicide to ensure death with dignity by precluding the continued indignity of living in such states.

The claim I wish to deny is exemplified in the Sue Rodriguez case. In 1993 the Supreme Court of Canada ruled 5–4 against Rodriguez's request for physician-assisted suicide. Her application was based in part upon "the right to live her remaining life with the inherent dignity of a human person."[3] Since a time would come when "she [would] no longer wish to face the indignity and agony of life in such a state,"[4] she asked for the assistance of a physician to commit suicide. Justice Sopinka summarized Rodriguez' plight: "Although palliative care may be available to ease the pain and other physical discomfort which she will experience, the appellant fears the sedating effects of such drugs and argues, in any event, that they will not prevent the psychological and emotional distress which will result from being in a situation of utter dependence and loss of dignity."[5]

HUMAN DIGNITY IS NOT SOCIAL DIGNITY

My interest in the concept of human dignity was aroused by a sign outside a pharmacy proclaiming the sale of "dignity pants," a new name for adult diapers. Such a term is a perversion of the concept of human dignity, a perversion that demeans human beings by identifying their dignity with control of their bowels and bladders. Slave owners and Nazis threaten human dignity, but the same cannot be said of incontinence and disease. In the mid-1990s Pankratz responded in *Humane Medicine* to the pro-euthanasia argument that there is "a right to prevent our dignity from being undermined by disability and suffering" in these terms: "To be accurate, euthanasia proponents should not refer to a person's dignity, but to that person's capacity for independent living. They could use such terms as decorum or modesty, which, in the perspective of some individuals, are dependent on external circumstances. (Perhaps this could be simply a misdirected sense of pride?)"[6]

I wish to draw a distinction between human dignity and social dignity. There is a cultural, largely aesthetic sense of dignity that imbues persons with dignity/worth according to their demonstrations of grace, composure, upright carriage, good manners, modesty, personal hygiene, and self-sufficiency. This sense is reflected in such phrases as "he conducted himself with great dignity," or "she carried herself with dignity." By contrast, ungainliness, rage, stooped shoulders, stained trousers, bumptiousness, body odour, and begging are thought to be undignified. I believe that these social norms represent a rather too zealous desire to distinguish ourselves from other animals – too zealous, that is, if they are confused with human dignity. Our essential worth, our human dignity, does not fluctuate according to some "gold standard" that measures our ability to transcend accident, fate, emotion, and bodily nature. Human dignity must be distinguished from social dignity, a concept that varies historically and culturally. Social dignity comes in degrees and fluctuates according to local standards involving the possession, or not, of composure, good manners, money, influence, prestige, title, or class membership. However, social dignity is distinguishable from human dignity – a morally relevant concept that accords human beings a common, equal worth that does not fluctuate: " 'Human Dignity' is not ... a matter of more or less, not a matter of virtue, accomplishment or refinement; rather it seems to be something 'inalienable' much like 'Rights of Man' and yet not quite in the same manner."[7]

HUMAN DIGNITY IS ...

Immanuel Kant, a German philosopher of the eighteen century, has written the only sustained defence of human dignity. His account remains the unchallenged exemplar of the concept and the authority to which we appeal, knowingly or not, in justifying our moral sentiments about when and why human dignity is threatened. Roughly speaking, Kant claimed that human dignity refers to the inviolable and incomparable moral worth of human beings, possessed in virtue of their autonomy – their capacity for rational self-legislation. In his most influential and well-known legacy, he asserted that we have a categorical duty towards ourselves and others in virtue of our worth/dignity: "Act so that you treat humanity, whether in your own person or in that of another, always as an end and never as a means only."[8]

Those who claim that human dignity is compromised by dependency, disease, disability, and suffering misconstrue the meaning of autonomy and ignore the essence of human dignity – unassailable human worth. Ignoring human worth and claiming that dignity is compromised by dependency, disability, and suffering would be consistent with treating those who are diseased and disabled as though they were commodities, things, mere means to other ends.

Human Dignity and Autonomy

Whether in terms of our "chameleon-like freedom" to make and re-make ourselves (Pico Della Mirandola, fifteenth century) or our capacity for rational self-legislation in the moral realm (Immanuel Kant, eighteenth century) or an existential freedom that denies us the status of *en-soi*, or mere things (Jean-Paul Sartre, twentieth century), the philosophical tradition concerning human dignity stresses, as the basis for that dignity, our freedom to create values and make choices and decisions uncoerced by completely controlling forces, either natural or divine: "Man alone can issue, recognize, obey, disobey (and not merely illustrate or fail to illustrate) laws. If he were a beast, he could neither create nor obey laws; were he a god he could create without having to obey; were he a slave, he would have to obey, but could not create laws. But the human being is, for good or evil, neither beast nor slave nor God."[9]

If we were merely puppets dancing on strings controlled by God, gods, other human beings, or instinct, we would lack the autonomy that renders us responsible for our actions and worthy of respect. However, this autonomy does not imply a responsibility to control what cannot be controlled: "ought" implies "can," and human dignity implies a realistic notion of autonomy. It would be absurd to suggest that human beings have dignity in virtue of a capacity to control what cannot be controlled, and it is equally absurd to suggest that human beings lose their dignity in virtue of an inability to control things such as death, aging, disability, and disease. Drooling doesn't threaten dignity; arbitrary or unreasonable interference with the reasonable decisions and choices of the drooler do.

To say that human dignity is diminished or lost owing to disease, disability, and suffering is equivalent to saying that, to possess human dignity with any degree of security, one must be forever free from adversity. Only immortals could be said to possess such dignity. We are humans and part of nature. To see natural processes as affronting, assaulting, or insulting human dignity relies on an antagonistic dualism between human dignity and nature, such that nature is other than, and the enemy of, our autonomy and dignity. Indeed, some versions of the death with dignity literature seem to suggest that, to exercise our autonomy, we must thwart such assaults by dying, dignity *intactus,* like chaste Christian virgins killing themselves to avoid defilement by Roman soldiers. Asserting one's autonomy by dying so makes sense only if one believes one's dignity to be a thing-like possession, like a membrane of the body or the soul, that can be torn or ruptured. However, both the literature on human dignity and common sense suggest that whatever it is, and however it is to be accounted for, human dignity is not a thing – wearable, washable, or tearable.

To say that human dignity is lost through disease, disability, and suffering either invokes the false interpretation of autonomy (criticized above) or reduces human dignity to a matter of well-being and ignores the importance of autonomy altogether. To be sure, well-being is a good and its moral importance is recognized in duties of beneficence, but duties of beneficence do not fully respond to human dignity. The history of the concept of human dignity suggests a common commitment to the view that human beings are different from animals and tractors, and that recognizing their dignity requires doing something more than merely preserving their well-being and oiling their engines. Had black persons and Jewish persons been treated kindly by their oppressors, been well fed and cared for, not overworked or jammed too tightly into cattle cars, but groomed, cleaned, and polished, it would not have removed the affront to the dignity of human beings epitomized by slavery and Nazism. Commitment to beneficence and nonmaleficence do not exhaust the duties entailed by human dignity. Respect for human dignity generates more complex duties. Sometimes "pulling the plug" is one of them. It is a peculiarity of human beings that they can muster their particularly human kind of dignity and say no with good reason to the impulses of beneficence: "Hands off, tubes out, let me be!" It is this barrel of autonomy in the double-barrelled concept of human dignity that thwarts attempts to reduce human dignity to a physiological state such as well-being or a psychological state such as happiness. Furthermore, identifying human dignity with states of well-being does not account for the symbolic dignity that we accord corpses, surely the antithesis of well-being, and the respect with which we treat them in deference to the dignity of the persons to whom the bodies formerly belonged.

Human Dignity and Equal Worth

The claim that dignity is lost or threatened when disease and disability strike implies that diseased or disabled persons lose their human worth. This is a profound error. Human dignity, a relational concept, embraces both recognition and response: recognition of the equal possession by human beings of a distinctive kind of worth, as well as the moral responses that such possession requires – negatively, by recognizing a duty not to regard or treat other human beings merely as means or objects, and positively, by acting so as to further the rational ends of others or to enhance their autonomy.[10] If our essential dignity/worth were to be undermined by aging, disease, and disability, then almost all of us could expect to be treated by others merely as means to other ends, as things unworthy of respect and equal consideration, at many points and for lengthy periods throughout our lives. We neither want, nor deserve, so fragile a dignity or so fickle a worth. Beneath the inflated pretences of social dignity lies an essential dignity ascribed equally to all human beings. It does not get lost: "While we might say that he has lost his dignity, we nonetheless recognize that this loss is not complete in this important sense: it does not provide others with the privilege to treat him like an object or deprive him of the status of a human being."[11]

The tradition concerning human dignity pronounces as equal our dignity, our essential worth. Kant accorded human beings incomparable and equal worth on the basis of our capacities to rationally legislate and execute a universal moral law. Sartre discovered our dignity in our *pour-soi/en-soi* nature that denies us the status of fixed things or objects that can be priced, compared, and marketed or used as means to other, more important ends.[12] We should take these views seriously in seeking contemporary consensus on what we mean by human dignity. We should take them seriously because, no matter how sceptical we may be about the general merits of human beings, we have seen the death camps, we have seen what happens when commitment to the tradition of human dignity is suspended: spontaneously and naturally we recoil from this sight into the deeper recesses of fellow feeling, to emerge with renewed commitment to human dignity. What is it about human beings that demands that we ascribe them equal worth, in health and in sickness, 'til death do us part? A convincing answer to this question requires more than the traditional responses about rationality, autonomy, or self-consciousness. These responses are only part of the story. Since we do not possess these capacities equally, they do not provide an ineluctable basis for a belief in equal worth. I believe we need to refine these traditional views in the light of the work in this century of the late Gabriel Marcel. Marcel asks us to look to our mortality and the human condition in order to grasp our equal worth and our all-too-human dignity.

Marcel's portrait of human dignity emphasizes the human condition as mortal and tragic, and human beings as receptive to these elements and called upon to react with compassionate fraternity – fellow feeling, as well as with reason: "What I wish to emphasize is that a careful examination of active receptivity can help us formulate our conception of man and what we have called human dignity."[13] Active receptivity to the human condition involves a compassionate response that levels our moral significance, our worth, our human dignity to that of other human beings, and strips us of pretentions to superior worth. In the following passage, Marcel describes a person with "a keen and exacting sense of human dignity [who] gives in his actions the most irrefutable proof of it":

He has an active and even poignant experience of the mystery inherent in the human condition and in everything which is hazardous, precarious, and, at the same time, tragic. And what we discover in this line of thought is compassion, in the strongest sense of the word, and consequently to the degree that it implies in the person who feels it nothing at all resembling a feeling of superiority. This would amount to saying, then, that dignity must be sought at the antipodes of pretention and rather on the side of weakness.[14]

Seeking this dignity "at the antipodes of pretension and rather on the side of weakness," Marcel asks us to "consider the human being in his nudity and weakness – the human being as helpless as the child, the old man, or the pauper."[15] To respond to these reminders of our mortality by declaring ourselves bankrupt of worth and "ridiculously insignificant" not only invites tyranny but evokes a fundamental resistance to this "disintegration and downward course": "We shall have to determine more clearly and precisely the significance and nature of this resistance, but even now it should be significantly clear that this resistance is founded, not on the affirmation of the self and the pretensions it exudes, but on a stronger consciousness of the living tie which unites all men."[16]

Marcel urges us to look to our common human condition to discover our equal worth and essential dignity. From this confrontation with finitude and mortality there comes the consciousness that equally we are bound together by the very processes and conditions of pain, disease, disability, aging, suffering, and death. I conclude that, from such a perspective, it is a contradiction in terms to hold that such processes and conditions threaten human dignity, understood as equal worth.

CONCLUSION

Human dignity is not a thing and nature doesn't destroy it. There is no moral obligation to die before nature violates our dignity, and no obligation to dispatch others before nature violates theirs. Nature does not violate our dignity; human beings do. Death does not preserve human dignity; only human beings can. We can preserve human dignity by careful elucidation of what we mean by it and cautious examination of the claims that appeal to it. Some of those claims, like the one examined here, are counterfeit. This does not mean that human dignity and the practices of assisted suicide and voluntary, active euthanasia are necessarily mutually exclusive. It just means that this particular version of the death with dignity conversation is unacceptable.

---

16 (b) Unpacking the Concept of Human Dignity in Human (e) Death: Comments on "Human Dignity and Disease, Disability, and Suffering"

With her focus on the word "dignity," Stolberg tries to answer the following question: Are we being manipulated by the use of special language in the euthanasia debate? In doing so, she raises as many questions as she answers. Warning that we should "respond cautiously to calls for *death with dignity*," she rejects the claim that human dignity is lost through disability, disease, dependency, or suffering. As she points out, "dignity is not a thing that can be lost."[1]

Stolberg presents several problems: the relation between dignity and autonomy and between dignity and control, or power; the different effects of extrinsic as compared with intrinsic definitions of dignity; the role of dignity in establishing the conditions and even the nature of dying; the relation between dignity and honour; and dignity as a concept that can permit the interpersonal relations of either superiority-inferiority or equality.

We are an intensely individualistic society. We value most those whom we believe are able to act independently and autonomously and who are not dependent on others. If dignity is the possession of these attributes, then, at the end of life, almost everyone loses dignity. And if we equate dignity with worth, as Stolberg points out, then we lose dignity and worth when we lose autonomy and independence. Although euthanasia is often promoted as essential to preserve the dignity of terminally ill people, this analysis suggests that euthanasia – when used for that purpose – could become a way of eliminating those whom we consider of less worth than we are. This possibility evokes the fears of many disabled people who oppose euthanasia: that their lives are sometimes seen to be of less value because they are seen as lacking dignity; that legalizing euthanasia would reinforce this view; and that they could become preferential subjects for (or objects of) euthanasia.

Stolberg rejects the equation of dignity with control. Euthanasia is closely associated with taking control[2] in some ways that are obvious and others that are much less so. Serious and debilitating illness obviously causes loss of control. People might try to redress that loss by seeking an alternative source of control, which euthanasia can be seen to provide. A much less obvious connection between euthanasia and control arises from the fact that to have control is usually to have power, and ours is a society in which power is often eroticized.[3] This association means that the sense of power and control can depend on perceptions of being sexually desirable (which is often connected with being seen as beautiful) and aesthetically pleasing; the unerotic and the ugly are characterized as undesirable and, therefore, suitable for elimination. It might also provide part of the explanation (though not the only or dominant one) for the fact that people with AIDS in the Netherlands, where euthanasia is legally available, have a much higher rate of death by euthanasia than other terminally ill people.[4] And it could help to explain why the groups most uniformly "pro-choice" on euthanasia in both Canada and Australia, for instance, are those living with AIDS and those who support them.[5] To the degree that the gay community emphasizes the erotic and the aesthetic as important elements of its lifestyle, seeing oneself as sexually undesirable and physically ugly could cause suffering beyond that directly associated with the loss of these characteristics themselves. For instance, it could cause people to feel excluded from the community. Euthanasia could provide a way to reaffirm membership through a last act that is seen as manifesting a combination of control, a courageous or heroic stance, and aesthetic sensitivity.[6] Because of these same perceived characteristics, they could see euthanasia also as a way of maintaining or restoring at least some form of dignity.

Stolberg points to the relation between dignity and autonomy. She sees autonomy as an important component of dignity. But she sees dignity as independent of both well-being and autonomy.[7] According to Stolberg, "autonomy does not imply a responsibility to control what cannot be controlled: *ought* implies *can*." It would be absurd to suggest that human beings have dignity in virtue of a capacity to control what cannot be controlled, and "it is equally absurd to suggest that human beings lose their dignity in virtue of an inability to control things like death aging, disability, and disease." Stolberg does not define autonomy even though, or perhaps because, it is highly debated.[8] This uncertainty would present difficulties, for instance, in assessing people's dignity and what is required to respect it if having dignity depended on having autonomy. And if so, then loss of autonomy would mean loss of dignity, the pro-euthanasia position. Depending on the definition of autonomy, moreover, one could regard some mentally incompetent people as lacking autonomy. And that could mean that they lack dignity, too. This line of reasoning is clearly the opposite of what Stolberg is advocating.

According to Stolberg, dignity is a "double-barrelled concept ... one barrel [of which] is autonomy."[9] Presumably, either autonomy or this "other barrel" would provide a good reason for claiming dignity. In her search for this other barrel, she makes a valuable contribution to the concept of dignity.

Stolberg describes dignity as a "relational concept, [which] embraces both recognition and response." There are two competing definitions of dignity: intrinsic and extrinsic; either it is an innate characteristic (intrinsic) or it exists in the eye of the beholder, one person conferring dignity on another (extrinsic). The idea of "recognition and response" incorporates an intrinsic approach to dignity, but with the addition of an extrinsic component. It says that we recognize innate dignity in others and respond to it; in doing so, we affirm it in others (and incidentally in ourselves as well). In contrast, the extrinsic approach permits someone to confer dignity on someone else – or to withhold it

People suffer when they experience a loss of control over what happens to them and perceive their own disintegration.[10] To view dignity as intrinsic, depending only on being human, does not deny that terminally ill people might suffer and describe their suffering as loss of dignity. Stolberg describes this situation as a loss of "*social* dignity," not human dignity. It causes intense emotional pain and elicits our deepest compassion, sometimes horror. We need to show that we understand the patients' perceptions of themselves, that they have lost their social dignity. At the same time, though, we need to show that we still see their *human* dignity. Some terminally ill people ask for euthanasia to test whether others still want them around, not because they want to be killed.[11] To agree that they have no dignity would be to give them a negative response; conversely, to assure them that they still have dignity is to affirm the value of their existence – to us and to everyone else.

If we do not see the dignity of terminally ill people despite their suffering, moreover, we prevent them from giving us a unique and otherwise unobtainable gift. This gift affirms perceptions of our own worth as human beings. In addition, though, it helps us come to terms with our eventual, inevitable dying. Furthermore, in preventing them from giving this gift, we deny them a major opportunity to find meaning in their own dying. Katherine Young describes the Greco-Roman period as one that approved of self-willed death; men who acted accordingly might have been trying, through their control, heroic stance, and aesthetic sensitivity, to offer their communities a gift. Doing so made it likely that they, too, would be remembered and so enabled them to find meaning in death.[12]

Some leaders of the campaign to legalize euthanasia, such as Sue Rodriguez, have expressed the sentiment that, by taking this position, they are leaving a legacy – offering a gift – and, in addition, finding some meaning in death. When people ask for euthanasia so as not to burden others, they might be trying to offer a gift to others by dying and thereby removing the burden. If so, then we need to show them that continuing to live until they die naturally will be experienced as the giving of a gift by those who are dying and will be received as one by others. Those of us who are against euthanasia need to ponder what would be required to achieve this objective. At the least, it would require us to be "present," in a broad and deep sense of the word, to receive the gifts that dying people cannot deliver if they feel unloved and abandoned. Our horror of dying alone might reflect a need to convert the last act of life, dying, into something of value to those we leave behind.

In contrasting human dignity with social dignity, Stolberg provides an important insight: the former is an intrinsic attribute and the latter an extrinsic one, a distinction we are in danger of losing when we speak simply of dignity. By moving from a concept of human dignity to one of social dignity, has our society journeyed along a "slippery slope" from seeing dignity as arising from recognition of the mystery and sacredness of human life, to seeing it as arising from the intrinsic worth of each person as a human being (a more individualistic concept than the former one), to seeing it as depending on attributes (the loss of which constitutes a loss of dignity)? In the last case, euthanasia can seem necessary to preserve dignity; it removes people from the affront to their dignity, when the affront itself cannot be removed. This position can be summed up as follows: We will provide you with death to preserve your dignity. It can be extended as follows: We will provide you with death, because your loss of some attributes is detrimental to our perception of our own dignity (because we see ourselves reflected in your undignified state).[13]

By way of contrast, as Stolberg points out, Gabriel Marcel asks us to "*to look to our mortality* and the human condition in order to grasp our equal worth and our all-too-human dignity."[14] If we call for the legalization of euthanasia because we have grave difficulties in accepting our mortality, as I have suggested elsewhere,[15] one would expect us to avoid or reject Marcel's approach to human dignity (which requires acceptance of mortality). Furthermore, under Marcel's approach, we have no control over who does or does not have dignity; everyone has it because everyone is human. To the extent that advocates of euthanasia want to exercise control over death, an intrinsic approach to dignity is likely to be less appealing than an extrinsic one; the latter incorporates an element of control, after all, control over who does or does not have dignity.

Stolberg argues that "traditional responses about rationality, autonomy or self-consciousness" are only some aspects of what we mean by the worth of human beings. Speaking of Marcel's portrait of human dignity, she emphasizes that he saw the ability to feel "compassionate fraternity [or] fellow feeling"[16] as integral to honouring human dignity in others. He proposed that the capacity to manifest this attitude depended on experiencing "the mystery inherent in the human condition and in everything which is hazardous, precarious, and, at the same time, tragic."[17] If real respect for human dignity requires "experience[ing] ... the mystery inherent in the human condition," and if – as I argue[18] – such respect requires us to exclude euthanasia, it is paradoxical to claim, as those who call for legalizing euthanasia do, that its availability is required to honour human dignity. And there is another lesson here. I have suggested elsewhere[19] that the current push to legalize euthanasia is connected with a loss in our society of a sense of the sacred and, with it, a sense of the mystery of human life (and death). A similar cause-and-effect relation might be reflected in the loss of that mystery as integral to the concept of human dignity. The loss converts human dignity from a concept that would disfavour euthanasia to one that would favour it.

Using a term whose meaning has become different from, or even the opposite of, its earlier one seems to be a prevalent *modus operandi* in arguing the case for euthanasia. The right to refuse treatment is characterized as a "right to die," which is then supposed to provide a basis for claims to physician-assisted suicide and euthanasia – that is, a "right to death." The concept of (human) dignity can be used to promote respect for human life. But if the content of this concept is replaced with that of social dignity, then the promotion of dignity can be used to support euthanasia as a requirement for the preservation of (social) dignity. A similar reversal has occurred in connection with the concept of quality of life. Originally, it was formulated to provide a basis for claims to some minimally adequate level of health care. People could claim a right to those health-care resources needed to sustain a basic quality of life. In stark contrast, the concept is now used as a basis for *denying* claims to health care. Some people have a quality of life so low, it is argued, that they do not merit the allocation of health-care resources.

The concept of dignity can be used to establish either that some people are superior to others or the opposite, that everyone is of equal worth. An extrinsic definition means that others can seem to lack dignity and are, therefore, inferior to us (a dignity-as-superiority concept); an intrinsic "mystery-dignity" definition cannot have that meaning; indeed, it means the opposite (a dignity-as-equality concept).

Historically, dignity has been seen as a derivative of, or a replacement for, honour, "which ... is intrinsically linked to inequalities."[20] Thus dignity's antecedents were based on worth. That concept of dignity shares another feature of honour: it can be lost. But as philosopher Charles Taylor explains, the modern notion of dignity in a democratic society is "universalist and egalitarian." Everyone has dignity because everyone is human – which is precisely the same approach as Marcel's. The connection between dignity and honour can help us understand the connection between dignity and death (and death with dignity). If we see death – more accurately, the process of dying – as "oddly shameful,"[21] and if we connect dignity with honour, then, by definition, dying involves a loss of honour and, therefore, of dignity as well. Some will call on society to stop this shame and loss of dignity by ending the process of dying through euthanasia.

In the context of exploring the links between honour-shame and dignity, we can examine other historical and anthropological evidence too. In some times and places, self-willed death, in prescribed circumstances and in compliance with the rules governing its legitimate availability,[22] was regarded as an honourable (dignified) death. Conversely, *not* dying in the same circumstances might involve dishonour (lack of dignity) and shame. In contrast, suicide in general was a cause of shame for the family and often taken to indicate mental illness (something else that was stigmatized) or even possession by the devil. In modern societies, on the other hand, advocates of physician-assisted suicide and euthanasia believe that legalization would promote dignity. Might legalization be sought in order to shift euthanasia and physician-assisted suicide from the shame of suicide to the honour of self-willed death? What impact would accepting the principle of such honour and enshrining it in law have on societal values and symbols?

The intrinsic/extrinsic concept of dignity can be described also in terms of defining dignity from the perspective of a focus on either the self or the other. Paradoxically, the extrinsic definition stems from the definer's focus on the self and the intrinsic one from a focus on the other. In the former, we see what is important to our own dignity and decide whether or not others have these characteristics. In the latter, without question, we see others as like ourselves and, therefore, as possessing dignity.

A discussion of the concept of dignity invites many further questions: Is compassion the way we can best experience the mystery of the human condition? Is experiencing it, by recognizing our shared mortality, the key to recognizing equal worth? Is the "mystery-dignity" concept "the living tie which unites all men"[23] not only in the present but also across all generations? Is this concept of dignity one of the most important or fundamental memes (units of cultural information passed from generation to generation) that the legalization of euthanasia would destroy?

Stolberg's article presents profound issues. We need deeper and broader research to decide how we should respond to them in the euthanasia debate. In particular, exploration of the concept of dignity and the questions it raises show that we need to be acutely aware of the complex nature of concepts, such as dignity, and the complex interrelations of many issues associated with euthanasia. I conclude with the simple but profound words of the Special Senate Committee on Euthanasia and Assisted Suicide of the Parliament of Canada:

Dying with dignity is not simply a matter of controlling the time or means of death but involves the right to receive, up to the end, the care to relieve one's suffering and to be surrounded by human attention and compassion. It is the right to feel one still has value as a person. Dignity exists when one faces the final stages of life with a feeling of self-worth and with the care, solicitude and compassion to which all human beings are entitled.[24]

17 (a) Prothanasia: Personal Fulfilment and Readiness to Die

CONSTANTINE JOHN FALLIERS

The steady spate of papers about euthanasia and physician-assisted suicide should remind us that death can be approached, as it were, from the opposite direction. Death (Gk *thanatos*, Lat. *mors, mortis*; Goth. *dauthus*) generally has been viewed as a "failure" (to survive); efforts to prevent – actually only to postpone – death have become a preoccupation of modem medicine, which indicates a widespread thanatophobia. Historically, in most societies, death has served as the ultimate penalty for evil and unlawful deeds, even though many have questioned both its deterrent and its ethical aspects. Ever since Diodotos' address to the Athenian Assembly – recorded by Thucydides nearly 2500 years ago[1] – national ideals have glorified a readiness to die for patriotic purposes and certain religious movements have promoted death as a way to attain transcendental bliss and eternal redemption. Also, many societies have accepted death as evidence of the fulfilment of principles, prophesy, or destiny – Socrates, Jesus Christ and others, and/or, more commonly, as the end of unbearable suffering (euthanasia). From an individual point of view, a "wish to be dead" has been the traditional expression of the lovelorn Sappho, quoted in Lesbos.[2]

This essay examines a conscious preparedness for death not from a sense of duty, or as a response to suffering, or as an attempt at redemption, but as a consequence of the fulfilment of a personal aspiration. The term, *prothanasia*, has been chosen to indicate such a readiness for or receptivity to the termination of an accomplished or blessed existence. I have selected citations from ancient Greek, biblical, Asian, and romantic European traditions that I encountered during literary research connected with the writing of a history of Lesbos and other transcultural and interdisciplinary studies[3] to demonstrate that, under certain circumstances, individuals anywhere may be ready to die.

READY TO DIE FOLLOWING LYRICAL PERFECTION: SOLON OF ATHENS, C.640–C.560 BC

Solon, the Athenian statesman, lawgiver, poet, traveller, and one of the Seven Sages of ancient Greece, heard his young nephew recite and sing a *melos* (poem with melody) of the famous Lesbian poet Sappho. "This is my translation of the original Greek story, recorded by Aelian (Ailianos) and quoted by Strobaeus (Strobaios) in his *Anthology*: When his nephew sang a *melos* by Sappho while they were drinking, Solon of Athens was so delighted with the melody that he asked the boy to teach it to him. Someone then inquired what was the reason he wanted so much to accomplish that and he replied: 'So that after I learn it I may die.'"[4]

The expression in Greek *ina mathon apothano* may also be translated as "so that having learned it I shall die," probably meaning "so that I may die – only after I have learned it." The "it," of course, was one of the hundreds of songs composed by Sappho. Many of these verses expressed deeply sentimental love for her young female students/ companions, and provided the basis for the modern term "lesbian."

THE FULFILMENT OF A PROPHESY: SIMEON AND CHRIST, FIRST CENTURY AD

In the Christian tradition, the Hebrew elder Simeon expressed his readiness to die once the infant Jesus was presented to him in the temple. His words have been rendered in English as "Lord, now lettest thy servant depart in peace ... for mine eyes have seen thy salvation" or "Now let your bondslave depart in peace, Lord ..." Closer, perhaps, to the text of the evangelist Saint Luke is my translation from the Greek:

The Gospel According to Saint Luke, First Century A.D.

And, see, there was a certain person (*anthropos*, a human being) in Jerusalem named Simeon; and this man was just and devout, looking forward to the consolation of Israel; and the Holy Spirit had been upon him. And to him it had been revealed by the Spirit that it was meant for him not to encounter death until he beheld Christ the Lord. And prompted by the Spirit he came to the holy temple; and when the parents brought the child Jesus to do for him as was customary by law, he received the child in his arms, praised *God and said, Now, Lord, do release your servant in peace, in accordance with your word, Because my eyes have seen your agent of salvation* ...

An essay on the "readiness to die" might focus on Simeon's word, *apolyeis*, rendered in Latin as *dimittis*. As English translations, "release" or "dismiss" may be acceptable, but equally appropriate would be the expression "let me go" or "send me forth." They all convey the message that life is an obligation, a commitment to serve. When this is achieved, the person may be released – that is, free to die.

ORIENTAL WISDOM: CONFUCIUS, 551–479 BC

The early Chinese sage, administrator and teacher, Confucius – a transliteration of Kung Fu-tzu, also known as Kong Zi, Kong the Master – equated the attainment of wisdom with the readiness to die.[5] Although exact interpretations in English remain questionable, the essence of the Confucian approach to life – and death – can be summarized in this dictum:

He who learns about the path in the morning
can die in the evening

Or, my version:

Those (not he or she!) who perceive the right way in the morning
may (be ready to) die in the evening.

The "path" is the understanding of life's purpose and pursuits. Confucian wisdom included the correct perception of the world, social order, and a proper equilibrium between the passive and the active (Yin and Yang) elements of the cosmos.

DEATH AS A ROMANTICIZED EROTIC SATIETY: TANNHÄUSER, AD C.1850

The life of Tannhäuser, the historical thirteenth-century troubadour (Minesinger) of Germany, was embellished to include a sojourn on the Mountain of Venus (Venusberg). When, in the mid-nineteenth century, Richard Wagner used the story for his opera, he dwelt on the "sin" of voluptuous cohabitation with the Goddess of Love and on the hero's need to escape and to be redeemed. The

young singer, Tannhäuser, saturated with the endless erotic embraces of Venus, begged the goddess to let him go, willing to face
death as a consequence.[6]

Tannhäuser and the Singers' Contest at Warburg
A "romantic opera" by Richard Wagner, first performed in 1845

Act 1, Scene 2 (my translation from the German)

Tannhäuser:
But mortal, yes, I still remain
and overwhelmed by your love ...
Bless'd forever who can stay with you
...
Yet I must leave for the world of the earth.
Near you I'll be only a slave
for Freedom, Freedom now I crave.
For struggle and challenge ready I am
To die and perish if I must.

Tannhäuser's readiness for death (Germ. *Tod*) might be considered a
reflection of the heroic Teutonic spirit, but Wagner's libretto declares a
desire to end aimless pleasure with a meaningful mortal confrontation.

DEATH FOLLOWING AN ELEGANTLY COMPLETED LIFE: SPAIN, AD 1994

A quotation from a recent book, *Locuras y Amores* (Madness and Love, in
plural), by Elena Ochoa, illustrates a readiness to die as the grand finale
of a fulfilled personal life. Dr Ochoa is an outstanding academic psychologist from Spain, a country notable for combining modern inquisi-
tiveness with a deep respect for tradition. The excerpt is my translation
from chapter 5, "Algunas razones y sinrazones de la muerte," which can
be rendered in English as "Some Reasons and Misconceptions–or, as
well, Rights and Wrong– of death."

He well knew the critical limit between life and death ... And decided to self
administer the sacrament of peace when he detected signs of the unfathom-
able void. He took the most irrevocable decision without ... any apparent
external motive, without the sharp pain of insanity, without a physical ailment that might have led him to the act of a final farewell ... He had been
saying that everything has a limit, which neither music nor any temporary

comfort can help overcome. Evidently life had taken so much out of him that he had no time to settle serenely in "these times of horror and cheapness."[7]

The last line may suggest a fatal depressive episode, but, clearly, such a departure is characteristic of a fulfilled human sensitivity, erudition, and culture, and of the virtues of educated elegance and style, beyond which life's end becomes rationally desirable. For those who consider death an unmitigated loss and who spare no effort to prolong even the least accomplished lives, the personal sincerity and the historical reality of a readiness to die (prothanasia) without regrets ought to provide some challenging and sobering examples.

SUMMARY

A number of historically prominent persons have reported a readiness, or preparedness for death, which can be called "prothanasia" (very different from the death wish due to severe depression and/or intolerable physical suffering) following an extremely satisfying or transcendentally fulfilling experience. The author has demonstrated the universality of this phenomenon, which may occur in many ordinary lives, by citations from diverse cultures and locations, retrieved in the course of a review of historical, religious, and musical documents. He contrasts it to a prevailing undue fear of death – or thanatophobia.

---

17 (b) Taming the Tiger: Reflections on "Prothanasia: Personal Fulfilment and Readiness to Die"

Death is a complex issue for us, both as individuals and as a society. Constantine Falliers's article, "Prothanasia: Personal Fulfilment and Readiness to Die,"[1] raises questions that add to our appreciation of this complexity.

What would it mean in personal, practical, emotional, and societal terms to interpret Simeon's words in St Luke's Gospel as "convey[ing] the message that life is an obligation, or commitment to serve [and that] [w]hen this is achieved the person may be released – that is, free to die"?[2] Do we regard life as an obligation or as something else? Is it something we own (the materialist view)? A script that each of us can write as we wish (the "intense individualism" view)? Or a gift, even a mystery (the "human spirit" view, which can, but need not, have a religious component)? Is life lived essentially alone (the "thin," or minimalist, view of the human condition)? Or is the human experience by its very nature immensely complex and necessarily interwoven with the lives of other individuals and social experience (the "thick" human condition view)? Each view can determine a stance on euthanasia. It can, for example, determine whether we see death as just a personal, private matter (the pro-euthanasia view) or as also affecting others, especially society (the anti-euthanasia view).

Does a good death require entering a neutral state in relation to the will to live? Or do we need to go even further and somehow elicit a will to die? What is the nature of this will to die? What is the difference between being neutral regarding the will to live and having a will to die? Is it the difference between being ready to die and asking someone else to cause death (physician-assisted suicide or euthanasia)? Or are the latter aberrant manifestations of the will to die (because others are involved in causing our death and, therefore, we no longer have complete personal control over it)? Is willing oneself to die and dying naturally the last great act of personal control? If so, would euthanasia mean diminishing rather than augmenting personal control?[3] In some circumstances, would we recognize suicide (as distinct from physician-assisted suicide) as a legitimate expression of the will to die? What would these circumstances be? These questions have been explored in depth elsewhere, in the context of eight major world religions, by Katherine Young in her landmark article "A Cross-Cultural Historical Case against Planned Self-willed Death and Assisted Suicide."[4] She shows how the attainment of spiritual perfection – which we can equate with Falliers's "attainment of wisdom" – could indicate "readiness to die,"[5] as he suggests, and be accepted by others as indicating this state.

We need to take great care in interpreting people's statements about readiness to die and to avoid the risk of being simplistic or of taking a unimodal approach to interpreting these statements, whether in literature or in response to patients in a palliative care unit or hospice. The context in which these statements are made can be as important as the words themselves. For instance, Tannhäuser's words, as quoted by Falliers,[6] could be more descriptive of the hero's need to engage in a male rite-of-passage than a willingness to die. The rituals and traditions of the Australian Aborigines provide a powerful example in this respect. Young boys live with the women until the beginning of their initiation, the process of "making them men." Up to this time, they have lived in "the joyfully carefree and erotic woman-based security of childhood."[7] The first step is for the men to seize the boys from the women. The whole tribe – men and women – act out what anthropologists describe as a group theatrical deception, which leads the boys to believe they will die and be reborn through initiation.[8] This transition is symbolized when their names are changed. The pre-initiation state of these boys and their initiation through a confrontation with death corresponds to Tannhäuser's description of leaving his erotic, woman-based security to face death.[9]

Robert Lawlor has suggested that the masculine psyche exhibits an innate need for initiation through a confrontation with death.[10] Traditionally, in the West, this confrontation occurs when young men go – or, more accurately, are sent – off to war. "Going off to war" and the deaths that ensue can affect not only the young men themselves and their families but also society. On 25 April each year, Australians celebrate ANZAC Day, which they refer to as "The One Day of the Year." This national holiday commemorates the landing of the Australian and New Zealand Army Corps troops at Gallipoli in 1915. Australians believe that their national character was born on this battlefield, where thousands of young Australian men were killed; in fact, though not in law, this event founded the nation. They identify as national characteristics that can be attributed to Gallipoli, "tenacity, determination, care for others and being prepared to go to the extra mile."[11] It is noteworthy that they see their nation and character as having been born out of an overwhelming defeat – not from victory, which is probably more often the case. This attitude brings to mind Thomas Jefferson's guiding maxim: "It is not our failures that count, but what we do with them." In short, how people die can be a crucial element in forming community and establishing values or symbols not only at the time of death but also in the future.

There has been a very strong movement in Australia to legalize euthanasia. The Northern Territory Legislature passed The Rights of the Terminally Ill Act 1995, which legalized it and authorized physicians to carry it out. Subsequently, the Australian Commonwealth Parliament invalidated this legislation amid great controversy. A wide variety of arguments and themes in support of euthanasia emerged. Some members of the gay community, which had been confronted with AIDS and generally approved of euthanasia, spoke about seeking a "noble death" through euthanasia – language others have often used to describe death in war. This language captures the idea of facing death courageously and of leaving a heroic memory. Some people have expressed concern to me, anecdotally, that the use of this rhetoric might be a form of peer pressure. Some gay men – particularly those with AIDS – might seek death through euthanasia because doing so would be seen as courageous; they would be seen as heroes for advocating the legalization of euthanasia and through their conduct promoting the likelihood of that outcome.

It has been said that we can easily give up only that which we have fully experienced.[12] This is probably true of life itself. Consequently, in order to reach a state of readiness to die ("prothanasia") and to avoid undue fear of death ("thanatophobia"), as Falliers urges us to do, it would be essential to have fully experienced life. In this regard, Falliers's article gives rise to two problems and two comments.

The first problem is found in Falliers's implicit critique of those "who spare no effort to prolong even *the least accomplished lives*."[13] Should we ever characterize some of us as "the least accomplished lives"? Does it mean that some people can never fully experience life and, therefore, cannot expect a state of readiness to die – and that we should not prolong their lives in the hope that they might do so? This view could be seen as a new twist on the concept of a "life not worth living," that of a "death not worth dying." There is a grave danger in applying extrinsic judgments of human worth in the context of dying. Apart from other considerations, those whom we might regard as the least among us could have the most profound experience of the mystery of death.

This discussion leads to my first comment. Could we see the experience of death, in the way Falliers describes and implies, as an immensely important and final life experience? Could we come to regard this experience as one that, beyond a specific point, we should not seek to avoid or control other than by doing all that we can (short of intentionally killing) to relieve pain and suffering? Is this an experience that dying people cannot have unless they are prepared to accept the idea of not trying to control death, but simply being deeply present at it accompanied by other deeply present people? If so, one argument against euthanasia would be that it deprives people of any possibility of experiencing death in this way. I hasten to add that this approach is not meant to glamorize or romanticize death; death is neither romantic nor glamorous. Both pro-euthanasia and anti-euthanasia proponents, including some people in the palliative-care community, have occasionally glamorized or romanticized it in order to advance their respective positions. Sometimes they almost compete over who can offer the best "fantasy death." In the spirit of Falliers's article, I aim, rather, to find ways of reducing the terror of death.

A second problem is the word "prothanasia," which could be misunderstood as a contraction of "pro-euthanasia." Language can sometimes be misleading. There is a vast moral and ethical difference between *letting go of life* and *being dispatched.* And it is not clear whether Falliers intends the word "prothanasia" to cover only the former or also the latter. Those who are anti-euthanasia might see the introduction of this term as a "soft move" towards euthanasia, as another step towards legalizing "euthanasia by degrees."[14]

Part of the consciously adopted approach of those who are pro-euthanasia has been a sophisticated choice of language. They have thought about what would persuade the general public to approve of the legalization of euthanasia and what would not. I have mentioned already that I interviewed Dr Roger Hunt, an Australian palliative-care physician, who was very influential in the legalization of euthanasia in the Northern Territory of Australia. He strongly objected to my use of the word "kill" to describe physicians' providing euthanasia to dying patients. He emphasized that this procedure should never be described as killing. I should not use this word, he argued, because it gave the wrong impression about euthanasia.[15] He favoured an acronym, VAE (voluntary active euthanasia). Note the transition from the language of killing to that of euthanasia, to physician-assisted suicide, to physician-assisted death, to an acronym (VAE) that is, on its face, neutral with respect to eliciting negative emotional reactions to euthanasia.

What Falliers describes as "thanatophobia" – the fear of death, which he wants to reduce – could be one cause of current moves to legalize euthanasia. Euthanasia can represent not only an attempt to control death itself but also a deliberate confrontation with death in order to control fear of it.[16] Whether or not euthanasia is effective in reducing fear is, of course, another matter.

Thus I conclude as I began: death is a complex problem for us, both as individuals and as a society.

18 Debating *A Gentle Death*: A Review Essay

As humans we need to engage in "death talk." But in modern Western societies many of us no longer participate in the religious ceremony and ritual that, traditionally, has accomodated and facilitated such talk. Consequently, some other form of death talk has become essential. One is the euthanasia debate, and an important voice in this debate is provided by books on how to manage one's own or another's dying. I would like to comment on one of these books: Marilynne Seguin's *A Gentle Death*.[1]

There is much in this book that everyone, whether pro-euthanasia or anti-euthanasia, would agree on. Some of the most important chapters include those on how to find physicians who will be partners in health care and how to interact with them. Those who are dying, in particular, need physicians who communicate well and who are willing to comply with advance health-care directives such as "living wills" and durable powers of attorney – the validity of which is now well recognized in Canada and elsewhere. In addition, Seguin offers good advice on palliative care, great sensitivity to the enormously important issue of pain control, and concern for care-givers and what they need to survive emotionally and physically in ministering to the dying.

It is disappointing, therefore, that her book starts with a sentence that focuses on the disagreement between pro-euthanasia and anti-euthanasia proponents: "This is a book about choice, about your right to choose the time and manner of your death. It would be both moral and just for our society to recognize this right, yet at present our laws do not do so."[2] As with all pro-euthanasia texts, "choice," "dignity," "autonomy," "self-determination," "control," and "rationality" are key words. It is not that these concepts are irrelevant to those who are anti-euthanasia or that they would disagree with them. Rather, the difference between the pro- and anti-euthanasia positions lies in whether there should be any *limits* on individual rights – in particular, the right to autonomy. We are a society based on individual rights, but we need to ask, and not only in the context of euthanasia, whether, in some circumstances, individual rights can be used in such a way that they do far more harm than good. If so, should some limits be imposed on them in order to preserve the fundamental basis of society? And should these restrictions include the prohibition of euthanasia? I believe that they should.

Seguin places strong emphasis on the obligation to relieve pain, which, unfortunately, is still something that health-care professionals need to hear. One vignette in the text describes the author arriving at the front door of the house of a dying person who was screaming in pain; she was nearly knocked down by the patient's physician rushing out of the house. This story is emotionally difficult to read, and it is extremely hard to find the words to describe the horror one feels in becoming aware of this incident. Whether we are pro-choice on euthanasia or anti-euthanasia, we can all agree that leaving patients in pain is abhorrent, ethically, and morally reprehensible, and should be punished severely by the law.

As in all pro-euthanasia texts, Seguin makes an argument on behalf of euthanasia based on the now widely accepted right of competent patients to refuse treatment. Her reasoning is that recognizing the right to refuse treatment involves recognizing a right to die. That, in turn, gives rise to a right to be assisted in dying. This help could include many measures – such as palliative care, which all of us would want – but it is interpreted as a right to be provided with euthanasia and, therefore, a right to be killed (which was Sue Rodriguez's argument). This argument can be extended, too, although Seguin does not do so. It is sometimes proposed that a right to euthanasia can found a right to kill someone else (or possibly an immunity for doing so), or even a duty to be killed when one is an unbearable burden on others, including society itself.

In other words, the argument is that there is no valid distinction to be made – at least in ethical, moral, or legal terms – between accepting a decision to refuse treatment on the one hand and the right to be killed and to have access to the necessary means for this right to be implemented on the other. Those who advocate euthanasia have adopted this blurring of the boundaries as a strategy for furthering acceptance of their position.

Another theme in the book is that brave people choose death and that brave physicians and nurses "risk all by helping a 'patient' to die."

Seguin speaks also, however, of "North Americans ... [being) fond of stories about the 'brave' person who carries on against all the odds. We glorify those who 'set an example' for the rest of society with their choice of courageous deeds. Our heroes are the 'winners' who beat disease, or, alternatively, those who die only after prolonged 'battles' with their particular disease."[3]

It is interesting that, in the case of those who choose euthanasia as well as those who reject it, the theme of bravery emerges. Could it be that whether we are pro-euthanasia or anti-euthanasia, we are looking for bravery in the context of death, particularly on the part of those who are dying? Perhaps we should be looking for something else in this context – meaning, for example, or even love.

As in Derek Humphry's well-known book on the subject of euthanasia, *Final Exit*,[4] there is much warm, cozy, friendly, and informal language in *A Gentle Death*. Both authors try to normalize not only death but also the infliction of death. There are frequent references to the brilliance of the day, the birds, gently falling snow, the "garden [that] paraded its best and brightest blooms" surrounding stories of death – especially (indeed, almost exclusively) those that occur through euthanasia.

One of the book's most chilling stories is that of the double suicide of an elderly couple who decided to die together at a time of their choosing. What is particularly disturbing about this story is that neither of them appears to be terminally ill or suffering at the time of death; their decision to commit suicide seems to have been fully supported by everyone with whom they came in contact, including members of their family. Seguin makes it clear that, provided this is a competent and rational decision – the choice was "fitting for them" – it was their right to decide the time and circumstances of their death.

It is worth quoting the end of this particular story in order to ask ourselves whether there are some emotional lacunae in both the reactions described and in the telling.

Mr. and Mrs. T ended their lives, as they had so carefully and considerately planned. The family was understandably saddened by their death, but all agreed that "they were proud of their parents and grandparents." When I attended a celebration of the lives of these two wonderful people, that was the expression I heard again and again: 'I am so proud of them. They died as they had lived, with careful thoughtfulness and, most of all, with dignity.'

I miss these dear friends as if they were my own family, and I also
       ·   · ·heir strength, determination and courage to live and die as they

This account raises several questions. First, many who ask about euthanasia are testing to see if others still want them around. They interpret an offer to help them die as a definite no, which probably encourages them to act accordingly. Second, stories of this kind emphasize that suicide is brave and courageous. Above all, it makes one of no trouble to anyone else – reflecting a society that has adopted an individualistic, materialistic, and consumeristic worldview – one that does not manifest any sense of community, to say nothing of "soul." Third, although Seguin is clearly compassionate and empathetic, there are times when one suspects that her attempts to help dying people, by facilitating their access to euthanasia, play an important role in fulfilling her own needs. The motivation for "doing good" is often, in part, to fulfil our own needs, so we need to be highly aware of that and extremely vigilant when these acts involve killing others.

It is interesting that a large portion of the text consists of stories about the deaths of individual people told from an intimate and personal perspective; thirty-nine people are identified, and there are other cases in the remainder of the text. As discussed in chapter 1, I believe we are in a period of unusually high activity in searching for a new societal paradigm (and the cultural basis for it) – the story that informs and gives meaning to our collective life and, through it, to our individual lives. Consequently, using the story mode might have more significance than its simply being an appropriate literary style to convey the information that Seguin wants to communicate. It could also elicit the emotional responses in favour of euthanasia that Seguin is seeking and help to incorporate euthanasia into the new societal paradigm.

The style in which the stories are written, too, makes it evident that, as mentioned often, our choice of language in the euthanasia debate is of the utmost importance; whichever side we are on, it is possible to use language, especially rhetoric, to manipulate the debate. That is acceptable if it is done in good faith. Indeed, it is inevitable and might be desirable. Euthanasia is not simply a matter of cognitive, rational, logical responses; it is one of the most deeply emotional issues that we have to deal with both as individuals and as a society. It is important, however, to acknowledge when we are acting from a cognitive base and when from an emotional one – and to recognize the way emotions can be manipulated through language. Seguin's arguments in favour of euthanasia focus predominantly on the appropriateness of euthanasia from a cognitive, rational, and logical point of view. In spite of this, a great deal of the text deals with descriptions of her empathetic emotional responses to those who are terminally ill and want to die.

Seguin argues that failure to relieve suffering, including failure to do so by killing suffering people who request assistance, "is inhumane and hypocritical in a free, democratic society ... [it] is to impose a sentence of suffering." This is strong rhetoric and reflects the position taken by the dissenting judges of the Supreme Court of Canada in *Rodriguez*.[6] Although pain and suffering must be relieved whenever possible, other than by intentionally killing, it is disingenuous and misleading to characterize powerlessness to relieve some suffering as the *imposition* of it.

Equally strong is the language Seguin uses to describe those who are anti-euthanasia. Their words are described as "graphic, dramatic and simplistic."[7] They are seen as resorting to "inflammatory rhetoric." In contrast, Seguin implies that those who advocate euthanasia are "responsible thinkers." In the same vein, people who oppose euthanasia are described as "a small vocal minority," "unthinking bigot[s]," "so called right-to-life campaigners," "anti-choice activists ... who would like to obstruct our work,"[8] and "over-zealous, self-styled arbiters of society's morals ... [with] a need for control and power, and a self-righteous conviction that they have a better knowledge of the will of the Almighty than others." Her failure to show respect for opponents sounds vaguely fanatical. Seguin sees only her adversaries as seeking power, not her colleagues.

Behind this debate, however, is a struggle between two ideologies competing for dominance in our society. Power, especially in the form of control, can be sought and exercised at both the individual and the societal level in the context of euthanasia. At the individual level, Seguin describes physicians who see themselves as "warriors crushing death" and, therefore, over-treating terminally ill patients. She is rightly critical of them. But physicians who are pro-euthanasia could be inspired by similar imagery and be motivated by similar attitudes. It is possible to see euthanasia as a way for physicians to feel like "winners," as opposed to "failures," in the face of their patients' deaths. Instead of accepting what they cannot and should not try to change – namely, that patients die despite all of their best efforts – they take control through euthanasia. It is the ultimate example of the "do something" syndrome. When faced with traumatic events, we feel better if we act – even if doing so is necessarily futile or even harmful.

At the societal level, the use of polls can be an exercise of power. Seguin states that "Canadians have voted" in favour of euthanasia and then quotes polls showing 76 per cent support. This information is misleading. Polls have consistently shown this level of support for euthanasia in Canadian and American communities, it is true. But whenever the question has been put to the *vote*, with the exception of approval of physician-assisted suicide in the state of Oregon, only about

46 per cent have approved it. (I refer to two referenda in California, for instance, and one in Washington State.⁹) One possibility to explain these discrepancies is that we are engaging in death talk when we are polled; when we vote, we are dealing with reality. There can be a big difference.

Both explicitly and implicitly, Seguin provides testimony throughout the book of the awful fear of being alone at the end of life, of feeling unloved and abandoned – which brings us back, again, to reflect on what Jay Katz has described in *The Silent World of Doctor and Patient*[10] as the experience of intense "pre-mortem loneliness." It is probably true that some people would rather be killed with another person present than die alone, and certainly Seguin is a powerful example of making oneself available as a presence for dying people. But people should not have to choose between being killed with others present or dying alone. They should be able to die with others truly present.

Seguin notes that important societal changes have changed our experience of death. Changes in family structure, in particular, have left many people alone in old age. She quotes philosopher Daniel Callahan, who describes in his book, *Setting Limits*, how he saw old ladies eating "alone [in a 'tearoom'], dining delicately and slowly, obviously drawing out as long as possible the ritual of nourishment and life in a public place ... at the restaurant ... [he] saw ... old age as isolation and loneliness." Seguin comments that it "does not have to be thus."[11] But, surely, the answer to loneliness is not to kill lonely people.

And yet this reaction is precisely what has happened. I was invited to the Netherlands to give a speech on the occasion of the twenty-fifth anniversary of the Dutch Medical Law society. My hosts, many of whom were strong advocates of the legalization of euthanasia, knew my stance on this issue. But, as is so often true for the Dutch, they are models of tolerance, and, consequently, invited me. I presented the case against euthanasia. At a cocktail reception that followed the lecture, a Dutch physician approached me and said: "I would like to tell you about a case in which we carried out euthanasia, and I think even you might agree this was not ethically wrong." I expected to hear some horrific story of highly invasive and destructive head-and-neck cancer, or something equivalent. Instead, the physician described how they had made home visits for three months to an elegant old lady in her eighties. She had been married to a diplomat and they had lived in many parts of the world. They had no children, but shared a passionate interest in music, art, and literature. Her husband had died and she was alone. She said she had nothing left to live for. After three months of her requests for euthanasia, the

physician gave her a lethal injection and she died peacefully. Spontaneously, I said to the physician: "Did you think of buying her a cat?"
The physician reacted with surprise and said: "No, we didn't. But
what an excellent idea, we will certainly think of that next time."

As with much pro-euthanasia literature, the book focuses on dignity
and concludes that what constitutes dignity is a matter of one's own definition. Certainly, if one could choose any word that has marked the
pro-euthanasia movement, it is "dignity." At the end of the book,
Seguin describes a death in which, she strongly implies, one of those
present gave a lethal injection to someone in an intensive care unit who
then died "with a 'thank you' in his eyes." Here are the final words of
her book: "Dignity. There is no more perfect word for it." As discussed
in chapter 16, the question is whether dignity is an *intrinsic* attribute of
human life – which means that all have it, no matter what the person's
current state – or whether only those people on whom we *confer* it have
dignity. The latter definition favours euthanasia; the former does not.

One major issue not addressed by Seguin, though inherent in her
book, is the logical discrepancy between arguing for what appears to
be an absolute right to autonomy in choosing the manner, time, and
place of one's death and then limiting access to euthanasia to "carefully regulated circumstances." If there is a right to choose suicide (as
the chief justice of the Supreme Court of Canada stated in *Rodriguez*),[12] and if the basis of this right is respect for competent adults'
absolute rights to self-determination and autonomy, then it would be
inconsistent to limit the exercise of this right to terminally ill people.

There is so much that has been and still needs to be said about euthanasia that it is extremely difficult to review a book, such as this one,
that raises so many questions. There is much of merit in the text, and
Seguin is deeply committed to the aim of providing "a gentle death."
But her book focuses almost entirely on the individual at an individual
level; it contains only distant sounds of the vast array of other issues
that we need to examine in great depth and with much care before we
decide whether or not to legalize euthanasia. We should remember
that changing what is arguably each of our society's most fundamental
rule – the rule against killing one another – to allow for killing one another in some circumstances would radically alter the ethical and legal
tone of our society, even if those circumstances were such that the exclusive motives were mercy or compassion. Such a change is perhaps
the most radical and fundamental one we could make.

Finally, Seguin sees pro-euthanasia activists as "fighting for a
cause," and herself as committed to "a noble cause." This appraisal is
one way to give meaning to one's death – to make it have significance

and impact, and not only to oneself. But death can have other meanings, too. Its imminence, as Florence Perella (a Montreal woman who, like Sue Rodriguez, has ALS) says, can give us "the ability to listen to what life wants to teach us."[13] The possibility of finding these other meanings is almost certainly conditional on excluding the possibility of euthanasia.

PART FIVE

Euthanasia in the "Public Square"

19 Euthanasia in the Media: Journalists' Values, Media Ethics, and "Public Square" Messages

MASS MEDIA AND THE SOCIETAL PARADIGM

It is not enough, even as an academic, to engage in the euthanasia debate only in academia. This debate must take place primarily in the public square. The media are the messengers – and, as Marshall McLuhan showed us – they can be the message too. Consequently, the ethics adopted by the mass media, and that govern the content and mode of their communications, will have an important impact on the outcome of the euthanasia debate.

Canada, like other postmodern, secular, Western democracies, is often called a "media society." People can have very disparate reactions to major controversies – such as euthanasia – depending on whether they learn about the from the mass media or from some other source. One could even come to the conclusion that events perceived through the mass media, especially television, are "more real" and more credible than the same events in real life. Reality at a distance – even virtual reality – has *become* reality; "real reality" has no credibility unless it is authenticated by the mass media. This transferance can be called the "mediatization" of controversies. We see them only, or mainly, through the eyes of the mass media.

Modern technology has meant that debates on important societal issues, such as euthanasia, are not carried out face to face and in person. The "baby boomers" are the first generation for which this has been true, and we have no idea of what the long-term impact on the content and outcomes of these debates might be. Changes caused by mediatization of these debates are important because they deeply affect the "shared story" on which we base our societal paradigm. By that, I mean (as I discussed in chapter 1) the store of values, attitudes, beliefs, commitments, and myths that inform collective life (and, therefore, individual lives) and help to give them meaning. Creating a shared story through the mass media could alter the balance among the various components that make up this narrative. In particular, we might engage in too much "death talk" and too little "life talk." We can be most attracted to what we most fear, and the mass media provide an infinite number of opportunities to indulge our fear-attraction reaction to death.

The mass media, especially television, favour some forms of narration, the results of which are woven together to create a shared story. It does not make "good television" to show all the participants in a debate in agreement, especially on some middle-of-the-road opinion. Most television producers choose participants who are polarized, profoundly disagreeing with each other. Moreover, in my experience, most people who work as researchers for the mass media and who screen potential participants are relatively young. Different generations have different views on important societal controversies, especially on important values. My impression is that most mass-media researchers are small-l liberals – civil libertarians who defend personal autonomy. This attitude reflects and generates a "pro-choice" world view with respect to abortion, euthanasia, and so on. In the context of religiously based media, however, I have often encountered mass-media researchers who have adopted a clearly "pro-life" world view. It is possible that many media researchers take care not to expose their own positions, adopting whatever stance they believe will elicit the real views of the person they are interviewing. My general experience is that these researchers try to act fairly in choosing a range of people to present their arguments for or against euthanasia. Indeed, their need for conflict to produce good television or radio demands that they do so.

VALUES AND LANGUAGE

At a less personal level, this approach reflects the important traditional journalistic value of objectivity. (It could be argued, however, that objectivity has been supplanted by conflicting aims, such as sensationalism, celebrity, or advocacy.) In achieving objectivity, the choice of interviewees can be a less crucial factor than others, especially when the controversy, as in the case of euthanasia, reflects deep societal tensions. These other factors include decisions as to what is newsworthy and what, therefore, will be covered; the amount of coverage; and, very important, the selection and amount of coverage of related matters. With respect to euthanasia, the quantity and nature of its coverage can be compared with that of pain-relief treatment and the right to refuse treatment or the accessibility of palliative care. The former is given far more attention than the latter. In dealing with euthanasia, then, we need to keep in mind that the mass media make an issue visible (or invisible) and define a "frame" that can determine which related issues are taken into account. And "media reports can set the policy agenda and significantly influence political decisions."[1]

Other factors, which can be only mentioned here, include the language, metaphors, and images that the mass media use. These factors can reflect values, set the tone of debate, trivialize something or render it important, marginalize or empower a different group, define something as an urgent or routine problem, assign blame or innocence, and affect policy and strategy.[2]

Language can become confused in the debate over euthanasia. Sometimes, this confusion is accidental; at other times intentional. For example, accidental confusion can be seen in reports that life-support treatment was removed from a brain-dead woman to allow her to die. If she was brain-dead, she was dead. Refusals of treatment that result in death are often innocently – but erroneously – described as euthanasia. As I discussed in chapters 3 and 7, pro-euthanasia advocates equate refusals of treatment and euthanasia and intentionally cause confusion in doing so. They argue that there is no difference between refusals that allow someone to die and euthanasia (a lethal injection); if, they say, the former is ethically and legally acceptable, as most people believe, so is the latter.

The mass media might be reluctant to take stands on some controversies for fear of losing readers or viewers. Some say there was such reluctance in the early days of the AIDS pandemic because this disease was linked with homosexuality and sexual transmission.[3] In this respect, it is interesting to note that the *Globe and Mail,* a national newspaper in Canada, first editorialized on the dangers of euthanasia,[4] but, within a relatively short time, came out in support of it.[5] To act with honesty and integrity, we must be open-minded and courageous enough to be willing to change our views when we decide that we were wrong (much as I was disappointed to see the later stance of the *Globe* and argued against it).[6] But could it also have occurred to the *Globe* that, by adopting these different positions, it could appease *all* its readers – or possibly none of them?

Speaking in the context of AIDS, but in words equally applicable to euthanasia, Dorothy Nelkin sums up the power of the mass media to influence us and our values: "The media can move issues to centre stage or keep them out of public view. They serve as filters through which people receive news and interpretations of events. The information they convey, their visual and verbal images, and the tone of their presentation can define the significance of events, shape public attitudes, and legitimate – or call into question – public policies."[7]

SOCIETAL ISSUES

On the whole, we have failed to give enough weight to societal issues related to euthanasia. This failure is connected with the mediatization of the euthanasia debate. Sue Rodriguez became a national celebrity in 1993 by taking her case for euthanasia to the Supreme Court of Canada. It made for dramatic television. Here was an articulate, courageous, forty-two-year-old, divorced woman who was dying of amyotrophic lateral sclerosis. She was begging to have euthanasia made available. She was threatening to commit suicide while still able to do so (and thus leave her eight-year-old son even sooner) if she was refused access. As I say elsewhere, the court denied her this right by a majority of five to four, with a plurality of dissenting judgments.[8]

To capture a reader's or a viewer's attention, the mass media need to personalize stories. This focus makes them resonate in some way with personal experience, especially for those people with experience of the problems being discussed. People need, or at least are perceived to need, personal entries into media presentations. This is one reason why medical stories and medical ethics are so popular in the media: we all strongly identify with the drama of illness, the hope for care and treatment, and the victory of cure. Some stories deal with situations, concepts or abstractions so vast in scope that people feel overwhelmed by the descriptions; these stories show complexities rather than reduce them to readily understood, black-and-white conflicts. This approach is usually described as "academic." It is considered incomprehensible to ordinary people and, consequently, of no interest to them. It causes serious problems in the euthanasia debate – which really does need in-depth, broad-based, consideration in both practical and theoretical terms, if we are to find a wise collective response.

The mass media both reflect and form attitudes. This role is relevant to another factor in the euthanasia debate: the impact of the intense individualism of postmodern, secular, Western democracies. It has been described in some instances as individualism run wild. How does individualism play out in the mass media? Rights to autonomy and self-determination are seen by small-l liberal researchers and journalists as being almost absolute. Consequently, any infringement on these rights – especially prohibiting access to something, such as euthanasia, that they believe pertains only to the individual – is unacceptable to them, although often they try not to communicate their disapproval to the person they are interviewing. The twentieth-century focus on respect for individual rights has done much good. Taken to an extreme, though, it can do harm that is not offset by any good achieved. Human beings cannot live fully human lives in isolation; they need also to be members of families, groups, communities, and societies. To maintain these forms of connectedness, we must sometimes infringe on the rights of individuals. It is seldom easy to justify this view in the mass media, partly because those justifications are not black and white. They require the balancing of competing benefits, harms, and interests. They often involve difficult and complex value judgments. And they also require the taking into account of societal concerns that are not easy to present in the mass media.

Some arguments against euthanasia, those based on potential harm to society in both the present and the future, are very much more difficult to present in the mass media than those for euthanasia. Anti-euthanasia arguments do not make dramatic and compelling television. Visual images are difficult to find. We do not personally identify with these arguments in the same way that we do with the pleas of dying people who seek euthanasia. Society cannot be interviewed on television and become a familiar, empathy-evoking figure to the viewing public. Only if euthanasia were legalized and associated with obvious abuses – such as proposals to use it on those who object to it and want to continue living – could we create riveting and gripping images that would be comparable in strength with those projected by Sue Rodriguez in pleading her case for euthanasia and that would adequately communicate the case against euthanasia. Or, perhaps, we need to present the case against euthanasia through the imagination of those who write and read prose and poetry. An example mentioned before is that in the first chapter of *The Children of Men*,[9] by P.D. James. The author describes the mass death of some old people by euthanasia in the year 2025, a scene that elicits a powerful reaction against euthanasia.

DESENSITIZATION TO DEATH

The impact of the media in desensitizing us to death has been discussed in chapter 6. This discussion is such an important element in considering the role of the media in the euthanasia debate that it is also included here. It is possible that our reaction to seeing death inflicted has been blunted through the vast exposure to death we are subjected to by the mass media in both news and entertainment programs. This could have overwhelmed our sensitivity to the awesomeness of death and, likewise, of inflicting it. Recent research has shown that human beings have an innate resistance to killing each other and that this is operative even among soldiers in battle – unless they have been systematically desensitised.[10] Could the mass media have desensitized us to death? If so, this is another difficulty in presenting the case against euthanasia in the mass media.

Ironically, among the most powerful ways in which the case *against* euthanasia has been presented on television is through Dr Jack Kevorkian's efforts to *promote* it. Kevorkian's advocy has produced a strong negative reaction in many people, including many of those who support euthanasia. Indeed, some of the latter worried that he was damaging the case for euthanasia. A Dutch documentary of a physician providing euthanasia to a terminally ill patient who had requested it[11] was shown on prime-time television in Canada and the United States. It elicited a chill in many viewers.[12] Moreover, it evoked condemnation as exploitation by the mass media of both the patient and of euthanasia itself.[13] Likewise, some people have suggested that, by seeing executions on television, viewers would be so horrified that they would demand the abolition of capital punishment. Disturbingly, it has been pointed out also that the opposite could occur; people might be as fascinated as they were in the past by public executions.

Personal closeness to, or distance from, inflicting death can affect how we perceive our own involvement and that of others in causing someone's death. The mass media can affect our perceptions of closeness by the way in which they present death. This factor of personal closeness distinguishes euthanasia from physician-assisted suicide. Everyone, especially "treating" physicians, can feel more distant from the infliction of death in the latter case than in the former. In the Northern Territory of Australia, where euthanasia was temporarily legalised,[14] a computer-activated "suicide machine" that could be triggered by terminally ill people was developed.[15] It was used for carrying out the first death that took place under that legislation. And even Dutch physicians, with long-term experience in carrying out euthanasia, have recommended that physician-assisted suicide be practised rather than euthanasia, whenever possible; the former is less emotionally stressful for physicians than the latter.[16]

POLITICAL CORRECTNESS

Political correctness is another factor influencing how the mass media deal with euthanasia. Conformity to its dictates is often a consideration in mass-media presentations. This late-twentieth-century concept, which can function as an ideology, articulates and can sensitize us to the rights of some people or groups and the wrongs done to them. But it can also, when taken to extremes, cause harm. One problem is that those who advocate its application sometimes deny that it can cause any harm.

A pro-choice position on euthanasia has been associated with political correctness. Reporting on euthanasia in the *New York Times*, Paul Wilkes quotes Herbert Hendin, a psychiatrist and executive director of the American Suicide Foundation, as follows: "[Euthanasia] became ... a politically correct issue ... [N]o thinking person would be caught talking against [euthanasia] ... and it became a red badge of courage for liberals ... to be so enlightened as to be for it. Supposedly, it was the thinking person's decision and statement of their independence so they wouldn't be looked upon as some unthinking, religious fundamentalist."[17] This comment raises the complex issue of the mass media's portrayal of religion and how religion, political correctness, and civil liberties are related (a topic I cannot explore here).

CHANGE AND NOVELTY

Consider as well the emphasis on change and novelty in mass-media reporting. It is easy to portray those who uphold traditional values as dinosaurs, lacking the ability to change and soon to become extinct. It is much more difficult to show how one can take important, newer values, such as those developed from concepts of human rights and civil liberties, and incorporate them with older ones. The image that best captures what we need to do is that of a spiral like the DNA helix, not simply a pendulum. A helix allows us to see that, in holding old values, we have not necessarily rejected new perceptions – for instance, those of personal autonomy, self-determination, human dignity, and respect for the individual – but have moved back over old values, taking the new ones with us to find insights that can result from amalgamating them.

REASON AND "OTHER WAYS OF KNOWING"

As I say elsewhere in this book, Western societies have focused, especially in public life, on reason to the exclusion of "other ways of knowing." The pro-euthanasia argument has been based largely on what is presented as a reasoned, utilitarian approach: if people are terminally ill and, therefore, going to die soon anyway, it makes no moral difference – and ought to make no legal difference – if they die naturally or through lethal injection. Yet these arguments are almost invariably presented, as I have already noted, in the context of highly emotional interviews with terminally ill people. It is difficult to assess in these situations the extent to which pro-euthanasia responses are elicited by reason or by emotion (especially powerful empathy with suffering people who want euthanasia). Arguments said to be based on reason can seem much easier to present well in the mass media and to be more authoritative than, for instance, those said to be based on moral intuition – important as the latter might be. Those who rely on intuition can seem to be "fuzzy thinkers," moreover, especially when faced with opposition based purely on reason. Reasoned arguments also seem less dependent for their validity on the need to trust and respect the person or the institution that is their source than is the case with arguments based on "other ways of knowing." As individuals and as a society, we have lost trust in authority figures and institutions and, in particular, their exercise of discretion. This means that the kind of latter arguments are unacceptable to many people.

BASIC PRESUMPTIONS

As I have noted elsewhere, basic presumptions, too, can affect controversies presented in the mass media. If the basic presumption is pro-euthanasia, then those arguing against it have the burden of proof in justifying their position. This could be the current situation. Daniel Callahan, formerly president of the Hastings Center in New York, sums up the situation as follows: "With physician-assisted suicide, we have a sea change: we are saying it is good, humane and dignified and that it can be handled in some systematic way, free from abuse."[18] In short, we have changed from a society that is based on a presumption that it is wrong to kill people to one that is based on a presumption that it is justified in the case of euthanasia. Has this change been caused by the way in which the issues surrounding euthanasia have been presented in the mass media?

MASS-MEDIA ETHICS

How do we draw the fine line, as ethics requires, between reporting adequately on those seeking euthanasia and allowing the mass media to exploit them in manipulative ways in order to attract public attention, discussion, debate and conflict, and ultimately to increase sales or ratings? In the same way, advocates of legalizing euthanasia can manipulate the mass media to further their cause. And sometimes they can use the dying person primarily for the same purpose. In the case of Sue Rodriguez, that was true of the Right to Die Society of Canada and its president, John Hofsess. After Rodriguez failed to obtain an order from the trial court, which would have allowed her access to physician-assisted suicide or euthanasia, Hofsess immediately went to the mass media and announced that Rodriguez would appeal the ruling. He did so without consulting Rodriguez, who was so angry that she terminated her relationship with him. Subsequently, Hofsess appeared in a CBC television documentary, where he seemed on the verge of tears. Now that he could no longer work for her and her cause, he explained, his life had lost its meaning. He had believed that his efforts on Rodriguez's behalf would be the only actions for which he would be remembered by posterity; that possibility was now destroyed. This admission was an unusually frank, though perhaps unwitting, disclosure of how even well-intentioned public actions, as I am sure was true for Mr Hofsess, can have many motivations.

After this event, Svend Robinson, a federal member of parliament from British Columbia, took up the Rodriguez cause. Robinson is an openly gay politician. In promoting freedom of choice on euthanasia, he reflected very powerfully the political and ideological stance on euthanasia of the gay community in Canada. Robinson stated that he was acting simply as a friend. And, as Lisa Hobbs Birnie and Sue Rodriguez make clear in *Uncommon Will*,[19] Rodriguez was certainly in deep need of friends. Robinson's involvement in the case culminated when he announced in Parliament that he had been present with Rodriguez when she died with the help of a physician. There was widespread debate in the mass media over whether any charges would be laid against him, but none was.

MASS MEDIA AS FORUMS FOR "DEATH TALK"

As I say in chapter 6, we are death-denying,[20] death-obsessed[21] societies in which the many people who no longer adhere to the practice of institutionalized religion have lost their main forums for engaging in "death talk" – namely, their places of religious worship. As humans, we need to engage in death talk if we are to accept as part of life the inevitable reality of death. Arguably, the extensive discussion of euthanasia in the mass media is another forum for contemporary death talk. Instead of being confined to an identifiable location and an hour a week, it has spilled out into the larger world. This exposure makes it more difficult to deny death, because it makes fear of death more pervasive and present. One way to deal with this fear is to believe that we have death under control. The availability of euthanasia can encourage that belief. Euthanasia moves us from chance to choice concerning death. Although we cannot make death optional, we can create the illusion that it is by making its timing and the conditions and way in which it occurs a matter of choice. The availability of euthanasia supports this illusion.[22] By acting as modern forums for death talk, the mass media both elicit expressions of fear of death and seek to deal with them – as do churches by the promise of eternal life. Does this role mean that the mass media are a form of religious institution?[23] After all, the word "religion" simply means binding together. And, in some ways, the mass media cause us to do so. Or is there a difference between people binding together and their cultural homogenization?

Finally, I can attest from personal experience how difficult it was to argue against the pleas of Sue Rodriguez when facing them in the mass media. It was impossible not to empathize deeply with her and her suffering, to admire her courage. I often thought of how societies that, appallingly, still engage in capital punishment give prisoners condemned to death some form of their last wish. But I was not prepared to do this for Rodriguez. She often implicitly asked why I would deny her what she wanted so much and what she saw as the only way to relieve her suffering. My answer was, and still is, that legalizing euthanasia would harm society and diminish the value of respect for human life. It would change the fundamental norm of society – that we must not kill one another – to one that we may do so in some circumstances, albeit for reasons of the utmost mercy and compassion.

CONCLUSION

In view of all these factors and forces, it is no wonder that the mass media have, and will have, a difficult time in presenting the euthanasia debate fairly, fully, deeply, and wisely, in facilitating and guiding the societal discussion that surrounds it, and, ultimately, in helping us to reach a wise decision about euthanasia.

20 Euthanasia and the Death Penalty

Two high-profile news stories in early 1998, which centred on the infliction of death, raise questions about the relation between euthanasia and the death penalty: the dismissal of first-degree murder charges against Canadian physician Dr Nancy Morrison in relation to the death of her patient Paul Mills; and the execution of Karla Faye Tucker by the state of Texas. Although the death penalty has been abolished in Canada, there are people – including some members of the Canadian Alliance, the official opposition party – who promote its reintroduction. They claim that most Canadians support it. Many of these same people are also strongly anti-euthanasia. Are people who support the death penalty consistent in their beliefs about the rightness or wrongness of killing other people? In particular, could support for the death penalty promote the legalization of euthanasia?

As I say many times in this book, one of the most important rules on which we base our societies and their legal systems is that we must not kill each other. We must take great care in derogating from this rule. Four exceptions to the rule against killing people have been recognized by the law: self-defence; just war; abortion; and the death penalty.

The primary justification that underlies all four traditional exceptions is that the infliction of death is necessary to save human life. In law, these exceptions are examples of a defence of necessity. The doctrine of *self-defence* applies only to the extent that those who have killed used reasonable force and believed on reasonable grounds that this degree of force was necessary to save their own lives or to protect the lives of others.

In international law, a stringent definition of a *just war* is that this characterization applies only to armed conflict that is necessary to avoid a serious threat to the lives of people facing an aggressor. This is a *collective self-defence* justification.

The original justification for *abortion* was that this intervention was necessary to save the mother's life or to avoid a very serious risk to her life or health. Today, abortion on demand is usually said to be justified on the grounds that the fetus is not yet a person and, therefore, killing it does not count as the taking of a human life. Once a fetus is seen as a person, however, its life is taken only when necessary to save the mother's life or avoid a serious risk to her life or health.

The *death penalty* was initially justified on the grounds that it was a merited and appropriate punishment. But as Western democracies became less comfortable with a straight punitive approach that involved the taking of human life, even in response to murder, capital punishment was viewed as necessary to protect people's lives. The underlying beliefs were that someone who had intentionally killed was likely to kill again and that the death penalty was a strong general deterrent to others who might kill. Consequently, these societies restricted the death penalty to murder. But most of these same societies now recognize that capital punishment is not an effective deterrent and that we no longer need to kill murderers to protect life. These changed perceptions mean that the justification of capital punishment could be used as a precedent for justifying euthanasia.

As with capital punishment today, euthanasia, were it to be legalized, would fall outside the traditional justification for taking life. It involves killing a person – though for reasons of the utmost mercy and compassion – but not to save another human life. The same is true for capital punishment, minus the reasons. But for those who agree with the taking of human life in capital punishment, these reasons should make euthanasia a more, not less, compelling case for justification than capital punishment.

Some people who oppose the death penalty do so on utilitarian or situational-ethics grounds. For instance, Greta van Susteren, the legal commentator on CNN, argued that the problem with the death penalty was that "we might get the wrong person" – make mistakes about whom we killed. As with the people who support capital punishment, those who adopt this view do not regard intentionally killing another human as inherently wrong – as wrong in itself. Rather, in some circumstances, it could be wrong because of error or abuse. This view is consistent with the situational-ethics approach to euthanasia taken by those who support its legalization. These views on the death penalty and euthanasia are consistent in that the taking of human life is not seen as inherently wrong; it all depends on the circumstances.

Before continuing, I should make it clear (as I do in chapter 3) that there are four possible combinations of positions on capital punishment and euthanasia. People can oppose both capital punishment and euthanasia; support capital punishment but oppose euthanasia; support both capital punishment and euthanasia; or oppose capital punishment but support euthanasia. Again as I say in chapter 3, the first is a true pro-life position in that it demonstrates a moral belief that all killing (except, usually, as a last resort in self-defence) is wrong. The second represents the view of some religious fundamentalists – that to uphold the sanctity-of-life value requires prohibition of euthanasia, but the death penalty is justified on the grounds that this punishment is deserved and just according to God's law. The third position is that of those neo-conservatives who see capital punishment as a fit penalty on the basis that one can forfeit one's life through a very serious crime, but one can also consent to the taking of one's own life in the form of euthanasia. The fourth view is that of those civil libertarians who believe that one may consent to the taking of one's own life, but must not take that of others.

The only killing we can justify while maintaining a profound respect for human life is that which is necessary to preserve human life. There is, therefore, a fundamental inconsistency in the approach of those who favour the death penalty but oppose euthanasia on the grounds that the latter derogates from a "sanctity of life" value.

This inconsistency might reflect another inconsistency in the attitudes that people who adopt this position have to individual rights. "Intense individualism" (individual rights always trump claims based on any harm to the community that exercising these rights involves) is operative in the service of the death penalty. In a radio interview, Richard Thornton, whose wife, Debra, was killed by Karla Faye Tucker, passionately proclaimed: "Don't ask for capital punishment, demand it. It's your right!"

Intense individualism also grounds the argument that euthanasia should be legalized because access to it is an essential element of one's rights to autonomy and self-determination. But many people who approve of capital punishment are highly critical of intense individualism in the context of euthanasia. They believe that claims to euthanasia based on individual rights are overwhelmingly outweighed by societal interests in maintaining the utmost respect for human life – which requires the prohibition of euthanasia. They do not recognize that the death penalty, too, necessarily derogates from this value; the harm it causes to society is of the same nature as that involved in legalizing euthanasia. Likewise, they regard the taking of human life through euthanasia as inherently evil. But they do not view the taking of human life through state-sanctioned killing in the same way.

Many people use the Bible to justify their distinction, in terms of acceptability, between capital punishment and euthanasia; the Bible does not prohibit capital punishment, which is deserved and just according to God's law, but it does prohibit euthanasia as contravening the sanctity-of-life value. Nevertheless, this justification of capital punishment does not hold in a secular society, and it is very difficult to find a widely accepted alternative that results in the same distinction. In its absence, those who are pro-capital punishment and anti-euthanasia must choose which of two positions they want to promote for society as a whole. Either capital punishment and euthanasia are both wrong, because both involve taking human life for reasons other than to protect human life, or both can be justified in some circumstances.

Of the four combined positions that can be taken on capital punishment and euthanasia, only the "pro-capital punishment–anti-euthanasia" one is inherently inconsistent (from a secular perspective) with respect to the rightness or wrongness of taking human life. Those who agree with both capital punishment and euthanasia adopt a situational ethics approach. Taking human life is not seen as inherently wrong; it all depends on the circumstances. Capital punishment, with safeguards to prevent error or abuse in its application, can be a just penalty; one must forfeit one's life after committing a very serious crime, and one can consent to being killed through euthanasia. Those who oppose capital punishment but approve of euthanasia give primacy to the value of personal liberty; they believe that one can consent to the taking of one's own life but must not take that of another. And those who oppose both capital punishment and euthanasia reflect a true pro-life stance: all killing (except, usually, as a last resort in self-defence) is wrong.

This analysis shows that, depending on the issue, the various groups can either agree or disagree with one another. We need to acknowledge the possible mixture of consensus and divergence if we are to assess properly the political realities and public-policy stances that will affect whether or not the death penalty continues to be allowed and euthanasia continues to be prohibited.

In conclusion, if one believes it is inherently wrong to kill other people, then (in a secular society) there are only two consistent positions. One can be either for both capital punishment and euthanasia or against both. Therefore, those who support the death penalty but oppose euthanasia are faced with a choice. We should all hope that they choose to uphold a value of the utmost respect for human life.

PART SIX

Ethical and Legal "Tools" in the Euthanasia Debate

21 Labels versus Contents: Variance between Philosophy, Psychiatry, and Law in Concepts Governing Decision-Making

For some time now I have been hearing noises, ranging from rumblings to thunder claps, to the effect that the practice of psychiatry is becoming impossible owing to the application of law. One psychiatric resident told me that she was thinking of leaving psychiatry because it seemed too difficult – not the profession itself but the intervention of law.

I suggest that psychiatry and law are not only essential to each other but complementary; they can and must be integrated. Both have a common goal: the relief of suffering. But, in some circumstances, they see this goal as being best achieved by different means, which are not always compatible. We must build bridges between the two disciplines, and that can be done only if they understand each other. Understanding requires a common language in terms of content, not only terminology. To achieve such understanding, we need to ask whether hidden differences in language could be blocking its realization. In this chapter, I examine four concepts: autonomy, self-determination, competence, and voluntariness. They are often explored in philosophy, including its subdiscipline of ethics, and govern decision-making in medicine, including psychiatry (which I use in this chapter as the example of clinical medicine), and law. This examination is relevant to the euthanasia debate because that is an important context in which ethics, medicine, and law are interacting. Most important, these disciplines govern decision-making about the treatment of people at the end of their lives.

But before moving on, I would like to address, very briefly, three preliminary matters. All are characteristic of, and relevant to, philosophy, psychiatry, and law. They involve words as tools of trade; discretion in decision-making; and the need to identify the essential requirements for an acceptable decision-making process.

WORDS AS "TOOLS OF TRADE"

Words are the "tools of trade" in philosophy, psychiatry, and law. They can be used to involve oneself and one's discipline in a situation or to distance oneself and one's discipline. Words can be used to "attach emotionally" to a situation (become involved), to "detach emotionally" (disengage), or to "dis-identify" (which does not always mean become uninvolved in). One can usefully compare being uninterested (not involved), disinterested (involved but not emotionally involved), and interested (emotionally involved). Each of these concepts is relevant to philosophy (in particular, ethics), psychiatry, and law.

The use of words can be merely descriptive or communicative. It can also be regarded as a "verbal act." The use of words in philosophy, psychiatry, and law is often of the latter nature. The difference between the two uses of words envisaged here can be summarized as one between "talking about" psychiatry and "doing" it (for example, practising psychoanalysis) or "talking about" law and "doing" it (for example, rendering a judgment). Verbal acts are seldom neutral; people seek an outcome, decision, or change, not simply a discussion.

The distinction between "talking about" and "doing" is of interest with respect to the relatively recent advent of the field of practical or applied ethics – especially clinical ethics, of which psychiatric ethics is an important part. Applied ethics can be regarded as "doing" philosophy, unlike the traditional practice of "talking about" philosophy.

Moreover, "doing" philosophy – applied ethics – is not neutral or detached in the sense that no identified people are involved or affected (unlike much theoretical philosophy, which really is neutral in that sense – at least on a direct and immediate basis). As a result, philosophy has a common characteristic with law and psychiatry – the lack of which used to be a distinguishing feature of philosophy as compared with law and psychiatry. There is still debate, in some circles, as to whether or not the evolution of applied ethics is a good development for philosophy. Some see it as a harmful vulgarization; others as saving the life of philosophy, in that the public can now see philosophy as useful and will be willing to continue to support it with their tax dollars and students will be attracted to study it.

The use of words, whether descriptively or as "verbal acts," can be a means of taking control and, therefore, of taking power. One can, by applying descriptive words, define a matter into one's orbit of control and take power as a result – for example, by both professionalizing it in general and bringing it within one's professional domain in particular. Moreover, as we have seen throughout the euthanasia debate, for instance, our choice of words is not emotionally neutral and strongly affects outcomes.

DISCRETION IN DECISION-MAKING

Autonomy, self-determination, voluntariness, and competence can all be discretionary concepts in the sense that their content, or their application when their content is defined, has a large discretionary component. Its presence, in turn, might allow them to be used for the protection of discretionary, unarticulated, perhaps even unarticulable factors.

That could be a valid function of these concepts. It means that they can be used to allow decisions that are justified in particular circumstances without setting precedents that could inflict harm. In future cases, any precedent could be avoided by a different exercise of the discretion with respect to the relevant factor (for example, in deciding whether people are competent or their decisions voluntary). But how are these concepts used in practice? How should they be used? These are the questions I will answer in this chapter.

In almost all decision-making situations, and certainly in those involving law, we operate from initial presumptions – although they are not always articulated. I propose that the initial presumption regarding the validity of persons' decisions concerning themselves (for example, in connection with medical treatment) should be like those governing sanity or competence, in which one presumes people sane or competent until the contrary is proven. In other words, the presumption should be that persons' decisions concerning themselves are valid and that those wanting to override these decisions should have the burden of proving they are justified in doing so.

The use of the concepts of autonomy, self-determination, competence, and voluntariness allows either the application or the exclusion of other principles and concepts to the decision-making of the person to whom they are applied. They can be regarded as "gate-keeping" concepts. When their requirements are fulfilled with respect to a given person, other concepts can be activated. They include liberty, justice, fairness, and respect for persons and their rights to inviolability, privacy, and confidentiality. In contrast, when the requirements for autonomy, self-determination, competence, and voluntariness are held *not* to be fulfilled with respect to a given person, still other principles and concepts can dominate in the decision-making. They include paternalism, protection, and beneficence, but, again, justice and fairness. The presence of the latter two in both cases – that is, regardless of whether the concepts of autonomy, self-determination, competence, and voluntariness are operative – provides an important insight. What constitutes justice can vary not only with the circumstances of a given situation but also with the people involved. It would be unjust to characterize competent people as incompetent in order, for instance, to override their decisions. But one might be just (or more just[1]) towards people by holding them to be incompetent when that is clearly the case, and unjust (or less just) by ignoring the incompetence or acting on a façade of competence. It should also be noted that decisions about the discretionary content concepts of autonomy, self-determination, and voluntariness depend on whether people are held to be competent or incompetent – which likewise involves a concept and decision of discretionary content. In one sense, therefore, competence can be regarded as the "gate-keeper" of "gate-keeping" concepts.

It is possible that, through their discretionary content, the concepts of autonomy, self-determination, voluntariness, and competence allow the introduction of non-cognitive factors into the decision-making situation. These factors could include examined or unexamined emotional reactions to the situation from which decision-making arises or intuitive responses.

We need to "unpack" the concepts of autonomy, self-determination, voluntariness, and competence to see how we use them in decision-making. In philosophy, there has been much talk about these concepts, but only very recently, with the development of applied ethics, has there been any direct, practical use of them. It is interesting that in both law and psychiatry, in contrast to philosophy, we have constantly used these notions – both descriptively ("talking about" law and psychiatry) and prescriptively ("doing" law and psychiatry) – but have seldom done in-depth analyses of their contents or tried to define them precisely. For example, most psychiatrists believe that they know what competence is, but cannot readily define it when asked to do so. This difficulty is surprising in view of the extensive and still evolving literature dealing with competence, especially in the area of psychiatry and law.[2] But a distinction should be made here between the definition of competence and the criteria for establishing it.[3] The literature deals with the latter, not usually the former, although it is true that exploration of criteria for the determination of competence necessarily, but indirectly, throws light on the definition of competence.

It could be – indeed, I suggest it is likely – that psychiatrists have difficulty defining competence because there are intuitive and other non-rational elements in deciding whether it is present or absent. These elements should not – indeed, must not – be excluded; but decision-making in which such unconscious components play a major role needs safeguarding. This need is demonstrated also by studies showing that values and other subjective elements are involved in establishing competence. According to one study, the more serious the outcome of a decision (in terms of life and death), and the more it differs from what psychiatrists think they would decide as a patient in the same circumstances, the more likely it is that people will be adjudged incompetent.[4] The effect is to take decision-making power away from patients and give control over to others.[5] The latter could be people whom psychiatrists can influence more easily than patients or even, in some cases (at least in the past), the treating psychiatrists themselves.

Exploring the content and definition of these four concepts governing decision-making in philosophy, psychiatry, and law – namely, autonomy, self-determination, competence, and voluntariness – is not a neutral activity. To the extent that it results in trying to define these concepts comprehensively and, as a result, has the effect of tying them down, they could lose their ability to function as discretionary mechanisms, which could be their most important function. This is yet another example of the dilemma faced constantly by law: how to balance certainty with flexibility. We tend to be uncomfortable with identified uncertainty (in this case, identified uncertainty in the definition and application of these concepts), but not with the very same uncertainty when *not* identified. Perhaps one of our tasks is to train ourselves to live more comfortably with a higher degree of identified uncertainty, when doing so would be more beneficial than either failing to identify it or, having identified it, trying to replace it with certainty.

Autonomy and its companion concepts are like icebergs; only the tips are visible. There is a need to explore what is submerged: how these concepts function unconsciously and symbolically, as well as consciously, with respect to both the individual and society. Increased awareness of the nature of these concepts will not necessarily mean that we would want to use them any differently. We might want and need to retain, for example, their ability to function in a discretionary manner. But we would choose to have them function in these "other" ways rather than having them do so without our recognizing this possibility because we failed to realise that we were dealing with an "iceberg concept" – one that has important functions at more than just the conscious level.

We must bear in mind that we might, in some circumstances, choose to have uncertainty present. We might do so, for instance, by choosing decision-making mechanisms that operate on the basis of chance more than choice. In summary, there is a difference between uncertainty being present and its being identified. There is a difference, moreover, between choosing to have uncertainty present and its being unavoidably present.

THE DECISION-MAKING PROCESS

I will mention only briefly the need to identify the essential requirements of the decision-making process used in philosophy, psychiatry, or law. But it must be recognized.

Form is no mere formality. The processes we use can have a major impact on the outcomes of decisions, particularly when faced with uncertainty as to the substantive principles that should be applied (which is often the case with issues presented at the intersections of philosophy, psychiatry, and law).

Law has by far the most formal decision-making processes of the three disciplines and the best articulated procedural rules. Among the most important are those of natural justice, which require impartial decision-makers and establish the right of all interested parties to be heard. These rules have become increasingly relevant to medicine and, therefore, to psychiatry. For example, when approval of an ethics committee is required before research involving human subjects may be carried out, these rules and others are applicable to the functioning of the ethics committee (although, at least in the past, that has seldom been recognized unless the committee's decision has been challenged in some manner). Much less formal rules, too, are relevant. Records of earlier decisions, including those taken by committees, can influence later ones. Keeping or not keeping records can affect future decisions owing to the availability or unavailability of precedents. Some people moreover, might decide one way or another merely because records are kept.

THE CONCEPTS

I will now try to define the content of autonomy, self-determination, competence, and voluntariness. I will do so, in part, by comparing and contrasting them. Both negative and positive definitions are relevant: what is not regarded as self-determination, for instance, can tell us much about what it is and *vice versa*.

Autonomy and Self-Determination

What is autonomy? What is self-determination? In law the terms "autonomy" and "self-determination" are used interchangeably, although reference to both is often made at the same time (usually in the context of rights to autonomy and self-determination). According to the rules of legal construction against redundancy (that is, if two terms are used instead of one, both are assumed to be necessary, neither being superfluous), this duplication would indicate that the two terms have different meanings.

What are these meanings and how are they relevant to the law? One possibility is that "self-determination" might refer to the ability of people to express their wishes. That is, people have the ability simply to say yes or no to proposals, and saying either constitutes a decision for the purposes of the law. With that approach, incompetent people could be self-determining; despite their incompetence, they might be able to respond positively or negatively when asked to make decisions. This is to propose that self-determination is a dispositional capacity: if people can do "x" (say yes or no), then they are "y" (self-determining), which relies on a behaviourist theory of mind. This approach would mean that the decisions of incompetent people could not be disregarded on the basis that they were not self-determining. Nevertheless, the decisions of incompetent, self-determining people could be overridden, but only with justification. The burden of proof of such justification (for instance, avoiding harm) would be on those seeking to rely on it. This means that, in cases of equal doubt as to whether or not a justification applies for overriding the decisions of incompetent people, the general rule – that the decisions of all people must be respected – would prevail. When incompetent people refuse medical treatment, and there is equal doubt as to whether either the harm that is avoided by intervening is serious or the benefits and potential benefits of the intervention outweigh its harms and risks, overriding their refusals would not be justified.

One important effect of adopting an approach that deals with competence and self-determination separately, as I say, is that it would require respect for the wishes of incompetent but self-determining people, unless there were good reasons to override them. This approach is the most person-respecting one. It would probably help overcome some of the very real dangers that exist in labelling people "incompetent" and, therefore, non-self-determining. One danger is that this labelling is either taken to indicate global incompetence of the person (which might be inaccurate) or treated as having the global effect of rendering people incompetent for all purposes (which leads to the same outcome). People might be incompetent in some ways and competent in others. A second danger is that labelling people "incompetent" is usually taken to indicate that they need no longer be consulted or have their wishes taken into account. This classification can lead to brutal disregard of their wishes in circumstances when they should at least be taken into account, though not necessarily respected. An effect of such attitudes and conduct is the depersonalization and dehumanization of incompetent people.

If self-determination is defined as above, but autonomy requires competence, then self-determination is a concept that has less exacting requirements than autonomy. Conversely, self-determination might be defined as a concept with more exacting requirements than autonomy. This position is reflected in another possible approach to the distinction between the two terms, which is that autonomy does not require for its exercise that a "self" be present, but self-determination does.

What would constitute a "self" for the purpose of deciding whether people are able to be self-determined? Must there be some minimal presence of the person? If so, what would constitute it? One question raised here is whether the concepts of "person" and "self-determination" are linked. If they are, and if the concepts of "autonomy" and "person" are linked as well, then the concept of "self-determination" and that of "autonomy" are necessarily linked. Indeed, they would be synonymous, although one could argue that "autonomy" refers to the capacity for self-determination (which can be present without being exercised) and "self-determination" to the exercise of it. If only autonomous beings are considered "persons," and the definition of autonomy is a "full," or "packed," one, then a "full," or "packed," definition of "person" will be the result. This reasoning represents the philosophical approach, which uses autonomy as the marker of personhood. Likewise, pursuant to such analysis, a minimalist definition of "autonomy" would result in a minimalist definition of "person." In other words, the word "person" could be treated as more or less equivalent to "human being" – which seems to be the approach of the law. This approach would result also in a minimalist definition of what is required for the presence of "self" – and, therefore, of "self-determination" – if the concepts of "person" and "self" are linked. This could be a return to the content of the first approach, that people are self-determining if they can say yes or no. But here the content of the definition of "self-determination" is made to depend on that of another concept, "personhood."

According to some philosophers, the word "autonomous" should be used to describe the decision of a free, self-realizing, self-directed agent; the decisions of people are autonomous, when these decisions are authentic ("theirs") and independent ("their own").[6] These philosophers refer also to greater and lesser degrees of autonomy.[7] To some extent, a value judgment is involved in deciding what constitutes greater or lesser degrees of autonomy: greater autonomy is said to be present when people act free of unacceptable influences, including unacceptable intrinsic psychological influences, and deciding what are acceptable and unacceptable influences is far from value-free. According to this philosophical view, people are regarded as more autonomous as they become more aware of what influences them and are more psychologically able to decide whether or not to allow these factors to operate – in a sense, they could be characterized as "psychologically free" – and *vice versa*. This concept of autonomy is value-laden in at least two other respects. First, greater autonomy is regarded as a "higher state of being." Second, it postulates a particular kind of person as being most autonomous – namely, self-aware, reflective, and insightful. Those who are impulsive, act on instinct, or are emotionally influenced (and, as a result, impetuous) are likely to be regarded as less autonomous. In other words, people whose cognitive functioning clearly dominates their emotional functioning are likely to be regarded as more autonomous. This distinction would matter if some rights or privileges were conditional on a person being regarded as having a certain degree of autonomy – or even if being less autonomous were believed to detract from the worth of these people or were seen as an implicitly or explicitly derogatory statement about them.

Unlike philosophy, the law has no definition of autonomy and, as I have noted, tends to equate the concepts of "autonomy" and "self-determination." The law does, however, seek to establish the conditions in which it is presumed or hoped that autonomy will be present or fostered (for instance, when it is used to articulate and implement rights to autonomy and self-determination in relation to decision-making). But what constitutes autonomy *per se*,[8] as compared with a right to autonomy, is not defined in law. In practice, whether or not people are autonomous seems to be treated as a question of fact more than of theory. It is determined, if at all, on a case-by-case basis, usually by a court, as a passing reference to someone's state of mind. This is probably because the determination of whether or not someone is autonomous is seldom of direct relevance to the law, whereas the determination of a person's competence and the voluntariness of his or her decision-making are considered relevant. These characteristics are linked to autonomy; they might reflect the presence or absence of autonomy in the philosophical sense. This is because decisions by incompetent people might not be authentic ("theirs") and those that are not voluntary might not be independent ("their own"). At issue for the law is the level of inauthenticity or dependence that would make people legally incompetent or their decisions involuntary from the law's perspective. People and their decisions might well be regarded as non-autonomous in the philosophical sense before they or their decisions are regarded as incompetent or involuntary by the law.

Likewise, if autonomous people are defined philosophically as those whose second-order desires endorse their first-order ones (that is, they not only recognize and act on their desires but also like being as they are), then people who are competent legally and whose decisions are voluntary – but whose second-order desires conflict with their first-order ones – might not be fully autonomous philosophically.

What Is the Relation between Autonomy and Other Person–Protecting Concepts?

I begin with informed consent. Autonomy is a purpose or goal of the doctrine of informed consent, not one of its elements. One might assume that if informed consent were being used to inhibit rather than promote autonomy, it would be a relevant consideration in relation to the validity of consent. But that might not be true from a legal point of view. Consider the psychological coping mechanism of denial. Patients might refuse to be given information so as to remain in a state of denial about their illnesses and the implications. But people need some minimal consciousness of a matter in order to be able to suppress consciousness of that matter so as to be in a state of denial.[9] Are we promoting or reducing autonomy by insisting on informing patients in order to obtain informed consent? Does the answer depend on the extent of the information we insist on providing? Can informed consent be present without informing? This is probably best described as a situation requiring application of the legal doctrine of waiver. Waiver applies when those who have the right to be informed give consent (*quaere*, informed consent) to *not* being informed in circumstances where those who have a legal obligation to inform are ready, willing, and able to do so and make that known. Waiver can be regarded either as an exception to requiring informed consent or as permitting informed consent to be obtained on the basis of less than the usually required scope of disclosure of information. The latter might seem to present a contradiction in terms. How can people give informed consent if they are not informed?

The confusion arises because, although information disclosure was the initial focus of the doctrine of informed consent, that doctrine is now much more all-encompassing, nuanced, and subtle in terms of what is sought to be achieved through its use and includes promotion of patient autonomy. In particular, patient autonomy could be promoted by accepting patients' waivers of the right to be informed and treating the resulting consents as valid – that is, as fulfilling the requirements of the doctrine of "informed consent."[10] To the contrary, there could be a detraction from patient autonomy by refusing to accept consent given pursuant to a waiver of information. In short, waiver can be regarded as another example of an exercise of autonomy by patients, because they choose not to be informed. But whether or not decisions made in these circumstances should be regarded as autonomous depends on one's definition of "autonomy." This distinction presents an interesting paradox, which I will not explore here: one could, through the same mechanism, simultaneously promote the autonomy of patients and detract from the autonomy of their decisions.

I turn now to inviolability. The law speaks of a "right to autonomy" – that is, a right to decide what happens to oneself, especially what is done with or to one's body. This right overlaps with that to inviolability, which comprehends the right not to be touched without one's consent. The right to inviolability can be regarded as a negative-content expression of the right to autonomy. The latter has positive content, too, such as the right to demand to be touched. That right exists in some jurisdictions, for example, in Quebec, by virtue of the legal right to necessary medical care.[11] If this care were refused without justification, such as a reasonably unavoidable shortage of resources, it could be demanded and obtained through legal action.

The right to autonomy encompasses a right to privacy, too. In fact, the most famous development of this right in Anglo-American legal systems was in the reverse order: American courts interpreted the right to privacy as requiring recognition of the right to autonomy in order to give adequate protection to the right to privacy. One of the landmark decisions in this regard is *Roe* v. *Wade*,[12] in which the United States Supreme Court held that a "penumbra" right of privacy was to be found in the United States Constitution. The court held that this right required recognition of a right to autonomy. In the circumstances of the case before the court, that right allowed a woman to decide for herself without any state interference, during the first trimester of pregnancy, what should be done with respect to her body. This meant that during that period the state could not interfere in any way with her decision not to continue a pregnancy by undergoing an abortion. (This right became slightly less absolute during the second trimester and very much more restricted in the third trimester.) This privacy-autonomy right is of negative content; it is a "right against." Positive-content rights of privacy – for example, the right to inspect and take a copy of one's own medical records[13] and have them corrected if they are in error[14] – implement rights to autonomy and self-determination in yet another sense. They allow one to exercise the ability to express one's wishes and to have them implemented when that requires action on the part of someone else. Both negative- and positive-content rights of privacy and autonomy reflect and implement the rights of freedom and liberty. This is a "freedom from" in the case of negative-content rights of privacy, which are rights not to be physically or mentally invaded. Such privacy rights might be necessary conditions precedent to autonomy and self-determination, to the extent that the latter depend on the power to control the inputs to which one is subject. Positive-content rights of privacy involve "freedom to" do, see, or change something – which are forms of control over what happens to one and, therefore, closely related to autonomy and self-determination. Both forms of freedom might be related also to autonomy in the broader philosophical sense described above: people who are free from unwanted interferences and free to act as they see fit have at least the circumstances present in which their psychologically free (that is, "their" authentic and "their own" independent) decisions can be taken and implemented. In short, autonomy, self-determination, liberty, and freedom have a common element: control of both what one does not want and what one does want to happen to one.

What Are the Dangers of Abuse of a Concept of Autonomy? It would be dangerous for the law to adopt the philosophical notion of autonomy if doing so were to mean that only autonomous people or autonomous decisions, in the philosophical sense, must be respected. Promoting a right to autonomy is intended to protect people's liberty, freedom, and right to self-determination – that is, the right to decide what should happen to themselves. But it could have the opposite effect for those adjudged to be non-autonomous. They could be deprived of their liberty, freedom, and right to self-determination on the basis of their non-autonomous state, when they would not necessarily be deprived of these rights if autonomy were irrelevant. In short, there is danger in promoting autonomy as a factor relevant to legal rights in relation to personal decision-making because doing so could result in the invasion of the human rights of, a lack of respect for, and wrongful discrimination against people characterized as non-autonomous.

The same phenomenon – a doctrine meant to promote respect for persons or to protect them being used to the opposite effect – can be seen in connection with the doctrine of informed consent (a doctrine that would be better named "informed choice"). That doctrine is meant to protect patients from unwanted or unconsented-to treatment and requires that patients be informed of the nature and consequences, including material risks, of the proposed treatment, of its alternatives, and of forgoing all treatment. But the doctrine can be used also to deny treatment. This can occur when it is argued that not enough is known about a treatment – such as an experimental drug for AIDS – to allow people to give their informed consent to its use or when it is argued that it is impossible for some people's consent to be sufficiently free or voluntary – which could be the case for prisoners – and, therefore, that they are incapable of giving their informed consent. In short, the doctrine of informed consent, which has a primary purpose of protecting people from the wrongful imposition of treatment, can, when stringently defined and applied in a particular way, be used also as a way of denying access to treatment. It is interesting to note, however, that such a denial is rarely a complaint on the part of mentally ill people – even though there are many new experimental psychopharmacotherapeutic agents that offer them hope of vastly improved treatment, and even though involuntarily hospitalized mentally ill people can be compared in some respects with prisoners. The reason is that most court cases involving the application of the doctrine of informed consent to mentally ill people concern their reliance on the doctrine to have their refusals of treatment respected, when health-care professionals regard this treatment as essential. These cases do not concern the use of the doctrine by health-care professionals to deny the claims of mentally ill people to access to treatment.

In the remainder of this chapter, I have adopted (unless otherwise stated), a minimalist definition of both "autonomy" and "self-determination."

Competence

What Is Competence?
In law, the doctrine of competence has two limbs: legal and factual. Adults are legally competent unless subject to a court order declaring them incompetent. On the whole, factual competence, which I will define, is of much greater importance to health law than legal competence. In the following discussion, I assume that all people are legally competent.

In law, only the decisions of factually competent people are binding. Factual competence is defined by cognitive mental functioning. People are functionally – and, therefore, factually – competent if they have the capacity to understand the nature and consequences of the proposed course of conduct. Competence does not depend on rationality or rational-decision outcomes. Irrationality is legally relevant in terms of voiding decisions only if the irrationality indicates defects in cognitive functioning (lack of capacity to understand the information required to be disclosed). At least in theory, competence is judged on the basis of cognitive capacity, not its exercise *per se* – and, therefore, not the content of the decision reached. In practice, the latter features often play a role in the determination of competence because they can be used as evidence indicating a lack of the necessary cognitive capacity.

At present, the law does not incorporate any separate or distinct concept of emotional competence or incompetence. Emotional functioning is relevant to the law and its definition of competence only if it affects cognitive functioning and, hence, capacity for understanding. There are arguments both for and against incorporating the notion of emotional incompetence into the law.[15] The dangers are those of abuse: decisions that should not be overridden will be on the basis of emotional incompetence. The benefit is that the decisions of some seriously emotionally disturbed – but cognitively competent – people could be overridden when their decisions are far outside any range that could be considered "normal." Many paranoid people are cognitively competent, but delusions dominate their decision-making, sometimes with seriously harmful results. If an approach that took emotional competence into account were to be adopted, strict safeguards would be needed. The presence of emotional incompetence should not, in itself, justify overriding the decision of cognitively competent people. The overriding must be clearly justified – necessary in that no less invasive or restrictive approach would suffice, serious harm would be avoided, and the benefits and potential benefits to the emotionally incompetent person clearly outweigh any harm and risks of harm to him or her. The intervention of a court, too, might be required as a safeguard in declaring cognitively competent persons emotionally incompetent in order to override their decisions concerning themselves.

The legal approach to competence does not function on a continuum, but on a bi-polar model: people are adjudged either competent or incompetent for the purposes of law. In fact, however, not all incompetent people are equally incompetent, and not all competent people equally competent. This variable is illustrated diagrammatically in figure 21.1.

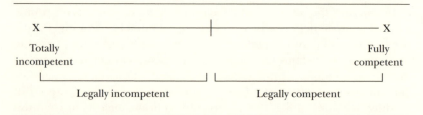

Figure 21.1
Competence

What Is the Relation between Competence and Self-Determination?

If the right of self-determination – the right to have one's decisions concerning oneself respected – depends on one's competence, then competence acts as a condition precedent to exercising the right of self-determination. According to this approach, the contents of the concepts of competence and self-determination are different, but related. On the one hand, determining competence involves an assessment of mental capacity in terms of cognitive functioning for decision-making. On the other hand, exercising the right of self-determination assumes, but does not demand, the exercise of that capacity in decision-making when it is found to be present. This means that irrational decisions of competent people will be respected, and respect will be accorded on the basis of respect for their right of self-determination. Using that model, competence has a prescriptive function, and self-determination a descriptive one. But if self-determination does *not* depend on the presence of competence, there is no necessary relation between competence and self-determination; they can be regarded as independent variables in a decision-making context. Such an approach means that an incompetent person could exercize a right to self-determination, and a competent person could lack this right in certain circumstances. Whether the concept of either self-determination or competence functions prescriptively or descriptively depends on how it is used. In law, competence tends, in practice, to be used prescriptively, and self-determination, descriptively. In practice, the outcome in law tends to be the same whether competence and self-determination are regarded as dependent or independent variables, which means that it is difficult to determine the theoretical approach of the law to this question. Which theoretical approach is taken becomes important when one theoretical base would give a certain outcome, and the other a different outcome in the same situation.

What Is the Relation between Competence and Autonomy? The analysis outlined above can be applied directly to a second comparison, that of the concepts of competence and autonomy, if the latter is regarded as interchangeable with self-determination – which is one possible definition of "autonomy."

But what is the relation between competence and autonomy when the latter is defined in the philosophical sense described above? One can regard competence as the beginning of a continuum that ends with "full autonomy." That philosophical concept includes, however, a great deal more than simply having full and free capacity for cognitive functioning and even exercising it. In addition, it contemplates having full and free emotional and psychological functioning in the sense that decisions, to be regarded as fully autonomous, must be free of what are classified, either by the people themselves or, sometimes, by others, as unacceptable influences – including intrinsic ones. Consequently, the continuum is better envisioned as including a triangle rather than as just a straight line. The triangle, the apex of which is competence, represents a series of factors overlying competence. It should be noted that legal competence can exist before autonomy in the philosophical sense is present. As well, the commencement of competence in the legal sense and autonomy in the philosophical sense can coincide, depending on the circumstances of the case. On the other hand, it is impossible for autonomy in the philosophical sense to exist before legal competence. But if autonomy is defined only to require that people be able to express their wishes, which is equivalent to the least demanding definition of self-determination, it would not depend on the presence of competence and could precede it. The general scheme contemplated here is illustrated diagrammatically in figure 21.2.

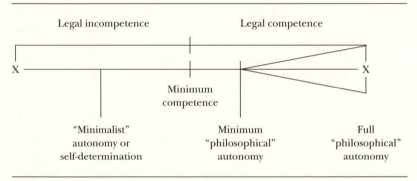

Figure 21.2
Autonomy and its relation to competence

Some authors (such as Jay Katz in *The Silent World of Doctor and Patient*[6]) have proposed that one may invade someone's rights to privacy and self-determination for the purpose of promoting autonomy. Promoting autonomy is seen as being undertaken, despite the invasion of autonomy involved in the intervention, when one gives people every opportunity – or even forces them – to achieve the fullest possible state of psychological freedom of which they are capable in relation to decision-making. When patients refuse treatment and their refusals carry material risk of serious harm unaccompanied by any compensating benefits, Katz (who is both a psychiatrist and a professor of law) argues in favour of imposing "clinical conversation" on patients for a limited time in order to ensure that they have the fullest possible perspective on their situations and every opportunity to change their mind. It is obviously open to debate whether that would promote or infringe on autonomy – even in the overall sense of whether this approach achieves the greatest net augmentation of autonomy, as compared with a non-interventionist approach that merely respects the refusals of competent patients. It could well be that law would see it as invading autonomy on the basis that it infringes the rights of patients in this respect, whereas psychiatry would see it as promoting autonomy on the grounds that it best responds to patients' needs in this regard. This distinction touches on one difference between law and psychiatry: when there is conflict between respecting the rights and needs of patients, law tends to give priority to the former and psychiatry the latter.

Voluntariness

What Is Voluntariness?
Voluntariness requires that decisions be the result of free acts of will; stated negatively, decisions must not be the result of coercion, duress, or undue influence. Voluntary decisions are those willed (freely made by decision-makers). Involuntary or non-voluntary decisions are those made by – but against the will of – decision-makers. "Avoluntary" decisions are those made in the absence of will – for example, in a state of automatism.

Factors with the potential to affect voluntariness can be classified as extrinsic or intrinsic. Holding a gun to someone's head and thereby forcing agreement to a course of action, is a clear example of extrinsic coercion. On the whole, these factors are easier to assess and to deal with than intrinsic ones. Intrinsic factors that could be regarded as coercive include some psychopathological states (for instance, obsessive disorders, megalomania, or paranoia) and drugs that affect the psyche in a way that causes people to make decisions they would not make otherwise. The former factors could be labelled "pure intrinsic coercion," and the latter "mixed intrinsic coercion"; both can be compared with "extrinsic coercion." Again, one has a continuum. And again, the law must draw a line below which coercion is not regarded as present and above which it is present.

Figure 21.3 indicates that "pure" intrinsic coercive factors do not in law render decisions involuntary, which is probably true. That does not mean, however, that these factors are irrelevant in establishing the legal validity of decisions by those who are subject to them. Factors that can be classified as "pure" intrinsic coercion, for example, could indicate incompetence. Or they could block sufficient understanding of the information required (by people, for instance, whose informed consent must be obtained), with the effect of rendering their decisions invalid in law on the basis of lack of information. It is not enough in law for information to be delivered. It must be received, too. The test

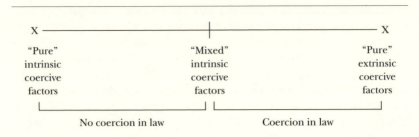

Figure 21.3
Coercion

for that, I suggest, is whether those who are legally required to inform others would, as reasonable people giving information, believe that the recipients of the information apparently understand it.[17] If the answer is negative, any consent of those receiving the information is legally defective; there has been no legally adequate reception of information. In summary, for legally valid decision-making in situations where the legal validity of the decision-making depends partly on the provision of information, the law has minimum requirements that must be fulfilled with respect not only to giving information but also to receiving it.[18]

In law, extrinsic coercive factors are more likely than intrinsic ones to be regarded as voiding decisions on the grounds of lack of voluntariness. The law has a pervasive doctrine of "take your victims as you find them," which means that defendants take the risk that their wrongdoing will cause much greater than expected damage because of the plaintiffs' personal susceptibilities or circumstances. In these cases, defendants must pay the full extent of the damage, not merely that which was reasonably foreseeable, although reasonable foreseeability, to which this approach is an exception, is the general principle governing both the imposition and limits of legal liability. In assessing the effect of intrinsic coercive factors on voluntariness, particularly those not generated by an identified external cause, one could compare psychopathological states that fulfill the criteria for an intrinsic coercive factor, with similar states induced by drugs: the latter are much more likely than the former to be held to give rise to a lack of voluntariness. With respect to intrinsic coercive factors, the maxim referred to above tends to adopt the form of "take yourself as you find yourself." That is, plaintiffs have more difficulty establishing "pure" intrinsic coercion than other forms of coercion as something that should be regarded by the law as invalidating their decision-making and, thereby, making defendants legally liable. Finally, it is worth noting that, when either extrinsic or intrinsic factors influence decision-making, a value judgment is required to decide when the factor reaches a degree of influence such that it becomes unacceptable in the sense of rendering a decision involuntary through coercion, duress, or undue influence. This is especially true in deciding, as figure 21.3 indicates is necessary, which "mixed" intrinsic factors amount to coercion and which do not.

What Is the Relation between Voluntariness and Self-Determination, and between Voluntariness and Autonomy?

The presence of voluntariness indicates that a decision is indeed self-determined, not other-determined. The absence of voluntariness indicates the opposite. Consequently, voluntariness can be regarded as a marker of, or test for, self-determination in decision-making. Stated another way, an ability to be self-determining is related to an ability to make voluntary choices. On the other hand, it is "the self" who still decides even when a decision is involuntary – for example, subject to coercion. According to this analysis, self-determination and voluntariness are not linked; rather, they are independent variables.

Voluntariness and autonomy, in the philosophical sense, are directly related. The more autonomous a decision is, the more voluntary it becomes. One can thus adopt a continuum of voluntariness from involuntary to avoluntary to voluntary, which parallels the continua described previously for both autonomy and competence. In fact, one of these continua exists in relation to voluntariness. But, again, only one point on it is relevant to the law: that below which decisions are characterized as involuntary and above which they are treated as voluntary. In neither case need a decision be at an end-point to be so characterized. This approach is represented diagrammatically in figure 21.4.

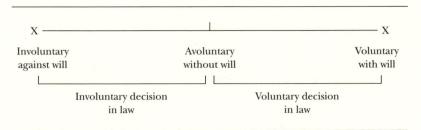

Figure 21.4
Voluntariness

As the diagram indicates, some avoluntary decisions could be characterized in law as involuntary and others as voluntary. Again, a value judgment is involved in making such determinations.

What Is the Relation between Voluntariness and Competence?

The relation between voluntariness and competence is similar to one version of that between voluntariness and self-determination: the two are independent variables. That is, they are not linked. Competent people can make voluntary or involuntary decisions, although whether they could make avoluntary ones is an interesting question. Does the absence of exercise of will necessarily mean that they are incompetent (that competent people cannot, by definition, act without will)? The answer, at least in a technical, legal sense, is probably that they can act in an avoluntary manner, because competence requires only the presence of the capacity to understand the information that must be provided in relation to any given decision. It does not require the exercise of that capacity. However, the cases in which competent people do something with no act of will would have to be carefully identified. Refusing to make a decision is not an example, because a refusal is in itself an exercise of will. In fact, it is an option resorted to, especially by older people making decisions about medical treatment.[19] Moreover, the distinction between acts and omissions could be relevant here. A decision outcome that results from an omission to decide is more likely to be characterized as avoluntary than one in which someone acts, whether verbally or otherwise, to render the decision.

Clearly, incompetent people can make both involuntary and avoluntary decisions. But can they make voluntary ones? The answer is just as clearly yes; their competence or understanding is defective, not their ability to will or "want" the decision outcome they articulate. These decisions can be voluntary, but they are not competent. It is important to recognize these factors, because recognizing that the decisions of incompetent people are voluntary could make us more ready than otherwise to respect them when this is appropriate – that is, when there is no adequate justification for overriding them. Here is a good example: a requirement to take into account the wishes of incompetent people when it comes to sexual sterilization. Too often, their decisions are regarded as totally defective. We might develop a different attitude if we were to recognize that some people's decisions can be defective because of involuntariness, although these people are competent, and other people's decisions can be voluntary but defective because of incompetence. In both cases there is a single defect, though a different one. In a sense, the decisions of people in one of these categories are no more defective than those of people in the other. That recognition could be important in order to obtain a balanced perspective on defects in decision-making and to decide what consequences, whether legal or other, should flow from their presence.

CONCLUSION

Exploring and comparing the decision-making concepts of autonomy, self-determination, competence, and voluntariness in philosophy, psychiatry, and law provides insights that can help us decide both which decisions we should respect and which we are justified in not respecting. However, just as we need to distinguish the sin from the sinner, we must distinguish the decision from the decision-maker. This is particularly important in ensuring respect for all people. There might be a tendency to respect only those whose decisions we respect; that is, respect is generated from respect for a decision and flows to the person who made it. The converse, too, should be true. We must respect all people, whether or not we can respect all of their decisions.

This leads me to a final point, one that has been made many times in this book. We need to identify the *prima facie* presumption from which we work. For that, I propose that the decisions of all people should be respected and that exceptions would have to be clearly justified. These exceptions could include a range of factors, one of which could be incompetence. But if the decisions of incompetent people were not harmful to them or seriously harmful to others, incompetence by itself would be an insufficient justification for ignoring or overriding them. The alternative *prima facie* presumption, and the one that might be in use currently, is that the decisions of all competent (or self-determining, or autonomous) people should be respected and that exceptions must be clearly justified. This means that incompetent (or non-self-determining, or non-autonomous) people would be classified separately from others, with the result that there would be no *prima facie* presumption that their decisions or wishes must be respected and exceptions justified. Even more important, this approach would mean that the decisions or wishes of incompetent people need not even be taken into account. The distinction between "not respecting" and "not taking into account" is important. There is a difference between not respecting decisions or wishes because they have been ignored and not respecting decisions or wishes after they have been taken into account. The latter is more person-respecting. I propose that decisions, not people, should be classified if we are not to run the risk of wrongfully discriminating against those whom we regard as less competent than we are and, therefore, less worthy of respect for their rights of self-determination and more needy of protection. The first of the presumptions outlined above distinguishes among, if anything, decisions, not people; the second distinguishes among people. By focusing on differences among decisions, and not on the people who make them, we are more likely to retain our respect for all people.

22 Human Rights and Human Ethics: Health and Health Care

The titles of colloquia, conferences, books or journals – for instance, "AIDS, Health and Human Rights," "Health and Human Rights," and "The Right to Health: A Human Rights Perspective" – and of academic centres for teaching and research reflect a relatively recent phenomenon. Human rights in relation to health ("rights to health," "rights to health care," or "rights to health protection")[1] have for some time been articulated in international law and conventions[2] and found by courts to be part of national and domestic law.[3] But the exploration of these rights – what is required to respect, protect, and fulfill them – is much more recent.[4] This linking of health and human rights is relevant to many important questions raised in the euthanasia debate. To give just one example: If there is no human right to health care, and if this means dying people lack care and treatment, especially for the relief of pain and suffering, euthanasia seems easier to justify. (If we believe that euthanasia is inherently wrong, it cannot in theory be justified. But we are likely to find it much more difficult to avoid euthanasia, in practice, if dying people are left in serious pain. And if we do not believe that euthanasia should always be prohibited, it is more readily justifiable when dying people have no access to palliative care.)

I am assuming here that most people agree with the principles and purposes of concepts of human rights and, therefore, that there is no need to justify them. (We do need to justify them, however, to those who challenge their validity or appropriateness.) Rather, I would like to discuss some difficulties that we are, or will be, facing with respect to both human rights and rights to health. These two areas of rights will be of critical importance to the way in which many ill people – people with HIV infection and AIDS, for instance – are cared for. But both are currently being challenged in terms of their appropriate content or use.

HUMAN RIGHTS

Calls to respect human rights have been a powerful rhetorical tool of late-twentieth-century democracies and emerging democracies. Promoting these rights – whether against something (torture; cruel or unusual treatment or punishment) or to something (life, liberty, and security of the person; freedom of association, religion, conscience, mobility; and so forth) – has been of enormous importance in setting the "ethical and legal tones" not only of individual societies but also of the world community. Moreover, we have come to recognize that human rights *per se* are inextricably connected with each other; in one sense, they form a community of rights. However, particularly in modern Western democracies, the emphasis on human rights has been very much on individual human rights; only more recently has there been a realization that, because most of us (hermits aside) need to live in communities if we are to be fully human, we need protection not only as individuals but also, sometimes, as communities.

This recognition has been used as the basis for a controversial concept, that of "collective rights." There is a serious danger in that approach – especially when the collectivity seeking protection is the state itself, and the state claims protection of its "rights" at the expense of individual human rights.

One response would be that, although the state has obligations with respect to human rights, it should not implement its "rights" at the expense of those of individuals.[5] In other words, collective rights, if they exist, should never be used to infringe the human rights of individuals.

Another response would be that collective human rights should not accrue to the state itself, arguably because the state is neither a human person nor simply a collection of persons as is true of some groups, but an incorporeal entity separate from those whom it governs.

Yet another response would be to accommodate respect for the human rights of both individuals and collectives (which might or might not include the state) in cases of either apparent or real conflict between them. This accommodation can sometimes be achieved by focusing on the fundamental principle underlying the requirement of respect for human rights: respect for persons. Sometimes, that requires respect for networks and communities even at a cost to some individuals and some of their rights. In other words, "some communitarian claims can actually underwrite liberalism and defend it from other traditional communitarian critiques."[6] Moreover, "liberalism [can be] grounded in community practice ... [that is,] can rest on communitarian underpinnings."[7] In any case, "it is generally accepted that collective rights may not infringe on universally accepted individual rights such as the right to life, freedom from torture, etc."[8]

As frequently happens, an idea or concept such as human rights, which breaks through previous barriers, causes us to reassess our thinking, stance, and conduct. It achieves enormous good. But it can, unless we are very vigilant, with time and use, lose its original impact and even its meaning and effectiveness. Moreover, it can be rejected, whether rightly or wrongly, for being tied to one particular political or cultural stance – and, therefore, not universally applicable – or simply for interfering with the "business of state." There is a real need to fear that the concept of human rights is currently endangered for these reasons. A cartoon in a Bucharest (Romania) newspaper captures the danger in one image, as cartoons so often do. It shows a man gluing a false door, made of paper, on the outside of a brick wall. The words "Human Rights" are written on the door, referring to the World Conference on Human Rights, which was taking place in Vienna. As Oswald Mitshali, the Soweto poet, has said, it portrays:

A wall without windows
for the spirit to breeze through
A wall
without a door
for love to walk in.[9]

The cartoon graphically demonstrates the opposite of what those involved in promoting human rights hope to achieve. Human rights punch out windows and doors through which the "human spirit" can travel in hope. In short, we need to be concerned that the concept of human rights might no longer have the impact that it had in the past (partly because it has lost the impact of newness), or that we would want it to have in the future (partly because its applicability or universality is more likely to be denied with the increase in its use and the expansion of its content). The more it is used, the greater the number and diversity of people there are to object to it. The more its content expands, the more likely it is that some people will object to the content.

What can we do? I propose that we talk about the universal need to respect persons and the need to recognize that one very important way to implement respect is through the concept of human rights. The language of respect for persons helps to avoid the danger of over-legalization.[10] Rights are tools of law. One way to implement human rights, therefore, is through law. But that is not the only (or even the principal) way – except, perhaps, in Western democracies. Retaining the use of rights language, but as part of a broader concept of respect for persons, is likely to counteract opposition based on the argument that the concept reflects only one particular cultural and societal reality, not a universal requirement. Further, we need to recognize that statements about human rights, including even when enshrined in law, are declarative, not constitutive, of the respect for persons they require. They articulate profound principles of human ethics. In other words, these principles exist as powerful moral claims, whether they are recognized by legal systems or not. Often, people who are strong advocates of human rights, but not lawyers, fail to recognize dangers inherent in the terminology of rights. Implementable rights are essentially creatures of law. Although they are very powerful tools wherever legal systems recognize them – indeed, the most powerful tool – they are in danger of being totally ignored by societies that are not "rights based." It is important to seek, to the greatest extent possible, implementation of the content of these "rights," even when they are not recognized as legal ones. This outcome is likely to be achieved only if we broaden our terminology and discourse beyond the language of rights (while not abandoning either the terminology or discourse of human rights) to that of respect for persons and, I suggest, *"human ethics."*

The relation of human rights to human responsibilities and "human ethics" – which I regard as interchangeable terms – is demonstrated in figure 22.1. It shows also that applied ethics and law are two scales of the same balance and that particular areas of ethics and law overlap when they are each relevant to a given issue. The diagram should alert us to the complex ethical and legal thought that can be needed to address some problems. In the remainder of this chapter I use the term "human rights." In doing so, however, I mean to include, first, human responsibilities. They are integral components of human rights, but are not often articulated as such for fear of opening up possibilities for the abuse of human rights. This would occur if a state justified the breach of people's human rights on the grounds that, as the state saw it, they were not fulfilling their human responsibilities. I mean to include human ethics, too. As the diagram shows, all these terms should be regarded as alternatives for each other. Which one is the most appropriate depends on the situation.

Respect for human rights is important both to individuals and communities. Not respecting them affects society and, therefore, harms everyone – even those people whose human rights, as individuals, are not breached. Likewise, we need to keep in mind that there is an inti-

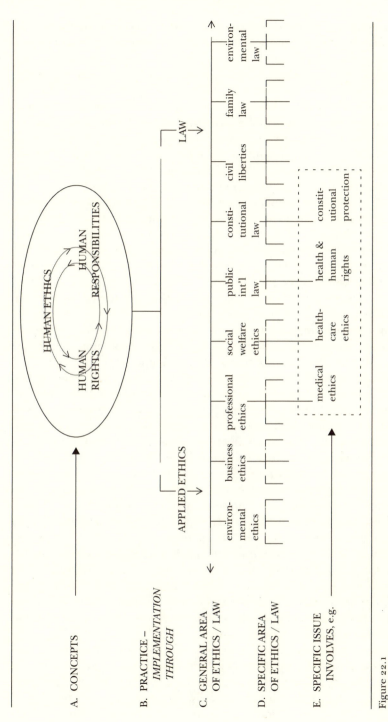

Figure 22.1
The Relation of Human Rights, Human Responsibilities, and Human Ethics

mate connection between respect for human rights in theory and in practice and that both are required. The rhetoric of human rights is important because it "draws on the moral resources of our belief in the significance of our underlying common humanity; human rights discourse then serves both as a potent source of radical critiques of actual social arrangements and also as a powerful basis for working out and presenting alternative institutional practices."[11] One way to view the rhetoric of human rights is that it is necessary to establish a reality of respect for these rights and helps us to define and decide what the right thing to do might be. But we must also be committed to doing so. In many recent cases of breached human rights we could engage only in the rhetoric of human rights because practice was impossible. Changed political systems in many parts of the world have radically altered the situation, so we will be challenged to show whether our commitment to human rights is an empty slogan or has real content.[12] A related matter is the danger of mistaking the rhetoric for the reality or even believing that the former is sufficient or substitutes for the latter. That we need to avoid this danger is a message of the cartoon I have described.

Another very important message can be inferred from the cartoon: it is more dangerous to have a facade of respect for human rights, if the reality is absent, than it is to know that human rights are not being respected. In the political sphere, especially, there is a tendency to use the language of human rights but not always, sadly, to implement the reality required to respect them. Again, the Vienna Conference itself provided a powerful example. As one report from a newspaper states: "The United Nations' acceptance of China's demand that the Dalai Lama be barred threatened to undermine the world conference on human rights. Charges that the UN is stifling the right to free speech swirled on the eve of today's official opening of the conference, attended by representatives of more than 100 governments and 150 human rights organisations. ... China ... pressured the United Nations to withdraw the offer [to the Dalai Lama to participate]."[13]

That incident brings to mind the exclusion of HIV positive people from international AIDS conferences because of restrictions on their entry to countries of which they are not nationals. In short, even conferences or other measures dedicated to promoting human rights can be used as vehicles for breaching them. We need to be aware of these possibilities, especially, in the context of health care.

Mental-health care provides some good examples. It is far more dangerous in terms of the potential for breaching human rights to maintain a facade of proper process in making some decisions – whether to hospitalize mentally ill people involuntarily, for instance, or to treat them forcibly with psychotropic drugs – than it is to know that these decisions are being made contrary to the requirements of respect for these people and their human rights. In other words, a "rubber stamp of human rights" – having mechanisms that purport to ensure respect but do not – can be more dangerous in terms of the likelihood of breaching human rights than not articulating the need to respect human rights. Moreover, it has been well said that human rights are often never more threatened than when we act purporting to do good to others – in part because those who act with such motives can be insensitive to the possibility that they could be doing the wrong thing, even breaching the human rights of others. Recognizing this possibility is particularly relevant to respect for human rights in the context of health care because, in general, we assume that, even though physicians and other health-care professionals do not always do good, at least they do no harm or intend to do no harm – in particular, harm in terms of breach of human rights. That is not necessarily true. Again, a facade of respect for human rights and of the respect for persons that it requires is more dangerous than knowing the reality when these qualities are absent.

I would like to sound a second warning, which comes from another cartoon. This one shows a group of men – brutal, militant thugs (a modern gang) – marching with banners that say "Stop xenophobia; xenophobes go home; death to the xenophobes." We must be aware that even our best impulses and actions, taken to an extreme, can be forms of fanaticism and do harm. I am not saying this to denigrate the "human rights movement" in any way or those involved in it. Rather, I do so as a warning. We must remember that, in promoting human rights, ethics, and the rule of law – all extraordinarily important and immensely worthy causes – there is a danger if any of these principles becomes a way of thinking that automatically overrides everything else – that is, even if thinking that way and using those benevolent principles actually causes serious harm that cannot be justified. For instance, we would have to be very sensitive to that possibility before accepting, as the Ontario Human Rights Commission has proposed, the idea that people accused of racism should be considered guilty until proven innocent. As the premier of Ontario said in commenting on the proposal, "The presumption of innocence is a fundamental legal principle which applies to people who are accused of an offence."[14] It is a foundational principle of a society that respects human rights. The warning that we can do harm even in seeking to do good requires a counter-warning. Some of those who correctly argue on the basis of liberal principles that "political correctness" (or, indeed, promotion of human rights) can become a form of fanaticism and infringe rights, sometimes do so to promote their own conservative political stance and maintain the "status quo" in terms of (in)equality behind a facade of liberal symbolism.[15] In summary, those involved in ethics, human rights, and law, like politicians, exercise power. And that power should be used ethically – in ways that respect human rights. Let us all be sensitive to our obligations in these regards.

Concepts created for entirely altruistic purposes are sometimes "turned on their heads" to achieve exactly the opposite results. One such concept is "quality of life." As I have discussed in a previous chapter, it was formulated with the aim of establishing a principle that all people have some claim to a minimum quality of life. Indeed, this claim was based on respect for persons and their human rights. People could use this principle to found a claim of access to the necessities required to fulfill basic needs that we all have – food, shelter, clothing and some minimally adequate level of education and health care. But "quality of life" is sometimes used now to deny access – for instance, to health care. The argument is that some people would not enjoy an "adequate" quality of life even if provided with medical treatment and, consequently, it would be wasteful to use medical resources on them; they have no claim to wasteful use of resources and, therefore, no right to these resources. In short, "quality of life" can be used to achieve an outcome that is exactly the opposite of the one for which it was formulated: to deny care rather than to grant access to it. This is not to say that withholding medical resources in some circumstances is unacceptable. Rather, it is to challenge the way in which the purported acceptability of doing so is sometimes established.

In the context of human rights, especially in health care, we must keep in mind that the concept of dignity can be used in the same way. Human rights are often linked with human dignity.[16] As I also point out in more detail elsewhere in this book, if the latter is seen as an intrinsic attribute of people, it is more likely to be a source of protection of the person whose dignity is in question than if it is seen as an extrinsic attribute (when dignity is in the eye of the beholder). It has been alleged, for instance, that although the availability of euthanasia is promoted as necessary for respecting dignity, in fact it can be motivated by a desire to dispatch those considered undignified.[17] In other words, though promoted as a human-rights-and-dignity-respecting approach to other people, euthanasia can reflect a narcissistic response.

A related problem could arise from connecting human rights with dignity if as has been claimed, "the obverse side of dignity is the dishonour of those whose dignity must be in their submission to others and in their willing acquiescence in their own degradation."[18] In short, like quality of life, dignity can be a "double-edged sword."

Finally, in the areas of both human rights and health care, we have moved past the time at which sweeping generalizations and analysis were sufficient. If we are concerned that a right to health, for example, in such contexts as AIDS, "becomes a right in action and not just 'a right on the books,' the content of the right must be elaborated, the duties and obligations implicit in the right must be clarified and means of implementing it must be developed. These tasks await human rights scholars if the rhetoric of the right to health is to have an impact on the resolution of contemporary issues concerned with health."[19] Likewise, "each AIDS epidemic – ... whether in New York, Hollywood, or Kinshasa, whether among American women, European hemophiliacs, or Asian prostitutes – demands its own analysis, its own history, and its own understanding. The frenzied general statements of the mid-1980's no longer suffice."[20] To the extent that we recognize our obligations in these respects, and take on the task of fulfilling them, we will make the legalization of euthanasia less likely. But the converse is equally true, which should sound a powerful warning to those people who oppose euthanasia.

RIGHTS TO HEALTH – RIGHTS

Can there be a "right to health"? In jurisprudential theory the answer is clearly no, because that would mean that somebody else would have an obligation to provide us with health. And that would not be possible for all of us or in all circumstances – and ultimately impossible for any of us. It could also mean that those who are viewed as not capable of being made "healthy" might be regarded as having no right. I see no need to emphasize the wider reverberations of this approach and its immense dangers. There might be circumstances, however, in which a non-legal, but moral, right to health would serve a useful purpose.

With the "medicalization" of modern societies, we have increasingly widened the definition of what constitutes health and, consequently, health care. On the one hand, this expansion has opened up access to health care. In many societies, people believe that they should provide necessary health care for each other – that is, they focus on obligations to provide health care rather than rights as such. On the other hand, broad definitions of health and health care have fostered the professionalization and medicalization of problems – at the societal level no less than the individual – such that someone with expertise in a particular area of health care can become a dominant force in dealing with problems that are defined as falling within this area and with people who have them. There is much debate over this phenomenon and criticism of the trend it represents, not least because one form of professionalizing societal problems, including those of health care, has been their legalization. In any case, it is clear that we need to be careful when talking about these issues to realize that health and health care are open-ended concepts. Therefore, who defines them is important. Also important, as I say elsewhere, is that we know precisely what they include in each situation. Whatever our definition of health, however, when we add the word "right" – "right to health" or "right to health care" – we need to be even more careful because we then have interactive uncertainty from three perspectives: that of rights, that of health, and that of health care.

Using a concept of rights can itself be challenged in the health-care context. It can be argued that health care systems should respond to needs, not rights, and function best when they do so. Basing claims to health care on rights rather than needs can result in sick people "rotting with their rights on."[21] Further, there has been a rapidly increasing practice of articulating responsibilities when speaking of rights – for example, in relation to patients' rights and responsibilities. Although doing so can be valuable in terms of broadening the scope and depth of our insights, knowledge, and approaches, care should be taken that the approach is not misused. If some illnesses are seen as self-inflicted (the consequences of alcohol or tobacco use, for instance), patients with these illnesses can be seen as having breached their responsibilities not to harm themselves and, consequently, as having forfeited their rights to at least some levels of health care (such as liver transplantation), which would have been provided were the condition not seen as self-inflicted.

Rights can be subdivided, which is especially important in the context of rights to health or health care. Two subdivisions are "negative-content rights" and "positive-content rights." Negative-content rights are rights against something. There are generally recognized rights, including some expressed as human rights, against having one's access to health care wrongfully inhibited. Wrongful inhibition would be constituted by wrongful discrimination – discrimination on the basis, for instance, of race, sex, sexual orientation, religion, ethnic origin, or mental or physical disability. Most jurisdictions do not have a problem recognizing these rights in connection with health care. Nonetheless, we do need to ask whether systems based primarily on ability to pay, indirectly at least, contravene even this negative-content form of right. For example, if a large segment of the population who cannot afford health insurance comes from one ethnic or racial group (or consists mainly of one sex or the very young or old), and if society provides health care only to those who can pay for it (or in connection with employment), there might, indeed, be discrimination – even though it is not overt and cannot be documented in any formal way. Indeed, this kind of discrimination might be skilfully hidden. It is interesting to note that "during the drafting of the right to health article in the Convention on the Rights of the Child, which has recently entered into force, the United States delegate was willing to accept the concept of the 'right to health' but not the right to 'health care,' thus suggesting that the 'right to health' did not encompass a right to health care."[22]

Likewise, indirect or hidden discrimination can occur if the "wrong kind of sick people" can be avoided. In a largely private health-care system, such as that of the United States, "hospitals can ... prosper by carefully choosing the doctors to whom admitting privileges will be granted. For example, an applicant's patient list can be given an instantaneous analysis by computer to determine whether a large number of patients live in postal code areas marked by poverty and uninsurance [or, I would add, certain illnesses such as AIDS or are an aged population that is likely to need palliative care]. These doctors can be (and have been) denied privileges."[23]

Other forms of discrimination, which are now being recognized in the area of health care, include not carrying out research on diseases that affect some groups, particularly when members of them are likely to be poor, disadvantaged, or vulnerable. The occurrence of discrimination is well recognized in connection with diseases that affect people only, or mainly, in developing countries. But it occurs elsewhere, too. For instance, "women's diseases" have been very under-researched as compared with diseases that affect mainly men. Similarly, we can wrongfully exclude people from participation in research that could benefit them, purportedly for reasons of protecting or even doing good to them. Women of child-bearing age have largely been excluded from acting as subjects in medical research, which can be to their disadvantage and has certainly been to the disadvantage of women as a group. As researchers have recognized, in implementing measures to rectify this situation in Canada and the United States, there is no guarantee that the results of medical research carried out on men are equally true for women. Discrimination can take place also within groups. Not all people with life-threatening diseases or who are terminally ill might be seen as entitled to the same level of health care. In one Canadian case, a court held that people with AIDS had no right to demand that the state pay for their drug treatment even though it did pay for comparable treatment for people with cancer. The people with AIDS had alleged that this refusal constituted wrongful discrimination, but the court rejected their argument.[24] Similarly, in practice, it might be more difficult for some dying people – for example, those with AIDS – than for other dying people to obtain access to palliative care.[25] Discrimination can occur even between people with the same disease. Some groups – such as HIV-positive women – might not have received the level of care provided for HIV-positive men (partly because, on the whole, these women had not organized politically).

A positive-content right to health care would be a right to have health care provided. Most countries – even Canada, which has an almost totally socialized health-care-delivery system – have not recognized that right. Governments and politicians are frightened of creating unfulfill-able claims and, in particular, those that could involve major economic cost. When there was very little that we could do in terms of treatment or cure, which was the situation until relatively recently, we did not face the dilemma of finding sufficient resources to provide health care. We could – as used to be true in Canada, for instance – sustain the illusion of providing all necessary health care for all people who require it, even though that has never really been true. But the current dilemma of the cost of health care is a cost of success, not of failure.[26] This recognition could alter the tone of the analysis. Still, labelling health-care resources as a product of success does not take away our human-rights obligations in dealing with them. People (but which ones can be a difficult question, especially in our globally connected world) have a right to share in the benefits of at least some successes (but which ones?) and not to be excluded by wrongful discrimination.

RIGHTS TO HEALTH – HEALTH

The terms "right to health," "right to health care," and "right to health protection" have all been used in the context of human rights, but "in international human rights literature, the term 'right to health' is more common than either of the other two terms."[27] International human-rights instruments refer to "the right of everyone to the enjoy-ment of the highest attainable standard of physical and mental health."[28] But what constitutes health and, correlatively, health care within these definitions?

Health care has been defined extensively to include services such as "protective environmental services, prevention and health promotion and therapeutic services, as well as related actions in sanitation, envi-ronmental engineering, housing and social welfare."[29] That broad def-inition, as Virginia Leary notes, almost makes the word health lose meaning.[30] We need to keep in mind that, if it does, so does the con-tent of any right to health. Promoting unfulfillable or generally unful-filled human rights, moreover, could set a precedent that human rights cannot or need not be fulfilled, a precedent that would damage respect for human rights in general. An inclusive term, but not as broad, is the right to "health protection." That would include not only the right to some minimum level of medical care but also the right to healthy conditions (such as "the purity and cleanliness of water, air, waste disposal, food, drugs, cosmetics, etc."[31]).

It has been suggested that the right to health is a shorthand expres-sion, in the field of human rights, for the right to the highest attainable standard of health. In this respect, its use is similar to that of terms such as the "right to work."[32] But it is noteworthy that the "right to work" does not imply the "right to be provided with work."[33] This limitation indicates that it is an inappropriate model for the right to the highest attainable standard of health – certainly as far as that relates to the provision of, and access to, health care. Arguably, the latter right is even more basic than the former, so it should be interpreted more broadly.

LEGAL BASES OF A RIGHT TO HEALTH

The bases on which a right to health in international law is founded include the assumption that the concept is implicit in the right to life, a provision binding on all states by virtue of customary international law as well as international human-rights instruments. Other bases in international human rights instruments include provisions in the Universal Declaration of Human Rights and the International Covenant on Civil and Political Rights that prohibit torture or cruel, inhuman, or degrading treatment[34] and subjecting people to medical or scientific experimentation without their free consent,[35] along with provisions articulating rights to a standard of living adequate for the health and well-being of people and their families – including medical care.[36]

Article 12 of the International Covenant on Economic, Social and Cultural Rights[37] is explicit not only in recognizing the right of everyone to the enjoyment of the highest attainable standard of physical and mental health, but also in setting out the steps that must be taken by State Parties to the Covenant to achieve the full realization of this right. One step is of particular interest in connection with infectious diseases such as AIDS, tuberculosis, or haemorraghic fevers such as Ebola, and people who are dying of these diseases. It requires "the prevention, treatment and control of epidemic ... and other diseases [and] ... [t]he creation of conditions which would assure to all medical service and medical attention in the event of sickness." The latter obligation can found an important claim for patients who are among the most likely to be abandonned. What palliative care and treatment might they be entitled to pursuant to this provision? It is important to note also that Article 24 of the Convention on the Rights of the Child[38] explicitly "recognizes the right of a child to enjoyment of the highest attainable standard of health" and lists measures to be taken by states to implement this right. Children can need special protection and assistance even beyond that which adults would require. And dying children have the strongest claims on palliative-care resources, in particular to fully adequate pain-relief treatment.

Finally, it is worth noting that the three "generations" of human rights, which have been described elsewhere,[39] are all relevant to a right to health care. The first "generation" are political and civil rights as expressed in Articles 2–21 of the Universal Declaration of Human Rights. The second comprises economic, social, and cultural rights as outlined in Articles 22–27 of the Universal Declaration. The third and most controversial is the "'emerging' generation of human rights, a result of demands [of the developing world] ... for a more equitable social and economic order. It includes collective rights to development, humanitarian assistance, information, and environmental well-being. The origin of this generation of rights can be found in Article 28 of the Universal Declaration: 'Everyone is entitled to a social and international order in which the rights set forth in this declaration can be fully realised.' "[40]

CONCLUSION: SEEKING INSIGHTS

What should we conclude about rights to health or health care? First, we must not view human rights in isolation from the context in which those rights arise or are claimed. Second, we must not view human rights to either health or health care in isolation from other human rights. Third, we must not view one kind of illness in isolation from either other illnesses or society itself.[41] Let us take AIDS as an example. It means that we should not view AIDS and human rights in that context, including a "right to health," in isolation from the larger health-care and societal contexts in which they arise. If we were concerned about compulsory testing for HIV, we would need to compare it with compulsory genetic screening. If we try to give all terminally ill people the option of palliative care, we would need to have a strong justification for not offering it to people dying of AIDS. And there can be problems related to human rights in the allocation of resources not only *within* the health-care context, for example by physicians, but also *to* this context, for instance by a government. Valid claims on resources that could be spent on health care can be made also on behalf of housing, education, and other social services.

It would be unwise to make claims founded on rights to health so broad and unfulfillable that they provide a basis on which all claims to a "right to health" are likely to be ignored. In short, well-intentioned but very broad claims might not be beneficial or even neutral; in terms of promoting a "right to health," they could be counter-productive and harmful.

People often feel a stronger obligation not to do harm (non-maleficence) than to do good (beneficence). This tendency can be manifested as feeling a stronger obligation to relieve suffering than to confer benefits. Consequently, depending on how claims to a right to health are presented, there might be different responses. One study,[42] which I discuss elsewhere in this book, showed that in some countries, such as the United States, if patients said they were in pain, health-care professionals or institutions did not necessarily respond by helping them. But if they said that their rights were being breached, assistance was more likely. In other countries, such as France, claims that rights had been breached had little effect on health-care professionals and the health-care system. But statements about suffering did elicit assistance. Not all cultures encourage people to react the same way. Each has a distinctive "trigger" that causes a distinctive response (in this case, either respecting human rights by providing health care or not doing so, by not providing it).

There is also an opportunity for promotion of human rights, in general, by examining human rights in relation to health. This chance arises, when it comes to health care, because everybody personally identifies with breaches of human rights in that context (which is not the case in other breaches of human rights that threaten people only in some countries). They do so because they perceive that they, too, could be victims of breaches – denial of health care, denial of access to investigative new drugs, wrongful use of people as research subjects, failures to relieve pain or to offer palliative care, and so on. The resulting personalized sensitivity can be generalized to help people not only to know but also to feel what it means to have one's human rights in general breached. This can be a very strong force for the promotion of sensitivity to breaches of human rights in general and, consequently, to the eradication of breaches.[43]

In a postmodern, secular society, health care – to some extent at least – has replaced religion as one forum in which people can relate to each other in such a way that they can experience a "coming together."[44] The symbolism that we create in this context functions not only within that context but also within society in general. What we do to, and for, each other when it comes to health care tells us much about what we do to, and for, each other in general. Nowhere is this test more revealing than in the context of our treatment of dying people. Whether we believe that health care is a public good on which everyone has a claim and to which everyone must contribute, or whether we regard health care as just another commodity, will be an important factor in determining how we think about rights to health and health care. Do we see the provision of health care as a community mission or simply a matter of private ends? Do we regard society as having an obligation to establish a social "safety net" that includes health care[45] (in which case one could postulate a collective right of persons as members of society to some basic level of health care[46])? The answers to these questions will affect recognition of rights to health and health care, including the rights of dying people to care and treatment.

We will need to do much exploration to evolve a balanced, effective, and – above all – humane and compassionate position on what respect for human rights to health and health care requires. This exploration, in turn, will lead us to ask more questions. Should needs precede rights and be the basis for defining rights? Why, apart from cost (and when is that an adequate justification?), would we not regard health or health care as a human right? We will need to focus not only on these rights *per se* but also on what it means if they are not recognized. To take one example, unless we recognize some rights to health care, dying people in unbearable pain would have no right to pain-relief treatment. As I have emphasized throughout this book, to leave them that way when their pain could be relieved would be a breach of the most fundamental principles of human rights and a grave affront to respect for persons and their dignity.

In one sense, the essence of respect for human rights is an expression of human solidarity. Although that is a powerful bonding and activating force for good, contemplation of it, especially in relation to health and health care, can easily cause us to be overwhelmed by a vision of ourselves as privileged people living in Western democracies, as nothing more than tiny specks in a vast sea of humanity, much of which is in great need, especially with respect to health care. Consequently, we might have to be modest in our original claims both on ourselves and on others as to what is required and what is an adequate expression of solidarity. As much as most of us would like to end the hopelessness, misery, and suffering of others, looking at all this pain globally can evoke a nihilistic response. We must avoid nihilism, and one way of doing so is to dis-identify from whatever might evoke it, whether people or issues. But we must also counter dis-identification because it is often the source of breaches of human rights. Dis-identification makes it much easier to treat others in ways that we would find appalling if applied to us, because it means that we do not see them as people like ourselves. This phenomenon explains why we are usually much more shocked by need and poverty at home than by the same situations far away.

If we can establish a sense of community (and an important question is whether, in recognizing that we are part of a global community, we can feel as well as think of ourselves that way), we probably could evoke caring responses that, on some level, would be expressed as requirements that rights to health and health care be respected as part of respect for persons and for their human rights. Recognition of these rights would, in turn, require commitment to implementing them. One major challenge to human rights in general, in the immediate future, will be how to respond as a global community to claims based on a right to health or health care. If we promote those rights but fail to fulfill them, we will damage the concept of human rights in general. In short, it will not be a situation only of failing to do good but one of doing harm. We will also need to consider carefully the much-less-spoken-about companion concept to human rights, that of human responsibilities. We are promoting the principle that human rights are universal and therefore that we may insist that they be respected by people in other countries. Logically, the same can be said for human responsibilities, which means that those people have justifiable claims on us.

Finally, as people deeply committed to human rights, we need to be open-minded enough to query whether the language of human rights is an adequate strategy in promoting claims to health and health care. I suggest, in addition, that we start to explore human ethics, in particular, an "ethic of care," in terms of both what that would require and how it could be safeguarded to avoid overly paternalistic use. Its aim is well summarised as follows:

Many traditional ethical theories are based on an understanding of human nature that sees people as individuals in competition with one another who need to protect their own interests and rights. Recent ethical thinking has questioned this view, and tries to take into account that we are all connected to one another in families, communities, and social bonds of all sorts, and that people who are connected in these ways care about each other's welfare – they know no one can enjoy their rights and interests by themselves. The ethic of care gives priority to this mutual care and connectedness and tries to foster it rather than starting by viewing individuals as adversaries. A large part of ethical deliberation therefore concerns how to build relationships and prevent the things that give rise to conflict. We ... [need to be] committed to finding creative ways to remove or reduce conflict, and ... [to] focus ... on helping society and human relationships to flourish by seeking to foster the dignity of the individual and the welfare of the community.[47]

Nowhere are the concepts of an ethic of care, human ethics, human rights, and human responsibilities more important than in relation to human dying and the care that all of us provide to each of us as, finally, we encounter the great mystery of human death in real time.

Epilogue

Contemporary death talk – the euthanasia and physician-assisted suicide debate – can only be properly understood within the much larger context of which it forms part.

In the last half-century we have crossed the barriers of time, space, sight, sound, genetic difference, immunological rejection, and species integrity. We have instant communication, rapid world-wide travel, and, as a result, globalization. At one end of the spectrum of our new knowledge we have opened up vast inner space. With genetic and molecular biology technologies we have the power to design our children – and, through them, far-off generations – and to asexually replicate our genetic selves – to achieve at least genetic immortality. At the other end of this spectrum we are exploring vast outer space, probing our galaxy and the cosmos.

At the same time, in Western societies, we have become intensely individualistic (possibly the unprecedented changes described above have made us feel that the only thing we can be certain of is ourself), and many of us complain of a loss of a sense of family, community, social cohesion, and the common good. With the decline in adherence to institutionalized religion (although, not necessarily, of religious belief and certainly not of spirituality), we have also lost a sense of belonging to something larger than ourselves – any sense of transcendence – and of a consensus on fundamental values. In many areas of our lives we have moved from chance to choice, including with respect to the values that we apply daily in our own actions, families, communities, and society. This change to choosing our values is embodied in situational ethics –

nothing is regarded as inherently wrong, it all depends on the situation. One extreme result of the combination of intense individualism and situational ethics is that the basic rule becomes that all persons can make up their own values as they go along.

The twentieth century was marked by the development of articulated concepts of human rights, especially the rights of individuals. The arguments for legalizing euthanasia are often expressed in terms of such rights. Rights protect the freedoms and liberty we need to live fully human lives. But these rights must be balanced by ethically acceptable responsibilities, because protection of these same freedoms and liberty also depend on fulfilling our human responsibilities. These responsibilities require that we limit what we can do by what we ought not to do – that is, we must adopt an ethics of wise restraint in relation to such age-old ethical questions as euthanasia. Living according to certain choices that limit what we do, even when living without such limits could be of personal advantage to us – for example, honouring principles of justice and tolerance at a cost to ourselves or our community – makes us more, not less, human.

Extraordinary scientific and technological developments have faced us with a vast range of unprecedented ethical choices. The widespread public debate and conflict that have surrounded these developments and the ethics that should govern them have, I believe, been important factors in precipitating the euthanasia debate. The ethics debate surrounding new scientific advances has made us very aware of a lack of even a working consensus on societal values, placed all our values on the line, and opened up all of them for reassessment, including those which relate to death.

The debates surrounding the new science and euthanasia are also linked in another way. The most important question that faces us in relation to the new science and technology is not what we will do among the extraordinary array of never-before-possible feats that it presents, but what we will choose not to do because we believe that to do it would be ethically wrong. What limits, if any, should we place on how human life may be passed on and changed; the genetic manipulation of animal and plant life; or the risks arising from new technological developments we will accept as a public? Transferred to the context of euthanasia, these same questions become: What limits should we place on how we may die? In deciding this, to what extent should we limit ourselves in order to protect future generations – How do we not want our great-great-grandchildren to die? And what effect will our decisions in these respects have on the "shared story" – the collection of values, attitudes, beliefs, and myths – that forms the paradigm on which we base our society?

Our greatest challenge, at present, is to create a sense of meaning, moral rules, and social order for ourselves as both local communities and a global society. In undertaking this daunting task, we cannot avoid travelling between hope and fear; we must map out both human rights and human responsibilities; and we need to provide both secular and religious routes to the same values' destinations. Our best chance of achieving some consensus on common values is for all of us to engage in the process of "doing ethics." Nowhere is this more important than in the euthanasia debate.

We often have a knee-jerk reaction that to reject old values and to change a traditional stance – such as the prohibition of euthanasia and physician-assisted suicide – is progress, liberal, and good, and refusing to do so is retrogressive, conservative, and bad. Moral and ethical progress may depend, however, on not making such a change. Sometimes, people criticize the imposition of ethical limits as being a return to a conservative, old-fashioned, or Luddite stance. They describe the process of developing these limits by using the image of a pendulum that swings back to a former position. This image is a mistake. A more appropriate one is that of the helix – like DNA – in which we move forward, taking our new knowledge, values, insights, and wisdom with us, to re-examine where we have come from, to recover from that earlier "knowing" what we still need ethically, and to integrate this "old knowing" with the new realities we face. This process, when ethically carried out, results in ethical progress. We need such progress in deciding on the values that should now and in the foreseeable future govern human death.

There is an old saying in law that freedom is to be found in fetters. The message this saying carries is that we must be very careful in using our freedoms to ensure that, in the process, we do not destroy the conditions that make freedom possible. Euthanasia and physician-assisted suicide are at the centre of an intense – and arguably the most important – current debate as to where the limits, if any, on our freedoms should be drawn, in this case on the freedom to choose the time, place, and manner of our death. In engaging in the euthanasia and physician-assisted suicide debate and establishing these limits, we will be deciding what is required of us if we are to respect dying people and human death, and are to uphold the value of respect for human life in our societies. These questions always have been and will remain central to how we perceive and find meaning in life. How we respond to them is, therefore, of unique importance.

Notes

PROLOGUE

1 In this introduction, I use the word "euthanasia" to include physician-assisted suicide.

2 R. Eckersley, "Universal Truths," *Sydney Morning Herald*, 8 January 2000, 4s.

CHAPTER ONE

1 An earlier version of this chapter was published as "Are We Just 'Gene Machines' or also 'Secular Sacred'? From New Science to a New Societal Paradigm," *Policy Options* 17, 2 (1996): 3.

2 M.A. Somerville, "The Song of Death: The Lyrics of Euthanasia," *Journal of Contemporary Law and Health Policy* 9 (1993): 1–76. See chapter 3 below.

3 M.A. Somerville, "Legalizing Euthanasia – Why Now?" *Australian Quarterly* 1 (1996): 1–14. See chapter 6 below.

4 M.A. Somerville, *The Ethical Canary: Science, Society and the Human Spirit* (Toronto: Viking/Penguin, 2000).

5 M.A. Somerville, "Weaving 'Birth' Technology into the 'Value and Policy Web' of Medicine, Ethics and Law: Should Policies on 'Conception' Be Consistent?" *Nova Law Review* 13 (1989): 515–608; "Birth and Life: Establishing a Framework of Concepts," *University of Connecticut Law Review* 21 (1989): 667–83.

6 The United States is a major exception; survey after survey finds that most Americans see themselves as religious in one way or another. There is, however, strict separation of church and state.

7 R. Wright, *The Moral Animal: Evolutionary Psychology and Everyday Life* (New York: Pantheon, 1994); P. Singer, *Animal Liberation: A New Ethics for Our Treatment of Animals*, rev. ed. (New York: Avon Books, 1990).

8 Bear in mind that the word "religion" derives from the Latin word meaning to bind together, and that binding together is necessary for the formation of any community.

9 Brian Swimme and T. Berry, *The Universe Story: From the Primordial Forth to the Ecozoic Era – A Celebration of the Cosmos* (San Francisco: Harper, 1992).

CHAPTER TWO

1 H. Kuhse and P. Singer, *Should the Baby Live? The Problem of Handicapped Infants* (Oxford: Oxford University Press, 1985).

2 G.J. Gruman, "Death and Dying: Euthanasia and Sustaining Life," in *Encyclopedia of Bioethics*, ed. Warren T. Reich (New York: Free Press, 1978), 1: 267.

3 A.L Howe, "Allocation of Resources in Care of the Aged," *BioEthics News* 5, 4 (1986): 13, 15.

4 M. Kaye et al., "Consent to Dialyzer Re-use: Is It Ethically Necessary?" *American Journal of Nephrology* 5 (1985): 138–41.

5 RSQ, c. S-5, s. 4.

6 Canada Health Act, SC 1984, c. 6, s. 7.

7 See, for example, Act to Revise the Family Law Reform Act, SO 1986, c. 4, s. 32.

8 Howe, "Allocation of Resources," note 3, at 16, citing D. Well and M. Sheehan, "The Allocation of Medical Resources," paper presented at the Conference on Distributive Justice and the Australian Medical Care System, Monash University, Australia, 1983.

9 E. Pellegrino, "Rationing Health Care: The Ethics of Medical Gatekeeping," *Journal of Contemporary Health Law & Policy* 2 (1986): 41.

10 P.G. Clark, "The Social Allocation of Health Care Resources: Ethical Dilemmas in Age-Group Competition," *Gerontologist* 25, 2 (1985): 119 (cited by Howe, "Allocation of Resources," note 3).

11 Pellegrino, "Rationing Health Care," note 9.

12 See C. Fried, *Medical Experimentation: Personal Integrity and Social Policy* (Amsterdam: North Holland, 1974), 107ff.

13 G. Calabresi, *The Cost of Accidents: A Legal and Economic Analysis* (New Haven: Yale University Press, 1970).

14 Howe, "Allocation of Resources," note 3.

15 Ibid., 26.

16 For an excellent discussion of this topic, see J. Katz, *The Silent World of Doctor and Patient* (New York: Free Press, 1984).

CHAPTER THREE

1 For a discussion of distinctions between the use of language to "talk about" an activity (e.g., law or psychiatry) and "to do" it, see M.A. Somerville, "Labels vs. Contents: Variance between Psychiatry, Philosophy and Law in Concepts Governing Decision-Making," *McGill Law Journal* 39 (1994): 179–99. See chapter 21 below.

2 D. Humphry, *Final Exit: The Practicalities of Self-Deliverance and Assisted Suicide for the Dying* (Eugene, Oregon: Hemlock Society, 1991).

3 M.A. Somerville, "The Definition of Euthanasia: A Paradoxical Partnership," *Bioethics Research Notes* 3, 3 (1991): 17–18. See chapter 5 below.

4 Ibid.

5 It could be argued that the inclusion of this last exception opens up the possibility of extending the range of interventions, which, I argue, should be permitted to include those that would constitute euthanasia, as defined below. I propose that this possibility will not occur, if we respect the principle of treating the patient's symptoms, not eliminating the patient in order to eliminate the symptoms. Also, treatment that might shorten life would be needed very seldom. Personal communication with Norelle Lickiss, director, Palliative Care Services, Royal Prince Alfred Hospital, Sydney, Australia, December 1992.

6 Normally, in law, one is responsible for acts that one intends. Intention to kill another person, in a legal sense, is present when there is a desire to kill the other person or when death is the certain or almost certain result of an act or omission (when there is a duty to act). The difficulty, in the context of this discussion, is to establish legal immunity for (1) giving adequate treatment for the relief of pain or other symptoms of serious physical distress, even when this treatment could shorten life, if it is reasonably necessary to relieve pain or other symptoms of serious physical distress (which would be given with an intention to kill, in the technical legal sense, if the treatment was certain or almost certain to shorten life); (2) respecting valid refusals of treatment; and (3) withholding or withdrawing futile treatment, when doing so would or could result in death, while prohibiting other interventions specifically intended to cause death. There are two possible approaches, each based on the definition of euthanasia: (1) have the definition include all interventions in which there is an intention to cause death (except the provision of reasonably necessary treatment for the relief of pain or other symptoms of serious physical distress, or respect for a valid refusal of treatment, or withholding or withdrawing futile treatment); and (2) have it include the motive to kill (which is not present in giving treatment necessary to relieve pain or other symptoms of serious physical distress, respecting a valid refusal of treatment, or withholding or withdrawing futile treatment). I have adopted the former approach. It should be noted that I use the terms

"primary intent," "primary purpose," and "motive" as synonyms. The term "direct intent" is not used, but it means the same thing.

7 In general, I use "to cause death" rather than "to kill," but these terms can be used as synonyms. It is interesting to consider the different nuances of these two terms and compare them with "to allow to die." People use "to kill" most often to describe interventions or non-interventions that cause death and that are regarded as unjustifiable. In contrast, people use "allow to die" most often to describe non-interventions that are regarded as justifiable. The provision of reasonably necessary pain-relief treatment that could or would shorten life is an intervention often referred to as causing death, but not in general as killing, probably because it is regarded as justified or even required.

8 The word "futile" is used to include both medically useless treatment and treatment in which the benefits, if any, are minimal and clearly outweighed by harms; that is, the treatment would be clearly "disproportional." These appraisals unavoidably involve value judgments, which are often a source of criticism. The solution is not to avoid these approaches when they are otherwise the best ones (which, I suggest, is the case with appraisals of when treatment is futile), but to surround them with adequate safeguards. I will not discuss safeguards here. See below.

9 A valid refusal of treatment is an informed refusal of treatment given by (1) a competent adult or a factually competent minor or (2) a refusal pursuant to a valid advance directive, whether in the form of a living will or a durable power of attorney for health care, or given by some other legally recognized substitute decision-maker (when the refusal is within the scope of the authority of this decision-maker).

10 Cited in H. Rigter, "Euthanasia in the Netherlands: Distinguishing Facts from Fiction," *Hastings Center Report* 19, 1 (Spec. Supp.) (1989): 31. Compare the term "deliberate action" with the one I use: "primary intention." They might or might not mean the same thing. One problem with "deliberate action" as one defining feature of euthanasia is that (at least, in legal systems based on Anglo-American common law) it has no specific meaning and would, therefore, probably lead to further confusion.

11 See A.M. Capron, "Euthanasia in the Netherlands: American Observations," *Hastings Center Report* 22, 2 (1992): 30, 31, referring to the Remmelink Report, which is summarised in P.J. van der Mass and others, "Euthanasia and Other Medical Decisions Concerning the End of Life," *Lancet* 2 (1991): 669–74.

12 M.A.M. de Wachter, "Euthanasia in the Netherlands," *Hastings Center Report* 22, 2 (1992): 23.

13 Rigter, "Euthanasia in the Netherlands," 31. On 9 February 1993 the Second Chamber of Parliament in the Netherlands passed, by a vote 91–45 in favour, a bill approving the regulatory system set up by these judicial guidelines. The bill was later rejected. Subsequently, the regulatory system was

officially approved, but not enacted in legislation. Legislation authorizing euthanasia has now been enacted. See below.

14 R. Doerflinger, "Assisted Suicide: Pro-Choice or Anti-Life?" *Hastings Center Report* 19, 1 (Spec. Supp.) (1989): 16, 18.

15 Rigter, "Euthanasia in the Netherlands," 31.

16 Ibid.

17 See, for example, H. Kuhse, *The Sanctity-of-Life Doctrine in Medicine: A Critique* (Oxford: Clarendon Press, 1987).

18 See Law Reform Commission of Canada, *Euthanasia, Aiding Suicide and Cessation of Treatment,* Working Paper 28, Protection of Life Series (Ottawa: Minister of Supply and Services, 1982), 7–8, 43.

19 See, for example, *Nancy B (N.)* v. *Hôtel-Dieu de Québec,* [1992] RJQ 361 (SC Qué.) [hereafter *Nancy B.*].

20 See, for example, *Malette* v. *Shulman* (1990), 67 DLR (4th) 321, 72 OR (2nd) 417 (CA Ont.), in which the Ontario Court of Appeal awarded $20,000 damages for battery to a woman who was given a blood transfusion, which saved her life, after being admitted to a hospital emergency room in a semiconscious state, but carrying a card stating that she was a Jehovah's Witness and refused all blood products or blood transfusions.

21 M.A. Somerville, "Birth and Life: Establishing a Framework of Concepts," *Connecticut Law Review* 21 (1989): 667–83.

22 Disproportionality – when the suffering inflicted by treatment outweighs any possible benefits it might offer – raises difficult ethical questions about who should make these decisions. In general, it should be the patient or the patient's substitute decision-maker. In some exceptional cases, though, it might be the physician.

23 See, for example, *Malette* v. *Shulman.*

24 I recognize that deciding when justification is or is not present and, consequently, when there is or is not causation in law involves a value judgment. But this does not mean that distinctions based on these judgments are illegitimate, arbitrary, or a matter of "semantics" (as is argued by some supporters of euthanasia).

25 See, for example, D.W. Brock, "Voluntary Active Euthanasia," *Hastings Center Report* 22, 2 (1992): 10, 19.

26 According to a newspaper report of a survey of nurses in the state of Victoria, Australia, the survey might have asked questions that could be interpreted in this way. See "Nurses Admit Helping Eighty to Die" (Adelaide, Australia) *Advertiser,* 2 March 1992, 3.

27 Notes: "Physician Assisted Suicide: The Right to Die with Assistance," *Harvard Law Review* 105 (1992): 2021.

28 See also G.P. Smith II, "All's Well That Ends Well: Toward a Policy of Assisted Suicide or Merely Enlightened Self-Determination?" *University of California Davis Law Review* 22 (1989): 275.

29 Notes: "Physician Assisted Suicide."

30 Unless otherwise indicated, "euthanasia" is used in the sense of the paradigm case in which we all agree that it is involved – that is, giving a lethal injection.

31 Capron, "Euthanasia in the Netherlands," 30.

32 Notes: "Physician Assisted Suicide."

33 Ibid., 2024.

34 Ibid., 2022.

35 See M.A. Somerville, "Refusal of Medical Treatment in 'Captive' Circumstances," *Canadian Bar Review* 63 (1985): 59–90.

36 For a discussion of the difference and the relation between the right to inviolability and the right to autonomy, see M.A. Somerville, "Consent to Medical Care," Law Reform Commission of Canada, Ottawa, 1983.

37 There is increasing evidence, however, that medically advanced pain-relief regimes do not shorten life. In that case, objections should become obsolete. Personal communication with Norelle Lickiss, director, Palliative Care Services, Royal Prince Alfred Hospital, Sydney, Australia, December 1992.

38 M.A. Somerville, "Medical Interventions and the Criminal Law: Lawful or Excusable Wounding?" *McGill Law Journal* 26 (1980): 82–96.

39 Also, consider whether establishing a system, such as the one described, could be regarded as "systems negligence" and, therefore, give rise to a possible action in negligence directly against the hospital for damages by patients who are harmed as a result.

40 M.A. Somerville, "Pain and Suffering at Interfaces of Medicine and Law," *University of Toronto Law Journal* 36 (1986): 286–317. See chapter 11 below.

41 De Wachter, "Euthanasia in the Netherlands," referring to arguments to the same effect presented by Capron.

42 See, for example, Notes: "Physician Assisted Suicide."

43 See M.A. Somerville, "New Perceptions, Old Values from Inner and Outer Spaces," *Canadian Speeches* 6, 5 (1992): 65–8; "Spacing-In and Spacing-Out: Searching for the Purple-Pink Middle," convocation address, University of Windsor, Windsor, Ontario, June 1992.

44 Garry Larson, *The Far Side*, Montreal *Gazette*, 7 November 1990, D10.

45 For example, in *Nancy B.*, an important court case in Canada, the request of a young, competent, quadriplegic woman to be disconnected from a respirator was upheld. The mass media discussed this case often in connection with euthanasia.

46 "California Voters Reject Doctor-Aided Suicides," Montreal *Gazette*, 5 November 1992, A11.

47 Bill C-203, "An Act to Amend the Criminal Code (terminally ill persons)," The House of Commons of Canada, 3rd Session, 34th Parliament, 40 Elizabeth II, 1991. First reading 16 May 1991; the bill failed on second reading in January 1992.

48 Bill c-261, "Euthanasia and Cessation of Treatment Act," The House of Commons of Canada, 3rd Session, 34th Parliament, 40 Elizabeth II, 1991. First reading 19 June 1991. The bill was withdrawn before second reading.

49 Katherine K. Young, "Euthanasia: Traditional Hindu Views and the Contemporary Debate," in H.C. Coward, J.J. Lipner, and K.K. Young, *Hindu Ethics: Purity, Abortion and Euthanasia* (Albany: State University of New York Press, 1989).

50 Somerville, "Spacing-In and Spacing Out."

51 R. Fenigsen, "A Case against Dutch Euthanasia," *Hastings Center Report* 19, 1 (Spec. Supp.) (1989): 24.

52 S.M. Wolf, "Final Exit: The End of Argument," *Hastings Center Report* 22, 1 (1992): 30-3.

53 Ibid., 30.

54 Ibid., 32.

55 Ibid.

56 Ernest Becker, *The Denial of Death* (New York: Free Press, 1973).

57 Quoted in de Wachter, "Euthanasia in the Netherlands."

58 J. Greenberg, "At Different Times, in Different Ways, We All Board the Same Train: The Management of Terror in Everyday Life," Plenary Address, 9th International Congress on Care of the Terminally Ill, 3 November 1992, Montreal.

59 E. Cassel, "The Nature of Suffering and the Goals of Medicine," *New England Journal of Medicine* 306, 11 (1982): 639-44.

60 See L. Israel, in interview with Jacques Nerson, "Pr. Lucien Israel: L'Euthanasie est un meurtre," *Le Figaro*, 6 mars 1993, 111.

61 Fenigsen, "A Case against Dutch Euthanasia," 26.

62 Brock, "Voluntary Active Euthanasia," 17, referring to Velleman.

63 Katherine K. Young et al., unpublished abstract (1992). Published as "A Cross-Cultural Historical Case against Planned Self-Willed Death and Assisted Suicide," *McGill Law Journal* 39 (1994): 657-707.

64 M. de Hennezel, "The Myth of the Perfect Death: The New Meaning of Death in the Context of AIDS," Plenary Address, Caring Together/Entraide: Conference Proceedings, Ottawa, 1991, 34.

65 Actually, this is not a myth in the technical sense. Myths are stories, not propositions. And they are by no means always false or childish.

66 Ibid., 35.

67 Israel in interview with Nerson, 112, referring to a statement by Bernard Rapp.

68 A. Parachini, "The California Humane and Dignified Death Initiative," *Hastings Center Report* 19, 1 (Spec. Supp.) (1989): 11.

69 H.J.J. Leenen, "Euthanasia in the Netherlands," in Peter Byrne, ed., *Medicine, Medical Ethics and the Value of Life* (New York: Wiley, 1990), 2.

70 W. Saletan, "There Is No Pro-Choice Majority Either," *Wall Street Journal*, 27 June 1990, A12.

71 L. Shelley, "Practical Issues in Obtaining Organs for Transplantation," *Law, Medicine and Health Care* 13 (1985): 37.

72 R. Carson, "Washington's 1–119," *Hastings Center Report* 22, 2 (1992): 8.

73 Ibid.

74 Fenigsen, "A Case against Dutch Euthanasia," 24.

75 T.G. Gutheil, "In Search of True Freedom: Drug Refusal, Involuntary Medication, and 'Rotting with Your Rights On,'" *American Journal of Psychiatry* 137, 3 (1980): 340–46.

76 De Wachter, "Euthanasia in the Netherlands," 27, quoting a 1972 pastoral manual of the General Synod of the Dutch Reformed Church, "Euthanasia: Meaning and Boundaries of Medical Treatment."

77 M.A. Somerville, "Messages from Three Contemporary Images of Medicine: Failed Medicine, Miracle Medicine and Science Fiction Medicine," in W.R. Shea and A. Spadafora, eds., *From the Twilight of Probability: Ethics and Politics* (Canton, Mass.: Science History Publications/ USA, 1992), 91–105.

78 The opposite situation can also apply. For instance, a primary purpose of the criminal law in protecting individuals was originally not to protect the individual, as such, but to maintain the king's fighting men in order to protect the community.

79 Young, "Euthanasia."

80 C. Levine, "AIDS and the Ethics of Human Subjects Research," in F.G. Reamer, ed., *AIDS and Ethics* (New York: Columbia University Press, 1991), 83.

81 See, for example, Federal Centre for AIDS (Canada) Working Group on Anonymous Unlinked HIV Seroprevalence, "Guidelines on Ethical and Legal Considerations in Anonymous Unlinked HIV Seroprevalence Research," *Canadian Medical Association Journal* 143, 7 (1990): 625–7.

82 For an argument to the contrary, see above; also Notes: "Physician Assisted Suicide," 28.

83 Involuntary euthanasia would be carried out despite someone's refusal of it.

84 Non-consensual euthanasia would be carried out without informing competent people about the nature of the intervention.

85 M.P. Battin, "Age Rationing and the Just Distribution of Health Care: Is There a Duty to Die?" *Ethics* 97, 2 (1987): 317–40.

86 See, for example, *Curlender* v. *Biosciences Laboratories*, 106 Cal. App. 3d, 811; 165 Cal. Rpt. 477 (1986) (Ct Appeal).

87 D. Margolick, "Patient's Lawsuit Says Saving Life Ruined It," *New York Times*, 18 March 1990, A24.

88 J.F. Fries, "Aging, Natural Death, and the Compression of Morbidity," *New England Journal of Medicine* 303, 3 (1980): 130–5.

89 See de Hennezel, "The Myth of the Perfect Death."

90 B. Campion, "Love and the Quality of Life," Toronto *Globe and Mail*, 4 August 1990, A-4.

91 If "dignity appears compromised, the argument goes, the patient's life no longer has the quality that obliges us to preserve it. Indeed, there may even be the obligation to end this caricature of human existence." Ibid.

92 B. Summer, "The New Crusade", Monteal *Gazette*, 23 September 2000, B5.

93 M. Kundera, *The Unbearable Lightness of Being* (New York: Harper & Row, 1984).

94 It is interesting to compare the trigger for this terror reaction (a fear of some specific kind of *life*) with that of the other terror reaction (intense fear of *death*) – fears that are arguably relevant to euthanasia. See, for example, Greenberg, "At Different Times."

95 Ibid. See also de Hennezel, "The Myth of the Perfect Death."

96 See de Wachter, "Euthanasia in the Netherlands," 25.

97 J. Katz, *The Silent World of Doctor and Patient* (New York: Free Press, 1986), 207ff.

98 Fenigsen, "A Case against Dutch Euthanasia," 22.

99 T.W. Gremmem and F.M. Van der Boom, "AIDS, Euthanasia and Grief," paper presented at First International Conference on Biopsychosocial Aspects of HIV Infection, Amsterdam, 22–25 September 1991, Final Program and Abstract Book, 203. See also J. Beckett et al., "Physician Attitudes towards Assisted Suicide and Euthanasia," ibid., 202.

100 It is very difficult to find undisputed statistics on the number and percentage of deaths occurring through euthanasia in the Netherlands. Figures are given, but "the extent … is not known. According to one report, there were some 200–300 cases of euthanasia in Amsterdam in 1987, 10 percent of which were reported to the public prosecutor. The frequently cited figure is 5000–8000 cases per year but the Amsterdam data suggests this figure is too high. According to one estimate, the average general physician has recourse to euthanasia once every three years" (Rigter, "Euthanasia in the Netherlands," 32). Reasons for this difficulty include non-reporting and possibly the under-exaggeration or over-exaggeration of "soft" data in order to promote a position either for or against euthanasia. Exaggeration in either direction can occur with respect to both positions – that is, for and against euthanasia. For example, it can be argued by those opposing euthanasia that so few people need euthanasia that society is not justified in legalising it; alternatively, it can be argued that the number of cases that have occurred or will occur is so large that euthanasia should not be legalized; the numbers indicate a great potential for abuse. Similarly, pro-euthanasia advocates argue that the numbers are so small that abuse is very unlikely. Or they argue that the number is or will be so high that it demonstrates a major need for euthanasia – and approval of it. One report (van der Mass and others, "Euthanasia") presents the results of three nationwide studies in the Netherlands (undertaken for the Dutch Remmelink Commission) on euthanasia and other medical decisions concerning the end of life. This report has elicited

further discussion. See, for example, *Hastings Center Report* 22 (March–April 1992), which features articles on euthanasia, including those in the Netherlands. But even that report does not resolve some important uncertainties. Its "findings require cautious interpretation, because there are no universally accepted definitions of such terms as 'euthanasia' and 'killing,' and what is 'euthanasia' for one person is but 'good medical practice' or the withholding of 'futile treatment' for another." H. Kuhse and P. Singer, "From the Editors," *Bioethics* 6, 4 (1992): iii–vi, v.

101 Paul Nathanson points out that the same was said by the Nazis about their exterminations and eugenic programs; also, the most obvious *linguistic* parallel, though, would surely be "ethnic cleansing" (personal communication, 24 February 2000). For a discussion of attitudes and behaviour in relation to HIV/AIDS and people with AIDS which serve functions other than their apparent or proclaimed practical ones – for instance, symbolic and ritual functions – see M.A. Somerville, "Law as an 'Art Form' Reflecting AIDS: A Challenge to the Province and Function of Law," in James Miller, ed., *Fluid Exchanges: Artists and Critics in the AIDS Crisis* (Toronto: University of Toronto Press, 1992), 287–304.

102 See M.A. Somerville, "Human Rights and Medicine: The Relief of Suffering," in Irwin Cotler and F. Pearl Eliadis, eds., *International Human Rights Law: Theory and Practice* (Montreal: Canadian Human Rights Foundation, 1992), 505–22. See chapter 13 below, "The Relief of Suffering: Human Rights and Medicine."

103 Campion, "Love and the Quality of Life."

104 Brock, "Voluntary Active Euthanasia," 21.

105 See Somerville, "Human Rights and Medicine." See also M.P. Battin, "Assisted Suicide: Can We Learn from Germany?" *Hastings Center Report* 22, 2 (1992): 44. Battin describes the situation in Germany, in which assisted suicide in terminal illness is regarded as de facto acceptable in some circumstances – provided it is carried out entirely outside the medical context. Assistance within that context, especially by physicians, is regarded as entirely unacceptable. This situation can be contrasted with that in the Netherlands, where assistance in euthanasia is regarded as acceptable only if provided by a physician. See also A. Tuffs, "Germany: Scandal over Euthanasia," *Lancet* 1 (1993): 551, in which it is reported that "under cover of humane euthanasia a network of couriers has been selling cyanide capsules for years and making a fortune out of it."

106 Bill C-261, "Euthanasia and Cessation of Treatment Act," sections 2, 8, and 12.

107 A. Hister, "Kevorkian Offers Cold Comfort on Euthanasia Debate," Toronto *Globe and Mail*, 14 September 1991, c8.

108 Since these events, legislation has been passed in Michigan making it a crime to assist a person to commit suicide.

109 "Doctor Charged with Murder in Assisted Suicide," *Globe and Mail*, 6 February 1992, A9; M. Betzold, "Cleared 'suicide doctor' Urges Other Physicians to Join Him," Montreal *Gazette*, 22 July 1992, B5; "Who Has the Final Choice?" editorial, *Gazette*, 28 July 1992, B2.

110 It is interesting that the way I wrote this sentence, initially, was "Does the use of technology somehow come between us and the person to whom the technology is applied?" – as though there were not necessarily a human agent involved in applying the technology. This demonstrates the point I am making here: that the use of technology (or even just imagining its use) causes (or at least allows) us to depersonalize situations in which it is used.

111 J.J. Lally and B. Barber, "The Compassionate Physician: Frequency and Social Determinants of Physician-Investigator Concern for Human Subjects," *Social Forces* 53, 2 (1974): 289–96.

112 G.J. Annas, "Killing Machines," *Hastings Center Report* 21 (1991): 33, 5.

113 This "quasi-legal" situation was maintained even after legislative approval in 1993 of the "Netherlands Reporting Procedure for Euthanasia." (It changed only in 2001 with the passage of legislation legalizing euthanasia.) A press release dated February 1993, provided by the embassy of the Netherlands in Ottawa, states that "euthanasia is a crime under Dutch Criminal Law" and that the 1990 guidelines "on the reporting procedure for euthanasia … have now been codified." In short, the existing situation was legislatively recognised, but not changed – except to the degree that recognition, itself, constituted change. For analysis of the operation and effect in law of the guidelines (an analysis which, though undertaken before codification of the guidelines, remained valid), see Leenen, "Euthanasia in the Netherlands"; Diana Brahams, "Euthanasia in the Netherlands," *Lancet*, 1 (1990): 591–2; H.D.C. Roscam Abbing, "Dying with Dignity, and Euthanasia: A View from the Netherlands," *Journal of Palliative Care* ("Special Issue on AIDS") 4 (1988): 71; Rigter, "Euthanasia in the Netherlands,"; de Wachter, "Euthanasia in the Netherlands,"; Capron, "Euthanasia in the Netherlands,"; H.A. ten Have and J.V.M. Welie, "Euthanasia: Normal Medical Practice?" *Hastings Center Report* 22, 2 (1992): 34.

114 Leenen, "Euthanasia in the Netherlands"; Brahams, "Euthanasia in the Netherlands." Prosecution, though unlikely, was still possible, even if the guidelines were followed – that is, euthanasia remained punishable and whether the physician had a defence was "assessed by the prosecution and the judge." However, see P.A. Singer and M. Siegler, "Euthanasia – A Critique," *New England Journal of Medicine* 322, 26 (1990): 1881–3, who imply the contrary. See also Rigter, who, speaking of the situation prior to the recent legislation legalizing euthanasia, states that "the present government has *not* adopted a long-standing proposal to legalise euthanasia. Instead, it has decided that physicians who terminate life on request of the

patient will not be punished only if they invoke a defense of *force majeure* and have satisfied ... criteria ... and then only on condition that the court accepts this defense. Such possible immunity from prosecution applies only to doctors." (Rigter, "Euthanasia in the Netherlands," 31.) This approach has now been codified in the new legislation.

115 Brahams, "Euthanasia in the Netherlands," 592.

116 ten Have and Welie, "Euthanasia," 36.

117 Rigter, "Euthanasia in the Netherlands," 31.

118 Brahams, "Euthanasia in the Netherlands," 591.

119 Ibid., quoting B. Levin, "Under Patient's Orders to Kill," London *Times*, 11 December 1989.

120 "Mercy Killing for Newborns Spurs Euthanasia Debate," Montreal *Gazette*, 30 July 1992, A6.

121 See Somerville, "Medical Interventions and the Criminal Law," for a discussion of the difference between justifications and excuses. The former renders conduct legally acceptable; the latter does not, but excuses the actor from liability for it.

122 Leenen, "Euthanasia in the Netherlands," 5.

123 Brahams, "Euthanasia in the Netherlands," 592.

124 Ibid., citing B. Sluyters, "Euthanasia in the Netherlands," *Medico-Legal Journal* 57 (1989): 34–43.

125 J. Keown, "On Regulating Death," *Hastings Center Report* 22, 2 (1992): 41.

126 de Wachter, "Euthanasia in the Netherlands," 27, quoting B. Dickens. See also Somerville, "Medical Interventions and the Criminal Law."

127 See note 100.

128 Studies showed widespread non-compliance with reporting provisions. See ten Have and Welie, "Euthanasia"; and Keown, "On Regulating Death," 40, who says that the prosecutor was notified in less than 2 percent of the Dutch cases. The subsequent "Reporting Procedure" guidelines (see notes 13, 113) were intended to solve that problem. If they did, they might have made euthanasia less, rather than more, available – despite its having been "recognized" by the Dutch Parliament. That could be seen as an ironic result. Enacting the euthanasia guidelines as legislation could have a similar impact.

129 Report, "French Health Ministry Supports Doctor over Euthanasia," *New Scientist*, 28 July 1990, 22 (emphasis added).

130 B. Sneiderman, Toronto *Globe and Mail*, 17 August 1992, A19.

131 See Keown, "On Regulation Death," 40, citing C.F. Gomez, *Regulating Death: Euthanasia and the Case of the Netherlands* (New York: Free Press, 1991), who states that the prosecutor was notified in less than 2 percent of Dutch cases.

132 Ibid.

133 For example, Brock, "voluntary Active Euthanasia," 20.

134 C. Mungan and G. Abbate, "Sentence Suspended in Euthanasia Case," Toronto *Globe and Mail*, 25 August 1992, A1. But see also Canadian Press,

"Euthanasia: M.D. Gets Suspended Sentence," Montreal *Gazette*, 4 April 1993, A1, a later case in which the judge gave a similar sentence without any such caveat.

135 "Nurses Admit Helping Eighty Die," Adelaide *Advertiser*, 2 March 1992, 3.

136 As reported in "One in Five Doctors Helps Death," *Weekend Australian*, 29 February – 1 March 1992, 13.

137 See Young et al., unpublished abstract.

138 The American Society of Law and Medicine, "Health Care Professionals and Treatment at the End of Life," 1992 Annual Meeting, 30–31 October 1992, Cambridge, Mass.

139 "Assisted Death," *Lancet* 2 (1990): 610–13.

140 M. Angell, "Euthanasia," *New England Journal of Medicine* 319 (1988): 1348–50. See also R.G. Twycross, "Assisted Death: A Reply," *Lancet* 2 (1990): 796–8.

141 See, for example, de Wachter, "Euthanasia in the Netherlands," 24, who quotes a Dutch physician as saying that "there are situations in which the best way to heal the patient is to help him die peacefully and the doctor who in such situation grants the patient's request acts as the healer *par excellence.*"

142 Quoted ibid., 29.

143 Fenigsen, "A Case against Dutch Euthanasia," 24.

144 Ibid., 23. The term "involuntary active euthanasia" is probably not intended (at least I hope not) to include euthanasia carried out despite someone's refusal of euthanasia. Rather, it probably intends to allow the possibility of euthanasia on those unable to consent or to refuse consent for themselves.

145 See, for example, correspondence in *Hastings Center Report* 19 (1989): 47ff.

146 See Keown, "On Regulating Death," 41–2.

147 "Open House," CBC Radio, conversation between David Lewis and M.A. Somerville. Lewis was a Vancouver psychologist with AIDS. He assisted eight other people with AIDS to commit suicide, and killed himself after announcing his intention to do so in the mass media.

148 B. Callaghan, correspondence on "Assisted Death," *Lancet* 2 (1990): 1012.

149 *Nancy B*, see note 19.

150 D. Callahan, "When Self-Determination Runs Amok," *Hastings Center Report* 22, 2 (1992): 52, 53.

151 See, for example, Notes, "Physician Assisted Suicide."

152 de Wachter, "Euthanasia in the Netherlands," 28, quoting R. Gillon.

153 See M.A. Somerville, "Autonomy in Health Care," proceedings of the 25th Anniversary Congress of the Dutch Association on Medical Law, "Healthy By Right (Met Recht Gezond)," Nijmegen, The Netherlands, May 1992.

154 Humphry, *Final Exit*, 36.

155 Ibid., 89.

156 Ibid., 96.

157 Ibid., chapter 20, "Going Together?" 100–2.

158 Ibid., 97–8.

159 Moreover, in wet weather, one's daily newspaper can even be delivered in a potential "suicide machine," a plastic bag secured with a large rubber band.

160 Ibid., 98–9.

161 Artificial hydration and nutrition, too, are forms of life-support treatment and have been characterised as no different from other forms. See, for example, *Cruzan* v. *Harmon*, 760 sw 2d 408 (1988) (ussc). In the past, though, their withdrawal has been regarded as different from that of other forms. In part, this was due to fear of inflicting serious suffering, by allowing patients to die from dehydration and starvation, and to fear of the effect on cultural symbols. Today, we see these treatments as artificial support for failed alimentary systems, just as respirators are for failed respiratory systems. Moreover, research has shown that, as people die and their bodies shut down, their normal thirst and hunger responses also cease.

162 D. Callahan, "Can We Return Death to Disease?" *Hastings Center Report* 19, 1 (1989) (Spec.Supp.): 4, 5.

163 Keown, "On Regulating Death," 40.

164 For a definition of intention in the law, see note 6 above.

165 See Battin, "Assisted Suicide," who says that, "because permitting assisted suicide would require a less dramatic change in the law, I think that the United States will come to accept assisted suicide in the relatively near future, officially as well as tacitly, but is likely to resist legalising active euthanasia for a longer time."

166 The Supreme Court of British Columbia (scbc) No. 4040/92, Victoria Registry, 29 December 1992, Melvin J.

167 rsc 1985, c. c-46 (as amended).

168 Constitution Act, 1982, Part i.

169 scbc, 9.

170 Ibid., 13, citing Lamer cj in *Reference re: ss. 193 and 195.1(1)(c) of the Criminal Code* (1990), 56 ccc (3d) 65.

171 Ibid., 15, 19, 21.

172 Court of Appeal for British Columbia, No. Vo1800, Victoria Registry, 8 March 1993, McEachern cj, Proudfoot J, and Hollinrake j (subsequently reported as *Rodriguez* v. *British Columbia (Attorney General)*, [1993] wwr 553 (bcca).

173 Ibid., 46, per Hollinrake j.

174 Ibid., 30, per McEachern cj.

175 Ibid., 66, per Proudfoot j.

176 See *Procureur Général du Canada* c. *Hôpital Notre-Dame et un autre (défendeurs) et Jan Niemic (mis en cause)*, [1984] CS 426 (Qué. SC); Somerville, "Consent to Medical Care"; M.A. Somerville, "Refusal of Medical Treatment in 'Captive Circumstances,'" *Canadian Bar Review* 63 (1985): 59–90.

177 BCCA, 68, per Proudfoot J.

178 *Rodriguez* v. *British Columbia (Attorney General)* (1993), 107 DLR (4th) 342 (SCC). There is a further discussion of this case in chapter 4 below.

179 SCBC, No. 4040/92, 16.

180 BCCA, 55.

181 *Rodriguez* v. *British Columbia* (1993), 366.

182 The Parliament of Canada voted 140–25 against considering a law to allow assisted suicide. Canadian Press, "MPs won't consider right-to-die law," Montreal *Gazette*, 23 March 1993, B1.

183 It is arguable whether there are duties to provide treatment in these circumstances and, indeed, it is likely that this matter will be litigated. One case in Quebec involved a comatose man. His family wanted life-support treatment continued, but the physician and hospital wanted to withdraw it. The case was settled out of court. An American case, *Wanglie*, raises the same questions. See M. Angell, "The Case of Helga Wanglie: A New Kind of 'Right to Die' Case," *New England Journal of Medicine* 325 1991: 511–12. And in February 2000 the report of a Quebec coroner's enquiry into the death of a Montreal man, Herman Krausz, from whom life-support treatment was withdrawn without his consent and against the family's wishes, was released. See M.A. Somerville, *The Ethical Canary: Science, Society and the Human Spirit* (Toronto: Viking/Penguin, 2000).

184 See S. Wolf, "Conflict between Doctor and Patient," *Law, Medicine and Health Care* 16 (1988): 197–203.

185 M.A. Somerville, "Justice across the Generations," *Social Science & Medicine* 29 (1989): 385–94.

186 The work of Mildred Solomon (presented at the American Society of Law and Medicine conference; see note 137) demonstrates this phenomenon. Solomon reported that she and her colleagues have found that two out of three physicians surveyed believe that there is a difference between withholding and withdrawing treatment; they are much more uncomfortable with the latter, despite the general consensus in bioethics and "medicine, ethics, and law" literature that these are ethically and legally equivalent. Solomon and her colleagues suggest this feeling might have a deeper ethical purpose: to keep us from becoming insensitive to the seriousness of withdrawing treatment and making it too easy. As she said, it should be a difficult decision and act, especially because cases of withdrawal are seldom ethically clear cut. In contrast, cases in which treatment is not begun are, in general, ones in which there is little doubt that non-treatment is justified; consequently, they do not present the same ethical problems.

187 *Cruzan* v. *Harmon*; see note 16.

188 Re *Quinlan,* 355 A. 2d 647 (NJ, 1976).

189 See, for example, Notes: "Physician Assisted Suicide."

190 Callahan, "When Self-Determination Runs Amok," 55.

191 With rapidly emerging, highly sophisticated medical diagnostic techniques, moreover, the well among us could be seen as the undiagnosed
sick. I am indebted to Dr Ken Flegel of the Royal Victoria Hospital in
Montreal for this insight.

192 See Brock, "Voluntary Active Euthanasia," 17–18, referring to Velleman.

193 "Conflicts in Managing Intractable Pain and Suffering," American Society
of Law and Medicine conference; see note 138.

194 Singer and Siegler, "Euthanasia."

195 S. Wolf, "Holding the Line on Euthanasia," *Hastings Center Report* 19,
1 (1989) (Spec. Supp.): 13–15.

196 Callahan, "Can We Return Death to Disease?"

197 Capron, "Euthanasia in the Netherlands," 32.

198 Ibid.

199 Kass as quoted in Brock, "Voluntary Active Euthanasia," 17.

200 Ibid., 16, quoting W. Gaylin and others.

201 Fenigsen, "A Case against Dutch Euthanasia," 24.

202 It has also been noted (see, for example, A. Trafford, "Wishing to Die: Are
Women Really More Open to Assisted Suicide?" *Washington Post,* reprinted
in Montreal *Gazette,* 15 March 1993, D5) that, to that time, *all* the highly
publicized cases of physician-assisted suicide in the United States have involved the deaths of women – historically a vulnerable group. But Paul
Nathanson, who is doing research with Katherine Young on attitudes to
and of men, suggests that another factor is involved. Men have always been
reluctant to seek help for any reason at all; they are afraid of being thought
unmanly. In fact, many men would rather risk premature death than consult their physicians on a regular basis. Does this behaviour indicate that
men are more suicidal than women? Nathanson documents that they are.
The male suicide rate is much higher than that of women. In fact, it is still
rising. It is true, he agrees, that euthanasia can be seen in heroic terms and
it is true that heroic imagery appeals to some men. But he proposes that
most men, in all likelihood, would be much more reluctant than women to
admit they need physicians to help them die (let alone to live). They would
see euthanasia as an "easy way out," not a heroic act; it would be incompatible with their notion of masculinity. Personal communication, January
2000.

203 Singer and Siegler, "Euthanasia," 1882.

204 Ibid., 1833.

205 Wolf, "Holding the Line or Euthanasia."

206 Ibid.

207 J. Rawls, *A Theory of Justice* (Cambridge: Belknap Press, 1971), 12, 137ff.

208 See Somerville, "Spacing-In and Spacing-Out."

209 D. Schulman, "Remembering Who We Are: AIDS and Law in a Time of
Madness," *AIDS and Public Policy* 3 (1988): 75–6.

CHAPTER FOUR

1 See the list of questions, below, for examples of these issues.
2 Together, these two images can be regarded as representing the two types
of analysis we must undertake regarding euthanasia. Vertical analysis (the
iceberg) requires that we examine not only the factual reality or conscious
level of an issue but also its unconscious (its broad and deep origins) and
its superego (the values and symbols it carries or affects). Horizontal analysis (the pond) involves examining the connections of an issue, at any of
the three vertical levels described, to others at the same level.
3 [1993] 3 SCR 519. (sub nom. *Rodriguez* v. *British Columbia* (AG)) 107 DLR
(4th) 342 [hereafter *Rodriguez* cited to SCR].
4 I have used the terms "euthanasia" and "physician-assisted suicide" interchangeably in this chapter. For a detailed discussion of the importance
and difficulty of defining euthanasia, see M.A. Somerville, "The Song of
Death: The Lyrics of Euthanasia," *Journal of Contemporary Health Law and
Policy* 9 (1993), 1. See chapter 3 above. This chapter also contains a brief
account of the *Rodriguez* case.
5 *Rodriguez*, 565, Lamer CJ.
6 In his *Rodriguez* judgment, the chief justice clearly anticipates that physician-
assisted suicide could involve assistance beyond actions that would normally
be characterized as suicide – the acts causing death would not be those of
the people themselves, but those of other people (ibid., 578). It is very difficult to distinguish some of these acts from ones that would constitute homicide – in particular, culpable homicide in the form of murder or
manslaughter. This raises the question of whether, in *Rodriguez*, we are really
discussing justification for what would otherwise be culpable homicide –
namely, that the motive is compassion; that the person is competent and
consenting and wants euthanasia; and that the circumstances are judged to
justify killing. It is important to make the distinction between homicide and
suicide, because it allows us to see how legalizing physician-assisted suicide
or physician-inflicted homicide would fit in with and affect both the
broader context of criminal law and some important principles on which
our society is based. If we are justifying homicide, we need to be clear about
that and not to confuse it with another situation – namely, suicide. Whether
homicide can be justified and whether suicide is justified are both questions
that can be regarded as open to argument. The important point is that the
answer to each of these questions will not be identical, and, therefore, we
need to be clear that we know which one we are discussing.
7 See the remarks of Chief Justice Lamer (ibid., 567), who implied that the
burden could be on those opposing physician-assisted suicide. In address-

ing the argument that legalizing it could place vulnerable people at risk of subtle and overt pressures (ibid., 566), he concluded that these are "speculative grounds ... The truth is that we simply do not and cannot know the range of implications that allowing some form of assisted-suicide will have for persons with physical disabilities" (ibid.). Consequently, the chief justice's position, allowing physician-assisted suicide, means that he held that the burden of proof is on those who oppose legalization of euthanasia; they would have to show that it would harm society – especially vulnerable members of society. This approach can be compared with one based on the position that those arguing for a change in the status quo (the prohibition on euthanasia) have the burden of proving that change is justified; they would have to show that the benefits of change would clearly outweigh its risks and harms. See Somerville, "The Song of Death," 63–7.

8 Canadian Charter of Rights and Freedoms, Part I of the Constitution Act, 1982, being Schedule B to the Canada Act 1982 (UK), 1982, c. 11 [hereafter Charter].

9 I am indebted to my colleague Katherine Young for raising this question. See also Linton Gifford-Jones, "We Need Society to Prevent Cruelty to Dying Patients," Montreal *Gazette*, 10 July 1994, C5. He was "asked to appear before a committee of Canadian senators to give [his] opinion on euthanasia." Speaking in strong support of euthanasia, he asks, rhetorically, "How could I convince them that there is a point in history when no army can withstand the strength of an idea whose time has come? How they had a unique opportunity to make history. And how other countries might listen to their decision."

10 M.A. Somerville. "The Right to Health: A Human Rights Perspective," in J. Mann and C. Dupuy, eds., *SIDA: Santé, droits de l'homme/AIDS: Health and Human Rights* (Veyrier-du-Lac (Annecy), France: Fondation Marcel Mérieux, Institut des Sciences du Vivant, 1993), 75. See chapter 22 below, "Human Rights and Human Ethics: Health and Health Care."

11 See the first chapter of the novel by P.D. James, *The Children of Men* (New York: Knopf, 1993), for a description of death by euthanasia in the year 2025.

12 I am indebted to my colleague Roderick Macdonald for articulating this insight.

13 Cognitive dissonance is the phenomenon experienced when one receives two sets of conflicting information, both of which appear to be correct.

14 Somerville, "The Song of Death," 74–5.

15 Sue Rodriguez's impact in this regard has not ceased with her death. Documentary programs about her and the litigation that culminated in the Supreme Court case are being made and shown on television. The Canadian Broadcasting Corporation screened a one-hour documentary on *Witness* on 2 August 1994.

16 See M.A. Somerville, "Justice across the Generations" *Social Science and Medicine* 29 (1989): 385.

17 M. Solomon, "Health Care Professionals and Treatment at the End of Life," address to the American Society of Law, Medicine and Ethics Annual Meeting, Cambridge, Mass., 30–31 October 1992 (unpublished).

18 *Rodriguez,* 552, 562.

19 One can speculate that the chief justice might have characterized the right in this way to emphasize the mental element of those who want to commit suicide and the act of choosing, and also to de-emphasise the importance of the acts of those who assist in suicide. In short, this approach could make choosing suicide the overwhelmingly dominant, relevant, fact, not its commission, which, in turn, could lead to a position that assistance with the latter is not in itself of major importance. It has the effect also of emphasizing that the situation is one of suicide, and de-emphasizing that it could be one that involves homicide.

20 For instance, would it mean that there is a duty not to treat someone admitted to an emergency room who has attempted suicide and refuses treatment?

21 *Rodriguez,* 595, Sopinka J.

22 RSC 1985, c. C-46 (as amended).

23 *Rodriguez,* 584, 585.

24 Ibid., 584, 598.

25 Ibid., 620.

26 Ibid., 629.

27 See Somerville, "The Song of Death," 63–4.

28 *Rodriguez,* 595 (emphasis added).

29 Ibid., 595–6.

30 Ibid., 598.

31 A statement of the majority of the Supreme Court of Canada, referring to the House of Lords case, *Airedale N.H.S. Trust* v. *Bland,* [1993] 1 All ER 821, [1993] 2 WLR 316, is interesting in this respect because it arguably adopts both positions: "The principle of sanctity of life, which was not absolute, was therefore found not to be violated by the withdrawal of treatment" (Rodriguez, 598).

32 See Somerville, "The Song of Death," 10–12.

33 S. 241 (b).

34 M.A. Somerville, *Consent to Medical Care,* Study Paper, Law Reform Commission of Canada (Hull, Que.: Supply and Services Canada, 1980).

35 *Airedale N.H.S. Trust* v. *Bland.*

36 Law Reform Commission of Canada, *Euthanasia, Aiding Suicide and Cessation of Treatment,* Report 20 (Hull, Que.: Supply and Services Canada, 1983).

37 *Rodriguez,* 601.

38 See, in particular, ibid., 605–6.

39 Ibid., 617 (emphasis added).

40 Ibid., 605.

41 Ibid., 593.
42 Ibid., 585.
43 See, for example, ibid., 554, 560–1, Lamer CJ.
44 Ibid., 598.
45 Ibid., 560. See also 554.
46 Somerville, "The Song of Death," 64–5.
47 Ibid., 44–56.
48 With regard to possible definitions of autonomy and self-determination, for example, see M.A. Somerville, "Labels versus Contents: Variance between Philosophy, Psychiatry and Law in Concepts Governing Decision-Making" *McGill Law Journal* 39 (1994): 179 (see chapter 21, below); and with respect to dignity, choice, and control, "The Song of Death."
49 *Rodriguez*, 589, quoting L. Tribe, *American Constitutional Law*, 2d ed. (Mineola, NY: Foundation Press, 1988), 1371.
50 Somerville, "The Song of Death," 27–9.
51 *Rodriguez*, 585 (emphasis added).

CHAPTER SIX

1 M.A. Somerville, "Song of Death: The Lyrics of Euthanasia," *Journal of Contemporary Health Law and Policy* 9 (1993): 1–76. See chapter 3 above.
2 New York State Task Force on Life and the Law, *When Death Is Sought: Assisted Suicide and Euthanasia in the Medical Context* (Albany: New York State Task Force on Life and the Law, 1994); G.J. Annas, "Death by Prescription: The Oregon Initiative," *New England Journal of Medicine* 331 (1994): 1240–3; House of Lords, *Report of the Select Committee on Medical Ethics* (London: HMSO, 1994); Report of the Special Senate Committee on Euthanasia and Assisted Suicide, *Of Life and Death* (Ottawa: Supply and Services Canada, 1995).
3 Editorial, "The Final Autonomy," *Lancet* 346 (1995): 259.
4 The Oregon Death with Dignity Act 1994 (Ballot Measure 16).
5 *Lee* v. *State of Oregon* 891 F. Supp. 1429 (D. Or. 1995).
6 *T. Quill and others* v. *Vacco* 80 F. Supp. 3rd. 716 (1996) (US Court of Appeals Second Circuit).
7 *Compassion in Dying* v. *State of Washington* 79 F. Supp. 790 (1996) (U.S. Court of Appeals, Ninth Circuit). The United States Supreme Court later overturned this decision. See chapter 7 below.
8 Somerville, "The Song of Death."
9 Rights of the Terminally Ill Act 1995, Legislative Assembly of the Northern Territory of Australia.
10 See references cited in note 2, Somerville, 'The Song of Death," and M.A. Somerville, "Euthanasia," correspondence, *Lancet* 345 (1995): 1240–1.
11 See Somerville, "Euthanasia," and "The Song of Death"; House of Lords, *Report*; Special Senate Committee, *Of Life and Death*.

12 J.J. Fins and M.D. Bacchetta, "Framing the Physician-Assisted Suicide and Voluntary Active Euthanasia Debate: The Role of Deontology, Consequentialism, and Clinical Pragmatism," *Journal of the American Geriatrics Society* 43 (1995): 563–8.

13 Katherine K. Young, "A Cross-Cultural Historical Case against Planned Self-Willed Death and Assisted Suicide," *McGill Law Journal* 39 (1994): 657–707.

14 Somerville, "The Song of Death."

15 *Lee* v. *State of Oregon.*

16 The Oregon Death with Dignity Act, 1994.

17 M.A. Somerville, "Unpacking the Concept of Human Dignity in Human(e) Death: Comments on 'Human Dignity and Disease, Disability, and Suffering,' by Sylvia D. Stolberg," *Humane Medicine* 11 (1995): 148–51. See chapter 16 (b) below.

18 *Rodriguez* v. *Canada (A.G.),* [1993] 3 SCR 519. (sub nom. *Rodriguez* v. *British Columbia (A.G.)* 107 DLR (4th) 342.

19 P.D. James, *The Children of Men* (New York: Knopf, 1993).

20 Gwynne Dyer, "Learning to Kill," Montreal *Gazette,* 15 December 1995, B3.

21 R. Rodriguez, "The Coming Mayhem," Los Angeles *Times,* 21 January 1996, M1.

22 "Death on Request," Ikon Television Network, 1994.

23 "Death on Request" (excerpts), *Prime Time Live,* 8 December 1994.

24 H. Hendin, "Selling Death and Dignity," *Hastings Center Report* 25, 3 (1995): 19–23.

25 Somerville, "Song of Death."

26 P. Parrs, "Suicide Program Makes Me Uneasy," Montreal *Gazette,* 25 May 1996, E21.

27 Somerville, "Song of Death."

28 M.A. Somerville, " 'Death Talk' in Canada: The Rodriguez Case," *McGill Law Journal* 39 (1994): 602–17 (see chapter 4); Somerville, "Song of Death."

29 G. Kolata, "Nurses Report Hastening Patients' Deaths," Montreal *Gazette,* 23 May 1996, A1, A2 (reprinted from the *New York Times*).

30 E. Becker, *The Denial of Death* (New York: Free Press, 1973); D. Callahan, *The Troubled Dream of Life: Living with Mortality* (New York: Simon & Schuster, 1993).

31 M.A. Somerville, "Just 'Gene Machines' or Also 'Secular Scared': From New Science to a New Societal Paradigm," *Policy Options* 17, 2 (1996): 3–6. See chapter 1 above, "Euthanasia, Genetics, Reproductive Technologies, and the Search for a New Societal Paradigm".

32 Somerville, "Song of Death."

33 Carol Gilligan, *In a Different Voice: Psychological Theory and Women's Development* (Cambridge, Mass.: Harvard University Press, 1982).

34 Somerville, "Just 'Gene Machines.' "

35 Some scholars in the field of religious studies point out that "religion" is
alive and well even in societies that purport either to be secular or to "separate church and state." Paul Nathanson, for example, has done a great deal
of research on what he calls "secular religion" (primarily in his book *Over
the Rainbow: The Wizard of Oz as a Secular Myth of America* [Albany: State University of New York Press, 1989] and in his article "I Feel, Therefore I Am:
The Princess of Passion and the Implicit Religion of Our Time," *Implicit Religions* 2, 2 [1999]: 59–87). By "secular religion," he refers to massively
popular world views that are secular in a technical sense (because they do
not mediate the sacred, which is the defining feature of religion), but religious in a functional sense. Secular religions function on both the individual level and the collective (but not necessarily official) level. They can take
either explicit forms (such as the movements based on political ideologies
and the public ceremonies of state-sponsored "civil religions") or implicit
ones (such as the neo-Romanticism that finds expression in phenomena as
different as television talk shows and public response to the death of Princess Diana). Directly or indirectly, secular religions explain universal features of the human condition (such as death, sacrifice, love, or home).
Directly or indirectly, intentionally or unintentionally, movies and even
television shows are often either "secular myths" or "secular parables"
(about the way things are now, the way things once were in some primaeval
golden age, and the way things will be again for those who "see the light").
Secular religions satisfy the universal need for rituals to mark the great
events of life (such as birth, death, and coming of age for individuals, and
independence or historic catastrophes for communities). They confer
identity, meaning, and purpose (as in the personal quest for self-realization
or the struggle for a common cause such as environmentalism). They provide exemplary heroes (such as movie stars and rock singers or political activists and martyrs). The only religious function they do not have is
mediating the sacred (which, being *sui generis*, is not a synonym for morality, justice, compassion, truth, or anything else that can be "understood" in
either emotional or cognitive terms).

36 M. Seguin, *A Gentle Death* (Toronto: Key Porter, 1994).

37 C.S. Lewis, *A Grief Observed* (London: Faber & Faber, 1961), 27–8.

38 H.R. Moody, *Ethics in an Aging Society* (Baltimore: Johns Hopkins University
Press, 1992), 86; cited in D.C. Thomasma, "The Ethics of Physician-Assisted
Suicide," in J.M. Humber et al., eds., *Physician-Assisted Death* (Totowa, NJ:
Humana Press, 1994),105.

39 Somerville, "Just 'Gene machines.'"

40 D.C. Dennett, "Darwin's Dangerous Idea," *The Sciences* 35 (1995): 34–40.

41 R. Wright, *The Moral Animal: Evolutionary Psychology and Everyday Life*
(New York: Pantheon Books, 1994); M. Ruse, "The Significance of Evolution," in P. Singer, ed., *A Companion to Ethics* (Cambridge, Mass.: Blackwell,
1991), 500–10.

42 Brian Swimme and T. Berry, *The Universe Story: From the Primordial Flaring Forth to the Ecozoic Era* (San Francisco: Harper, 1992).

43 Somerville, "Just 'Gene machines.'"

44 I am indebted to Paul Nathanson for this insight (personal communication, June 2000).

45 G.J. Annas and M.A. Grodin, eds., *The Nazi Doctors and the Nuremberg Code: Human Rights in Human Experimentation* (New York: Oxford University Press, 1992), 3.

46 R.N. Proctor, "Nazi Doctors, Racial Medicine, and Human Experimentation," in G.J. Annas and M.A. Grodin, eds., *The Nazi Doctors and the Nuremberg Code* (New York: Oxford University Press, 1992), 18–19.

47 Thomasma, "The Ethics of Physician-Assisted Suicide," 118 (emphasis added).

48 Somerville, "Just 'Gene machines.'"

49 Ibid.

50 Institute of Medical Ethics Working Party on the Ethics of Prolonging Life and Assisting Death, "Assisted Death," *Lancet* 336 (1990): 610–13.

51 W. Gaylin et al., "Doctors Must Not Kill," referred to, without citation, in D.W. Brock, "Voluntary Active Euthanasia," *Hastings Center Report* 22, 2 (1992): 16 and note 14.

52 N. Lickiss, untitled piece, in S. Chapman and S. Leeder, eds., *The Last Right? Australians Take Sides on the Right to Die* (Sydney: Mandarin, 1995), 92–8.

53 Editorial, "Doctors and Death Row," *Lancet* 341 (1993): 209–10; R.D. Truog and T.A. Brennan, "Participation of Physicians in Capital Punishment," *New England Journal of Medicine* 329 (1993): 1346–50; H. Wolinsky, "U.S. Physicians Debate Capital Punishment," *Lancet* 346 (1995): 43.

54 *Roe* v. *Wade* 410 U.S. 113 (1973 USSC).

CHAPTER SEVEN

1 M.A. Somerville, "The Song of Death: The Lyrics of Euthanasia," *Journal Contemporary Law & Health Policy* 13 (1993): 9. See chapter 3 above.

2 Unless otherwise indicated, the term "lethal injection" is used throughout this book to mean an injection given with the primary intention of killing someone.

3 State Committee on Euthanasia, *Report on Euthanasia* (The Hague: Government Printing Office, 1985). The definition was used also in the 1991 Remmelink Report and in the summary brochure, "Medical Practice with Regard to Euthanasia and Related Medical Decisions in the Netherlands," Ministerie van Justitie, 1991, 3. Despite the requirement for "explicit consent," recent research has shown a large number of cases of non-voluntary and involuntary euthanasia occurring in the Netherlands. See notes 5, 15, and 16 below.

4 Termination of Life on Request and Assistance with Suicide (Review) Act, 2001.

5 H. Hendin, C. Rutenfrans, and Z. Zylicz, "Physician-Assisted Suicide and Euthanasia in the Netherlands," *Journal of the American Medical Association* 227, 21 (1997): 1720–22.

6 See the text below, for a discussion of other cases of false association.

7 A.M. Capron, "Euthanasia in the Netherlands: American Observations" *Hastings Center Report* 22 (1992): 30.

8 Report of the Institute of Medical Ethics Working Party on the Ethics of Prolonging Life and Assisting Death, "Assisted Death," *Lancet* 2 (1990): 610–13.

9 Somerville, "The Song of Death."

10 Ian McLaren and Michael Piper, "Searching for Ethics 2001," transcript of pilot segment for a video, Uluru, Australia, April 1997.

11 The distinction was articulated in this way by Chief Justice Renquist, speaking for the United States Supreme Court in the landmark judgment *Vacco* v. *Quill*, US Supreme Court Docket No. 95–1858, 26 June 1997 (*United States Law Week*, 65 LW 4695, 24 June 1997).

12 M.A. Somerville, "Unpacking the Concept of Human Dignity in Human(e) Death: Comments on 'Human Dignity and Disease, Disability and Suffering' by Sylvia D. Stolberg" *Humane Medicine* 11 (1995): 148–51. See chapter 16 (b) below.

13 Hendin, Rutenfrans, and Zylicz, "Physician-Assisted Suicide."

14 G. van der Wal and P.J. van der Maas, *Euthanasia en Andere Medische Beslissingen rond het Levenseinde* (The Hague: Staatsuitgeverij, 1996).

15 P.J. van der Maas et al., "Physician-Assisted Suicide and Other Medical Practices Involving the End of Life in the Netherlands, 1990–1995," *New England Journal of Medicine* 335 (1996): 1609–1705; G. van der Wal et al., "Evaluation of the Notification Procedure for *Physician-Assisted Death in the Netherlands*," ibid., 1706–11.

16 L. Lagnado, "Top Journals Divide over Assisted Suicide," *Wall Street Journal*, 4 June 1997, B1.

17 Pilot sequence, per Professor Norelle Lickiss, Sydney, Australia, and Professor Aranda Sanchez, Melbourne, Australia, in McLaren and Piper, "Searching for Ethics 2001."

18 The Parliament of the Commonwealth of Australia, Senate Legal and Constitutional Legislation Committee, Consideration of Legislation Referred to the Committee: Euthanasia Laws Bill 1996, Senate Printing Unit, Department of the Senate, Parliament House, Canberra, 39–55.

19 The Rights of the Terminally Ill Act, 1995 (NT). Subsequently, the Commonwealth Parliament passed the Euthanasia Laws Act, 1997 (Cth) overriding the Territory legislation.

20 T. Quill, "The Case for Euthanasia," "Searching for the 'Soul' of Euthanasia," 11th International Congress on Care of the Terminally Ill, Montreal, 1996.

21 R.M. Sade and M.F. Marshall, "Legistrothanatry: A New Specialty for Assisting in Death," *Perspectives in Biology and Medicine* 39, 4 (1996): 547–9.

22 H. Shepherd, "Unity Council Sets New Direction," Montreal *Gazette*, 21 June 1997, J7: "Late last year … a group of churches including the Catholics, some evangelical churches and some in between, publicly criticized a trend toward acceptance of euthanasia – a statement that the United Church of Canada and the Quakers did not support."

23 I. Berlin, *Four Essays on Liberty* (London: Oxford University Press, 1969).

24 J. Katz, *Silent World of Doctor and Patient* (New York: Free Press, 1984).

25 See M. Seguin, *A Gentle Death* (Toronto: Key Porter Books, 1991).

26 For an example of this approach, see D.P.T. Price, "Assisted Suicide and Refusing Medical Treatment: Linguistics, Morals and Legal Contortions," *Medical Law Review* 4 (1996): 270–99.

27 Somerville, "The Song of Death."

28 J.A. Billings and S.D. Block, "Slow Euthanasia," *Journal of Palliative Care* 12 (1996): 21–30.

29 Ibid.

30 B. Mount, "Morphine Drips, Terminal Sedation, and Slow Euthanasia: Definitions and Facts, Not Anecdotes," ibid., 31–7; B. Dickens, "Commentary on 'Slow Euthanasia,'" ibid., 42–3; R. Portenoy, "Morphine Infusions at the End of Life: The Pitfalls in Reasoning from Anecdote," ibid., 44–6; H. Brodie, "Commentary on Billings' and Block's 'Slow Euthanasia,'" ibid., 38–41.

31 M.A. Somerville, "Death of Pain: Pain Suffering and Ethics," in G.F. Gebhart, D.L. Hammond, and T.S. Jensen, eds., *Progress in Pain Research and Management*, vol. 2, Proceedings of the 7th World Congress on Pain, International Association for the Study of Pain (Seattle, Wash., IASP Press, 1994), 41–58. See chapter 14 below.

32 See J. Keown, "Restoring Moral and Intellectual Shape to the Law after Bland," *Law Quarterly Review* 113 (1997): 484, note 10, citing the House of Lords Select Committee on Medical Ethics, Report of the Select Committee on Medical Ethics HL Paper 21-I of 1993–4, [242]. It is noteworthy that many criminal law texts – for example, E. Colvin, *Principles of Criminal Law*, 2nd ed. Toronto: Carswell, 1991), and D. Stuart, *Canadian Criminal Law*, 2nd ed. (Toronto-Carswell, 1987) – do not discuss this doctrine or even refer to it.

33 Dickens, "Commentry," 43.

34 Colvin, *Principles of Criminal Law*, 48.

35 Ibid., 200.

36 *R.* v. *Maloney*, [1985] AC 905 (UK).

37 It should be noted that medically appropriate pain-relief treatment properly titrated to the patients' pain is unlikely to kill them. Indeed, it can prolong life. I have taken here the strongest pro-euthanasia argument against

the anti-euthanasia case: that those who agree with pain-relief treatment that would shorten life, but not with euthanasia, are inconsistent at best in their use of the law and, more realistically, hypocritical.

38 See, for example, the Canadian Criminal Code, RSC 1985, chapter C-46 (as amended), section 222(5)(a).

39 See Somerville, "The Song of Death," 4, note 7, for a discussion of the concept of primary intent, which is a synonym for motive.

40 See the text below and note 68.

41 The one exception to this statement is that the analyses and arguments presented on pain-relief treatment that would or could shorten life apply, with changes as necessary, to similar treatment for relieving symptoms of serious physical distress (such as acute breathlessness or intractable vomiting) experienced by some dying people.

42 B. Sneiderman and M. Verhoef, "Patient Autonomy and the Defence of Medical Necessity: Five Dutch Euthanasia Cases," *Alberta Law Review,* 34, 2 (1996): 374–415.

43 Parliament of Canada, *Report of the Special Senate Committee on Euthanasia and Assisted Suicide* (Ottawa: Supply and Services Canada, 1995).

44 See the discussion, above, in which necessary pain-relief treatment is wrongly characterized as "slow euthanasia."

45 See, for example, Lagnado, "Top Journals Divide over Assisted Suicide."

46 Colvin, *Principles of Criminal Law,* 80–2.

47 The criminal law tends not to use, overtly, the distinction between causation-in-fact and causation-in-law, a distinction that is well developed in tort law. See J. Fleming, *The Law of Torts* (Sydney (Australia): Law Book Company, 1992), 192–204. Rather, in deciding criminal cases, courts speak simply of causation. Their reason for doing so is probably to avoid the appearance of using judicial discretion or any arbitrariness in relation to their decisions on causation. But the result is greater confusion in the theory and sometimes in the application of the law governing causation in the criminal law than in tort law. See Colvin, *Principles of Criminal Law,* 78–95; Stuart, *Canadian Criminal Law,* 102–16.

48 Fleming, *The Law of Torts,* 192–3, 202–4.

49 Stuart, *Canadian Criminal Law,* 110.

50 Ibid., 110–16; Colvin, *Principles of Criminal Law,* 84–90.

51 *R. v. Knutsen,* [1963] Qd R 157 (CCA), as cited in Colvin, *Principles of Criminal Law,* 87–8.

52 *Overseas Tankship (UK) Ltd* v. *The Miller Steamship Co Pty Ltd (The Wagon Mound) (No 2),* [1966] 2 All ER 709 (PC).

53 *Overseas Tankship (UK) Ltd.* v. *Morts Dock and Engineering Co Ltd. (The Wagon Mound) (No 1),* [1961] AC 388; 1 All ER 404 (PC).

54 Ibid.

55 One expression is the presumption of innocence.

56 Colvin, *Principals of Criminal Law,* 84–5.

57 In comparison, the American Model Penal Code's definition of causation [section 203] requires that the consequence for which one seeks to hold the accused liable must not be "too remote or accidental in its occurrence to have a just bearing on the actor's liability or on the gravity of his offence."

58 Fleming, *The Law of Torts,* 203, citing *Palsgraf* v. *Long Island RR* 248 NY 339 (1928) at 352, per Andrews J. Compare Lord Wright: "The law must abstract some consequences as relevant, not perhaps on the grounds of pure logic but simply for practical reasons." *Liesbosch* v. *The Edison,* [1933] AC 449 at 460.

59 *Richardson* v. *Mellish* (1824), 2 Bingham 229 at 252, Burrough J.

60 See, for example, *R* v. *Donovan,* [1934] 2 KB 498, 25 Cr App R 1 (CCA). See also *R* v. *Jobidon* (1991), 66 CCC (3d) 454 (Supreme Court of Canada).

61 *Vacco* v. *Quill,* per Renquist CJ.

62 J.K. Mason and D. Mulligan, "Euthanasia by Stages," *Lancet* 347 (1996): 810–11.

63 As a primary justification for euthanasia, Mason and Mulligan's proposal moves the focus from the right to self-determination and autonomy of the patient to the disease from which the patient suffers. This shift raises important questions about the impact that legalizing euthanasia would have on disabled people, who suffer from the same or equally debilitating conditions.

64 *Nancy B* v. *Hôtel-Dieu de Québec,* [1992] RJQ 361, 86 DLR (4th) 385 (Sup. Ct) (translation from French).

65 *Rodriguez* v. *Canada (AG),* [1993] 3 SCR 519, 107 DLR (4th) 342.

66 Criminal Code, 1985, section 241.

67 This argument presents an interesting issue, which I cannot discuss in detail here: the basic presumption from which we should assess obligations to give medical treatment. In brief, it can make a difference (especially in difficult cases, when we are unsure of whether treatment should be withdrawn) if we start from a basic presumption that a treatment should be continued unless it can be shown that it is useless, or a presumption that only a treatment that might be useful (or, even more stringently, is reasonably likely to be useful) must continue to be given. In cases of equal doubt about usefulness or futility, the basic presumption governs. Therefore, in the same circumstances, the first presumption would mean that treatment must be continued; the second presumption would mean that it could be withdrawn. See Somerville, "The Song of Death," 63–7.

68 It merits noting that if a similar situation arose with respect to a competent person who refused to consent to the withdrawal of the treatment, but it was withdrawn anyway, we would unhesitatingly call this murder – not euthanasia. Moreover, withdrawing medically futile treatment from competent

patients against their will (or in the case of incompetent patients, contrary to the will of their substitute decision-makers) presents complex legal issues. These issues likely to be faced by courts in the near future, as we experience severe restrictions on health-care budgets in many jurisdictions.

69 Mason and Mulligan, "Euthanasia by Stages."

70 *Nancy B* v. *Hôtel-Dieu de Québec.*

71 *Rodriguez* v. *Canada (A.G.).*

72 Civil Code of Quebec, Article 19. (Now Article 10.)

73 Ibid, Article 19.1. (Now Article 11.)

74 *Nancy B* v. *Hôtel-Dieu de Québec*, 390–1 (DLR).

75 Ibid., 392 (DLR).

76 Ibid., citing *Re Conroy* 486 A 2d 1209 (NJ 1985) at 1224.

77 Criminal Code, 1985.

78 *Nancy B* v. *Hôtel-Dieu de Québec*, 934 (DLR).

79 Part 1 of the Constitution Act, 1982, being Schedule B to the Canada Act 1982 (UK) 1982, chapter 11.

80 See M.A. Somerville, "'Death Talk' in Canada: The *Rodriguez* Case," *McGill Law Journal* 39 (1994): 602–17. See chapter 4 above.

81 *Rodriguez* v. *Canada (A.G.)*, 365.

82 Ibid., 363.

83 Ibid., 365.

84 Ibid., 384.

85 Mason and Mulligan, "Euthanasia by Stages," 811.

86 *Roe* v. *Wade* 410 US 113 (1973) (USSC).

87 *Cruzan* v. *Director, Missouri Department of Health* 497 US 261 (1990) (USSC).

88 *Roe* v. *Wade.*

89 *Compassion in Dying* v. *Washington* 79 F 3rd 790 (9th Cir 1996).

90 *Quill* v. *Vacco*, 80 F 3rd 716 (2nd Cir 1996).

91 *Vacco* v. *Quill*; *Washington* v. *Glucksberg*, US Supreme Court Docket No. 96–110, 26 June 1997 (United States Law Week, 65 LW 4669, 24 June 1997).

92 In Australia, the Rights of the Terminally Ill Act, 1995, of the Northern Territory, which authorized euthanasia and physician-assisted suicide, was overridden by legislation (the Andrews Bill, 1997) passed by the federal Parliament. The power of the Parliament to override Territory legislation could well be different, however, from its power with respect to state legislation. This question would be tested if any of the pro-euthanasia bills that have been before Australian state legislatures were passed into law and these laws were subsequently challenged.

93 M.A. Somerville, "Legalising Euthanasia: Why Now?" *Australian Quarterly* 68, 3 (1996): 1–14. See chapter 6 above.

94 M.A. Somerville, "Genetics, Reproductive Technologies, Euthanasia and the Search for a New Societal Paradigm," editorial, *Social Science & Medicine* 42, 12 (1996): ix–xii. See chapter 1 above.

CHAPTER EIGHT (a)

Torsten O. Nielsen, PhD, MD, CM, was a resident in anatomic pathology at the Health Sciences Centre, University of British Columbia.

1 S.J. Genuis, S.K. Genuis, and W.C. Chang, "Public Attitudes toward the Right to Die," Canadian Medical Association Journal 150 (1994): 701–8; R. Hassan, "Euthanasia and the Medical Profession: An Australian Study," Australian Journal Social Issues 31 (1996): 239–52.

2 J.L. Bernat, B. Geri, R.P. Mogielnicki, "Patient Refusal of Hydration and Nutrition: An Alternative to Physician-Assisted Suicide or Voluntary Active Euthanasia," Archives of Internal Medicine 153 (1993): 2723–8.

3 M.M. Burgess, "The Medicalization of Dying," Journal of Medical Philosophy 18 (1993): 269–79.

4 Ibid.

5 S.D. Block and J.A. Billings, "Patient Requests to Hasten Death: Evaluation and Management in Terminal Care," Archives of Internal Medicine 154 (1994): 2039–47.

6 E.J. Emanuel, "Pain and Symptom Control: Patient Rights and Physician Responsibilities," Hematology and Oncology Clinics of North America 10 (1996): 41–56.

7 A. Mullens, "The Dutch Experience with Euthanasia: Lessons for Canada?" Canadian Medical Association Journal 152 (1995): 1845–52.

8 Block and Billings, "Patient Requests to Hasten Death."

9 Hassan, "Euthanasia and the Medical Profession."

10 Block and Billings, "Patient Requests to Hasten Death"; Mullens, "The Dutch Experience with Euthanasia."

11 H. Kuhse and P. Singer, "Active Voluntary Euthanasia, Morality, and the Law," Journal of Law and Medicine 3 (1995): 129–35.

12 The Oregon Death with Dignity Act. Available from http://www.rights.org/~deathnet/ergo_orlaw.html.

13 Lee v. State of Oregon, 869 F. Supp. 1491 (D. Or. 1994).

14 Washington v. Glucksberg, 65 USLW 4669 (US 26 June 1997); Vacco v. Quill, 65 USLW 4695 (US 26 June 1997).

15 Rodriguez v. A.G. of B.C., 3 SCR 519 (30 September 1993).

16 Hassan, "Euthanasia and the Medical Profession."

17 Legislative Assembly of the Northern Territory, Rights of the Terminally Ill Act and Associated Materials. Available from http://www.nt.gov.au/lant/rotti/.

18 Kuhse and Singer, "Active Voluntary Euthanasia."

19 Emanuel, "Pain and Symptom Control."

20 Canadian Medical Association, "CMA Policy Summary: Physician-Assisted Death," Canadian Medical Association Journal 152 (1995): 248 A–B.

21 Genuis, Genuis, and Chang, "Public Attitudes."

22 Canadian Medical Association, "CMA Policy Summary."
23 Bernat, Geri, and Mogielnicki, "Patient Refusal."
24 J.R. Williams, "Physician-Assisted Death: Suicide Prevention and Patient Autonomy. CMA's Director of Ethics and Legal Affairs Responds," ibid., 1750–1.

CHAPTER EIGHT (b)

1 Torsten O. Nielsen, "Guidelines for Legalized Euthanasia in Canada: A Proposal," *Annals of the Royal College of Physicians and Surgeons of Canada* 3.1, 7 (1998): 314–18. See chapter 8 (a) above.
2 G. van der Wal and P.J. van der Maas, *Euthanasia en Andere Medische Beslissingen rond net Levenseinde* (The Hague: Staatsuitgerveris, 1996). For an English version, see P.J. van der Maas et al., "Physician-Assisted Suicide and Other Medical Practices Involving the End of Life in the Netherlands, 1990–1995," *New England Journal of Medicine* 335 (1996): 1609–1705; or G. van der Wal et al., "Evaluation of the Notification Procedure for Physician-Assisted Death in the Netherlands," *New England Journal of Medicine* 335 (1996): 1706–11. For critical commentary on the Remmelink study, see H. Hendin et al., "Physician-Assisted Suicide and Euthanasia in the Netherlands," *Journal of the American Medical Association* 227(21) (1997): 1720–2.
3 *Rodriguez* v. *Canada (A.G.),* [1993] 3 SCR 519 (SCC).
4 *R.* v. *Morgentaler,* [1998] 1 SCR 30 (SCC).
5 *Vacco* v. *Quill,* 117 St. Ct 2293 (1997).
6 M.A. Somerville, "The Song of Death: The Lyrics of Euthanasia," *Journal of Contemporary Health Law Policy* 9 (1993): 1–76. See chapter 3 above.

CHAPTER EIGHT (c)

1 P.J. van der Maas et al., "Euthanasia, Physician-Assisted Suicide, and Other Medical Practices Involving the End of Life in the Netherlands, 1990–1995," *New England Journal of Medicine* 335 (1996): 1699–705.
2 M. Angell, "Euthanasia in the Netherlands – Good News or Bad?" ibid., 1676–8.
3 *Rodriguez* v. *Canada* (A.G.), 3 SCR 519 (30 September 1993).

CHAPTER NINE

1 James M. Humber, Robert F. Almeder, and Gregg A. Kasting, eds., *Physician-Assisted Death* (Totowa, NJ: Humana Press, 1994), i–ix, 155.
2 Ibid., 75.
3 S. Gevers, "Physician Assisted Suicide: New Developments in the Netherlands," *Bioethics* 9 (1995) 309–12; M.A. Somerville, "The Song of Death:

The Lyrics of Euthanasia," *Journal of Contemporary Health Law Policy* 9 (1993): 1–76. See chapter 3 above.

4 Somerville, "The Song of Death."

5 Gevers, "Physician Assisted Suicide."

6 D.E. Meier, "Doctors' Attitudes and Experiences with Physician-Assisted Death: A Review of the Literature," in Humber, Almeder, and Kasting, eds., *Physician-Assisted Death*, 7–8.

7 Ibid., 8–9.

8 G.A. Kasting, "The Nonnecessity of Euthanasia," ibid., 25.

9 Ibid., 42.

10 Ibid., 40.

11 Canada, Senate, Report of the Special Senate Committee on Euthanasia and Assisted Suicide, *Of Life and Death* (Ottawa, 1995).

12 Kasting, "The Nonnecessity of Euthanasia," 41.

13 M.A. Somerville, "Would You Buy Yourself If You Were for Sale?" (unpublished manuscript); Pharmaceutical Manufacturers Association of Canada, Semi-Annual General Meeting, "Towards Quality of Life," Orlando, Florida, 1992.

14 G. Steven Neely, "The Constitutionality of Elective and Physician-Assisted Death," in Humber, Almeder, and Kasting, eds., *Physician-Assisted Death*, 53.

15 Ibid., 55.

16 Ibid., 61.

17 Ibid.

18 Somerville, "The Song of Death."

19 Ibid.

20 Neely, "The Constitutionality of Elective and Physician-Assisted Death," 63.

21 Notes: "Physician Assisted Suicide and the Right to Die with Assistance," *Harvard Law Review* 105 (1992): 2021–40.

22 Neely, "The Constitutionality of Elective and Physician-Assisted Death," 63.

23 Ibid., 66–7.

24 R. Schoof, "China using prisoners' organs for transplants: Group," Montreal *Gazette*, 29 August 1994, A1.

25 F.G. Miller and J.C. Fletcher, "Physician-Assisted Suicide and Active Euthanasia," in Humber, Almeder, and Kasting, eds., *Physician-Assisted Death*, 75.

26 Ibid., 76.

27 Ibid., 77.

28 Ibid., 81 (emphasis added).

29 D. Humphry, *Final Exit: The Practicalities of Self-Deliverance and Assisted Suicide for the Dying* (Eugene, Ore.: Hemlock Society, 1991).

30 Somerville, "The Song of Death."

31 Miller and Fletcher, "Physician-Assisted Suicide," 90–4.

32 Ibid., 90.

33 D.C. Thomasma, "The Ethics of Physician-Assisted Suicide," in Humber, Almeder, and Kasting, eds., *Physician-Assisted Death*, 125–6.

34 Ibid., 126.

35 Ibid., 101.

36 M.A. Somerville, "Legalizing Euthanasia: Why Now?" *Australian Quarterly* 68 (1996): 1–14. See chapter 6 above.

37 K. Young, "A Cross-Cultural Historical Case Against Planned Self-Willed Death and Assisted Suicide," *McGill Law Journal* 3 (1994): 657–707.

38 Somerville, "Legalizing Euthanasia."

CHAPTER TEN

1 N. Cherny and R. Catane, "Professional Negligence in the Management of Cancer Pain: A Case for Urgent Reforms," editorial, *Cancer* 76 (1995): 2181–5.

CHAPTER ELEVEN

1 I am indebted to my research assistants, John Kennedy and Galina Mikhlin, for assistance with the paper on which this chapter is based. It originated in a speech presented at the Sixth World Congress on Medical Law, Ghent, Belgium, in August 1982, and reported in the proceedings of that conference at volume 1, 246–56. The idea of writing this paper was suggested by my father, the late George P. Ganley, and arose from the problems he experienced in obtaining adequate pain-relief treatment and the concern he had for others in similar situations. Many people from many parts of the world discussed personal and professional experiences with me, which contributed to the final text. But I am particularly indebted to Dr Joel Paris for discussions that were fundamental to its production.

2 Any loss could be a source of suffering, but the type of loss contemplated here is limited to that which affects people's perception of themselves as individuals and persons. Consequently, to the extent that this perception depends on maintaining relationships with other members of a family or social network, then the destruction of these connections could give rise to the type of loss and consequent suffering being addressed here.

3 It could be argued that giving these people a choice would increase their suffering; it would put them in a situation of doubt as to what to do. Accepting that this ambivalence might be true, one would then have to decide which approach would lead to the greatest overall reduction in suffering. This decision would probably vary on a case-by-case basis, and there would be an obligation to make a subjective inquiry and assessment of each patient in this respect and then to act accordingly. The question of

whether the provision of a button could ever be construed as the crime of aiding and abetting suicide will not be explored here.

4 As a tentative suggestion, could it be that the use of these two words is connected with the fact that the common law has traditionally been reluctant to compensate for purely mental injury – for example, negligently inflicted pure nervous shock or mental anguish (suffering) – and yet would award damages for this type of harm (in the form of an award for non-pecuniary loss) if associated with physical injury (pain)? The policy decision not to allow compensation for negligently inflicted pure mental suffering was implemented by way of a principle to the effect that either there was no legal duty not to cause pure mental injury or, alternatively, that pure mental injury did not constitute damage recognized by the law as being of a compensable nature. For a discussion of tortious liability for negligent infliction of nervous shock, see John Fleming, *The Law of Torts*, 6th ed. (Sydney: Law Book Company, 1977), 146–53. This approach has, however, been subject to change. Canadian courts (see, for instance, *Marshall* v. *Lionel Enterprises* (1971), 25 DLR (3d) 141 (Ont. HC) and, later, the House of Lords in England (see *McLoughlin* v. *O'Brian*, [1982] 2 All ER 298) broadened the basis on which recovery of damages for pure nervous shock – that is, nervous shock unaccompanied by physical injury – is allowed. They adopted as the test of liability whether it was reasonably foreseeable that the plaintiff would be injured by nervous shock as a result of the defendant's negligence.

The rationale for the traditional refusal to award damages for pure nervous shock was probably a fear of fraudulent claims and, possibly, of unjustified interference with the liberty of those who might cause pure mental injury (see Fleming, *The Law of Torts*). These reasons might explain why loss was compensable when associated with physical injury – that is, as so-called parasitic damages – but not otherwise, which seems anomalous. The presence of physical injury, and one presumes of *pain*, could be regarded as constituting a threshold condition, or condition precedent, to recovery of damages for negligently inflicted mental harm or *suffering*, in order to reduce both the likelihood of fraudulent claims and the incidence of claims. According to this analysis, it is no accident that the law uses the conjunctive terminology of "pain and suffering."

Although the law is generally more expansive with respect to what injuries it regards as constituting damage when injury has been intentionally (rather than negligently) inflicted, some physical manifestation of the mental injury that founds the plaintiff's claim is required, at least traditionally, even for recovery of damages under the tort of "intentional infliction of mental suffering" (see *Wilkinson* v. *Downton*, [1897] 2 QB 57). But this requirement positions "physical injury" as a consequence rather than as a cause of the mental pain and suffering – and, in contrast, it is such a causal link that is required for recovery of pain and suffering damages associated with negligently inflicted physical injury.

5 For instance, the courts in the cases cited in note 4 made it clear that damages are recoverable only for "nervous shock," as compared with "mental distress" or "normal grief." When negligently inflicted mental injury stands alone, only nervous shock constitutes damage for the purposes of the law. Furthermore, judges use a wide discretion in deciding whether a plaintiff's injury should be characterized as nervous shock or as some other category of mental injury.

6 These three categories are all quality-of-life factors.

7 This head of damages is a quantity-of-life assessment.

8 This situation prevails under Quebec civil law. See Jean-Louis Baudouin, *La Responsabilité civile délictuelle* (Montreal: Les Presses de l'Université de Montréal, 1973), 116ff.

9 In contrast with Quebec, the common law provinces of Canada deal with these factors in this way. See, for example, *Andrews* v. *Grand & Toy Alta. Ltd*, [1978] 2 SCR 229, [1978] 1 WWR 577, (1978) 3 CCLT 225, (1978) 83 DLR (3d) 452, (1978) 8 AR 182, (1978) 19 NR 50 (SCC).

10 See, for example, in the English context, *Benham* v. *Gambling*, [1941] AC 157, 1A11 ER 7 (HL). It should be noted that this head of damages has been abolished in England by the Administration of Justice Act 1982, c. 53, s. 1(1)(a). However, the act provides that damages shall be awarded under the head of "pain and suffering" for suffering caused or likely to be caused to the person because of his or her awareness of reduced life expectancy (s. 1(1)(b)).

11 *Andrews* v. *Grand & Toy Alta. Ltd.* Lower courts have expressed hesitancy about applying this rule in all cases. Some have tried to avoid it, usually by holding that there were exceptional circumstances. One factor that can always be taken into account in order to exceed the $100,000 limit, and that the Supreme Court mentioned expressly, is "changing economic circumstances." In general, that has meant inflation. Canadian courts have adjusted the upper limit for damages for non-pecuniary loss on this basis. See, for instance, *MacDonald* v. *Alderson and Manitoba* (1982), 3 WWR 385 (Man. CA), in which the upper limit was placed at $130,000, and *Knutson* v. *Farr* (1984), 12 DLR (4th) 658 (BCCA), in which the upper limit was adjusted to $154,000.

12 *Lindal* v. *Lindal* (1981), 129 DLR 3d 263 (SCC) at 269, citing *Andrews*, SCR 261.

13 See, in general, A. I. Ogus, *The Law of Damages* (London: Butterworths, 1973) 194ff. See also the (British) Law Commission's *Report on Personal Injury Litigation – Assessment Damages*, No. 56, 1973; and Great Britain, *Royal Commission on Civil Liability and Compensation for Personal Injury Report* (Pearson Report), cmnd. 7054 (1978).

14 Ogus, *The Law of Damages.*

15 Ibid., 195.

16 Ibid.

17 Ibid.

18 In this respect, see *Bracchi* v. *Horsland* (1983), 25 CCLT 146, in which the British Columbia Court of Appeal held that it is not proper, when directing a jury on the question of non-pecuniary damages, to invite members to compare the case before them with *Andrews.* The court reasoned that, in the light of the functional approach to non-pecuniary damages now decreed by the Supreme Court of Canada, any such approach was inappropriate – whether damages are assessed by a judge alone or, as here, by a jury. Only when the injuries are devastating would any reference to cases such as *Andrews* or the $100,000 upper limit be proper matters to mention to a jury. This ruling indicates that the court was using the $100,000 limit only as a cut-off point and not in any way as a tariff.

See also *Hohol* v. *Pickering et al.,* [1984] 3 WWR 673 (Alta. CA), in which the majority of the Alberta Court of Appeal rejected a "comparative approach" (tariff approach), but considered the seriousness of the plaintiff's injuries (and compared them with those of the plaintiffs in "the trilogy of cases" of the Supreme Court of Canada) for the purpose of calculating what amount constituted fulfilment of "the need for solace" – a subjective assessment. The court held that "the conventional award is an arbitrary figure. It cannot be interpreted as meaning that pain, suffering and loss of amenities cannot be 'worth' more than $100,000. It was established in recognition of the impossibility of evaluating losses of this nature in monetary terms. Damages under this head cannot be assessed on a purely mathematical basis using the maximum of $100,000 as a starting point." The minority judgment on this point was that the award in "the trilogy" was a benchmark to which all awards for non-pecuniary damages in personal-injury cases must be proportionately scaled. The plaintiff's injuries and their consequences on his enjoyment of life and need for amenities were substantially less than those of the plaintiffs in "the trilogy." Clearly the courts are grappling with a problem here, and it probably arises from the fact that more seriously injured plaintiffs must receive only the same amount of damages for pain and suffering as less seriously injured ones. This result is consistent with both a "functional assessment of pain-and-suffering damages" as the basis for assessment and a cut-off limit, rather than a tariff scale. But in deciding the amount, there might be a psychological reaction, when comparing awards in different cases, which could give rise to a perception of unfairness.

19 (1982) 36 OR (2d) 653 (CA Ont.).

20 Ibid., 657.

21 Ibid.

22 *Thornton* v. *Board of School Trustees of School District No. 57 (Prince George) et al.*, [1979] 2 SCR 267, 83 DLR (3d) 480 at 284 (SCR), cited in *Mulroy*.

23 This view was taken by the Court of Appeal of British Columbia in *Blackstock & Vincent* v. *Patterson et al.*, [1982] 4 WWR 519 (BCCA). The Court of Appeal interpreted the Supreme Court's limit on damages for non-pecuniary loss as "based on the premise that in the case of all 'severely injured plaintiffs,' in order to avoid extravagant claims, an upper limit of $100,000 should be imposed" (526). Moreover, the Court of Appeal expressly stated that the limit "was not based on the view that the awards made by the lower courts in the trilogy [of] cases were excessive or that there was no distinction between the cases" (ibid.).

24 *Mulroy* v. *Aqua Scene et al.*, 657.

25 Alan Tyree, "Assessment of Damages," Medico-Legal Seminar, University of New South Wales, Sydney, Australia, 17 July 1982. Tyree demonstrated that awards calculated – for example, in 1970 to cover an anticipated life expectancy of forty years – were, in fact, exhausted in under twenty years.

26 It should be noted that Canadian courts are not now empowered to award periodic payment of damages (see *MacDonald* v. *Alderson and Manitoba*), although the parties can agree on a settlement to this effect, as was done in *Yepremian* v. *Scarborough General Hospital* (1980), 110 DLR (3d) 513 (Ont. CA); terms of settlement reported in (1981) 120 DLR (3d) 341.

27 See *Lindal* v. *Lindal.*

28 See, for example, M. Angell, "The Quality of Mercy," *New England Journal of Medicine* 306 (1982): 98–9.

29 Part of the section that follows was originally published in the *New England Journal of Medicine* 307 (1982): 55.

30 The definition of terminal illness can present difficulties. In The Natural Death Act of California (Cal. Stats. 1976, c. 1439, Health and Safety Code, c. 39, §. 7187(f)), " 'terminal condition' means an incurable condition caused by injury, disease, or illness, which, regardless of the application of life-sustaining procedures, would, within reasonable medical judgment, produce death, and where the application of life-sustaining procedures serves only to postpone the moment of death of the patient."

31 See M.S. Pernick, "The Calculus of Suffering in Nineteenth-Century Surgery," *Hastings Center Report* 13, 2 (1983): 26.

32 Ibid., 32.

33 Ibid., 33.

34 Criminal Code, RSC 1970, c. C-34, s. 14.

35 In this respect, see Legal Advisors Committee, "Concern for Dying, the Right to Refuse Treatment: A Model Act," *American Journal of Public Health* 73, 8 (1983): 918.

36 See M.A. Somerville, "Medical Interventions and the Criminal Law: Lawful or Excusable Wounding," *McGill Law Journal* 26, 1 (1980): 82.

37 For a discussion of competence – and, in particular, of emotional as compared with cognitive competence (noting that the former might be very relevant in relation to people in pain) – see M.A. Somerville, "Refusal of Medical Treatment in 'Captive' Circumstances," *Canadian Bar Review* 63 (1985): 59.

38 I have limited the discussion to physicians' duties with respect to relieving pain, but these duties could be applied more widely to health-care professionals in general. Note that all these duties would not be of the same content.

39 See *Knutson* v. *Farr*.

40 D. Waddell and R.V. Brody, "Inadequate Treatment of Pain in Hospitalized Patients," (correspondence), *New England Journal of Medicine* 307 (1982): 55, citing Shizukoy Fagerhaugh and Anselm Strauss, *Politics of Pain-Management: Staff-Patient Interactions* (Reading, Mass.: Addison-Wesley, 1977).

41 See *Yepremian* v. *Scarborough General Hospital* (1978), 88 DLR 3d 61 (Ont. HC) per Holland J, reversed on appeal (1980) 110 DLR (3d) 513 (Ont. CA). Note of settlement after leave given to the plaintiff to appeal to the Supreme Court of Canada cited in note 26. See also P.-A. Crepeau, "La responsabilité civile de l'établissement hospitalier en droit civil canadien," *McGill Law Journal* 26, 4 (1981): 673; Ellen Picard, *Legal Liability of Doctors and Hospitals in Canada* (Toronto: Carswell, 1978), 247ff.

42 D.A. Graves et al., "Patient-Controlled Analgesia," *Annals of Internal Medicine* 99 (1983): 360.

43 See text below.

44 See, for example, Linton Gifford-Jones, "Let Us Follow U.S. Example," Montreal *Gazette*, 10 April 1982. It has been reported since then that the Bureau of Drugs of Health and Welfare Canada has given permission for the trial use of heroin to relieve the pain of terminally ill patients. See "Medical Use of Heroin to Be Studied," ibid., 18 September 1982. Compare editorial, "Heroin for Cancer: A Great Non-issue of Our Day," *Lancet* 1 (1984): 1449.

45 J. Gagne, D.E. Bresler, and W. Sanders, "Inadequate Treatment of Pain in Hospitalized Patients," *New England Journal of Medicine* 307 (1982): 55.

46 For a discussion of the legal doctrine of "loss of a chance," see Georges Boyer Chammard and Paul Monzein, *La responsabilitié médicale* (Paris: Presses universitaires de France, 1974), 92–105.

47 Gagné, Bresler, and Sanders, "Inadequate Treatment."

48 *McGhee* v. *National Coal Board* (1972) 3 All ER 1008 (HL) (UK).

49 See J. Fleming, *The Law of Torts*, 136ff. For an example of the ease with which a court is sometimes willing to find that a physician-patient relationship has been established, see *St Germain* v. *R.*, [1976] CA 185 (Qué.). In this case, it was held that the physician, accused of manslaughter for failing to treat a patient who subsequently died, had entered a physician-patient relationship by

standing in the courtyard of the hospital, 2 feet away from an ambulance stretcher on which the patient lay, and directing the ambulance attendants to take the patient to another hospital.

50 See M.A. Somerville, "Changes in Mental Health Legislation: An Indicator of Changing Values and Policies," in Martin Roth and Robert Bluglass, eds., *Psychiatry, Human Rights and the Law* (Cambridge: Cambridge University Press, 1985), 156.

51 I am indebted to Michael A. Wolff (Saint Louis University School of Law), Lance Tibbles (Capital University Law School), and Sheila Taub (University of Bridgeport), for comments that caused me to address the issues discussed here.

52 Michael Wolff suggested this line of reasoning.

53 See above for a discussion of some questions raised in relation to non-terminally ill patients and whether pain-relief treatment that might shorten life may be offered to them.

54 The actors have the usual full criminal *mens rea*, or guilty mind, because they have a *mens rea* of either intention or recklessness in relation to the prohibited *actus reus* that they perform. As a general rule, it is irrelevant in proving or disproving *mens rea* what the motive was. See M.A. Somerville, "Criminal Liability in Canadian Law for Risk-Taking and Risk-Creating Conduct," textes présentés par l'Association québécoise pour l'étude comparative du droit au XIe Congrès International de Droit Comparé, Caracas, 1982, 203.

55 *Commonwealth* v. *Capute*, as cited by Angell, "The Quality of Mercy."

56 Even in 1980, when I first made this proposal, there was authority that this approach might already have been recognized by a court in England and, possibly, in the common law in general; see *R.* v. *Bodkin Adams* (unreported), cited by Bernard Dickens, "The Right to Natural Death," *McGill Law Journal* 26, 4 (1981): 868–70, quoting a transcript of the summing up of the case in Glanville Williams, *Sanctity of Life and the Criminal Law* (New York: Knopf, 1958) 289.

57 Criminal Code, RSC 1970, c. C-34, s. 14.

58 Law Reform Commission of Canada, "Euthanasia, Aiding Suicide and Cessation of Treatment," Working Paper 28 (Ottawa: Supply and Services Canada, 1982), 71.

59 President's Commission for the Study of Ethical Problems in Medicine and Biomedical and Behavioural Research, "Deciding to Forego Life-sustaining Treatment" (Washington, DC: U.S. Government Printing Office, 1983), 77–82.

60 Ibid., 73.

61 This topic is too broad and complex to be discussed here. However, this point – that care should be taken not to disguise euthanasia as pain-relief treatment – should be noted.

62 Paul Ramsey, *The Patient as Person: Explorations in Medical Ethics* (New Haven: Yale University Press, 1970).

63 This idea was first presented in summary form in the *New England Journal of Medicine* (see M.A. Somerville, "The Nature of Suffering and the Goals of Medicine," correspondence, ibid., 307 (1982): 758–9), and parts of that publication appear here.

64 Eric J. Cassel, "The Nature of Suffering and the Goals of Medicine," *New England Journal of Medicine* 306 (1982): 639–45.

65 Ibid.

66 For further elaboration of this distinction, see S. Hagg and Y.D. Kosskoff, "The Nature of Suffering and the Goals of Medicine," correspondence, *New England Journal of Medicine* 307 (1982): 759: "The observation made more than 30 years ago that neurosurgical procedures that affect personality can relieve suffering without affecting the perception of pain clearly demonstrated the existence of a syndrome of suffering separate from pain. (Y.D. Kosskoff et al., "Psychological Effects of Frontal Lobotomy Performed for the Alleviation of Pain," *Research Publications – Association for Research in Nervous and Mental Disease.* 27 (1948): 723–53.) We have previously advanced the view that the experience of loss is the essential antecedent of the syndrome of suffering. (Y.D. Kosskoff and S. Hagg, "The Syndrome of Suffering: A Pragmatic Approach," *American Journal of Clinical Biofeedback* 4 (1981): 111–16.) It is loss – whether actual or symbolic, perceived in the present or anticipated in the future – that provides the observable behaviours that we call suffering."

67 See Margaret A. Somerville, "Consent to Medical Care," study paper prepared for the Law Reform Commission of Canada, 1979.

68 Cassel, "The Nature of Suffering."

69 Margaret A. Somerville, "Structuring the Issues in Informed Consent," *McGill Law Journal* 26, 4 (1981): 740.

70 The difference between viewing patients as individuals rather than simply as members of a class called "patients," and viewing them not only as individuals but also as members of their own families and social networks should be noted. To some extent, the individualistic emphasis in the doctrine of informed consent does not reflect reality. Patients are seldom isolated beings. However, although it is not always recognized, the law must start from some basic presumption. A choice must often be made as to which presumption will be basic. In the doctrine of informed consent, it is the rights of the individual person. This does not mean that the rules derived from a basic presumption may not be modified by competing considerations such as the need to take account of the fact that patients are members of families and social networks. The important point, however, is that the basic presumption is most influential and, in cases of unresolvable conflict, overriding. Derogations from it must be clearly justified.

71 A.R. Dyer, "Informed Consent and the Non-autonomous Person: The Dynamics of Dependency Relationships," *IRB: A Review of Human Subjects Research* 4, 7 (1982): 2.

72 H.K. Beecher, "Consent to Clinical Experimentation – Myth and Reality," *Journal of the American Medical Association* 195 (1966): 124.

73 Somerville, "Structuring the Issues in Informed Consent," 767–73; M.A. Somerville, "Therapeutic Privilege: Variation on the Theme of Informed Consent," *Law, Medicine and Health Care* 12, 1 (1984): 4.

74 Ibid.

75 There could be situations in which the concurrence of cognitive and emotional functions is not so easily assumed. Some (even if only a few) competent Jehovah's Witness patients in serious need of blood transfusions give informed refusals, but are constantly accompanied by members of the sect; they might want to have their refusals overridden by medical authority. They might not want that, of course, but the possibility of coerced refusals should be kept in mind.

76 Law Reform Commission of Canada, "Sterilization: Implications for Mentally Retarded and Mentally Ill Persons," Working Paper 24 (Ottawa: Minister of Supply and Services, 1979).

77 Ibid., 119, recommendation (5)(e)(v). Further, the rule of successions law that, in order to be adjudged competent to make a valid will, the testator must be able to appreciate the range of persons who have just claims to be considered as beneficiaries of his or her bounty (see *McKewert* v. *Jenkins* [1958] SCR 719), could be regarded as establishing some requirement of emotional competence.

78 See, for example, *Superintendent of Belchertown State School et al.* v. *Saikewicz* 370 NE 2d 417 (Mass. SC 1977) at 430–2.

79 T.G. Gutheil, H. Bursztajn, and A. Brodsky, "Malpractice Prevention through the Sharing of Uncertainty: Informed Consent and the Therapeutic Alliance," *New England Journal of Medicine* 311 (1984): 50–1.

80 P.S. Jellinek, "Sounding Board: Yet Another Look at Medical Cost Inflation," *New England Journal of Medicine* 307 (1982): 496–7.

CHAPTER TWELVE

1 Law Reform Commission of Canada, *Euthanasia, Aiding Suicide and Cessation of Treatment*, Working Paper 28 (Ottawa: Supply and Services Canada, 1982).

2 See R. Fein, "What Is Wrong with the Language of Medicine?" *New England Journal of Medicine* 306 (1982): 863.

3 For a general discussion, see I.B. Corless, "Physicians and Nurses: Roles and Responsibilities in Caring for the Critically Ill Patient," *Law, Medicine and Health Care* 10, 2 (1982): 72.

4 In one case, a young diabetic woman, whose renal failure resulted from her diabetic condition, was being treated by haemodialysis and suffered a cardiac arrest. She was resuscitated and placed on a respirator, but had suffered

irreversible brain damage. The relatives agreed that she should not be dialysed, but refused permission to switch off the respirator. The patient's physician respected this request to avoid inflicting additional emotional trauma on the family, and artificial respiratory support measures were not discontinued until after the patient had died.

5 I am indebted to John Schuman, medical director, Providence Villa, Scarborough, Ontario, for this perspective.

6 M.A. Somerville, "Death of Pain: Pain, Suffering, and Ethics," in G.F. Gebhart, D.L. Hammond, and T.S. Jensen, eds., *Proceedings of the 7th World Congress of Pain: Progress in Pain Research and Management* (Seattle: ISAP Press, 1994). See chapter 14 above.

7 RSC 1970, c. C-34, as amended.

8 Ibid., ss. 203, 205, 212, 213, 214.

9 Ibid., s. 224.

10 Ibid., s. 14.

11 It might appear theoretically inconsistent to suggest a duty on the part of physicians, and then allow them to abrogate it in some circumstances. However, there are precedents in other areas of medical care – for example, in relation to conscientious objection in carrying out therapeutic abortions. Furthermore, the approach suggested for conscientious objection by the physician does not totally eliminate a duty of physicians to their patients with regard to making pain-relief treatment available. Rather, it changes its content.

CHAPTER THIRTEEN

1 Note that we often take for granted the universality and self-evident nature of these concepts. Unfortunately, for those of us who believe strongly in human rights, there is not always agreement on the origins of, and philosophical foundation for, these rights. This is a very serious problem in ensuring the basic respect for people that we implement through respect for their individual rights.

2 M.A. Somerville and A.J. Orkin, "Human Rights, Discrimination and AIDS: Concepts and Issues," *AIDS* 3 (suppl. 1) (1989): S 283–7.

3 United Nations, "Universal Declaration of Human Rights," in *United Nations, Human Rights: A Compilation of Human Rights Instruments* (New York: United Nations, 1988) (UN Doc. ST/HR/1/Rev. 3).

4 "International Covenant on Civil and Political Rights" (1976), ibid.

5 "International Covenant on Economic, Social and Cultural Rights" (1976), ibid.

6 "Universal Declaration of Human Rights."

7 RSQ, c. C-12, s. 2.

8 RSQ, c. S-5.1.

9 E. Cassel, "The Nature of Suffering and the Goals of Medicine," *New England Journal of Medicine* 306 (1982): 639–45.
10 Constitution Act 1982, Part I.
11 Ibid.
12 Ibid., section 7.
13 Ibid., section 1.
14 Ibid., section 15.
15 [1988] 1 SCR 30.
16 RSC 1970, c. C-34 (as amended).
17 I am indebted to Paul Nathanson for suggesting this term.
18 B. Arcand, *Le Jaguar et le Tamanoir* [The Jaguar and the Anteater] (Quebec: Boréal, 1990).
19 M.A. Somerville, "The Nature of Suffering and the Goals of Medicine," correspondence, *New England Journal of Medicine* 307 (1982): 758–9.
20 See, for example, *Nancy B* v. *Hôtel Dieu de Québec* (1992), 86 DLR (4th) 385 (Quebec Sup. Ct).
21 M.A. Somerville, "Pain and Suffering at Interfaces of Medicine and Law," *University of Toronto Law Journal* 36 (1986): 286–317. See chapter 11 above.
22 "Freedom from Cancer Pain," *Lancet* 1 (1985): 179; "Cancer and the Third World," ibid., 1 (1984): 1136.
23 See, for example, N. Gilmore and M.A. Somerville, *Physicians, Ethics and AIDS* (Ottawa: Canadian Medical Association, 1988).

CHAPTER FOURTEEN

1 See M.A. Somerville, "The Song of Death: The Lyrics of Euthanasia," *Journal of Contemporary Health Law and Policy* 9 (1993): 1–76, and references cited therein. See chapter 3 above.
2 B. Barber et al., *Research on Human Subjects: Problems of Social Control in Medical Experimentation* (New York: Russell Sage Foundation, 1973).
3 M.A. Somerville, "Pain and Suffering at the Interfaces of Medicine and Law," *University of Toronto Law Journal* 26 (1986): 286–317. See chapter 11 above.
4 J. Katz, *Silent World of Doctor and Patient* (New York Free Press, 1984), 207ff.
5 Somerville, "The Song of Death."
6 M.S. Pernick, "The Calculus of Suffering in Nineteenth Century Surgery," *Hastings Center Report* 13 (1983): 26.
7 Personal communication, Dr E. Corin, director of the Psycho-Social Research Unit, Douglas Hospital Research Centre, Montreal, Canada.
8 See K.J. Anand and P.R. Hickey, "Pain and Its Effects in the Human Neonate and Fetus," *New England Journal of Medicine* 317 (1987): 1321–9; and M.C. Rogers, "Do the Right Thing: Pain Relief in Infants and Children," ibid., 326 (1992): 55–6.

9 Pernick, "The Calculus of Suffering."

10 See J. Lally and B. Barber, "The Compassionate Physician: Frequency and Social Determinants of Physician-Investigator Concern for Human Subjects," *Social Forces* 53, 2 (1974): 289–96; Barber, *Research on Human Subjects*, 113, 133–43; and B.H. Gray, *Human Subjects in Medical Experimentation: A Sociological Study of the Conduct and Regulation of Clinical Research* (New York: John Wiley, 1975).

11 E. Scarry, *The Body in Pain: The Making and Unmaking of the World* (New York: Oxford University Press, 1985).

12 Editorial, "Conscience and Complicity," *Lancet* 336 (1990): 720; M. Grodin, book review of *Medicine Betrayed: The Participation of Doctors in Human Rights Abuse*, Report of a Working Party, British Medical Association (London: Zed Books, 1993), in *Social Science & Medicine* 37 (1993): 277–8.

13 R.D. Truog, and T.A. Brennan, "Participation of Physicians in Capital Punishment," *New England Journal of Medicine* 329 (1993): 1346–9.

14 D. Schulmann, "Remembering Who We Are: AIDS and Law in a Time of Madness," *AIDS and Public Policy* 3 (1980): 75–6.

15 *Rodriguez* vs. *Attorney General of British Columbia* and *Attorney General of Canada* (unpublished) no. 23476, 30 September 1993, Supreme Court of Canada.

16 RSC 1980 c. C-46 (as amended), section 241 (b).

17 Ibid.

18 Somerville, "Pain and Suffering."

19 See *Teno* v. *Arnold*, [1978] 2 SCR 287. The Supreme Court of Canada limited such damages to $100,000, as adjusted for inflation since the ruling in 1978.

20 President's Commission for the Study of Ethical Problems in Medicine and Biomedical and Behavioral Research, Deciding to Forego Life Sustaining Treatment (Washington, DC: U.S. Government Printing Office, 1983), 77–82.

21 Law Reform Commission of Canada, *Euthanasia, Aiding Suicide and Cessation of Treatment*, Working Paper 28 (Ottawa: Supply and Services Canada, 1982), 71.

22 *Airedale NHS Trust* v. *Bland*, [1993] 1 ALL ER 821; [1993] 1 HLJ 7.

23 Dr Mildred Solomon, presentation at the American Society of Law and Medicine, "Health Care Professionals and Treatment at the End of Life," 1992 Annual Meeting, 30–31 October 1992, Cambridge, Mass.

24 I have focused on physicians here because they are the least complicated category of health-care professionals, from a legal point of view, with respect to imposing liability. This is the case because physicians have full authority to order and administer pain relief treatment. Other health-care professionals will have correlative obligations and liability.

25 "Cancer and the Third World," *Lancet* 1 (1984): 1136.

26 See Katz, *Silent World*.

27 E. Cassel, "The Nature of Suffering and the Goals of Medicine," *New England Journal of Medicine* 306 (1982): 639–44.

28 M.A. Somerville, "Human Rights and Medicine: The Relief of Suffering," in Irwin Cotler and P. Pearl Eliadis, eds., *International Human Rights Law: Theory and Practice* (Montreal: The Canadian Human Rights Foundation, 1992), 505–22. See chapter 13 above.

29 Ibid.

30 Although it is proposed that relief of suffering is an important starting point for analysis, this principle is not absolute in its operation. For instance, euthanasia in the form of the administration of a lethal injection, even though it is intended to relieve suffering, would not be justified. See Somerville, "The Song of Death."

31 See ibid.

32 R. Fenigsen, "A Case against Dutch Euthanasia" *Hastings Center Report* (Spec. Supp.) 19, 1 (1989): 24.

CHAPTER FIFTEEN (b)

1 Engelbert L. Schucking, "Death at a New York Hospital," *Law, Medicine and Health Care* 13 (1985): 261–8.

2 M.A. Somerville, "Refusal of Medical Treatment in 'Captive Circumstances,'" *Canadian Bar Review* 63, 1 (1985).

3 B. Barber et al., *Research on Human Subjects: Problems of Social Control in Medical Experimentation* (New York: Russell Sage Foundation, 1973), 30.

4 H. Jonas, "Philosophical Reflections on Experimenting with Human Subjects," in P. Freund, ed., *Experimentation with Human Subjects* (New York: Braziller, 1970), 1.

5 Physicians might refrain from saving lives that could be saved if, for example, their patients' beliefs lead them to refuse treatment.

6 Legal documents are usually perceived as instruments of cold, hard reality, needed because they govern relationships between strangers, not intimates. (See C. Gilligan, "New Maps of Development: New Visions of Maturity," *American Journal of Orthopsychiatry* 52, 2 (1982): 199; S. Toulmin, "Equity and Principles," *Osgoode Hall Law Journal* 20, 1 (1982).) Yet testamentary wills and marriage contracts could, ideally, be characterized, like the living will and the durable power of attorney, as instruments of love and trust.

CHAPTER SIXTEEN (a)

Sylvia Stolberg wrote her PhD dissertation on human dignity at McMaster University in Hamilton, Ontario.

1 M.A. Somerville, "'Death Talk' in Canada," *Humane Medicine* 11, 1 (1995): 11. See chapter 4 above.

2 Ibid., 14.

3 *Rodriguez* v. *British Columbia*, [1993] 17 CRR at 203.

4 "Goldblatt-Mitchell Sack: The Supreme Court Rules on Physician-Assisted Suicide," *Ontario Medical Review*, October 1993, 57.

5 *Rodriguez* v. *British Columbia*, [1993] 17 CRR at 204.

6 H.R. Pankratz, "The Sue Rodriguez Decision: Concerns of a Primary Care Physician," *Humane Medicine* 11, 1 (1995): 17.

7 A. Kolnai, "Dignity," *Philosophy* 51 (1976): 258.

8 I. Kant, *Foundations of the Metaphysics of Morals* (Indianapolis: Bobbs-Merrill Company, 1976), 47.

9 L.W. Beck, "Kant's Two Conceptions of the Will in Their Political Context," in R. Beiner and J.W. Booth, eds., *Kant & Political Philosophy: Contemporary Legacy* (New Haven-Yale University Press, 1991), 46.

10 T.E. Hill Jr, *Dignity and Practical Reason in Kant's Moral Theory* (Ithaca: Cornell University Press, 1992), 50–5.

11 M.J. Meyer, "Dignity, Rights and Self-Control," *Ethics* 99 (1989): 529.

12 J.-P. Sartre, *Existentialism and Humanism* (London: Methuen, 1948), 44–5.

13 G. Marcel, *The Existential Background of Human Dignity* (Cambridge: Harvard University Press, 1971), 127–8.

14 Ibid., 134.

15 Ibid., 128.

16 Ibid., 135.

CHAPTER SIXTEEN (b)

1 S.D. Stolberg, "Human Dignity and Disease, Disability, Suffering: A Philosophical Contribution to the Euthanasia and Assisted Suicide Debate," abstract, *Humane Medicine* 11 (1995): 144–7. See chapter 16(a) above.

2 M.A. Somerville, "The Song of Death: The Lyrics of Euthanasia," *Journal of Contemporary Health Law and Policy* 15, 9 (1993): 1–76. See chapter 3 above.

3 R. Eisler, *Sacred Pleasure: Sex Myth and the Politics of the Body – New Paths to Power and Love* (San Francisco: Harper, 1995).

4 Somerville, "The Song of Death."

5 See, for example, the statement from ACON (the AIDS Council of New South Wales) accompanying the Voluntary Euthanasia Bill, which they drafted and submitted to the New South Wales Parliament in Australia in 1995.

6 For a description of self-willed death playing a similar role for some men in the Greco-Roman period, see Katherine K. Young, "A Cross-Cultural Historical Case against Planned Self-Willed Death and Assisted Suicide," *McGill Law Journal* 39 (1994): 657.

7 Stolberg, "Human Dignity."

8 M.A. Somerville, "Labels versus Contents: Variance between Philosophy, Psychiatry and Law in Concepts Governing Decision-Making," *McGill Law Journal* 39 (1994): 179–99. See chapter 21, below.

9 Stolberg, "Human Dignity."

10 E. Cassel, "The Nature of Suffering and the Goals of Medicine," *New England Journal of Medicine* 306 (1982): 639–44.

11 M.A. Somerville, review of Marilynne Seguin, *A Gentle Death*, in *Canadian Forum* 74, 935, 36–9. See chapter 18, below.

12 Young, "A Cross-Cultural Historical Case."

13 B. Campion, "Love and the Quality of Life," *Globe and Mail*, 4 August 1990, A4.

14 Stolberg, "Human Dignity," emphasis added.

15 Somerville, "The Song of Death"; M.A. Somerville, "'Death Talk' in Canada: The Rodriguez Case," *Humane Medicine* 11, 1 (1995): 10–15.

16 Stolberg, "Human Dignity."

17 Ibid., quoting G. Marcel, *The Existential Background of Human Dignity* (Cambridge: Harvard University Press, 1971).

18 Somerville, "The Song of Death."

19 Somerville, "Death Talk."

20 Charles Taylor, "The Politics of Recognition," in A. Gutmann, ed., *Multiculturalism: Examining the Politics of Recognition* (Princeton: Princeton University Press, 1992), 26–8. I am grateful to Katherine K. Young for bringing Taylor's work on this point to my attention.

21 R. Paden, "Death and the Limits of Medicine," *Medical Humanities Review*, 9 (1995): 60.

22 Young, "A Cross-Cultured Historical Case."

23 Stolberg, "Human Dignity," quoting Marcel, *The Existential Background*.

24 *Report of the Special Senate Committee on Euthanasia and Assisted Suicide: Of Life and Death* (Ottawa: Minister of Supply and Services Canada, 1995), 72.

CHAPTER SEVENTEEN (a)

Constantine Failiers, MD, is a physician at the Allergy and Asthma Clinic and a member of the board of the Humanities Institute at the University of Denver, Colorado.

1 Thucydides, *History of the Peloponnesian War.* Greek text edited by C.F. Smith (Cambridge: Harvard University Press, 1920–75), Book III, xli–xlix (also quoted in note 2, 91–4).

2 K.I. Fallieros, *Lesbos – 3000 Years on an Aeolian Island* (Denver: Isos Internat, 1994), vii, xv–xvi.

3 K.I. Fallieros (aka C.J. Falliers), *Enduring Torches–and Dilemmas–of classical Medicine from Homer to Hippocrates*, Proceedings of the First International Medical Olympiad, Kos, Greece, 1 August – 2 September 2 1996, 53–9; K.I. Fallieros

(aka C.J. Falliers), *Notes on Health and Healing from Mythical to Medieval Times*, 35th International Congress on the History of Medicine, Kos, Greece, 2–8 September 1996.

4 D.A. Campbell, *Greek Lyric* (Greek text with English translation), vol. 1 (Cambridge: Harvard University Press, 1982), 12.

5 J. Legge, *The Philosophy of Confucius* (New York: Crescent Books, 1974), 32.

6 R. Wagner, *Tannhäuser*, The Opera Libretto Library (New York: Avenel/Crown, 1939/80), 34–59.

7 E. Ochoa, *Locuras y Amores* (Madness and Love, in plural) (Barcelona: Plaza y Janes, 1994), 143–5.

CHAPTER SEVENTEEN (b)

1 Constantine John Falliers, "Prothanasia: Personal Fulfilment and Readiness to Die," *Humane Health Care International* 13, 2 (1997): 35–7. See chapter 17 (a) above.

2 Ibid., 3.

3 I am indebted to Professor Norell Lickiss, M.D., director of palliative care, Royal Prince Alfred Hospital, Sydney, Australia, for this insight.

4 Katherine K. Young, "A Cross-cultural Historical Case against Planned Self-Willed Death and Assisted Suicide," *McGill Law Journal* 36 (1994): 657–707.

5 Falliers, "Prothanasia," 3–4.

6 Ibid., 5.

7 A. Lawlor, *Voices of the First Day* (Rochester, Vt: Inner Traditions International, 1991), 185.

8 Ibid., 184–202.

9 Falliers, "Prothanasia," 5.

10 Lawlor, *Voices of the First Day*, 185.

11 R. Yallop, "The Anzac Future," *Australian*, 21 April 1997, 9.

12 Dr J. Paris, Jewish General Hospital, Montreal, personal communication, 1994.

13 Falliers, "Prothanasia," emphasis added.

14 K. Mason and D. Mulligan, "Euthanasia by Stages," *Lancet* 347 (1996): 810–11.

15 Ian McClaren and Michael Piper, "Searching for Ethics 2001," videotape, pilot segment, Uluru, Australia, April 1997.

16 M.A. Somerville, "The Song of Death: The Lyrics of Euthanasia," *Journal of Contemporary Health Law and Policy* 9 (1993): 1–67. See chapter 3 above.

CHAPTER EIGHTEEN

1 Marilynne Seguin, *A Gentle Death* (Toronto: Key Porter, 1994).

2 Ibid., xi.

3　Ibid., 10.

4　Derek Humphry, *Final Exit: The Practicalities of Self-Deliverance and Assisted Suicide for the Dying* (Eugene, Ore.: Hemlock Society, 1991).

5　Seguin, *A Gentle Death.*

6　*Rodriguez* v. *British Columbia (Attorney General)* (1993), 107 DLR 342 (SCC).

7　Seguin, *A Gentle Death*, 134.

8　Ibid., 214.

9　See chapter 3 above, "Song of Death," and Chapter 6, "Legalizing Euthanasia: Why Now?" In 1996, Oregon enacted legislation permitting physicians to prescribe drugs for terminally ill people, for the express purpose of allowing their patients to use these drugs to commit suicide.

10　J. Katz, *The Silent World of Doctor and Patient* (New York: Free Press, 1986).

11　Seguin, *A Gentle Death*, 143, citing Daniel Callahan, *Setting Limits: Medical Goals in an Aging Society* (New York: Simon and Schuster, 1987), 13.

12　*Rodriguez* v. *British Columbia.*

13　Personal communication to the author, Montreal, 1994.

CHAPTER NINETEEN

1　D. Nelkin, "AIDS and the News Media," *Milbank Quarterly* 69 (1991): 293–307.

2　Ibid., 303.

3　Ibid., 297–302.

4　Editorial,"Parliament's moral challenge," *Globe and Mail*, 6 March 1995, A12.

5　Editorial, "Time to Empower Angels of Mercy," *Globe and Mail*, 6 April 1996.

6　M.A. Somerville, "Societal Risks of Physician Angels of Death," *Globe and Mail*, 22 April 1996.

7　Nelkin, "AIDS and the News Media," 302.

8　*Rodriguez* v. *Canada (A.G.)* [1993] 3 SCR 519 (sub nom. *Rodriguez* v. *British Columbia (A.G.)* 107 DLR (4th) 342.

9　P.D. James, *The Children of Men* (New York: Knopf 1993).

10　Gwynn Dyer, "Learning to Kill," Montreal *Gazette*, 15 December 1995, B3.

11　*Death on Request*, Ikon Television Network, 1994.

12　"Death on Request," excerpts, *Prime Time Live*, 8 December 1994.

13　H. Hendin, "Selling Death and Dignity," *Hastings Center Report* 25, 3 (1995): 19–23.

14　*Rights of the Terminally Ill Act 1995*, Legislative Assembly of the Northern Territory of Australia. This legislation is discussed in more detail elsewhere. See chapters 6 and 7 above.

15　P. Parrs, "Suicide Program Makes Me Uneasy," Montreal *Gazette*, 25 May 1996, E21.

16 "Dutch Doctors Revise Policy on Mercy Killing: New Guidelines Urge Terminally Ill to Take Matters into Their Own Hands," *Globe and Mail*, 26 August 1995, A2.

17 Paul Wilkes, "The Next Pro-lifers," *New York Times Magazine*, 21 July 1996, 22.

18 Daniel Callahan, as cited ibid., 25.

19 Lisa Hobbs Birnie and Sue Rodriguez, *Uncommon Will: The Death and Life of Sue Rodriguez* (Toronto: Macmillian Canada, 1994).

20 E. Becker, *The Denial of Death* (New York: Free Press, 1973).

21 D. Callahan, *The Troubled Dream of Life: Living with Mortality* (New York: Simon & Schuster, 1993).

22 M.A. Somerville, "Unpacking the Concept of Human Dignity in Human(e) Death: Comments on 'Human Dignity and Disease, Disability, and Suffering,' by Sylvia D. Stolberg," *Humane Medicine* 11 (1995): 148–51. See chapter 16 (b) above.

23 See Paul Nathanson's research on what he calls "secular religions" and others call "implicit religion." (On public response to the death of Princess Diana, see "I Feel, Therefore I Am: The Princess of Passion and the Implicit Religion of Our Time," *Implicit Religions* 2, 2 [1999]: 59–87). Secular religions, he argues, are world views – often institutionalized – that function in most ways as religions (the major exception being that they do not mediate the sacred, a principal defining feature of religion). Included in this category are political ideologies on both the left and the right; examples would be Marxism, nationalism, or fascism, and – for some women – even feminism. Also included, however, are vaguer mentalities that are pervasive and deeply rooted, but seldom articulated consciously or systematically; a major example, he says, would be the kind of neo-Romanticism – propagated by countless talk shows, magazines, television programs, and novels – that glorifies emotion as an end in itself and at the expense of reason.

CHAPTER TWENTY-ONE

1 It is interesting to consider whether justice is a digital or binary concept (that is, either present or absent) or an analogue concept (there can be degrees of justice and injustice). For a discussion of that, see M.A. Somerville, "Justice across the Generations," *Social Science & Medicine* 29 (1989): 385–94.

2 See, for example, K.C. Glass, "Elderly Persons and Decision-Making in a Medical Context: Challenging Canadian Law" (PhD thesis, Faculty of Law, McGill University, March 1992); G. Sharpe, *The Law and Medicine in Canada*, 2d ed. (Toronto: Butterworths, 1987), 394–406; D.N. Weisstub, *Law and Psychiatry in the Canadian Context: Cases, Notes and Materials* (New York: Pergamon Press, 1980), 175–253.

3 The distinction being made here can be compared with that made between the definition of death (which is generally not undertaken in law) and the criteria for the determination of death (which is). See Law Reform Commission of Canada, *Criteria for the Determination of Death*, Working Paper No. 23 (Ottawa: Supply & Services Canada, 1979); Law Reform Commission of Canada, *Criteria for the Determination of Death*, Report No. 15 (Ottawa: Supply & Services Canada, 1981).

4 L.H. Roth, A. Meisl, and C.W. Lidz, "Tests of Competency to Consent to Treatment," *American Journal of Psychiatry* 134 (1977): 283.

5 M.A. Somerville, "Determinations of Competence as a Mechanism for Control of Persons," in D. Greig and E. Berah, eds., *Civil Rights in Psychiatry, Psychology and Law*, Proceedings of the 6th Annual Congress of the Australian & New Zealand Association of Psychiatry, Psychology and Law (Melbourne, 1985) 37.

6 G. Dworkin, "Autonomy and Behavior Control," *Hastings Center Report* 6 (1976): 24.

7 Ibid.

8 For discussion of the concept of autonomy, see below. See also M.A. Somerville, "Refusal of Medical Treatment in 'Captive' Circumstances," *Canadian Bar Review* 63 (1985): 59.

9 See E.E. Shelp and M. Perl, "Denial in Clinical Medicine: A Reexamination of the Concept and Its Significance," *Archives of Internal Medicine* 145 (1985): 697–9.

10 Jay Katz would disagree that it promotes autonomy (*The Silent World of Doctor and Patient* [New York: Free Press, 1984], 127). His concept of autonomy is closer to the philosophical one (see text accompanying note 6) than the legal one (such as it is) or what I propose here.

11 An Act Respecting Health Services and Social Services, RSQ c. S-5., s. 4.

12 410 U.S. 113 at 152–4 (1973).

13 An Act Respecting Health Services and Social Services, s. 7.

14 Privacy Act, RSC 1985, c. P-21, s. 12(2)(a).

15 See Somerville, "Refusal of Medical Treatment," 65ff.

16 Katz, *The Silent World*, 141.

17 M.A. Somerville, "Structuring the Issues in Informed Consent," *McGill Law Journal* 26 (1981): 776ff.

18 Ibid., 753ff.

19 R.M. Ratzan, "Cautiousness, Risk, and Informed Consent in Clinical Geriatrics," *Clinical Research* 30 (1982): 351.

CHAPTER TWENTY-TWO

1 See V. Leary, "Implications of a Right to Health," in K.E. Mahoney and P. Mahoney, eds., *Human Rights in the Twenty-First Century: A Global Challenge* (Dordrecht: Martinus Nijhoff, 1993), 484.

2 For example, a "right to health" is said to be contained within the "right to life" recognized in the Universal Declaration of Human Rights (1948), GA Res. 217A (111), art. 3 (UN Doc. ST/HR/l/Rev. 3) (hereafter Universal Declaration) and is expressly referred to in the International Covenant on Civil and Political Rights (1976), 999 UNTS 171, part IV, art. 28; art. 6 (UN Doc. ST/HR/l/Rev3) (ibid., 487).

3 For example, Canadian courts, including the Supreme Court of Canada (see *Morgentaler, Smoling et al. v. The Queen*, [1988] 1 SCR 30), have interpreted Canadian law in this way – in particular, the Canadian Charter of Rights and Freedoms, Part 1 of the Constitution Act, 1982, being Schedule B to the Canada Act 1982 (UK), 1982, c. 11; Quebec Charter of Human Rights and Freedoms, RSQ c. C-12; and the Ontario Code of Human Rights, 1981, c. 53.

4 In this regard, it is interesting to note that the "Human Rights Reference Handbook" of the European Community, dated 10 December 1992, does not include the right to health among the specific human rights issues addressed.

5 In this respect, it is relevant to consider the rights claimed by some collective entities other than the state, and misuse of them. For instance, multinational companies have sought to rely on rights to privacy in order to avoid disclosure of the details of their operations. Dennis Thompson, director of the Program in Ethics and the Professions at Harvard University, has argued that collective entities such as companies are not governed by the same ethical principles and claims (do not have the same rights) as individuals. Therefore, they do not have any such right to privacy. He calls the direct translation of ethical and legal claims from the micro to the macro "level" the "individualist mistake." D.F. Thompson, "The Politics of Professional Ethics," Astra Lectures in Ethics, 4 May 1992, McGill Centre for Medicine, Ethics and Law (unpublished).

6 D.R. Ortiz, "Saving the Self?" *Michigan Law Review* 91 (1993): 1018.

7 Ibid., 1021.

8 "Human Rights Reference Handbook," 7.

9 Reprinted in Rian Malan, *My Traitor's Heart: A South African Exile Returns to Face His Country, His Tribe and His Conscience* (New York: Vintage Books, 1990), 272.

10 I am indebted for this insight to Dean Yves-Marie Morissette and the text of his recent speech, "Does the Law Deserve so much Trust?" address to the Graduate Society of McGill University, 9 June 1993 (unpublished).

11 Leary, "Implications," citing T. Campbell, "Introduction: Realizing Human Rights," in Campbell et al., eds., *Human Rights from Rhetoric to Reality* (1986), 3.

12 I am grateful to Knut Hammarskjold for this insight.

13 J. O'Neill, "UN Rights Conference Opens under a Cloud," Montreal *Gazette*, 14 June 1993, B-1.

14 "Rae Keeps His Distance," ibid., 16 July 1993, B1.

15 S. McIntyre, "Backlash against Equality: The 'Tyranny' of 'Politically Correct,'" *McGill Law Journal* 38 (1993): 1.

16 It is interesting to consider the difference and the relation between the concept of respect for persons, which is discussed above, and those of respect for a person's dignity. Sometimes these concepts are used interchangeably, but I propose that the former is broader and more protective of persons than the latter, which can often be regarded as included within the former. A conflict between the two could arise, however, if respect for the person were interpreted as requiring protection of the person (for instance, in the form of medical treatment that the person had refused), and respect for the person's dignity required respect for that person's wishes (for example, the person's informed refusal of treatment).

17 See M.A. Somerville, "The Song of Death: The Lyrics of Euthanasia," *Journal of Contemporary Health Law and Policy*, 28, in particular, references to B. Campion, note 97, and pages 28–9. See chapter 3 above.

18 R. Howard, "Health Costs of Social Degradation and Female Self-Mutilation in North America," in Kathleen Mahoney and Paul Mahoney, eds., *Human Rights*, 515.

19 Leary, "Implications," 482.

20 A. Zuger, "AIDS Becomes Ordinary" *Medical Humanities Review* 7 (1993): 39.

21 T. Gutheil, "In Search of True Freedom: Drug Refusal, Involuntary Medication, and 'Rotting with Your Rights On,'" *American Journal of Psychology* 137, 3 (1980): 346.

22 Leary, "Implications," 486 (notes omitted).

23 D. Wikler, "Privatization and Human Rights in Health Care: Notes from the American Experience," in Mahoney and Mahoney, eds., *Human Rights*, 499.

24 *Brown* v. *British Columbia (Minister of Health)* (1990), 42 BCLR (2d) 294 (Supreme Court of British Columbia).

25 Meeting of the Advisory Committee for Palliative Care in the McGill Teaching Hospitals, Montreal, June 1993.

26 M. McGregor, "Technology and the Allocation of Resources," *New England Journal of Medicine* 303 (1989): 118–20.

27 Leary, "Implications," 484.

28 For example, the International Covenant on Economic, Social and Cultural Rights (1976), 993 UNTS 3, part IV, art. 12 (1) (UN doc. ST/HR/1/ Rev. 3). Similarly, the Constitution of the World Health Organization states that "the enjoyment of the highest attainable standard of health is one of the fundamental rights of every human being without distinction of race, religion, political belief, economic or social conditions."

29 Leary, "Implications," 485, citing R. Roemer, "The Right to Health Care," in H.L. Fuenzalida-Puelma and S. Connor, eds., *The Right to Health in the*

Americas: A Comparative Constitutional Study, Scientific Publication No. 509, Pan-American Health Organization (Washington DC, 1989) (hereafter PAHO Study).

30 Leary, "Implications," 486, quoting the PAHO Study (599).

31 Ibid., 486, quoting PAHO Study.

32 See "Human Rights Reference Handbook," 133.

33 Leary, "Implications," 487.

34 Universal Declaration, art. 5.

35 International Covenant on Civil and Political Rights, art. 7.

36 Universal Declaration, art 25.

37 See note 28 above.

38 Convention on the Rights of the Child, adopted by the UNGA Res. 44/25 on 20 November 1989, entered into force 2 September 1990.

39 See, for example, M.A. Somerville and A. Orkin, "Human Rights, Discrimination and AIDS: Concepts and Issues," *AIDS* 3 (1989) (suppl. 1): s283–7.

40 Ibid., s283.

41 M.A. Somerville, "AIDS: A Challenge to Health Care, Law and Ethics," in D. Snowden and D.F. Cassidy, eds., *AIDS: A Handbook for Professionals* (Toronto: Carswell, 1989), 216.

42 Personal communication, E. Corin, director of Psycho-Social Research Unit, Douglas Hospital Research Centre, Montreal.

43 M.A. Somerville, "Human Rights and Medicine: The Relief of Suffering," in I. Cotler and F.P. Eliadis, eds., *International Human Rights Law Theory and Practice* (Montreal: Canadian Human Rights Foundation, 1992), 515. See chapter 13 above.

44 The word "religion" has its origins in a word meaning "to come, or bind, together." See M.A. Somerville, *The Ethical Canary: Science, Society and the Human Spirit* (Toronto: Viking/Penguin, 2000).

45 Wikler, "Privatization," 498.

46 Collective rights might be linked to claims that can be fulfilled only if there are collective services – which is true, in general, of health care. That definition of "collective rights" might be useful also to limit the potential for abuse in recognizing the existence of these rights.

47 Royal Commission on New Reproductive Technologies (Canada), "Framework for Decision Making," (April 1993), Editorial Page Feature, (press release).

Permissions and Places
of Publication

- "Executing Euthanasia: A Review Essay of *Physician-Assisted Death* edited by James M. Humber, Robert F. Almeder, and Gregg A. Kasting." *The Quarterly Review of Biology* 70 (1995): 491–5.
- "Genetics, Reproductive Technologies, Euthanasia." *Social Science and Medicine* 42 (19): ix–xii. Reprinted with permission from Elsevier Science.
- "Human Rights and Medicine: The Relief of Suffering," in Irwin Cotler and F. Pearl Eliadis, eds., *International Human Rights Law: Theory and Practice*, 505–22. Montreal: Canadian Human Rights Foundation, 1992.
- "Labels versus Contents: Variance between Philosophy, Psychiatry and Law in Concepts Governing Decision-Making" *McGill Law Journal* 39 (1994): 179–99. Reprinted by permission of the McGill Law Journal.
- "Legalising Euthanasia: Why Now?" *Australian Quarterly* 68 (1996): 1–14.
- "Pain and Suffering at Interfaces of Medicine and Law." *University of Toronto Law Journal* 36 (1986): 286–317. Reprinted by permission of University of Toronto Press Incorporated.
- "'Should the Grandparents Die?': Allocation of Medical Resources with Aging Population." *Law, Medicine & Health Care* 14 (1986): 158–63. Copyright 1986. Reprinted with the permission of the American Society of Law, Medicine & Ethics. All rights reserved.
- "The Song of Death: The Lyrics of Euthanasia." *Journal of Contemporary Health Law and Policy* 25 (1993): 1–76. Reprinted with permission of the Journal of Contemporary Health Law and Policy.

Index

or others, 130; and self-defence,
130; true, 129
Neely, Steven, 162–4
negligent systems. *See* systems negligence
"negotiated dying," 164
Nelkin, Dorothy, 291–2
neonatology, 212
nervous shock: legal damages for,
184
Netherlands State Commission on
Euthanasia (1985), 27
Netherlands, euthanasia in, 50–2,
60, 105, 123, 147, 161, 352n,
358n, 361n, 371n; de facto legalization, 168; as flawed, 144; hidden, 53, 55; judicial guidelines,
161; non-voluntary and involuntary cases, 371n; reporting procedures, 359n, 360n; underlying
presumptions, 74. *See also* legalization of euthanasia; physician-
assisted death
neurological disease: and euthanasia, 138
newborn babies, 50; disabled, and
feeding on demand, 191; duty to
treat premature, 212
New England Journal of Medicine, 157
Nielsen, Torsten, and guidelines for
legalization of euthanasia, 144–
53; author's rebuttal of, 153–6;
response to rebuttal, 156–8;
author's response to response,
158–9
nihilism, 89, 113; and suffering,
342n
"no harm" (*primum non nocere*), 211,
248, 254
non-consensual euthanasia, defined, 356n
non-maleficence, defined, 206; vs
beneficence, 17, 79, 340

non-pecuniary loss, 173–6, 381n;
and "aesthetic prejudice," 175;
and approaches to legal assessment, 174, 176–9; and basis of
award, 176; categories of damages, 175; compensatibility, 174–
5; and compensation calculation,
177; conceptual approach, 176;
and discretion, 176–7; extravagant claims, 384n; and facial scarring, 177; functional approach,
176; and global limits on, 177;
and inconvenience, 175; and legal limits on damages for, 175,
382–3n; and legal liability for
pain-relief treatment, 180, 185;
and long-term compensation,
179; and "loss of amenities of
life," 175; *Mulroy* v. *Aqua Scene et
al.,* 177–8; and nervous shock,
381n; and pain and suffering,
175; and pecuniary loss, 179; personal approach, 177; and quality
of life, 175; *resitutio in integrum,*
176; subjective or objective approach to, 176;
non-terminally ill patients, and severe chronic pain, 182
Northern Territory Legislature,
Australia, 106, 108, 111,122, 144,
149, 168–9, 277; and suicide machine, 294; and Rights of the Terminally Ill Act, 1995, 275
Not Dead Yet (U.S.), 82

obiatry and obiatrists, 155, 164
Ochoa, Elena, 272–3
omission: treatment, 28–30, 95;
mere omission, 62; and law, 188
oncology, 169
Ontario Court of Appeal, and award
for non-pecuniary loss, 178;
fixed-total system, 178; and injury